Europe in Its Own Eyes, Europe in the Eyes of the Other

Cultural Studies Series

Cultural Studies is the multi- and inter-disciplinary study of culture, defined anthropologically as a "way of life," performatively as symbolic practice, and ideologically as the collective product of varied media and cultural industries. Although Cultural Studies is a relative newcomer to the humanities and social sciences, in less than half a century it has taken inter-disciplinary scholarship to a new level of sophistication, reinvigorating the liberal arts curriculum with new theories, topics, and forms of intellectual partnership.

Wilfrid Laurier University Press invites submissions of manuscripts concerned with critical discussions on power relations concerning gender, class, sexual preference, ethnicity, and other macro and micro sites of political struggle.

For more information, please contact:

Lisa Quinn
Acquisitions Editor
Wilfrid Laurier University Press
75 University Avenue West
Waterloo, ON N2L 3C5
Canada
Phone: 519-884-0710 ext. 2843
Fax: 519-725-1399
Email: quinn@press.wlu.ca

Europe in Its Own Eyes,
Europe in the Eyes of the Other

David B. MacDonald and **Mary-Michelle DeCoste**, editors

**WILFRID LAURIER
UNIVERSITY PRESS**

Wilfrid Laurier University Press acknowledges the financial support of the Government of Canada through the Canada Book Fund for our publishing activities.

LAURIER
Inspiring Lives.

Library and Archives Canada Cataloguing in Publication

Europe in its own eyes, Europe in the eyes of the other / David B. MacDonald and Mary-Michelle DeCoste, editors.

(Cultural studies)
Includes bibliographical references and index.
Issued in print and electronic formats.
ISBN 978-1-55458-840-4 (bound).—ISBN 978-1-55458-867-1 (epub).—
ISBN 978-1-55458-866-4 (pdf)

  1. Group identity—Europe. 2. National characteristics, European. 3. Political culture—Europe. 4. Collective memory—Europe. 5. Europe—Civilization—20th century. 6. Europe—Civilization—21st century. I. MacDonald, David B., 1973–, editor of compilation II. DeCoste, Mary-Michelle, editor of compilation III. Series: Cultural studies series (Waterloo, Ont.)

D1055.E97 2014   306.094   C2013-905940-7   C2013-905941-5

Cover design by Blakeley Words+Pictures. Front-cover image by AP Photo/Pier Paolo Cito. Text design by Sandra Friesen.

This book is printed on FSC recycled paper and is certified Ecologo. It is made from 100% post-consumer fibre, processed chlorine free, and manufactured using biogas energy.

Printed in Canada

RECYCLED
Paper made from
recycled material
FSC
www.fsc.org   FSC® C103567

Contents

Contents

Introduction

Identity, Memory, and Contestation in Europe

David B. MacDonald and Mary-Michelle DeCoste

During the eight years of the George W. Bush administration, Europe seemed to represent a more positive, prosperous, stable, and culturally enlightened antipode to the United States. A large volume of books during this period extolled the virtues of Europe, which was seen as the next super-power, a model of what countries could do when they put narrow national self-interest aside and worked together, promoted ethical forms of foreign policy, and maintained a strong welfare state. Sadly, by the time Barack Obama became president, the myth of an economically prosperous, stable, and progressive Europe was been shattered by the Greek bailout, economic problems in Italy, Spain, Ireland, and other countries, and fractious debates about monetary union. The rise of ultranationalism of the Pim Fortuyn or Jorg Haider variety during the 1990s and after also seemed to indicate that the European experiment was not working perfectly, and that lingering racism and xenophobia continued, despite decades of new myth-making. German Chancellor Angela Merkel's pronouncement in 2010 that multicul-turalism had "utterly failed" in her country, followed by negative reactions toward the phenomenon in other core EU countries, underscored the reality that European identity remains unsettled and contested, especially in an era of high immigration, low birthrates, a failed EU constitution, and the steady erosion of the welfare state. All this has come alongside ballooning debt and uncertainty about the limits of the eastward expansion of the Union, par-ticularly toward religiously dissimilar states like Turkey.

What it means to be European, however, has always been unsettled. What is Europe, and how can one define where it begins and ends? Our fo-cus in this book is European identity, a crucial topic as Europe undergoes a plethora of challenges. But what precisely does Europe mean? As Jacobs and Maier have argued, "positively, Europe can be defined as a jagged and ragged end of the Eurasian landmass. But there is no agreement at all where this part begins, and to call it a continent is certainly an abuse of language. To situate Europe geographically is therefore already problematic, but it is even more difficult to define Europe historically and culturally" (1998, 13).

The focus on Europe as it is seen through its own eyes and through the eyes of the other (a label problematized by many of the chapters in this volume) in a variety of different kinds of texts helps us to understand the contested nature of European identities in the plural, as well as allowing us to engage with the shifting sands of identity contestation from inside and outside of Europe. The idea that there are many forms of identity competing with dominant homogenizing conceptualizations is at the root of this work. We agree with Thomas Risse's view that "it is wrong to see 'European' identity as compared to national, regional, or local loyalties in a zero-sum fashion as either/or propositions. Individuals hold multiple identities and, thus, can identify with Florence, Tuscany, Italy, and Europe or with Munich, Bavaria, Germany, and Europe without having to face conflicts of loyalties. Which of these identities becomes salient or important in a given moment depends on the context in which people act" (2011, 2).

The chapters presented here reflect the tensions and ambiguities about both what being European might imply as well as what *not* being European can mean. The book features sixteen chapters divided into four thematic sections, drawn from a selected group of Canadian, American, and European contributors. We as editors hope the thematic divisions will allow academic researchers and course instructors to easily find what will be of interest to them. Two key themes unite the chapters: first, the politics of identity construction involving self and other, and second, the politics of memory, that is, how history is understood and interpreted.

Throughout much of European history, nations and states were formed on the basis of inclusive and exclusionary identity practices. Deciding the borders of the nation and demarcating identities was a crucial political project. In many cases, identities were defined both positively and negatively. On the positive side, Anthony D. Smith has noted the central importance of national myths, heroes and legends, and ideals of a "golden age" that national leaders strived to recapture from the eighteenth century in a wide variety of political projects. For Smith, nations are based on "an ideal of authenticity which presupposes a unique culture-community, with a distinct and original character." Each nation possesses its own "peculiar historic genius" which nationalists are tasked with rediscovering and possessing (Smith 2001, 442). A nation's view of the world must be both "culturally distinct" and "rooted." Clear-cut territorial boundaries need to be established, and a "keen eye" is required to determine the identity of "'alien' objects throughout trade and exchange, as well as for successive migrations, invasions and colonization." Throughout, images of cultural purity, of distinctiveness, of originality, of what is "'our very own' and nobody else's" form a crucial part of identity construction (Smith 2001, 442–43).

At the same time, the development of European nationalisms implied deciding who was not part of the nation, and in a larger sense as the supranational experiment evolved, who was not a part of Europe. A focus on others in group and national identity has been recognized as an important part of identity formation. For example, Hugh Trevor-Roper's "normal nationalism" included a sense of persecution and danger, comprising such things as "great national defeat," and "danger of being swamped by foreigners" (1962, 12). As Marc Howard Ross has further explained the phenomenon, the isolation of enemies who "contain unwanted parts of ourselves" can allow the nation to purge itself of many negative attributes, leaving only the good characteristics. Images of the world and plans for action are predicated on a shared conception of difference between one's own group and others. As he has described, "outsiders can then serve as objects for externalization, displacement and projection of intense negative feelings like dissenting perspectives, which are present inside the group but denied" (Ross 1995, 533).

Historian Eric Hobsbawm has also observed that otherization has proven central to the mass appeal of nationalism and other forms of group identity. This "democratization" of nationalism, as Hobsbawm recalls, often implies an era when "popular nationalist, or at all events, xenophobic sentiments and those of national superiority preached by the new pseudo-science of racism, became easier to mobilise." Reviewing nineteenth-century nationalism, Hobsbawm draws a positive correlation between nationalism and out-group violence, arguing, "there is no more effective way of bonding together the disparate sections of restless peoples than to unite them against outsiders" (1995, 91). In this approach, modernity creates the conditions for a more xenophobic and racially based nationalism. Further, his analysis prescribes nationalism as a potential cure for the onset of modernity, and its concomitant alienation of various groups in society, looking for some form of identity. The fear of losing traditional ways with the onset of increased urbanization made it easier for national elites to gain support by convincing the populace that they were being persecuted because of their national group.

How real are these actual differences? In many cases, the differences between nations are as manufactured as the putative similarities between co-nationalists. Michael Ignatieff employed Sigmund Freud's "narcissism of minor differences" to analyze the conflict in Yugoslavia during the 1990s, observing that "the smaller the real difference between two peoples, the larger it was bound to loom in their imagination.... Without hatred of the other, there would be no clearly defined national self to worship and adore" (1993, 14). What these theorists share generally is a view of national identity that needs an other, an external enemy, to consolidate support for an exclusive "in group." Of course, national loyalty is also derived from positive aspects as well—national symbols, characteristics, and shared memories worth preserving. Nevertheless, it is only when these positive aspects are threatened that they become truly appreciated.

What we see in the development of both European nationalisms and a sense of pan-European identity is a mixture of positive myths of the self, combined with negative portrayals of others, whether they be Americans under George W. Bush, Muslim immigrants from North Africa during the 9/11, London, and Madrid bombings, or more recent fears about the loss of European cultures and traditions in the face of new demographic realities. Like the nation, regional identity such as a sense of "Europeanness" is also best seen as socially constructed. At one level it is, as Andrew Hurrell suggests, "politically contested," since what a region is or is not rests on "mental maps whose lines highlight some features whilst ignoring others" (2008). We might understand regions to be based on selective interpretations of geography, history, culture, race, religion, and other forms of collective memory. We can add to this Katzenstein and Hemmer's conclusion that regions are hardly "material objects in the world, nor is geography destiny." Rather, "regions are social and cognitive constructs that can strike actors as more or less plausible" (2002, 578). From an ideational perspective, regions share certain features, including perceptions of common interests, similar values that contribute to their identity, and "confidence in common norms and procedures of conflict resolution" (Kivimaki 2001, 7–8). Regions, like nations, might be said to share similarities that are identified by regional members as being meaningful. The larger point is that regions can be seen as "imagined communities" in that they exist in the minds of those who profess to be part of them. These mental constructs help operationalize identity, and reinforce the legitimacy of regional practices. Shared conceptions of history, morality, similar threat perceptions, models of governance, and other ideational factors will play a key role in whether a region can be successfully imagined or not.

Memory also plays a crucial role in forging some identities while excluding others, and constitutes another central theme in this work. In 1822 Ernest Renan famously observed, "the essential element of a nation is that all its individuals must have many things in common but it must also have forgotten many things." More recently, Stanley Cohen has noted how societies deliberately forget uncomfortable knowledge, which then becomes a series of "open secrets" known by everyone but not discussed. This is "social amnesia": "a mode of forgetting by which a whole society separates itself from its discreditable past record." Alternatively, one can see this as a practice of "chosen amnesia," when societies deliberately exclude unwanted or unsavory aspects of their national past (qtd. in Buckley-Zistel 2006, 132–34). And Smith, as we discussed earlier, certainly highlighted the centrality of selective remembering in the creation of national myths. In transmitting cultural practices and identities, as Jennifer Milliken has rightly noted, national discourses "work to define and to enable, and also to silence and to exclude, for example, by limiting and restricting authorities and experts to some groups, but not others, endorsing a certain common sense, but making other modes of categorizing and judging meaningless, impractical, inadequate or otherwise disqualified" (2001, 139). The politics of memory, of selective remembering and forgetting, plays a key role in our book alongside the importance of building identities around self and other.

Section I: Politics, Philosophy, and Sociology

In the first section, six chapters consider various aspects of European identity through engagement with conceptualizations of self and otherness. A central theme connecting these contributions concerns how Europeans have often defined themselves against various "others," not only historically but also in the present. The other plays a central role in defining by opposition who is or is not European, and perhaps more importantly, sets out what being European actually means.

Andrei Markovits has a particular interest in understanding the role of self and other in European identity through the lens of sport, which both reflects and helps constitute group identities. In comparing Western European sporting traditions to those in the United States, Markovits convincingly demonstrates that soccer has evolved in Europe in opposition to various others. Sports constitute a shared language that binds groups together against those who are perceived to be different. Markovits presents us with a conundrum: while the United States is a more violent society, soccer stadiums in many European countries remain cauldrons of racism, xenophobia, and physical assault, whereas comparable phenomena remain virtually unknown among American spectators. Even though sports, on balance, foster forms of cosmopolitanism and inclusiveness, counter-cosmopolitanism has equally been part of sports culture. In a historically informed comparison, Markovits proposes several hypotheses to explain why partisanship includes violence in Europe, but not in the US. These reasons include the very localized sporting traditions (and rivalries) of Europe, the close ties between sports clubs and strong political identities, and the lack of widely supported national sports teams in the US competing against other countries, which has provided in Europe the immensely potent collective of nationalism as a further forum for hatred and disdain of the "other." Openly racist invectives and hatred of the disempowered that remain common fare in virtually every European soccer stadium have all but disappeared in the US. Markovits presents an intriguing analysis of why this is the case. Despite these positive features of American sports, the author notes the continued problems of homophobia on both sides of the Atlantic.

Sally Charnow focuses on how European identity has worked to exclude some groups in society, in this case, French Jewish people. She is interested in how being the target of homogenizing French nationalism influenced the development of French Jewish identity in Europe, viewed through the interwar experiences of Edmond Fleg, a writer, poet, and playwright whose work was steeped in Jewish and Christian biblical history, liturgy, and legend. Fleg's story reminds us of the multiple forms of identity in Europe, and the influence of growing nationalism in the nineteenth century and its impact on other forms of nationalism, such as Zionism. The European influence helped cement the sense of Judaism as a cultural fact, with Jewish people tied together through shared history and traditions. Fleg's work challenged the view that there was hegemonic French identity, and his writings also explored the potential for reconciliation between the Catholic Church and European Jewry, as well as among individual Jews, Christians, and Muslims. In the same vein, Charnow posits, he articulated a pluralistic concept of national belonging, one that accepted the possibility of multiple attachments, which contrasted sharply with the "blood and soil" definition of national identity that Markovits convincingly argues still exists at the local level of European identity.

William Conklin's contribution also retains a strong focus on European conceptions of self and other. Certainly, the German philosopher Georg Friedrich Hegel never visited the so-called New World, but his work, which denigrated Indigenous peoples and demonstrated an obnoxious form of xenophobia, played an influential role in justifying colonialism. Conklin examines how and why Hegel postulated that Europeans were "civilized" and why Indigenous peoples primarily of North America were "uncivilized" in his narrow conceptualization of nations. Creating a series of dichotomies, Hegel sought to promote European society as civilized, with Indigenous societies as their uncivilized antipode. The author outlines the process by which Hegel made this move. First, Hegel claimed that uncivilized societies lacked self-reflection, meaning that their peoples acted from biological motives alone. Second, Hegel took it for granted that human beings lived in a higher level of civilization than animals, because animals were said to lack language. Uncivilized societies, as exemplified by Indigenous peoples according to Hegel, lacked language and they therefore resembled animals. Third, because uncivilized peoples lacked self-reflection mediated by concepts, they lacked a state, which was crucial to a civilized society. Conklin concludes by examining Hegel's perception of Indigenous legal traditions, which he described as "pre-historical" or "pre-legal" in shape. Law and justice only become possible when individuals in a society become self-reflective with mediating concepts, Hegel argued. This chapter is particularly interesting because it presents a snapshot of European views about Indigenous peoples characterized by deep ignorance and outright falsehood. Despite the positive contributions of Hegel's work, Conklin provides a useful contextualization of how Hegel approached societies he knew nothing about, using Indigenous peoples as a foil to proclaim the superiority of European society and thought.

Picking up similar themes, David MacDonald, one of the editors of this book, highlights how the creation of historical retrospectives on twentieth-century Europe and its role in the world presented our past century as the most atrocious, while similarly glorifying and whitewashing earlier centuries of colonialism and destruction of Indigenous peoples. In his chapter, MacDonald argues that the twentieth century is often portrayed as the most atrocious century in human history in terms of totalizing ideologies, moral abandonment, technological horror, and mass death. The nineteenth and earlier centuries, by contrast, emerge as progressive and enlightened eras, characterized by morality, rationalism, and the absence of war. Creating a dramatic contrast between old and new ignores the historical reality of colonialism and violence outside Europe's borders. Retrospectives have acted to create nostalgia for the past, when in reality, we need to stress the important elements of continuity and evolution between the nineteenth and later centuries.

Fractured by war, Europe emerged after 1945 with a blueprint for improving equality across the board. Kimberly Earles' contribution demonstrates the positive aspects of the European Union in overcoming some of the otherization of its more patriarchal past. Gender discrimination seems less salient in Europe than it was historically, and despite many drawbacks, the EU has presented a relatively progressive model of gender representation, certainly when compared to North America. Earles argues that the critical mass of women in EU decision-making positions since the early 1990s has promoted the creation of a "European gender equality identity" related to citizenship rights and equal opportunities in the economic, political, and social spheres. Over time, the EU has come to offer an additional, supranational level for European women and women's organizations to lobby for change, and today there are an increasing number of EU bodies dealing with gender equality. The author explores and analyzes the creation of these bodies, the various campaigns, strategies, and projects intended to promote gender equality and EU gender equality legislation, and the overall trajectory toward the creation of a gender equality identity within the EU.

In a fitting end to this first section, Dirk Nabers highlights how Orientalist impulses continue to play a role in European identity formation, especially in debates about the cultural and geographical limits of European Union expansion. While issues of gender have become far less salient than in the past, discrimination based on ethnicity and religion continues. A fear and misunderstanding of the mythical "East" has been manifest in the last three decades in antipathy to Turkish membership in the EU. In a theoretically oriented approach, Nabers employs poststructuralist insights to redefine the concept of identity, and uses such notions of identity to quantitatively and qualitatively analyze discourse on Turkish EU membership between 2005 and 2013. For poststructuralists, there is never any fixed identity—identity is always seen as both unstable and negative, and cannot be complete. Identity is only confirmed through relationships, which are established by equivalence and difference, by drawing out similarities and differences between the self and others. Nabers provides a revealing exploration of conflicting discourses among EU member states about what Turkey represents, as Europe continues to enlarge its borders and reimagine itself in a continually unfolding process.

Section II: Memory and Identity in Europe

Section II continues with the focus on ideas of self and other, here more centred in the context of European literature. Memory plays a central role here, as characters measure what is against what has come before in an attempt to forge personal, cultural, and political identities.

Like Charnow's work on Fleg, Stephen Henighan explores the relationship between Jewish identity and national identity, focusing on Mihail Sebastian's novel *The Accident*. Sebastian was a secular Jew whose literary career in post–First World War Romania was aided by his assimilation of the discourse of Romanian nationalism. In the 1930s, when this discourse turned anti-Semitic, Sebastian was spurned by his former friends and allies and oppressed by government legislation. Henighan's chapter reads *The Accident* as a contradictory response to this changed environment. Set in multicultural Transylvania, whose territorial incorporation into Romania in 1920 was regarded as a triumph by nationalists, the novel reprises many of the 1930s nationalist tropes of mystical attachment to the landscape of the homeland. In Sebastian's treatment, however, this nationalist homeland also becomes a place of diversity, as collaborative relations between the region's German minority and its Romanian majority are integral to the recuperation of the protagonist's sanity.

Spenser Morrison's chapter takes us in very different directions. With an emphasis on an earlier period of European history, he invites us to consider the violent creation of otherness through the exported American-style capitalism that was part of the Marshall Plan's rebuilding of Italy after the devastation of her cities during the Second World War. Morrison proposes that Joseph Heller's novel *Catch-22* (1961) uses the image of European cities destroyed in the war and subsequently reconstructed in part through American aid as a lens through which to view America's Cold War–era "urban crisis." Morrison examines the significance of protagonist Captain John Yossarian's night walk through bombed-out Rome as a means to argue that capitalist liberal democracy, the social mode championed by America's postwar Marshall Plan for reconstructing war-ravaged Europe, acquired a violent quality through administrative, commercial, and militaristic structures. The urban spaces of annihilated Europe, where human life became (in Giorgio Agamben's phrase) "bare life" under a state of emergency, illuminated a violence wrought upon citizens by an American complex of government and commerce, whose modernity emanated primarily from urban centres. In Heller's novel, he argues, we see an ideologically tinged American "ruin-gazing," the image of a destroyed Europe used to better understand the violence of America.

The next chapter features Oana Fotache's exploration of Romanian identity in a later period. In her chapter on the representations of Europe as a cultural space in travel writings by Romanian intellectuals published between 1960 and 2010, she ruminates not upon the destruction of identities that must be painfully reconstituted in an altered or destroyed landscape, but rather upon the creation of a national identity, conceived also as a European identity, when met with resistance from a larger European context. The synchronization of Romanian civilization and culture with more general Western European patterns has been at the centre of numerous ideological disputes. These occur against the background of Romanian society's modern development. Being part of Europe has not been a legitimate claim for Romania unless it was supported by self- and others' representations of this status, and thus Western Europe emerges from these travel writings as a privileged and idealized cultural space of almost mythical character, an object of admiration at times frustratingly remote, and yet at the same time a cause of nostalgia.

Jeannine Pitas' chapter on the Warsaw uprising explores memories troubled by trauma as they are fished up from the past and used in the creation of a national myth. Memory is a theme that runs through all of the chapters in this section. The present, and the demands it makes on already constituted identities, often forces them to change or to reimagine themselves in significant ways. If the remembered city of Rome can be so cavalierly overwritten by the pressures and demands of modern American-style capitalism, if the physical evidence that corroborates a memory is no more reliable than the memories themselves, what hope is there for imagination to make useful contributions to the creation of a nation or European identity? These poignant questions form the root of Pitas' thought-provoking analysis. Her chapter addresses problems of memory, both personal and historical, in Miron Białoszewski's *A Memoir of the Warsaw Uprising*. Exploring the ways in which the Warsaw Uprising was adopted as Poland's national myth, Pitas examines the challenge Białoszewski's narrative poses to that mythmaking. Instead of reifying the historical event, the author seeks to describe it honestly. And yet time, space, and even personal identity become confused, and some memories inevitably get buried under the rubble. Under these traumatic circumstances, the attempt to remember becomes as much a compulsion as it is a conscious strategy of resistance against totalizing meta-narratives.

Section III: Geography and Cartography

In Section III we continue the focus on self and other in European identity formation, but shift the lens to maps and representations of Europe's geography, seeking to understand where Europe is geographically situated and what lies beyond its socially constructed borders. Fernando Clara begins with his analysis of "The Dynamics of European Identity: Maps, Bodies, Views." The author uses critical cartographical analysis to understand how European identity is made up of a series of discourses that divide, differentiate, dissect, and order it. Clara's project is located with a larger movement to challenge the hegemony of elites who have controlled cartography for several centuries. As Crampton and Krygier have argued,

> Elites—the great map houses of the west, the state, and to a lesser extent academics—have been challenged by two important developments. First, the actual business of mapmaking, of collecting spatial data and mapping it out, is passing out of the hands of the experts. The ability to make a map, even a stunning interactive 3D map, is now available to anyone with a home computer and an internet connection.... [Second] a more social theoretic critique, which we argue is a political one, situates maps within specific relations of power and not as neutral scientific documents. (2006, 12)

Besides providing Europe with a geographical, representational existence, discourses-maps-icons also allow important insights into the dynamics involving the historical constructions of European identity. Taking a historical approach, Clara focuses on the changes that Europe and European identity underwent between the sixteenth and the nineteenth centuries. The author, through an in-depth exploration of a small number of well-known allegorical and symbolic maps of Europe, shows how it was imagined through cartographic representation. In particular, Clara focuses on the *Königin Europa* by Johann Putsch (1570), popularized in Sebastian Münster's *Cosmographia Universalis*, and the *Nouvelle Carte d'Europe Dressée Pour 1870* (originally published in Paris in 1870) by Paul Hadol.

Gordana Yovanovich examines Emir Kusturica's film *Underground* not as it has been read by most Balkan intellectuals, that is, as a film that perpetuates stereotypes about the Balkans for a Western audience, but rather as one that explores the relationship between a local identity and a larger sense of national identity. Yovanovich finds in *Underground* not the creation of an image for the consumption of the other, but rather a self-reflexive identity construction. At the same time, the film engages in the larger context of world cinematic language, mixing regional Balkan metaphors and ethnic music with cinematographic language and tropes from world cinema, questioning the relationship between the centre and the periphery and re-examining the hierarchy of notions such as "civilized" and "primitive." Yovanovich argues here that the film questions and subverts rather than promotes the official world view of the Balkans.

Mary-Michelle DeCoste, one of the editors of this volume, contributes a chapter that, like the others in this section, examines a text to define one geographical space as distinct from another. Exiled from Italy for his Counter-Reformation sympathies, Giacomo Castelvetro sought the patronage of Lucy, Countess of Bedford, through a text describing the splendours of Italian produce. He paints for Lucy a picture of an Italy almost spontaneously fecund that nourishes its citizens on the most delightful fruits and vegetables, skilfully prepared for the table. In damp, chilly England, Castelvetro writes with nostalgia for his sunny Italian home, showing the profound attachment to the landscape described by Henighan in his chapter in Section II of this volume. Yet Castelvetro's love of his native land is coloured by his experiences of religious persecution. DeCoste shows how, through the narration of a linguistic misunderstanding centring around food while visiting Germany, Castelvetro distinguishes for his reader what is Italian, what is German, and what is English by combining what he views as the best elements of the three countries.

Section IV

Section IV takes up genres of fashion and dance along with a second chapter on film to explore the packaging of national identities for export. While this theme has already been explored in DeCoste's chapter, here we turn to visual representations. These chapters all seek to understand the role of the audience in the creation of national identities, and how an awareness of that audience colours the understanding of national culture.

Elena Benelli's focus is on the space of the Mediterranean as it figures in Italian cinema's exploration of migration and Italy. Benelli discusses the central role that film plays in resisting the negative image of immigration to Italy created by the Italian mass media. Cinema, Benelli argues, is particularly well-suited to the task of creating a more nuanced and complex view of migrants than is otherwise seen in Italian culture. She examines a number of films that focus on one particular space, central to Amelio's *Lamerica* (1994), Giordana's *Quando sei nato non puoi più nasconderti* (2005) and Melliti's *Io, l'altro* (2007), and fundamental to the encounter with the other:

the Mediterranean Sea, the natural border and the symbolic fluid threshold to be crossed before arriving on Italian shores. Benelli argues that the Mediterranean Sea plays a crucial function in the visual narrative because it represents the centre of an intricate crossroad of identities, languages, and cultures still to be mapped in Italian culture.

Susan Ingram's chapter explores the Bread & Butter fashion trade fair in Berlin, a city that has attempted to maintain its traditional strength in the fashion and media sectors while adapting them to the globalized twenty-first century. After outlining the contours of brand Berlin, Ingram then identifies and analyzes some of the factors that have contributed to its recent success, such as supporting fashion trade shows that foster anti-national European identities, or more specifically, fashion-oriented identities that can be coded "European." She contrasts brand Berlin with brand Barcelona, the city that tempted Bread & Butter to hold its trade fair there for a number of years before losing it to Berlin when its brand no longer conformed to the Euro-chic ideals of the trade fair. As Ingram demonstrates, the Europeanness of the identities produced and promoted at these fashion trade shows is a kind of "New Europe," with the potential to reconfigure the way we think about who we are and how places and their histories figure in that process. For Bread & Butter, being European means identifying with an urban culture constructed both discursively and materially on the basis of the historical and material traces these centres contain.

Alla Myzelev's chapter focuses on dance, and together with Susan Ingram's chapter on fashion that it follows, showcases performative constructions of identity. In conjunction with Berlin's XI Olympiad (1936) celebrations, German officials organized an international dance competition and extended an invitation to Canada to participate. The Canadian committee chose Russian émigré dancer Boris Volkoff to choreograph four dances for the event, two of which were based on Inuit and Aboriginal folklore. Myzelev argues that the costumes and set designs played upon European interests in Native subjects and on the lack of knowledge among Canadians and Europeans of real Aboriginal culture. Volkoff, a Russian immigrant to Canada sensitive to the desire of the Germans to showcase their own folk culture, wanted to find a way to showcase something that was uniquely Canadian. He had to interpret the ways in which other European dance traditions used the folkloric traditions of their countries in dance. He had to find, although himself an outsider in Canada, a way to package Canadian native culture through dance. This nexus of Russian, European, white Canadian, and Native Canadian typifies the ways in which national identities can never be wholly separated from the motives behind their construction.

References

Buckley-Zistel, S. 2006. "Remembering to Forget: Chosen Amnesia as a Strategy for Local Coexistence in Post-genocide Rwanda." *Africa* 76 (2): 131–50.

Crampton, Jeremy W., and John Krygie. 2006. "An Introduction to Critical Cartography." *ACME: An International E-Journal for Critical Geographies* 4 (1): 11–33.

Hobsbawm, Eric J. 1995. *Nations and Nationalism since 1780: Programme, Myth, Reality*. Cambridge: Cambridge University Press.

Hurrell, Andrew. 2008. "Playgrounds of Regional Powers: Regional Powers and the Global System." Paper presented at the first Regional Powers Network (RPN) conference in Hamburg, Germany, 15–16 September.

Ignatieff, Michael. 1993. *Blood and Belonging: Journeys into the New Nationalism*. Toronto: Viking Books.

Jacobs, Dirk, and Robert Maier. 1998. "European identity: construct, fact and fiction." In *A United Europe. The Quest for a Multifaceted Identity*, edited by M. Gastelaars and A. de Ruijter, 13–34. Maastricht: Shaker.

Katzenstein, Peter, and Christopher Hemmer. 2002. "Why Is There No NATO in Asia? Collective Identity, Regionalism, and the Origins of Multilateralism." *International Organization* 56 (3): 575–607.

Kivimaki, Timo. 2001. "The Long Peace of ASEAN." *Journal of Peace Research* 38 (1): 5–25.

Milliken, Jennifer.1999. "A Study of Discourse in International Relations." *EJIR* 5 (2): 225–54.

Risse, Thomas. 2011. "Nationalism and Collective Identities: Europe versus the Nation-State?" In D*evelopments in West European Politics*, 2nd edition, edited by Paul Heywood, Erik Jones, and Martin Rhodes. London: Palgrave.

Ross, Marc Howard. 1995. "Psychocultural Interpretation Theory and Peacemaking in Ethnic Conflicts." *Political Psychology* 16 (3): 23–44.

Smith, A.D. 2001. "Authenticity, Antiquity and Archaeology." *Nations and Nationalism* 7 (1): 144–49.

Trevor-Roper, Hugh. 1962. *Jewish and Other Nationalism*. London: Weidenfeld and Nicolson.

Section I
Politics, Philosophy, and Sociology

Chapter 1

Yet Another American Exceptionalism: The Minor Role of Counter-Cosmopolitan Fan Behaviour in North American Venues Compared to Their Salient Quotidian Existence in Europe's Soccer Stadiums

Andrei S. Markovits

In this chapter I will continue to compare Europe and America, a topic that has been central to my work for decades. I will look at the following fascinating puzzle: soccer stadiums in many European countries continue to remain cauldrons of racism, xenophobia, and physical assault, whereas comparable phenomena remain virtually unknown among North American spectators. Can this really be? Why are physical violence, racist invectives, and abusive language and behaviour among spectators of North American major team sports much rarer and less salient than in Europe?

What renders this discrepancy so interesting is the fact that by virtually all statistical measures, these European countries exhibit a much lower level of violence than does the United States. The question, of course, is why do we see such a sports exception in terms of the norms of violence governing the public cultures on these two continents? Clearly, in all competitive endeavours such as agonistic team sports, every team's supporters will do their best to become "the twelfth man," to use the world of football and soccer, or "the sixth man" in basketball, or "the seventh man" in ice hockey. Spectators will do pretty much anything to get into an opponent's head, to get under her or his skin, to render her or him insecure. This constitutes the very essence of fandom. But why has such partisanship come to include violence as routine in Europe and not in the United States, an otherwise more violent society? In a historically informed comparison, I will propose a few hypotheses as plausible reasons for this fascinating discrepancy.

To be sure, I fully believe that sports, on balance, have performed an enlightening function in human history, that precisely by dint of their inherently competitive and agonistic nature, they foster a profound meritocracy that few other venues in social life do. And as I have argued emphatically in my book *Gaming the World: How Sports Are Reshaping Global Politics and Culture,* co-authored with Lars Rensmann, I firmly believe sports foster a cosmopolitanism that is an indispensable ingredient to all the good that the editors of this volume believe sports to have. Indeed, my chapter's second argument consists precisely in the feting of just such cosmopolitanism by contrasting favourably the largely non-violent and non-racist discourses and demeanors of North American sports spectators with their European counterparts. But alas, just like in most realms of human activity, so too in sports do cosmopolitanism and inclusiveness meet with resistance by forces that could best be characterized by what Kwame Anthony Appiah has so aptly termed "counter-cosmopolitanism" (2007, 137–53). Newcomers, challengers, immigrants, and "alien" languages are often met with ridicule, as well as harsh, hostile, or even violent reactions by the natives. Since cultural changes inevitably imply some threat to entrenched identities, such changes exact tensions and defensive responses. Nowhere is this clearer than in the world of sports, since adversity, opposition, competition, contest and thus conflict—in short, sports' inherent agonistic if not necessarily antagonistic nature—are the most essential markers of identities. Without them, sports do not exist. By their very nature, by demanding winners and losers, sports possess a zero-sum essence that extols tensions, rewards the victors and punishes the vanquished.

One of the characteristics of any entrenched sports culture is its initial suspicion of and hostility toward any newcomers from within the sport itself, and by a rival sport. In both cases, the established sport perceives the intra- or inter-sport newcomer as inferior in any number of ways. First, the newcomer lacks toughness, and is not sufficiently manly. For example, "true" English and Scottish football supporters perceive continental players and others hailing from outside the British Isles as weak "divers" who "feign injury"—in short, they are not as manly and tough as "real" footballers ought to be. Northern Europeans see Latin American and Southern European soccer players as "fakers," "frauds," and "sissies." Or, reflect on how Canadian hockey fans and self-appointed guardians of the game, even beyond the provocative showmanship of Don Cherry, have continued to belittle the skill and very presence of European NHL players by calling them "soft." And to millions of "manly" sports fans of the North American Big Four, soccer is basically a sport for patsies, fakers, and women.

While soccer lacks masculinity in the eyes of American sports fans, baseball and basketball are viewed the same way by their European counterparts. Some European football supporters doubt the masculinity even of American football—or "gridiron," as the game has come to be labelled dismissively and derisively in Europe—which is most certainly a brutal and violent sport by any measure. However, to European machos, American football's alleged "softness" comes from its players wearing protective gear—unlike "real" men in the related rugby games—and in its being performed by players who are so big they are often perceived as "freaks of nature," not real men. For Europeans, football, more than any of the other American sports, has also become synonymous with American power, capitalism, commercialism, and crudeness. Moreover, it has become the American sport most associated with the ills of television culture. To its European critics, American football assumes a cartoon-like quality, something unreal that is a mere byproduct of America's money-making culture. In other words, all the threatening dimensions associated with an alleged American takeover of European culture and identity have become associated with football. This is odd, because this sport has been the least internationally successful among the North American Big Four, and has proved to be no threat to soccer's dominance in Europe, contrary to all kinds of alarmist and protectionist worries tinged with a fine dosage of anti-football rhetoric.[1] Behooving the massively gendered nature of all hegemonic sports cultures, the alleged absence of any requisite manliness of all rivals clearly helps to lower their legitimacy.

In addition to the perceived "unmanliness" of any newcomer to an existing sports space—be it the same sport performed by outsiders (European hockey players in the NHL; Latin footballers in Europe's northern, particularly British, leagues) or a different sport (soccer coming to America; American sports going to Europe)—the establishment denigrates the challenger for being facile and aesthetically displeasing. "How hard is it really to kick a ball?" is the frequent criticism made by America's Big Four fans levelled against soccer. "After all, any little kid can do so! What about any measurable statistics that convey each player's actual contribution to the game?" And most emphatically, "what is it with the deranged time-keeping by the referee who, in this day and age when we are able to measure time with precision to a tenth of a second—as is commonplace in three of the Big Four North American sports—decides totally arbitrarily and for no discernible reason to anyone else in the stadium when to end a game?"

Conversely, European soccer fans grumble about the alleged facility of American sports: "how hard can it be to hit this ball with this odd stick?" Or they state, "there is absolutely no skill to playing American football—big guys just hit each other indiscriminately and pile up on each other." And even basketball cannot be hard since it basically entails "seven-foot-tall giants dunking a ball into a ten-foot-high basket."

And lastly, of course, insiders invariably denigrate the new rival by labelling it boring: to millions of American sports fans, soccer is totally boring by dint of the paucity of goals during a match and what they perceive as endless passing in the middle of the field, apparently with little aim and all the more turnovers. Conversely, Europeans find the number obsession of Americans that characterizes all their sports boring, none more than baseball, which most Europeans completely fail to understand and remain unwilling to engage in. They also find basketball boring by dint of its high scoring, which devalues each incremental score.

The point is clear: high scoring can be as boring to an outsider as low scoring. Both bespeak a lack of appreciation for and often irritation with the new and threatening language, all sports being akin to languages: systems of communication with their own codes, cultures, grammar, metrics, and texts, from apparent to meta and sub. After all, the very same American baseball fan that categorizes soccer as boring by virtue of its lack of scoring revels in a pitchers' duel that results in a 1–0 game, which he most assuredly finds downright thrilling and aesthetically pleasing; ditto with the reverse. A true soccer fan will rejoice in the excitement of a 0–0 draw (in the British jargon of these games; "tie" in its American variant) and will dismiss American sports as boring due to an excess of scoring in basketball, paucity of action in baseball, and weird melees and unskilled mayhem in football.

That a different sport appears to be boring to the uninitiated makes complete sense. After all, a lecture delivered in any language the audience cannot understand would, by definition, be quite boring for its members. As we know from the world of languages, one needs to further denigrate any rival by diminishing its level of difficulty and beauty. Only one's own language has the requisite complexity, nuance, and aesthetics to render it incomparably superior to any other. Just like all language communities have their purists and chauvinists, whose very essence is to lord it over others by extolling their particular language's purity and expressive superiority, rail against any contamination by outsiders, and tout its advantages vis-à-vis all rivals, so too do established sports cultures protect their domain against newcomers on all possible levels of contestation.

Counter-cosmopolitanism's ugliest expression is resilient racism and random violence against "others." It is no coincidence that radical counter-cosmopolitan sentiments and activities frequently exhibit pronounced anti-Semitism: traditionally, Jews have been identified with cosmopolitanism in Europe, and anti-Semites have always seen cosmopolitanism as their enemy because (like Jews) it presumably undermines the rootedness of the local and traditional, especially as manifested by the *Volk* (Appiah 2007, xvi; Benhabib and Eddon 2007, 44–61). Since the 1970s, counter-cosmopolitan extreme-right groups and movements have re-emerged across Europe. Over the last two decades, new extreme-right parties with counter-cosmopolitan agendas have enjoyed significant inroads in the public spheres and political landscapes of Western and Eastern Europe.[2]

Some hooligan and extreme-right groups deliberately choose the sports arena as the place to act out their racist prejudices, committing violent deeds and agitating for the politics of exclusion. The quantity and quality of such counter-cosmopolitan activities varies over time and space. The very nature of sports is competition, where one favours one's own side as best one can while at the same time attempting to fluster and impede one's opponent. Since shaking an opponent's confidence will remain an integral part of sports, it is safe to assume that taunting will never disappear from any competitive sport. Indeed, it is the power of such taunting, distracting, unnerving, and intimidating, meant to impede the effectiveness of the opponent's efforts, that comprises one of *the* most cherished ingredients of all sports: home field (or court) advantage.[3] And as we know from all sports, this advantage is huge, constant, and ubiquitous! Winning away from home, on the opponent's field, court, or gym is arguably one of the most daunting tasks in any team sport. Human beings, even well-paid megastars, prefer playing in front of thousands of adoring fans who desperately want them to succeed, instead of thousands of ill-wishers who delight in their failures and will do everything in their power to foster them.

And where does one draw the arbitrary line of what is acceptable fan support of the home team and what is not? Why is it okay to distract a foul-shooting player in basketball by waving thousands of multicoloured plastic sticks to obstruct his view, but not to shout insults at him? Is it acceptable to set off the fire alarm in the visiting team's hotel at four a.m. the morning before the big game, and prevent it from being shut off for more than one hour? Is it fine to turn on the heat full blast on a hot day in June in the visiting team's locker room while providing air conditioning in the home team's? Does the throwing of cigarette lighters, heated coins, spittle, and animal feces on the visiting players—as happens regularly in basket-ball arenas of the Mediterranean and soccer grounds in Europe and Latin America—represent a legitimate expression of home field advantage?

The content of this taunting has varied widely and continues to this day. Thus, as I will argue, there is perhaps no greater difference between American and European hegemonic sports culture today than in the expression of counter-cosmopolitanism in those cultures. While in America, overtly racist taunts accompanied by violent acts against players and viewers have all but disappeared and lack any kind of legitimacy in contemporary sports, this, alas, is not the case in Europe. Soccer grounds have become perhaps the last bastion where the worst kind of racist, sexist, anti-Semitic, xeno-phobic—in short, counter-cosmopolitan—language and behaviour have not only been tolerated but actually extolled. I offer my own extensive ex-periences as cases in point. In my sixty-odd years of living a bi-continental life, I have attended many hundreds of baseball, basketball, football, and hockey games at virtually all levels in the United States since 1960. While I have encountered the occasional incident of ugly taunting (often of the sexist and homophobic variety) at the high school and college levels, and very rarely at the professional level, I have never experienced overt racism and anti-Semitism at any of these events. Nor have I witnessed major acts of violence among spectators beyond the occasional beer-fuelled fistfight between two fans that invariably was stopped very quickly either by people in the immediate area or by the stadium authorities, most often both.

Alas, this has not been the case with my European experiences where—especially beginning in the mid-1970s—my numerous visits to soccer grounds from Germany to England, from Austria to Spain, from Italy to Holland were regularly marred by overt racist and anti-Semitic language and behaviour. Worse still, whenever I or others tried to quell these ugly outbursts, we were met either with total indifference or indignation, and sometimes with outright hostility because we dared to challenge the norm and rock the boat. No one wants to stand out in the crowd, or dare to chal-lenge the loud and violent minority, and too few seem sufficiently offended by the hegemony of this counter-cosmopolitan behaviour and discourse in their stadiums to combat it effectively. In other words, it is not so much the activities of a committed minority that differentiates the European case from the American, but rather their de facto approval by the rest of the pub-lic. Once again, as is so often the case, it is the silent majority that defines the overall tenor and texture of the pervasive atmosphere and accepted behaviour.

In contrast to many European cases, violence is a very marginal occurrence in present-day American sports culture, and open racism is practically taboo and socially unacceptable in the stands and among players. While discrimination and racism undoubtedly remain major issues in American sports and society, explicitly worded overt racism has, for all intents and purposes, been banned from contemporary American sports.[4] In fact, any of the vile racist remarks and gestures that remain commonplace in many European stadiums—even where fan violence has been successfully contained if not completely eliminated over the last few years, such as in England—have virtually disappeared from all major league and college-level sports venues in the United States. Moreover, the rare cases of fan violence that have existed in America—and will always exist in any context where large numbers of people gather for emotionally charged events in a relatively small and confined space—have had a completely different substance and tone from their European counterparts. Thus, violence at American sports venues has almost never been a premeditated, organized activity implemented by a small group of well-trained street fighters whose primary, perhaps sole purpose is to engage in fights and cause havoc rather than to watch the game.

More than forty years ago, Philip Goodhart and Christopher Chataway observed that in America, "so often characterized as a land bubbling with violence, sporting hooliganism, apart from racial disturbances, seems to be largely unknown" (1968, 144).[5] Riots before and after games have occurred upon occasion; however, even these incidents have been on the decline for decades. While some scholars had observed a temporary rise in sports-related fan violence at American venues in the 1970s and 1980s—to some extent due to more extensive media coverage and public sensitivity toward the issue—occurrences since then have become few and far between.[6]

By far the most prevalent forms of violence in connection with any sports in America belong to the category best captured by the terms "celebratory violence" or "celebratory riots." Typically this involves unruly and often rather inebriated fans celebrating their team's victory by rioting in the streets, burning cars, turning over and igniting garbage cans, and fighting the police who are dispatched to quell the disturbance. Interestingly, it is exclusively fans of the winning teams that engage in such behaviour, never the losing teams. This was the case following the Tigers' World Series triumph in Detroit in October of 1984; in Chicago after the Bulls' championship victory in June of 1992; in Los Angeles after the Lakers regained their title in June of 2009 and then defended it one year later, with the latter two occasions witnessing crowd-induced violence immediately following the title-clinching games; in October of 2004 in Boston when the home-town Red Sox overcame a three-game deficit to beat their hated long-term tormentor the New York Yankees in the series by four games to three; in November of 2002 in Columbus, Ohio, when Ohio State fans stormed the field of the Horseshoe after their team had defeated arch-rival Michigan on the last play of the game; and in east Lansing in early December 2013, when Michigan State fans celebrated their team's long-awaited winning of the Big Ten championship in college football by burning couches, setting bonfires, overturning cars, and engaging in other types of unruly and vio-lent behaviour.

In each of these cases, the victories released much pent-up frustration by the winners' fans. The Boston Red Sox had not only won their series in a manner never achieved by any sports team in the history of major league baseball, professional football, and basketball (down three games to none in a best-of-seven series and winning it by triumphing in four must-win games in a row) but they did so against the very team that had constantly outshined them and was their ever-present nemesis since 1918, the last time the Red Sox had won the World Series.[7] Ohio State had been domi-nated by Michigan throughout much of the 1990s and the Buckeyes had just concluded an entire "Beat Michigan week" on campus that preceded the game and catapulted much of the student body into a frenzied state of mind. But even in these instances, one needs to differentiate between the "celebratory riots" that occurred immediately following the victories largely in and around the venues themselves, and subsequent physical as-saults and lootings that were connected only loosely, if at all, to the sports events that served as convenient pretexts to engage in violent acts ("Vio-lence Amid Celebration" 1992). Moreover, unlike in Europe, where virtually all of the violence in the stadiums is premeditated, prepared, and designed well before the actual games, "celebratory violence" at American venues occurs spontaneously and in an improvised fashion. Above all, these riots are not directed against the fans of the opposing teams as much as they are random acts of destruction against whatever constitutes their immediate surroundings.

In perhaps the greatest contrast to its European counterparts, these American instances of fan violence were not accompanied by overt racism, anti-Semitism, or any discourse or activity directed against a particular minority. Jeering the New York Yankees and deriding the Michigan Wol-verines using vulgar language might not be pretty, but it surely is in a whole different category from spewing hatred and venom against Jews, blacks, and other non-white minorities, tactics that have remained commonplace in Europe's stadiums since the 1970s. Jerry M. Lewis, author of one of the most comprehensive studies of fan violence in North American sports, summarizes the situation: "For North America, and particularly the United States, the data on fan violence at the collegiate and professional levels of competition are clear. The typical rioter is likely to be a young, white male celebrating a victory after a championship or an important game or match" (Lewis 2007, 69).

This also pertained to occasions of fan violence in Canada, such as the disturbances in Vancouver in June 2011 after the Canucks suffered defeat on their home ice in an all-decisive Game Seven against the Boston Bruins, thus continuing their inability to win the team's first Stanley Cup. While clearly not induced by the usual American-style celebration but instead by its opposite, namely disappointment and chagrin, the disturbances in Vancouver, though ugly and reprehensible, were quite American in nature in that they consisted of random acts of destruction and mayhem as opposed to clearly aimed European-style attacks on anybody perceived as the "other," in whatever guise this might be.

I do not mean to downplay the ugliness of occasional fan violence such as the post–Stanley Cup riots in Vancouver, Canada and similar ones in the United States caused by these so-called celebratory riots in any way. After all, a young Emerson College journalism student lost her life totally senselessly and tragically in the mayhem following the Red Sox's defeat of the Yankees. I certainly see its occurrence as detrimental to American sports and society. Yet it is noteworthy that European-style violence and hooligan-type riots have never emerged at American sport venues and events. Why has this been the case? Why has fan violence largely been absent from American team sports, when the United States suffers from a much higher level of violence in virtually every other aspect of its society than any country in Europe?

There have been many rather speculative scholarly responses to this puzzle in the social sciences. For example, the Leicester School on hooliganism, which has often provided first-rate studies and interpretations of this phenomenon in Britain and Europe, argues that in "welfare state" Europe, sections of the working class were more fully integrated into the overall "consensus" of society. Thus, these welfare states incorporated workers more fully into sports than has been the case in the United States. In contrast, according to the Leicester School, America's free market principles and "federal and state policies based to a greater degree on *laissez faire* values may have resulted in a greater proportion of the lower classes being less incorporated into dominant values and, consequently, less integrated into sports. In its turn, a consequence of this may have been to insulate American sports to a greater degree from the lower-class pattern of gang fighting" (Murphy, Williams, and Dunning 2002, 208).

The authors rightly conclude that in contrast to the European cases, where violent street gangs have conquered soccer stands in many places, gangs also exist in America but have not chosen to make sports the loci in which to fight and act out their aggression (Murphy, Williams, and Dunning 2002, 207). Yet I disagree emphatically with the Leicester School's interpretation on two counts: first, that fighting and hooliganism are somehow the (possibly exclusive) purview of the working classes; and second, that the American working class has been excluded from the world of American sports. That is factually incorrect as any reading of baseball's history, or the early days of the NFL, or basketball's ubiquitous reach into playing and following, and hockey's attraction to the industrial working classes of large Canadian cities and those of the Midwest and Northeast of the United States, reveals. Football was a way of life for the coal miners and steel workers of the Ohio Valley and western Pennsylvania, and had every bit the equivalent socializing function as Rugby League and soccer did in England's Yorkshire and Lancashire.

To the Italian, Irish, Polish, and Jewish workers of New York, Boston, Chicago, Detroit, and Cleveland, their baseball (and football) teams had the same cultural meaning and social importance as soccer teams did to their English and continental comrades. But by dint of ethnicity superseding class as a major signifier of collective identity in the United States, one might think of class as less important to America's sports culture than to Europe's. After all, people think of Hank Greenberg's exploits or Joe DiMaggio's feats as having helped Jews and Italians, respectively, to integrate into America's mainstream culture. Few note the modest social milieu from which these two American icons arose and what they meant to Jewish and Italian workers.

American sports have emerged over time into a particularly powerful medium for broadly inclusive cultural, social, and national integration that cuts across class divisions and increasingly transcends ethnic conflicts. In doing so, American sports have functioned as an integrative substitute for other forms of social (welfare) mechanisms. With the disproportionate success of minority athletes in America's hegemonic sports culture, sports have turned into a major model that facilitates exposure to cosmopolitan diversity and enhances broader recognition of ethnic and cultural multiplicity in American immigrant society. If anything, the much more pronounced prevalence of sports-related terms and metaphors in American English's vernacular compared to any of its European counterparts bespeaks the deeper penetration and broader proliferation of popular team sports in American culture than has been the case in Europe.

I now want to address conditions in American sports that I see as less favourable for sport-related collective violence than they have been in Europe. America is a country of continental proportions. The long distances inhibit travel to accompany one's team for an away game (Murphy, Williams, and Dunning 2002, 209). In addition, there is less of a tradition in following one's team across the country for a regular season or even play-off game than in Europe. Only year-end bowl games in college football, traditionally played on neutral sites, and the March Madness tournament in men's college basketball also played in neutral arenas strewn across the country, witness American sports fans traveling in large numbers to follow their teams. Rivalry games (or derbies, to use soccer parlance)—Auburn vs. Alabama, USC vs. UCLA, Ohio State vs. Michigan, Florida vs. Florida State, Stanford vs. California, Duke vs. North Carolina, Yankees vs. Red Sox—constitute exceptions to the American norm. And sure enough, these emotionally charged encounters do on occasion yield fan violence before and after the games in bars and streets near the relevant stadiums, and sometimes even during the games themselves, particularly in the bleacher seats.

These altercations are invariably quelled quickly by surrounding spectators, and the authorities are also at hand to nip things in the bud. But fights do happen at these emotionally charged games. With the exception of the rivalry games, however, American sports venues feature few visible "enemies" or outsiders. This drastically reduces the chance of clashes between large groups of opposing fans. By contrast, European soccer matches are more local affairs, and there is a tradition of clubs travelling with a large coterie of fans even to distant games. Geographic proximity in team sports breeds rivalries, which in turn fosters contempt and hatred that then increase the likelihood of violence.

Many European cities have had a long-standing tradition of featuring a number of clubs in close proximity, which intensifies rivalries and mutual hatreds: Vienna once furnished ten soccer clubs in Austria's top-level league of twelve teams well into the 1960s and continues to have three or four to this day; Budapest has had six; Bucharest, Istanbul, and Moscow four;

London still boasted six clubs in the English Premier League's 2013–14 campaign; and many cities have at least two. Because American sports teams began as businesses with their owners explicitly disallowing the establishment of any rivals in their territory, no cities other than New York, Chicago, and Los Angeles have more than one team per sport. And in those rare cases where cities have multiple teams per sport, they originated in different leagues (as in baseball) and led parallel but rarely overlapping existences. Or, they arose at vastly disparate time periods (as in basketball and hockey), both of which mitigated rivalries.

But let us recall that the intense mutual dislike on the part of Giants and Dodgers fans in baseball hails precisely from their proximate histories in New York City, where they played each other repeatedly in the very same league. Their antipathy stems not from their post-1958 West Coast incarnation, representing NorCal and SoCal respectively. The bad blood between New York Rangers fans and their counterpart supporters of the New York Islanders and the New Jersey Devils in hockey also attests to the ubiquitous phenomenon in all competitive team sports that proximity breeds competition and hatred, not respect and harmony. Distance may not foster affection, but it most certainly decreases the acerbity of conflict. And the larger distances of America's spaces—both in sports and geography—contribute considerably to a less violent atmosphere in American sports compared to their European counterparts.

In contrast to European clubs, many of which to this day have strong political identities, sports teams in the United States—tellingly called franchises—possess virtually none of this. In Europe, many clubs have been close to political parties or movements, which in turn reflect often bitter social, economic, religious, ethnic, and linguistic cleavages that divide people. And thus *any* contest, even a football match between a club identified as representing a "red" (i.e., socialist) subculture confronting a rival "black" club (i.e., Catholic-conservative)—such as Celtic Glasgow standing for Irish Catholicism confronting its crosstown rival Glasgow Rangers, which represented Scottish Protestantism—attains a vicarious dimension. The actual events on the field stand for something completely different, alas usually something divisive, precisely because these games are inherently contested between "us" and "them."[8]

Crucially, American sports have virtually no national dimension to them. There are no national baseball, basketball, football, and hockey teams that represent the country on a regular basis in constant contests with neighbouring countries. Americans are not familiar with the emotionally charged identification with a national team commensurate to what the Brazilians experience for their *selecao*, Germans for their *Nationalmannschaft*, Italians for their *squaddra azzurra*, or Argentinians for their *albiceleste*. Of course, there are "Team USA"s participating in quadrennial global competitions such as world championships and the Olympics, but these are far away and few in number, and have virtually no relevance for Americans' emotional investment in their sports and teams. American sports and the accompanying emotions are completely insular because they exist in an intercity and intracountry environment where international dimensions are secondary at best. Tellingly, it has been mainly in the least of American team sports, soccer, that the national teams—both on the women's and the men's side—play an integral role in that sport's presence in the country. They have developed intense rivalries with the Mexicans on the men's side and the Norwegians, Brazilians, and Germans on the women's. These could slip into violent altercations between opposing fans at future contests, though this is very unlikely, especially in women's soccer.

Furthermore, in contrast to the high emotional investment in soccer's dominant monoculture in Europe, the multiplicity of America's hegemonic sports culture tends to spread a fan's emotional involvement and allegiances over three, possibly four teams, thus easing the pain and frustration accompanying a lost game or, God forbid, an entire season. If as a New Englander, one is (very likely) a passionate Red Sox fan, and the season goes badly, there are always the New England Patriots, the Celtics, and the Bruins to hope for. Ditto in many American cities and regions where a multiplicity of teams representing the Big Four of American sports culture split loyalties to some degree, thereby lowering passions and fanaticism. This is less the case in sparsely populated areas with no major professional teams, where a single college or even high school team assumes a fan base of quasi-European proportions. Indeed, being a Cornhusker fan in Nebraska is more similar in its intensity and commitment to being a European soccer club's supporter than that of an American professional team (at the risk of slighting the legendary devotion by Oakland Raiders' fans populating the team's famed Black Hole).

While sports as a whole are much more popular and prevalent in American than European culture, the distinct history of soccer's club and national team cultures in Europe have, as a rule, created deeper ties and long-term local attachments to communities with "their" clubs than what exists between American franchises and their fans. For one thing, American teams have regularly moved from location to location, even from league to league, something that is unthinkable in the European context. On average, contests between two American teams connote proxy battles between two rival communities on a much feebler scale than has been the case in Europe (Murphy, Williams, and Dunning 2002, 208–09).

Professional leagues, club authorities, and owners in American sports have increasingly assumed major responsibility in violence prevention and commonly play an active role in an effective, spectator-friendly security system (Dubner 2007) that comprises programs to eliminate hostility among fans—in contrast to their counterparts in European soccer, at least until recently. These measures never included the creation of virtual cages in which fans at European venues had been perilously confined. The constant modernization of the venues in America, in better condition than their European counterparts, and the reshaping of the sports themselves that renders a stadium visit a more congenial experience to the general public, coincides with the search for new solutions to minimize fan violence in the United States. With excessive alcohol consumption posing the biggest problem in terms of fan violence and unruliness, many arenas have come to stop the sale of beer either in its entirety or after a certain period in the game, such as the seventh inning in baseball.[9]

If violence does occur among fans of the North American Big Four, it is not articulated in racist language and activities. Lest I be misunderstood here, I am *not* arguing that racism has disappeared from American sports, let alone among spectators, culture, and society. Far from it! Alas, it is alive and well. What I am saying, however, is that overt racist taunts have become completely unacceptable in the vocabulary of American sports in the major leagues and at the college level. The reason for this, I am convinced, lies in the fact that in sports and other realms of public life, "the United States has worked harder and gone farther than any other advanced majority-white nation in confronting and righting the wrongs of its racist past" (Patterson 2009).[10]

This is much less the case with "classism." Thus, in sports, various "classist" taunts continue to flourish, with "ho, ho; hey, hey; you will work for us some day" being on the milder side; nor have misogynist slurs disappeared, though they too have become rarer as the number of women as athletes, spectators, and viewers has consistently increased since the 1980s. Any offensive language, let alone action, directed toward a collective that is perceived to be disempowered and/or a minority—be they blacks, Latinos, or women—has been effectively banned from American sports at the top levels, with racism now a total taboo.

In college sports, for example, each conference and association has in its bylaws a requirement that a "crowd control statement" must be read over a public announcement system, or a printed version of the statement must be distributed to fans. Different variants of the crowd control statement are permitted, as long as there is one of some kind made at the event. Telling of the state of public discourse at American sporting venues, everything but the prohibition of alcohol is largely followed and accepted as legitimate.

Of course, personalized slights directed at individual players continue to flourish, be it about habits, posture, demeanor, language, friends, and associates. Deriding a player for making a mistake and continuing to irk him or her about it, sometimes in aggressive, if not necessarily vulgar, language, also continues unabated in American arenas. Such taunts and "trash talk" will always remain part of competitive sports. But it is telling that even foul language such as the use of four-letter curse words, has decreased of late in the stadiums of major league teams. It is not uncommon to have spectators reprimand a fan for repeated usage of foul language, usually with statements like, "Hey, my kids are here, and my wife: cool it with the swearing!" I have witnessed these types of admonitions at many baseball, football, basketball, and hockey games. It is also not unusual to have the public announcer declare before the beginning of the game that "foul language" will not be tolerated and its usage might lead to being expelled from the venue. Any such reprimand and subsequent desistance remains unthinkable on any of Britain's football grounds, where foul language continues to constitute a well-accepted lingua franca among all spectators.

Racist songs, slogans, and banners, let alone Nazi salutes—these have become commonplace in Europe's football stadiums—are unthinkable in contemporary American sports. This is not only because the authorities would not allow such behaviour and punish it promptly and severely, but much more important, because the fans would never countenance it. I regard such massive change in language and behaviour in contemporary America—including its male-dominated sports culture—as one of the many success stories that the civilizing agents of the 1960s and early 1970s (mostly, of course, the women's and the civil rights movements) wrought to enhance institutional and cultural inclusiveness and thus augment the country's democratic cosmopolitanism.

Moreover, size matters! When there were very few black players on the sports fields and in the stands, racist language and behaviour flourished. The same pertains to Latinos, when only a few of them plied their trade in baseball's major leagues in the 1950s and 1960s. But with the proliferation of both among the ranks of top-level players—to the point where African Americans comprise nearly 80 per cent of all NBA players and close to 70 per cent of the NFL's; and when Latinos exceed 30 per cent of major league baseball players—racism by necessity fades into the background.

Lastly, in notable contrast to Europe, where most countries until recently had few, if any, sizable non-white populations, it was American sports that played a vanguard role in the progress toward racial equality and colour-blindness in the country.[11] Beginning with Jackie Robinson's integrating America's pastime in 1947 by joining the roster of the National League's Brooklyn Dodgers (followed eleven weeks later by the oft-forgotten Larry Doby in the American League), the changes to more inclusion and diversity in America's sports world regularly preceded and anticipated similarly inclusive changes in other cultural, social, and political spheres. These were necessitated not by the enlightened and egalitarian inclination of its practitioners but rather by the inherently meritocratic, competitive, result-oriented, and profit-seeking nature of major league professional team sports, where winning wasn't everything but the only thing. Today, one can argue that the fame of African Americans in the sports world such as basketball stars like Magic Johnson and Michael Jordan or golf legend Tiger Woods helped expand the social acceptance of blacks and thus constituted the precursors to Colin Powell, Condoleezza Rice, and eventually Barack Obama's ascendancy to the presidency in 2008. Though racial discrimination in American sports has certainly not disappeared—a quick glance at the paucity of black team owners, front-office leadership, coaches, and managers will corroborate this point—the environment for racism has become socially taboo. Black athletes, as well as some coaches and managers have achieved so much, and minorities of all kinds have become widely respected heroes of these hegemonic sports and via them in American society as a whole. It is now much harder for the exclusionary counter-cosmopolitans, who have most certainly not disappeared from American society and sport, to spew their racist venom openly. Above all, their surroundings no longer countenance it. I agree with Orlando Patterson that the remaining pernicious racial divide in contemporary America pertains much more to our private than our public lives.

Just as in matters of diversity and racial integration in sports, so, too, has America been ahead of Europe in terms of the presence of women as spectators at major sporting events. With the presence of women hovering around 40 per cent of spectatorship in American stadiums, and reaching 50 per cent in college sports, the threat of violence has been substantially

reduced. More important still, women and families constituting a significant percentage of spectators in American sports has raised the threshold
of shame for exhibiting violent behaviour and voicing racially offensive language in sports venues across the board. Though England's and Germany's
top soccer leagues have not yet experienced the influx of women that has
reached American proportions, there is now such a critical mass that the
acceptability of fights and other acts of physical violence has declined.
The role of women as civilizing agents, as active carriers of cosmopolitan
thought and behaviour, of curtailing men from behaving badly should not
be underestimated as major contributors to the reduction of violence at
soccer matches.[12]

Indeed, as we know from various academic studies as well as literature—recall Huck Finn's escape from the women who wanted to "sivilize
[sic] him"—men have often not taken kindly to such developments, believing they are emasculating and threatening to their manhood. They often
responded to such measures by receding to male-controlled domains such
as fishing, hunting, and soccer hooliganism of one kind or another. One
cannot escape the feeling that in today's "humane," "social democratic," and
"politically correct" Europe, where a powerful force I call the "discourse of
compassion" has reigned supreme since the 1970s, the soccer stadium remains the last bastion of unbridled maleness. Here, one can really behave
badly, one can really be "a man" in one's element, unconstrained by the
feminized discourse of compassion that many men feel to be ubiquitous,
hegemonic, and ultimately an expression of weakness and submission.

Lastly, there is one additional reason for the prevalence of violent and
counter-cosmopolitan behaviour of soccer spectators as opposed to those
in other sports, including in Europe: the paucity of that sport's scoring.
By rendering a goal so rare and thus so dear, a soccer spectator's level of
anxiety—thus potential hostility and anger—is so much higher than any
other sport's. With soccer being a total outlier among any major team sport
in terms of the paucity and rarity of its scoring, the game fosters a tension
among its fans and spectators that high-scoring sports create only in the
contest's closing stages.

To end this contribution on a positive note, there have been many
commendable developments in recent years, not least of which was the
overwhelmingly favourable reception to the coming out of gay athletes
in professional basketball, rugby leagues in Australia and England, and
cricket. To be sure, these were all individual cases that have not yet led
to a larger movement of the full-fledged acceptance of gay athletes in the

predominantly male and macho hegemonic sports cultures, as opposed to less culturally salient sports like figure skating, platform diving, or any number of sports in which women have been long-standing and numerically as well as culturally significant participants. Moreover, there remains a long way to go, as demonstrated by the deeply homophobic policies pursued by the Putin-led Russian government which—very sadly—enjoys overwhelming popularity among the Russian people and probably the majority of other nations as well. But in the long run, progressive forces will not succumb to these reactionary measures. The underlying inclusive nature of sports, their inherently meritocratic tendencies fostered by the desire and necessity to win and be the absolute best, will ultimately prevail. I believe that the comparative study of sports-related racism and violence confirms and reinforces my broader argument that hegemonic sports constitute an important force within popular culture, and do in fact facilitate cosmopolitan change. Compared to other social spheres, hegemonic sports provide relatively easy access to (and for) immigrants and ethnic minorities in the global age. In the long run, ethnic minorities are able to enhance their visibility, and gain respect and social recognition through sports in increasingly multi-ethnic post-industrial societies. Despite the continued threat by counter-cosmopolitans in societies where immigrant sports heroes have acquired considerable standing over time, sports' merit-based cosmopolitanism has furthered progressive developments in culture, society, and politics.

Notes

1   Murphy, Williams, and Dunning have long expected that "soccer is a threat to gridiron football in the country of its origin, too." While American football is the "embodiment and display of male aggressiveness and power" and "based on sheer size and strength," in soccer the "warlike element is less obvious, more muted and controlled." They also lament that football is "more overtly capitalistic than is the case with most professional sports in Western Europe," and they claim that football is a "game which could only have grown up and taken root in a society where there is considerable support for ideals of masculinity which celebrate or at least tolerate a greater amount of overt physical violence than is considered desirable by the dominant and majority groups in the societies of Western Europe." Lastly, the rise of American football's popularity is situated in the context of the Vietnam War and attributed to the concurring "brutalization of society," while the authors view the new success of soccer as a participant sport in terms of a "civilizing process." Yet its civilizing social interventions "may be hampered in its competition with its

intrinsically more violence, but capital-packed and superbly media-packaged North American rival." See Murphy, Williams, and Dunning, (2002: 15–19). The impressive scholarship by the Leicester School scholars on sports and fan culture notwithstanding I am, frankly, quite baffled how knowledgeable authors hailing from the land of such global mega clubs as Manchester United, Chelsea, Arsenal, and Liverpool claim that European sports, in this case soccer, are "more overtly capitalistic" than American sports, in this case football, especially since if any quasi-socialist arrangements exist anywhere in American economy, society and culture, they have flourished in the country's four major sports leagues, the NFL included. Moreover, I am equally baffled how authors hailing from a continent that has had its fair share of mass atrocities throughout its history, including the twentieth century, can claim a greater reticence in its culture's and population's penchant for "overt physical violence" than they allege to exist in America's. Lastly, as this chapter's topic demonstrates, violence "outside the lines"—that is, by the spectators and fans—is much more pronounced in allegedly more civilized and less macho Europe than it is in the United States. The point here is simple: I do not think it empirically accurate or normatively desirable to attribute questionable national characteristics to the gestalt of any particular sport. After all, the very same allegedly violent American males whose essential being some claim to be so well reflected in the bellicose game of football also delight in playing and following baseball and basketball, both essentially non-contact sports, with the latter being explicitly so (and thus a consciously designed anti-football) that Europeans, including Beckenbauer, invoke derisively when they want to emphasize the legitimacy of soccer's rough manners and demeanours.

2 For on overview on the European extreme right, see Cas Mudde, *Radical Right Populist Parties in Europe*, and Lars Rensmann, "The New Politics of Prejudice: Comparative Perspectives on Extreme Right Parties in European Democracies."

3 A number of studies in soccer and in the Big Four American sports demonstrate, however tenuously, that referees favour the home teams in their calls. It is unclear as to the reasons for such actions, but most likely referees, being human themselves, fear abuse and threats.

4 See Reid Cherner and Tom Weir, "Longhorn cut because of Obama slur." Bernette wrote, "All the hunters gather up, we have a Nigger in the White House."

5 The "racial disturbances" to which Goodhart and Chataway refer are the fights between black and white youths that led to a temporary ban on high school night matches in parts of the United States. In an early, yet methodologically controversial study, Jerry Lewis observed 312 incidents he classified

as "riots" at American sports events between 1960 and 1972, 97 in baseball, 66 in football, 55 in basketball, and 39 in hockey; quoted in Allen Guttmann, *Sports Spectators*, 119. The scale and seriousness of these incidents, however, are not weighted, measured, or elaborated.

6 See Jerry M. Lewis, *Sports Fan Violence in North America*; Harry Edwards and Van Rackages, "The Dynamics of Violence in American Sport"; "Why Are There No Equivalents of Soccer Hooliganism in the United States?" in Murphy, Williams, and Dunning, *Football on Trial: Spectator Violence and Development in the Football World*, 200 and 203. Murphy, Williams, and Dunning cite an example of massive forms of disorderly conduct and assault during a Monday Night Football game between the New England Patriots and the New York Jets in 1977 that led to several arrests, while eighteen people had to be taken to the hospital.

7 The Toronto Maple Leafs of 1942, the New York Islanders of 1975, and the Philadelphia Flyers of 2010 in the National Hockey League were down by three games to none in a best-of-seven series and still managed to win. These were the only times in North American major team sports that such an amazing feat had been accomplished prior to the Boston Red Sox's defeat of the New York Yankees in 2004.

8 In a colleague's regularly taught sports and society class, which attracts 150 University of Michigan undergraduates, I always ask his students the day before Michigan's game against Ohio State how high their antipathy toward Ohio State is. It is quite clear from the answers that, not surprisingly, there is little love lost for the Buckeyes among his students. Then I inform the students that there is virtually no difference between University of Michigan undergraduates and their Ohio State counterparts, with the exception of a few points on various tests and grade averages—no serious religious, political, social, or economic differences worthy of mention. And then he tells the students to imagine their animosity for Ohio State were Michigan a predominantly Protestant school with students hailing from a wealthy East Coast social background voting largely for the Republican Party (perish the thought for most contemporary Michigan students, we are sure) as opposed to Ohio State being largely a Catholic university whose student body was mainly working class that voted heavily for the Democrats. In other words, what would happen if there were *real* differences between these student bodies? How much more intense would their enmity be toward Ohio State? And would not the upcoming contest stand for much more than just a standard rivalry game between two very similar American institutions of higher education? That exactly is the situation in European soccer.

9   Major League Baseball and the National Basketball Association participate in
    TEAM (Techniques for Effective Alcohol Management), which is a program
    for training everyone from vendors to ushers in handling people who have
    had too much to drink. See www.teamcoalition.org.

10 Patterson has argued this point emphatically in some of his scholarly work as
    well.

11 In basketball and football, where the universities took the lead, African
    Americans found earlier access than in the exclusive, resilient, and stubborn
    world of baseball. It took racial slurs by the New York Yankees outfielder
    Jake Powell in 1938 to lay bare the game's racism and break the silence that
    protected segregated baseball until then; see Chris Lamb, 2008, "Public Slur
    in 1938 Laid Bare a Game's Racism." The first African American football
    player was active for the University of Michigan in the 1890s. And virtu-
    ally all Jewish football stars had their breakthrough because they attended a
    college: for instance, Benny Friedman and Harry Newman at the University
    of Michigan, Sid Gillman at Ohio State University, Marshall Goldberg at the
    University of Pittsburgh, Charles Goldenberg at the University of Wisconsin,
    Sigmund Harris at the University of Minnesota, Benny Lom at the Univer-
    sity of California at Berkeley, Sid Luckman at Columbia University, Ron
    Mix at the University of Southern California, and Edward Newman at Duke
    University.

12 I experienced a particularly poignant instance where the presence of women
    most definitely prevented a tense situation from mutating into a violent one.
    At the end of the Croatia vs. Turkey quarterfinal match at the European
    National Championship in Vienna's Ernst-Happel Stadium, Croatian fans
    in the section where I sat were taunting and insulting the victorious Turk-
    ish players. They had come to greet their fans a few rows in front of the irate
    Croatian fans, whose team had just lost the game in a real heartbreaker.
    Things were getting heated and turning quite ugly when a particularly
    distraught Croatian fan appeared ready to descend to the Turks and escalate
    the confrontation. At that point, one of the women among the Croatian fans
    just placed her hand on this man's shoulder, gesturing to him to cool down
    giving him a pat and indicating to him to just let it go, that it was painful
    for the Croatians to lose but not worth starting a fight with all its adverse
    consequences. And sure enough, the man, still hurt, irate, and upset about his
    team's loss, did just that. He and his friends simply walked away. Had the situ-
    ation not taken place at such a major event that women in Europe have come
    to attend in greater numbers over the past few years, and had this been a
    regular club game, the man's girlfriend, wife, or sister would have been much

less likely to attend (since such games still attract mainly male fans), things could have easily and probably would have escalated into violence.

References

Appiah, Kwame Anthony. 2007. *Cosmopolitanism*. New York: W.W. Norton.

Benhabib, Seyla, and Raluca Eddon. 2007. "From Anti-Semitism to the 'Right to Have Rights': The Jewish Roots of Hannah Arendt's Cosmopolitanism." *Babylon* 22: 44–62.

Cherner, Reid, and Tom Weir. 2008. "Longhorn cut because of Obama slur." *USA Today.com*. Retrieved November 8, 2008. http://blogs.usatoday.com/gameon/2008/11/longhorn-cut-be.html.

Dubner, Stephen J. 2007. "Why Aren't US Sports Fans More Violent?" *Freakonomics*, February 9. Retrieved October 30, 2008. http://freakonomics.blogs.nytimes.com/2007/02/09/why-arent-us-sports-fans.

Edwards, Harry, and Van Rackages. 1977. "The Dynamics of Violence in American Sport." *Journal of Sport and Social Issues* 7 (2): 3–31.

Goodhart, Philip, and Christopher Chataway. 1968. *War without Weapons*. London: W.H. Allen.

Guttmann, Allen. 1986. *Sports Spectators*. New York: Columbia University Press.

Lamb, Chris. 2008. "Public Slur in 1938 Laid Bare a Game's Racism." *New York Times* July 27, p. Sports 5.

Lewis, Jerry M. 2007. *Sports Fan Violence in North America*. Lanham, MD: Rowman & Littlefield.

Mudde, Cas. 2007. *Radical Right Populist Parties in Europe*. Cambridge: Cambridge University Press.

Murphy, Eric, Patrick Williams, and John Dunning. 2002. *Football on Trial: Reflections on the Future of Soccer as a World Game*. New York: Routledge Chapman & Hall.

Patterson, Orlando. 2009. "Race and Diversity in the Age of Obama." *New York Times Book Review*, August 26.

Rensmann, Lars. 2003. "The New Politics of Prejudice: Comparative Perspectives on Extreme Right Parties in European Democracies." *German Politics & Society* 21 (4): 93–123.

Spitaler, Georg. 2006. "*Lads* vs. Metrosexuals Fußball als maskulines Melodrama am Beispiel des Fowler-Le Saux Zwischenfalls." In *Ritualisierungen von Geschlecht*, edited by Birgit Sauer and Eva-Maria Knoll. Vienna: Facultas Universitätsverlag.

"Violence Amid Celebration." 1992. *New York Times*, June 15.

Chapter 2

French Jewish Identity, 1898–1931:
The Story of Edmond Fleg

Sally D. Charnow

France was the birthplace of a historic revolution in Judaism at the dawn of the nineteenth century, when Napoleon Bonaparte liberated Jews from ghettos and granted them full citizenship. For the first time anywhere in Europe, Jews enjoyed full equality before the law, along with full freedom to practise their religion. They were also free, if they wished, to refrain from practising religion at all, as emancipation had ended the temporal power of rabbis and rabbinic law over Jews. France recognized Judaism as a legitimate religion, but only in terms of its specifically religious elements. In Napoleon's France, the cultural and ethnic aspects of Judaism as a nation in exile were relegated to history. Although Jews were "to be made into French men and Frenchwomen," the process was an uneven one, often taking several generations. Still, the emancipation paradigm was a powerful one; throughout the nineteenth century, Franco-Judaism was deeply engaged with republicanism. Educated Jews proclaimed that the principles of 1789 "were one and the same as the essence of Judaism, of the prophets of justice" (Rodrigue 1996, 3).

A century later, in the wake of the First World War, native French Jewish writers and poets such as Aimé Pallière, André Spire, and Edmond Fleg articulated a new cultural definition of what it meant to be a Jew. They considered Judaism a cultural fact akin to an ethnicity; what tied the Jewish people together, they argued, was their shared history and traditions. By defining Jewish identity in such a way, they challenged the popular, if rigid, conceptualization of an exclusively French national identity. One could, as Nadia Malinovich has argued, be both French and Jewish (2008). One could experience a "double consciousness," as W.E.B. Du Bois insightfully claimed in 1903.

As part of this notion of Jewishness, many of these writers consciously linked themselves to pacifist, internationalist postwar politics that aimed to foster friendship among all peoples. Some even suggested reworking the traditional notion of "choseness," that Jews themselves were historically positioned to spearhead such an initiative.

The emergence of cultural Judaism was part of a broader public discourse over the meaning of Jewishness that erupted in Paris in the 1920s with the publication of various books, including Edmond Fleg's *Pourquoi Je suis juif* and André Spire's *Quelques juifs et demi-juifs*, the performance of *Les Juifs* at George Pitoeff's Vieux Colombier theatre, and the screening of films with Jewish themes on the *grands boulevards*. There was a large appetite among Jews and non-Jews alike for publications and performances on Jewish themes.[1]

This essay is part of a larger study, still in its early stages, of the writing and activism of one of the most important figures of this French Jewish awakening: Edmond Fleg, whose personal evolution exemplifies some key themes of his age. As a young man, Fleg abandoned his family's Jewish religious practices. However, the anti-Semitism unleashed by the Dreyfus Affair compelled him to reconsider and ultimately embrace his Jewish roots. Best known as a writer, poet, and playwright, much of Fleg's literary oeuvre is steeped in Jewish and Christian biblical history, liturgy, and legend.[2] In his exploration of religious texts, Fleg reached for the most universalistic interpretations. His universalism found voice not only in his writings but also his actions. Fleg was a founding member of the Société l'Amitié judéo-chrétienne; he was also the president of the Eclaireurs Israelites Français, a Jewish youth movement that emerged in the 1920s and was defined by its defiantly pluralistic concept of Judaism that could even include "non-Jews." Through a close reading of Fleg's published texts and personal correspondence, I examine his depictions of Jews and non-Jews seeking spiritual fulfillment in a world often satisfied with material comfort and financial gain, and of the potential for reconciliation between the Catholic Church and European Jewry, as well as among individual Jews, Christians, and Muslims. Fleg's body of work suggests a dynamic relationship between the Jewish renaissance in interwar Paris and a wider French interest in neoclassical forms, the emerging discourse on "French civilization," and the meaning and value of spirituality.

This essay depicts Fleg's complex understanding of nationalism and national identity. During the Dreyfus Affair, when ideas of national identity were becoming the domain of right-wing ideologues and hardening into rigid unitary beliefs about "blood and soil roots," Edmond Fleg articulated a more flexible, even pluralistic concept of national belonging, one that accepted the possibility of multiple attachments.[3] Recent events in modern France—such as the outlawing of the burka in public spaces for citizens and even tourists, and the expulsion of the Roma—encourage a heightened interest in Republican universalism and French identity.

The Impact of the Dreyfus Affair

In the last years of the nineteenth century, Edmond Fleg was a student at the prestigious École Normale Supérieure in Paris. He was a "triumph of assimilation," according to André Elbaz, the editor of a compilation of Fleg's correspondence from the period (Maudale 1976, 2). Fleg had rejected the Judaism of his childhood and was even drawn to what he saw as the austere beauty and solemnity of Catholicism. Although a new, racialist form of anti-Semitism was on the rise in Russia and then in Germany, for most French Jews these happenings seemed remote, their confidence hardly shaken even by the 1886 success of Edouard Drumont's caustic anti-Semitic polemic *La France Juive*.[4] It was the trial of Captain Dreyfus, condemned in the public eye precisely because he was a Jew that inspired Fleg's "conversion" back to Judaism. As it was for so many others in his generation, the Dreyfus Affair was a decisive, watershed moment for Fleg.[5]

During the academic year 1897–98, Fleg was studying German and philosophy in Leipzig. At the time, Fleg was described by his friend Julien Luchaire as "detached from the realities of daily life," refusing to read newspapers, and "lost in the ethereal spaces of sentiment" (Maudaule 1976, 16). In contrast to the prevailing mood among many fellow students (known as Normaliens) who were concerned with the problems of the day and drawn to the socialist platform promoted by the Catholic writer and socialist, Charles Péguy, Fleg was something of an aesthete, interested in art for art's sake. It was during that same year that the Dreyfus Affair erupted into French public consciousness; Fleg soon admitted that the focus of his life had ceased to be literary. "I am living with more sincerity and with less clarity," he wrote on July 1, 1898 (Fleg 1976, 95).

The Dreyfus Affair put the question of national belonging centre stage in France. For Fleg, not even a French-born Jew, the problem of national identity was even more complicated. His parents, Alsatian Jews, had left that province for Switzerland after it was annexed by Germany in 1870. He was born in Geneva in 1874, but developed a yearning to be a French national after he moved to Paris to complete his education. He studied at the prestigious lycée Louis-le Grand in 1892 before entering the the Ecole Normale Supérieure in 1895. "I feel too estranged in Switzerland," he wrote, "because all of my intellectual life I have distanced myself from it.... I have desired to become French for a long time" (Fleg 1976, 95–96). Wrestling with his yearning to belong somewhere and aware of the rising tide of anti-Semitism in France, he wrote to his mother from Leipzig: "It is not the moment for a Jew ... to choose a new country where he will hear cried out: Death to the Jews" (Fleg 1976, 69). Regardless, his desire for some kind of attachment intensified. After reading Israel Zangwill's *Dreamers of the Ghetto*, a compilation of biographies of Jewish writers and poets dating back to the beginning of the eighth century, Fleg wrote again to his mother, "the reading of this awoke in me an urge to return to this prohibited race, beautiful in spite of its miseries, by studying its history and philosophy" (1976, 94).

A few years older than Fleg but of the same generation, André Spire was also deeply effected by Zangwill's text, especially one story in the collection, *Chad Gadya*, a devastating critique of assimilation. He wrote, "Chad Gadya!... played the role of a crystal in an over-saturated liquid, and brought about a return, a conversion: distress, fits of crying, a sudden change in the direction of life, the birth of a calling. Did I rediscover religion? No. My ancestors, my race, the Judaism of my childhood. I had become a Jew with a capital J. And, a French poet, [I became] a Jewish poet too" (qtd. in Rodrigue 1996, 9).[6]

Born into a wealthy, non-practising Jewish family in Lorraine, Spire had a career in the French civil service as an auditor in the Conseil d'État. But he is remembered for experiments in free-verse poetry and his essays and books on literary, social, and political topics—Jewish as well as non-Jewish. A social activist, Spire was deeply engaged with the squalid living conditions of the working poor. In 1898 he founded a Université populaire with Daniel Haléy in the eighteenth arrondissement of Paris. Through his activism, Spire became an associate of Péguy's well-known *Cahiers de la Quinzaine*. In contrast to Fleg, Spire was first sensitized to French anti-Semitism through the publication and popularity of Drumont's *La France Juive*. Spire and his Jewish colleagues at the Conseil, Léon Blum and Paul Grunebaum, became involved in the Dreyfusard campaign, not out of "Jewish national sentiment" but in the spirit of "of a French citizen loyal to the principles of 1789, who had feelings about justice and political equality offended" (Spire qtd. in Rodrigue 1996, 6).[7]

Writing to Lucien Moreau, a close friend from his days at the Lycée Louis-le-Grand, Fleg reiterated his acute desire for attachment: "I feel a need to reattach myself to a stimulating ensemble, to a past, to a tradition, to something that is me and more than me—to work on a piece of work begun by others and that can be continued by others." Fleg revealed to Moreau that he had found a past: "the past that I have discovered, asleep deep inside me, is the past of my race.... I regret that I haven't studied it and now don't have any time because of the 'stupid' [referring to his studies] path I follow" (1976, 96).

Fleg's use of the word race was not unusual or essentialist. At the time, people used the word "race" to describe groupings of family, profession, psychological type, and the like, not just to designate an ethnic group. Jews, as we see here, also used it to describe themselves. Anti-Semitic French nationalists at the time exploited the term in a negative sense when they described France as being invaded by an alien race, by which they meant especially Eastern European Jewish immigrants (Weber 1987, xxvii).

Unhappy with his current scholarly path and powerfully drawn to learning about Jewish history, religion, and Hebrew, as well as contemporary Jewish social problems, Fleg wrote, "all I know is that if I devote myself to another subject, or to a life of a dilettante egoist, or to a life as father of a family without religion and without ideals to teach to his children, I would have remorse and the feeling of having failed at a task." At that juncture Fleg reflected on his own father: "I didn't understand all that he was" (1976, 97).

By identifying as a Dreyfusard and actively joining the struggle against anti-Semitism in France, Fleg found himself in disagreement with his friend Moreau, even as they maintained an extensive correspondence. Moreau, influenced by Maurice Barrès and the radical Right, believed that the innocence or guilt of Dreyfus was only of secondary importance to the damage done to France by the attacks on the army. For Moreau, any notion of justice needed to be grounded in the "contingency of the all-encompassing 'national'" (Rodrigue 1996, 10).[8] As an anti-Dreyfusard, Moreau was adopting increasingly anti-Semitic views, even going so far as to argue that Jews should be excluded from French public life. By 1900, Moreau had become a follower of the nationalist Charles Maurras and was eager to introduce Fleg to him.[9] However, Fleg always refused to meet the man he referred to as a "fanatic," who inspired only hatred (1976, 14). In spite of their political differences, the two men were able to maintain a friendship, albeit strained, in part because Moreau, perhaps in a self-serving way, distinguished between his ability to have personal relationships with certain Jews, Protestants, and "intellectuals," and the political importance of limiting the influence of these groups in France (Fleg 1976, 143). By 1905 Moreau held the Maurice Barrès Chair at the newly founded Action Française Institute associated with Maurras.

Creating a Jewish self

As Fleg increasingly identified as a Jew, he became less tolerant of Jews who tried to hide their Jewishness. He wrote, "I have never seen anywhere the hatred of anti-Semitism comparable to that which reigns in this place [Paris]....We try to glide about unperceived in the crowd. Our hypocritical humility makes us even more in the wrong. The more I advance, the better I understand my dear father's sentiments; he didn't hide being a Jew, and didn't run after the Christians" (1976, 145). In November 1898, Fleg made an important professional choice: he decided to focus his doctoral thesis on *Literary and Philosophical Anti-Semitism in Nineteenth-Century Germany.* He wrote to Bernard Lazare, a French journalist, anarchist, Dreyfussard, and early Zionist, to tell him of this decision and seek his advice.[10] "Until now," he wrote, "I have searched in vain for an intellectual occupation that would engage me entirely: I have suffered to live, not as a dilettante, but as a man for whom social problems weren't a living reality. I have begun to find in the dreams of the Zionists an ideal that satisfies all of my intellectual and moral tendencies ... and if I devote myself to this work, I will discover in myself new forces of will and abnegation" (Fleg 1976, 111).

Bernard Lazare has been described as the first Jew to make the transition from an almost self-hating assimilationist to a full-fledged Zionist. Although this rigid distinction between assimilationist and Zionist has been analyzed with greater nuance in recent years, Lazare's notion of "Jews as a nation" had a powerful impact on Fleg's thinking at the time (Harris 2010, 66). Lazare's reputation as the "first Dreysuard" was encouraged by Péguy, who dubbed him a "Jewish prophet, an incarnation of the essence of the Jewish 'mystique,' of the Jewish 'prophetic' tradition" (Rodrigue 1996, 2). Although Lazare initially had no sympathy for the wealthy Dreyfus family, he (with urging from them) became their polemicist, instituting a campaign in favour of Captain Dreyfus among writers and journalists. In 1896 he published the pamphlet *Une erreur judicaire, la vérité sur l'affaire Dreyfus* that, according to historian Ruth Harris, presaged almost uncannily the arguments and tone of its much more famous successor, Zola's *J'accuse* (2010, 55).

In the critical autumn of 1898, Fleg was constructing a Jewish identity from his memories of the Jewishness expressed by his father, the anti-Semitism unleashed by the Affair, and the appeal of the nascent Zionist ideal. He would spend much of the next twenty years delving deeply into each of these strands.

Moreau, believing nationalism would provide the answer to the disloca-
tions of modernity, encouraged Fleg toward Jewish nationalism. Fleg also
moved toward Zionism, but his journey was not a smooth one. "I find in
Zionism," Fleg wrote to Moreau, "the calm and the force that I have been
missing for a long time.... I find an end point to which I can apply my intellectual effort which is necessary to direct my life, to give it social significance. And I feel, like you, that I have definitively left individualism" (1976,
128). Fleg "left individualism" in search of a Jewish self, but unlike Barrès,
Moreau, or Spire, his attachment to the particular, to Frenchness or Jewishness, was not rooted in fixed, immutable ethnic markers. Even for Spire, the
"real" or "authentic" Jew was poor, Eastern European, lived in the "ghetto"
and "ate matzah, gefilte fish, and kugel" (Rodrigue 1996, 8).

In a letter to Moreau, Fleg outlined the plot of a novel he planned to
write on a Zionist theme. Though brief, it gives us a sense of his developing ideas: the story is focused on a young Jew who spends most of his life
in Alsace. His mother was French Alsatian, indifferent to Judaism; his
father was a religious German Jew but wanted his children to assimilate
with ease. The young Jewish protagonist tries, at first, to become German
but does so without success. Instead, like so many of his co-religionists, he
finds himself drawn toward France because of its universalistic values and
its history of Jewish emancipation. In love with and engaged to a Christian
woman, he experiences anti-Semitism; he renounces his marriage and she
sadly accepts his sacrifice. He will end his days as a master of a school in
the Palestinian colony and as an agricultural worker at the same time. Fleg
understood his story to be about a young Jew who rejects his Jewish identity
when he recognizes it as either a religion or a race. He wrote, "the young
man only returns to Judaism when he finds in it a 'nation'" (Fleg 1976, 29,
128).

In this narrative, the idea of the Jewish nation takes on an ideal form, imbued with the possibility of reconciliation between the spiritual dimension
of identity and the material world of work, both intellectual and physical.
Writing at the height of the Dreyfus Affair, Fleg posited that this young Alsatian Jew, neither German nor French, was able to construct a new identity
as a Jew only in the Palestinian colony.

While attaching himself to an idealistic, almost mystical Zionist vision, Fleg continued to reject the sort of irredentist nationalism espoused
by Moreau. He wrote to Moreau, "I understand your spirit, your traditional soul, your statist, rationalist, reactionary positions ... but I am not
anything of all that, or at least, I am of it in a totally other way and not essentially" (Fleg 1976, 121). In letters written after the turn of the century,

he acknowledged being drawn to some forms of nationalism and even admiring the journal of the reactionary Action Française for its incisive discussions of philosophy and politics. He was often frustrated with what he called the "destructive egoism" of French Jews. He continued to struggle with his Jewish identity during the years leading up to the First World War as he made his way in the Parisian literary scene writing plays that had no Jewish content, including *Le Message, Le Trouble-fête,* and *La bête.*

In 1908, the same year his first son was born, Fleg wrote to his friend and collaborator Ernest Bloch, "is it necessary that we choose between two kinds of traditions: the Jewish tradition and the tradition of the countries in which we are established? One sees them [the French Jews] dividing the true force of France, so precious for civilization. I cannot tell you to what point these questions torment me" (Fleg 1976, 155).

His friend Bloch experienced a less tormented awakening of his Jewishness in the early years of the twentieth century. Although both Fleg and Bloch were born in Geneva (Bloch in 1880), they did not share a similar social background. While Fleg's family was prosperous and encouraged his educational pursuits in Paris, Bloch's father owned a retail store geared to tourists. Bloch's family had not been religious but he, according to one biographer, "venerated the sense of Jewish family life, the candle-lighting on Friday nights, the Seders on Passover" (Brody 1982, 64). Bloch wrote to Fleg in 1906, "I have read the Bible. I have read fragments from Moses, and an immense sense of pride surged in me. My entire being vibrated, it is a revelation.... I would find myself as a Jew, raise my head as a Jew.... Perhaps you and I will find this a release of our bonds. The music is in us ... we must show the greatness and destiny of this race."[11] The music Bloch referred to was not only symbolic. The two friends collaborated on an opera, *Macbeth,* with Bloch composing the score and Fleg writing the libretto that premiered in 1910 at the Opéra-Comique in Paris. With the birth of his son, Fleg abruptly turned his attention to what must have felt like pressing issues of cultural and religious continuity from generation to generation. He stopped reading the *Action Française* and began a three-year intensive study of Jewish texts. A few years later, Fleg published his epic biblical poem *Écoute Israël* in Péguy's *Cahiers de la Quinzaine* (1913).

The First World War had a profound impact on French Jews and their sense of belonging, including Edmond Fleg. Like many of his Jewish contemporaries, he fought for France during the war and became a naturalized French citizen in 1921. This greater integration into French society gave Fleg and many in his generation, including Spire, the ability to embrace their

Jewishness with less angst, Albert Cohen suggested in 1925 (qtd. in Malinovich 2008, 201). After the war, Fleg also became more closely aligned with Zionism; it was, however, a rather mystical, liberal mode of Zionism, distinct from the territorial and repatriating claims made by Chaim Weizmann or the more combative, anti-assimilationist stance of the André Spire. Fleg transposed the universalist values that nineteenth-century liberal French Jews saw as integral to Judaism—equality, justice, and peace—to his understanding of the Zionist project.

Zionism

Even after the Dreyfus Affair infused the various Zionist factions in France with energy and the reality of the Balfour Declaration recognizing a Jewish state, the established French Jewish leadership, represented by the Alliance Israélite Universelle, did not support Zionist initiatives.[12] In 1919, Fleg criticized the Alliance's anti-Zionist position. Although no longer a young man and still imbued with many nineteenth-century liberal, Enlightenment, universalist values held firmly by native French Jews,[13] Fleg argued that the Alliance was out of touch with Jewish youth.[14] Despite the fact that a Jewish state was only a faraway hypothesis, he cautioned Sylvain Lévi, the president of the Alliance Israélite Universelle, "[t]he Alliance must not sacrifice the success of a movement that has really awakened the Jewish soul merely because it might pose the theoretical danger of inciting anti-Semitism." This was how he saw the future: "The constitution of a Jewish state would end the equivocation that makes Judaism simultaneously a religion and a nation. Palestinian Jews will constitute a Jewish nation of themselves." Jews who remained in their countries would increasingly disengage from ethnic traditions to "develop Judaism's universal character, its universal mission" (1976, 168–71). Fleg foregrounded the universal character of Franco-Judaism, signalling what historian Lisa Moses has described as the prevailing nineteenth-century ideal of secular "choseness." Jews in their various homelands would take the lead in creating a peaceful world order, guiding all nations to embrace liberal values like tolerance, equality, and freedom (Leff 2006, 3). "The creation of a Jewish homeland is only one of the three possible solutions to the Jewish question," Fleg continued. The future, he believed, depended on "developing harmony between assimilationists and Zionists" (1976, 168–71).

For Fleg and many Western Jews, including Spire, the Zionist movement was first and foremost about providing a land of refuge for Jews persecuted elsewhere. Malinovich explains: the principal arguments that French Jews used to promote and defend the Zionist "movement among their compatriots were centered on discourses of dualism" common to French Cartesian thinking more generally. "Rather than rejecting either the Jews' loyalty and attachment to France or a commitment to 'universal' human values, French Zionists developed a variety of arguments intended to illustrate that these ideals were perfectly compatible with support for Zionism and the ethnic understanding of Jewish identity that it entailed" (Malinovich 2008, 203).[15] However, Fleg's particular conception of the Jewish homeland was a type of parallel construction to his notion of Franco-Judaism's universality infused with a profound spiritual mission.

Fleg was not alone in his commitment to the transcendent ideal of universality during the interwar years. Although Ernest Bloch and André Spire, like Fleg, flaunted their Jewish identity, they also identified, like Bloch's mentor and confident Romain Rolland, with universalist republican principles and a deeply felt internationalism. In 1925 Rolland wrote to Bloch, "we are everywhere citizens, everywhere strangers" (Brody 1982, 79). This profound, even contradictory understanding of being both insider and outsider knotted these artists together in a shared concern in seeking the universal, the bonds of commonality across the human community.

In the early 1930s Fleg travelled to Palestine, ostensibly to do research for his biography of Jesus.[16] In *Ma Palestine*, a travelogue he published upon his return, he presented multiple and conflicting voices describing the Zionist project on the ground (Fleg 1932). The text is constructed as a series of dialogues between Fleg and various figures, from Theodore Herzl (in a dream sequence) to a cab driver showing him the cultivated landscape. Fleg was proud of the Jewish settlements and did not shy away from describing Jewish agricultural practices with well-tread hyperbole: they turned the sand to gold, the land of milk and honey, the pioneers drained the swamps, cleared the roads (1932, 181–83).

Fleg's depiction of Arabs acknowledged the presence of various tensions, including violence, but looked toward a future of fraternity between Jews and Arabs: "this will never become a Jewish ghetto: between Jews and Arabs, the differences are only accidental. Soon you will understand why it will all end harmoniously" (Fleg 1932, 77). "It is necessary that in this country, two fraternal civilizations fraternize" (80). "I want to cry from my balcony," he wrote, "brother Arabs, brother Arabs, when are we going to become brothers?" (138).

Pointing to the contradictions of daily life in Palestine, he recalled, "a taxi driver recounted to me the horrors of a recent massacre of nine Jews in Hebron and claimed he will defend Jewish Palestine to the end. Then he stops and helps an elderly Arab woman pick up her scattered barley and drives her to the market to replace the eggs that she broke" (Fleg 1932, 100–1). He described an engineer who explained, "I am fine with the Arabs. My work as an agricultural engineer obliges me to travel everywhere, I know everyone, I live with them, eat with them; I spend the night with them. Politics is not my domain" (103). With these anecdotes, Fleg suggested that it was through everyday life and work that bonds of compassion were forged. In a sense, politics—British, Arab, and Jewish, as he understood them to operate under the Palestinian Mandate—only got in the way of uncovering the deep affinities between Arabs and Jews as human beings.

Fleg warned against extremism. To underscore his criticism of irredentist nationalism, he gave voice to a representative of dissident leader Vladimir Jabotinsky's Zionist Revisionist program: "the Arabs only understand force. The Arabs are the Arabs, you will not change them" (Fleg 1932, 85). The representative goes on to say that Jews, upon the establishment of the Mandate, should have "immigrated en masse and expelled the Arabs, transferred them elsewhere, installed ourselves everywhere on the land that is ours by every means" (87). Fleg compared this kind of thinking to that of the Zealots, Jewish fanatics in Roman-ruled Palestine who refused all entente with the Romans, patriots without limits who, through their patriotism, lost their country (89). Thus, Fleg rejected irredentism first in France and subsequently in Zionism.

Even as he refused revisionist Zionism, he was perplexed by his feelings of belonging in Palestine. "I felt like I was chez moi," he announced after a Passover seder (Fleg 1932, 129). He asked "am I, who in Paris can't suffer nationalism, going to become a nationalist in Jerusalem...? Where will I be me? Without any of myself destroyed?" (136, 143). These questions inspired Fleg to develop his understanding of the possibility of a parallel attachment, a double consciousness. His view echoed that of Du Bois, who stated that "he simply wishes to make it possible for a man to be both a Negro and an American" (1903). Fleg wrote, "one can be French and Jewish in Palestine. There is a harmony in being Jewish and French! One enriches the other" (163). Not only could one be simultaneously Jewish and French; one could be a French national and a Zionist *without* repatriating to a Jewish homeland.

Fleg was not alone in "turning the idea of 'double loyalty'" so criticized by right-wing French nationalists into a positive association for French Jews. Socialist minister Anatole de Monzie and active non-Jewish member of the Zionist organization Franco-Palestine praised the spiritual benefits that he imagined the establishment of a Jewish homeland would bring the Jews of the diaspora. The possibility for Jews "to feel the same visceral connection to their history and ancestors as other Frenchmen would in fact enable them to be more genuinely French" (de Monzie qtd. in Malinovich 2008, 215).

Fleg's Zionism was infused with spirituality.[17] Palestine was not merely the land of the British mandate; it was the "Promised Land," imbued with God-given holiness. This land and those who live upon it, according to Fleg, needed "carriers of this new message," and Jews with such a "double love" as he held would be those messengers (1932, 290). Even though he reckoned that Jews had a particular investment in the Jewish homeland, Fleg believed that Zionism had a universal, quasi-messianic mission benefiting all humanity with its "new message." The Jews in Palestine were preparing a new mode of life, creating "a new type of Jew, a new type of man" (Fleg 1932, 273). Akin to Louis Brandeis' notion that being a Zionist would make one a better American or de Monzie's assessment that being a Zionist would make one a better Frenchman, Fleg argued that being a Zionist would make one a more humane person, a divinely inspired person.

Conclusion

Edmond Fleg: Swiss-born, of Alsatian parentage, Paris-educated, naturalized French, Jew, and Zionist. His life was one of constant boundary crossings. Continually critical of any exclusive identity, he always reached for the most expansive sense of self. In Jewishness, Fleg discovered a new form of universalism. Rediscovering it, he exclaimed that he wanted to sing it not for a limited congregation, but for all the French, for all men.

For Fleg, Jewishness was another aspect of Frenchness. He envisioned Jewish literary and scholarly works as becoming part of the French canon. And by imagining French Republican culture in such a flexible way, he redefined French identity itself as capable of embracing particular traditions and incorporating them within the national body. Republican universality did not obliterate cultural difference; on the contrary, it was able to incorporate it, even celebrate it.

Fleg made the same case for Zionism: it offered a humanitarian, internationalist vision. But Fleg's Zionism (like his Republicanism) was discursive, and his discourse was profoundly shaped by an idealist philosophy that sought reconciliation. For him, Jewishness lived on the page or maybe on the stage—it was not about turf or political or economic power. He seemed to be able to write his way into universals that resolved tensions so keenly experienced on the ground, such as being a Zionist while being a loyal Frenchman, being a Zionist and not having any conflict with Arabs, and being a Dreyfusard who was friends with anti-Semitic French nationalists whom he admired, in a way. This kind of discourse-based identity certainly has limitations, but it also has strengths as a cultural strategy, especially in relation to the rise of Jewish political activism, self-defence, immigration, and colonization. Edmond Fleg's writing on nationalism might offer a kind of discursive emancipatory challenge to both irredentist Zionists and xenophobic French republicans today.

Today, Fleg is overwhelmingly remembered for his poem "Why I Am a Jew," which is used in the newly revised prayer book of the North American Reform Movement. The last two stanzas read:

I am a Jew because Israel places humanity and its unity above the nations and above Israel itself.

I am a Jew because, above humanity, image of the divine Unity, Israel places the unity, which is the divine.

Notes

1 For the "Jewish awakening," see Catherine Nicault, ed., "Le 'Reveil Juif' des annés vingt."

2 For an insightful discussion of Jewish writers and their writing including Edmond Fleg in 1920s Paris, see Catherine Fhima, "Au Coeur de la 'renaissance juive' des années 1920: littérature et judéité"; and Nadia Malinovich, *French and Jewish Culture and the Politics of Identity in Early Twentieth-Century France.*

3 Ruth Harris makes the point more broadly, arguing "many French citizens will continue to face the problem of living comfortably with multiple identities. This tension is one of the many aspects of French political culture that were strengthened, and in some measure created, by the Dreyfus Affair" (2010, 385).

4 *La France Juive* was a landmark development in the history of modern anti-Semitism. It introduced and popularized the use of Gobineau's terminology to distinguish the "Aryan" and "Semite races": "while the Aryan race includes an infinite variety of organizations and of temperaments, the Jew always resembles another Jew," recognized by "that famous hooked noose, blinking eyes, clenched teeth, protruding ears ... the fleshy hand of the hypocrite and the traitor" (Drumont 1938, 1: 24, 34).

5 For a discussion of the impact of the Affair on the French Jewish community, see Michael Marrus, *The Politics of Assimilation: A Study of the French Jewish Community at the Time of the Dreyfus Affair*; Paula Hyman, *From Dreyfus to Vichy: The Remaking of French Jewry, 1906–1939*, 42–46; Perrine Simon-Nahum, *La Cité investie: La "Science du judaïsme" française et la République*, 285–311; Harris, *Dreyfus, Politics, Emotion, and the Scandal of the Century*, especially 52–72; 187–200.

6 For more on Spire's "conversion" moment see André Spire, *Versets: Et vous riez: Poèmes juifs.*

7 Many Jews (and non-Jews) including Joseph Reinach defended Dreyfus in the name of Republicanism and patriotism. Anti-Semitism was the enemy of Republican universal morality and of Franco-Judaism. Dreyfus himself does not mention his Jewishness in his long letters to Lucie, his wife. He maintained his belief in the values and principles of the French Republic. See Harris, *Dreyfus: Politics, Emotion, and the Scandal of the Century*, 94–95, 39.

8 The literature on Barrès is enormous. For Barrès and the Affair, see Harris, *Dreyfus: Politics, Emotion*, especially Chapters 4, 5, 6. For Barrès and nationalism, see Zeev Sternhell, *Maurice Barrès et le nationalisme française.*

9 Charles Maurras was founder of the Action Française, a political movement that infused monarchism with Drumont's anti-Semitism and xenophobia, developing the idea that ethnicity was the only genuine source of French identity and nationhood, thus providing a basis for future political movements that abandoned monarchism for modern authoritarianism. Eugen Weber, *Action Française: Royalism and Reaction in Twentieth Century France*, 199.

10 Harris, 2010, *Dreyfus: Politics, Emotion*, 51–56. On Bernard Lazare also see Jean-Denis Bredin, *Bernard Lazare: De l'anarchiste au prophète.*

11 Bloch, cited in Brody, "Romain Rolland and Ernest Bloch," 64. Romain Rolland heard about *Macbeth*, and in the role of "paterfamilias" visited and encouraged Bloch in 1911. For a fuller discussion of their subsequent relationship, see Brody's article.

12 For a discussion of French Jews and Zionism see Micel Abitbol, *Les Deux Terres promises: Les Juifs de France et le sionisme.*

13 For an in-depth discussion of Franco-Judaism in nineteenth-century France, see Lisa Moses Leff, *Sacred Bonds of Solidarity: The Rise of Jewish Internationalism in Nineteenth-Century France.*

14 For a discussion of interwar French Jewish youth and Zionism, see Nadia Malinovich, *French and Jewish Culture and the Politics of Identity in Early Twentieth-Century France.*

15 On the particular humanitarian and pacifist values of French Zionism, see Catherine Nicault, "L'accultration des israélites français au sionism après la Grande Guerre."

16 Published as *Jésus, raconté par le Juif errant* (Paris, 1933).

17 Fleg works to reconcile his faith with his reason discursively. He acknowledged a conflict, and as a believer in God argued that he should not worship the "visible" nations but only the invisible, the spiritual (1932, 286).

References

Abitbol, Micel. 1989. *Les Deux Terres promises: Les Juifs de France et le sionisme.* Paris: Oliver Orban.

Bredin, Jean-Denis. 1992. *Bernard Lazare: De l'anarchiste au prophète.* Paris: De Fallois.

Brody, Elaine. 1982. "Romain Rolland and Ernest Bloch." *Musical Quarterly* 68 (1): 60–79.

Du Bois, W.E.B. 1903. *The Souls of Black Folk: Essays and Sketches.* Chicago: A.C. McClurg & Co.

Drumont, Edouard. 1938. *La France juive.* Vol. 1. Paris: Flammarion.

Fhima, Catherine. 2006. "Au Coeur de la 'renaissance juive' des années 1920: literature et judéité." *Archives Juives* 39: 29–45.

Fleg, Edmond. 1932. *Ma Palestine.* Paris: Reider.

———. 1976. *Correspondance d'Edmond Fleg pendant l'Affaire Dreyfus*, edited by André E. Elbaz. Paris: Librarie A.-G. Nizet.

Harris, Ruth. 2010. *Dreyfus: Politics, Emotion, and the Scandal of the Century.* New York: Henry Holt and Company.

Hyman, Paula. 1979. *From Dreyfus to Vichy: The Remaking of French Jewry, 1906–1939.* New York: Columbia University Press.

Leff, Lisa Moses. 2006. *Sacred Bonds of Solidarity, the Rise of Jewish Internationalism in Nineteenth-Century France.* Stanford, CT: Stanford University Press.

Madaule, Jacques. 1976. Preface. In Edmond Fleg, *Correspondance d'Edmond Fleg pendant l'Affaire Dreyfus,* edited by André E. Elbaz, 2. Paris: Librarie A.-G. Nizet.

Malinovich, Nadia. 2008. *French and Jewish Culture and the Politics of Identity in Early Twentieth-Century France.* Oxford: Littman Library of Jewish Civilization.

Marrus, Michael. 1971. *The Politics of Assimilation: A Study of the French Jewish Community at the Time of the Dreyfus Affair.* Oxford: Oxford University Press.

Nicault, Catherine. 2006a. "L'acculturation des israélites français au sionism après la Grande Guerre." *Archives Juives* 39 (1): 9–28.

———. 2006b. "Le 'Reveil Juif' des années vingt." *Archives Juives* 39:

Rodrigue, Aron. 1996. "Rearticulations of French Jewish Identities after the Dreyfus Affair." *Jewish Social Studies* New Series 2 (3): 1–24.

Simon-Nahum, Perrine. 1991. *La Cité investie: La "Science du judaïsme" français et la République.* Paris: Editions du Cerf.

Spire, André. 1908 (2010). *Versets: Et vous riez: Poèmes juifs.* Paris: Nabu Press.

Sternhell, Zeev. 1972. *Maurice Barrès et le nationalisme française.* Paris: A. Colin.

Weber, Eugen. 1962. *Action Française: Royalism and Reaction in Twentieth-Century France.* Stanford, CT: Stanford University Press.

———. 1987. Foreword. In *The Dreyfus Affair, Art, Truth, & Justice,* edited by Norman Kleeblatt. Berkeley: University of California Press.

Chapter 3

The Legal Culture of Civilization: Hegel and His Categorization of Indigenous Americans

William E. Conklin

The notion of "civilization" in European Enlightenment and post-Enlightenment writings has recently been reassessed. Critics have especially reread the works of Immanuel Kant (1724–1804) by highlighting his racial categories.[1] However, something is missing in this contemporary literature: how European legal culture developed a racial and ethnic hierarchy of societies, and how they understood "civilized society." This chapter highlights this connection by engaging with the work of one of the most important jurists of the nineteenth and twentieth centuries, Georg W.F. Hegel (1770–1831). Hegel took for granted a sense of a legal culture that excluded the Indigenous inhabitants of the Americas.

This focus upon the relation of a legal culture to an understanding of what one took as civilization in Hegel's day, to my knowledge, has largely been left to the side.[2] Unlike Kant and other Enlightenment writers, Hegel did more than concentrate upon the identity of a discrete law; he offered a theory as to why such a law was binding or obligatory to a self-reflective inhabitant. Kant, for his part, considered such a consideration as treasonous (Kant 1797/1996, 95). Hegel's explanation of the binding character of an identifiable law rested in the character or ethos of a community. An ethos, or what Hegel called a *Sittlickeit*, embodied the social assumptions and expectations shared in a community. The most important assumption of a community concerned how thinking subjects reciprocally recognized one another in the content of the identifiable laws. Today, we might better describe an ethos as a culture. A family, village, religious group, nation-state, or even an international community may possess an ethos or culture. I aim to outline what Hegel understood as a legal culture, because he considered the legal culture as a hallmark of civilization. Such a legal culture, in Hegel's understanding, excluded the Indigenous inhabitants of the Americas from the very beginning of his analysis.

The starting point of Hegel's legal theory required an intellectual "leap" from the traditional societies, in this case of the Americas, into the legal culture of a civilized society, as Hegel conceptualized the latter. Traditional societies were described as "lawless." Lawlessness, though, took Hegel's view of "law" for granted. From his standpoint, a law had to be inscribed in codes (rather than in unwritten customs); authored by a state; the state had to possess a patriarchal structure of departments, offices, judges, and the like; each institutional office had to possess a jurisdiction or legal space separate from the next; a singular Head had to symbolize the whole structure; and territorial knowledge as well as an international legal objectivity independent of a state had to characterize legal norms. The traditional communities of the Americas lacked such attributes, according to Hegel. Without them, the Indigenous social life of the Americas could not be protected against the violence of the "civilization" of European intruders. The jurist could not even begin to understand, study, or reflect about the complex and sophisticated legal cultures of the traditional communities of the Americas, since the latter lacked the character of a law—at least as Hegel understood the nature of law. Accordingly, in his view, laws only took form *after* inhabitants leapt from a felt or immediate identity with nature to a culture of self-reflection about concepts. Hegel read this leap into his "conception" of the inhabitants of the Americas. A rupture radically separated the legal culture of the Europeans from the "lawless" "passive" "mass" of Indigenous individuals on the American continents. The implicit legal culture which he used to understand and "conceive" a civilization excluded Indigenous societies from the very start of his analysis.

This essay aims to explain why Hegel separated civilization from traditional societies. Section 1 will outline several features of what Hegel took to be a legal culture. Such features concerned Hegel's focus upon *Bildung* and an ethos, the representation of a law in writing, a self-creative author (the state), territorial knowledge, and a hierarchy of societies based upon their progress toward the legal culture. Section 2 will highlight the importance of "the leap" in Hegel's legal theory. Section 3 will outline why Hegel considered the traditional societies of the Americas as lacking the European sense of a legal culture before the leap. I shall end by returning to his view of legal culture in order to highlight why he characterized traditional societies as lacking social progress.

Hegel's Conception of European Legal Culture

Ethos and *Bildung*

Hegel's conception of a legal culture had several features. For one thing, he identified two elements that one needs to appreciate in order to understand his sense of a legal culture and of civilization. The first is his emphasis upon the contextualization of a legal rule or legal institution in the ethos of a society. Such assumptions and expectations work to confer form (that is a concept) onto a social bond among inhabitants. The challenge for the jurist, Hegel suggested, was to examine the presupposed social content of a codified rule in order to identify the extent to which the content manifests the ethos in which the rule is nested.

The second element pinpointed what Hegel considered the crucial feature of the ethos of a modern European civilization: *Bildung*[3] (that is, "cultivation" or "education") (1991a, 187). *Bildung* manifested a wide, context-specific perspective about the world external to oneself, as well as one's role in constructing such a world by her or his concepts. One's life experiences were as important as one's formal education. *Bildung* would render one aware of the separation of one's self-conscious thinking from an objective world.

Before a discrete coded law was enacted, legal objectivity was synonymous with nature (Hegel 1991a, 13R). After the leap into a legal culture, the objectivity of nature was displaced in favour of an objectivity of legal consciousness. The latter represented civilization. The objectivity of legal consciousness was the consequence of reflection about concepts. The more one became self-conscious of her or his relation to a reflective objectivity, the more one became autonomous or free from the legal objectivity. Legal knowledge, then, was not to be found in the discrete rules of some external world of statutes and treaties, but in one's subjectivity as one came to recognize the external world as the objectivity of his (Hegel had little space for women) legal consciousness (1991a, 13R). Accordingly, what was crucial was the substantive social content of a legal rule, legal procedures, legal institutions, and general attitudes toward legal objectivity.

Such social content represented the extent to which the legal culture (or ethos, to use his term) represented the *Bildung* of a civilized society. The social life of Indigenous inhabitants of the Americas lacked such an ethos, according to Hegel. This was so because the *Bildung* of a civilized society (and its legal culture) began only after individuals started to become self-conscious—that is, conscious of the relation of one's self to a legal objectivity.

A state's legal order represented such an objectivity. An international legal order represented a further advanced shape of self-consciousness than that of a state-centric legal order. Officials had to relate any discrete provision of a code to the ethos (that is, a culture) in which he was situated.

With one's self-conscious separation from legal objectivity, legal objectivity became the object of one's own thinking. Legal objectivity here was not fixed in calendar time and territorial space. Rather, one constantly developed with multiple possibilities to choose this or that personal action. Statutes and institutions were considered *indicia* of the self-conscious choices of individuals in an organic ethos. The competent jurist, then, had to be self-aware of his role in the very construction of a series of historically contingent shapes of legal objectivity. Accordingly, any legal objectivity was conditioned and historically contingent by boundaries of a structure (or what Hegel called a "shape") of legal consciousness shared with others in an ethos. Such shapes permeated one's analysis of property, contract, crimes, legal rights, legal duties, the family, civil society, the state, and international law.[4] Hegel described how the individual subtly became conscious of himself inside the socially constructed boundary of each such shape. The crucial point is that Hegel attempted to explain what a legal culture would resemble if social life represented and were the consequence of *Bildung*. *Bildung* would characterize the ethos of a civilized society. Let us identify how *Bildung* entered into Hegel's view of a legal culture.

Writing

For one thing, the legal culture of civilization, according to Hegel, was represented by codes—that is, by written laws. Hegel's idea was that an unwritten custom, as advocated by his contemporary Friedrich Carl von Savigny, lacked a discrete, assignable, and self-conscious author, such as a legislature. An unwritten law existed from "time immemorial." A custom was just "there" in a society. One could not change or "amend" a custom as a consequence of reflection, deliberation, and inscription of the custom in a statute. An author had to reflect and deliberate about the social content represented by a written law. As such, the code could reform what inhabitants had accepted as a custom since time immemorial.

The Self-creative Author of a Civilized Society

Writing highlighted a second and related feature of the legal culture. This was the presupposed importance of the author as self-creative and self-determining. Hegel assumed that a civilization was composed of self-conscious authors. Although the author figured in Thomas Aquinas' legal theory, the author of legal authority prominently emerged in the early legal theories (Thomas Hobbes' being important) (Conklin 2001, 2011b). Michel Foucault, in his genealogical approach, asserted that the author became so important in European culture that discourses were believed to have been founded by authors (Foucault 1984, 113–17; Conklin 2001, 84–85, 107–10). Interestingly, even today, a leading twentieth-century Anglo-American legal philosopher has insisted that "in a developed legal system" a rule is legal if it refers to "the writing or inscription as 'authoritative'" (Hart 1994, 93). Hegel too articulated the importance of self-conscious writing by an author, in this case a self-creative and self-determining state. When the Europeans arrived on the shores of the Americas, Hegel claimed, indigenous inhabitants lacked self-consciously authored laws to which they were obligated. Writing again, for Hegel, expressed the will of authors who reflected about concepts.

Indigenous inhabitants would only be civilized if they came to recognize that they were separate from nature. At that moment, they would become aware of concepts that mediated between their own subjectivity and legal objectivity. And at that point, they would construct a state, the state being the product of self-conscious autonomous individuals. Inside the territorial boundary of a state, the sources of laws would be state institutions such as legislatures and courts. Such sources were surrogates or "actors," to use Hobbes' latter term. An author signified its will (or intent) in writing. The author willed concepts. The writing in the form of a statute or judicial precedent was the product of a reflective deliberation about concepts. Such writing contrasted with unstated and unwritten customs. A custom just happened unselfconsciously. One simply followed a custom while by contrast, a statute or judicial decision was the product of reflection and expression by a legislature or a court.

Now, Hegel did not attribute self-creative authorship only to civilized human beings. He also attributed such a character to the state as a product of legal consciousness. So there were two types of authors: the self-originating and self-determining human authors, and the self-creative and self-determining states constructed by the human authors. The state's statutes and treaties expressed such a state's will. The very drive to become increasingly self-conscious, whether on the part of the autonomous individual human being or of a state, created the need for self-consciously written laws and for the state that authored such laws, according to Hegel: "but we must not for a moment imagine that the physical world of nature is of a higher order than the world of the spirit; for the state is as far above physical life as spirit is above nature" (1991a, 272A). The state, as author, was "far above physical life" because the state was the product of self-conscious thought about concepts. The state, being a self-conscious author, was not constructed by nature but by self-conscious human beings.

As such, the leaders of a stateless society, which was how Hegel viewed Indigenous governance in the Americas, might sign a treaty and its members might believe that the European state party to the treaty was obligated to adhere to its terms. But the "treaty" would be considered a "political," not a legal obligation, since the individuals of a traditional society had not yet become self-conscious of law as a humanly constructed objectivity. A treaty was considered non-binding to the European parties as a consequence. Interestingly, only as recently as 1984 did the Canadian Supreme Court hold that treaties with Indigenous leaders were "legally" obligatory rather than "political oughts."[5] As a consequence, a national government became legally obligated to abide by the terms of the treaties. Negotiation of their enforcement had to proceed in good faith as with other treaties between state parties.

Both the state and human beings, again, were subjects of the objectivity of legal consciousness. Once constructed in the collective consciousness, the state and its laws were an objectivity vis-à-vis human beings as authors of signified concepts. Indeed, the state was greater than the aggregate of the individual wills of human beings. Thus, crimes could be caused against the state, aside from crimes against other individual human beings. In the same way that the individual came to recognize that she or he was separate from nature, and then separate from the condition of legal consciousness, so too the state was separate from the objectivity of international law. The institutions and written laws were projected into objectivity of consciousness so that an individual's will would be rationally guided and constrained.

The State

The third element manifesting Hegel's sense of a legal culture highlighted the state. Human beings represented an advance over animals because we could reflect about concepts, whereas animals acted from the passions of their bodies. Unless one could think about concepts and thereby become conscious of her or his separation from nature, one could only live a "fragmented" or atomistic existence without the unifying concepts needed for a reflective *Sittlichkeit* (Conklin 2008, 43–48). A state represented such a product of human consciousness. Once a legal culture took hold in North

America, Hegel stated, slavery would be a mere "phase in man's education ... whereby he gradually attains a higher ethical existence and a corresponding degree of culture" (1975a, 184). With a capacity to think about concepts, individuals could socially recognize one another by sharing concepts with the other thinking beings (Conklin 2008, 162–87).

The state, itself a concept, needed institutions to represent its will. Hegel highlighted a series of such institutions. One was the legislature, another the courts, and a third an administrative structure in which a Head (or monarch) symbolized the whole. Such institutions mediated between the human beings, as authors, and the legal objectivity of codes, treaties, and state institutions. Officials had to reason and act in a detached way, as if the written laws existed in a legal objectivity. Such institutions symbolized civilization. Each of the three structures, organized in a "patriarchal" way, was separate from the other. A monarch would join the organization into oneness at the pinnacle of the pyramidal organization, although he or she would do little but say "yes" and "dot the i" (Hegel 1991a, 280A). Hegel associated the organic character of the state with such a governmental organization (Conklin 2008, 243–54). The legal organization as a whole developed into an organic constitution.

Territorial Knowledge

This suggests a fourth element of Hegel's understanding of legal culture. Legal knowledge in European legal culture had a territorial character about it (Hegel 1975a, 122–23). Hegel's territorial knowledge had two features. First, knowledge in legal culture took territorial borders as the limit of the state's jurisdiction. Inside its own borders, the state had a totality of legal authority over all human subjects and things. Because legal objectivity was invariably separate from the author or subject, the state, as an author of such a legal objectivity, had an unlimited desire to acquire more and more territory in order to protect and widen its own self-conscious authority. The European legal culture completed itself by geographically expanding to all parts of the globe (Schmitt 2006). By Hegel's projection of his category of a consciousness of nature onto geographical areas of the globe, racial and ethnic categories became part and parcel of his exclusion of traditional societies, lacking a state-centric legal structure from what he considered "civilization" (1971, 393).

In his earliest writings, Hegel placed the Mongols and Arabs at the bottom of his hierarchy of social development because they lived a nomadic life (1975a, 156). Nothing could be more alien to the self-conscious construction of a territorial state than a territory inhabited by nomadic inhabitants, Hegel believed. We know now that most of the traditional societies east of the Rocky Mountains were nomadic (Albers 1996). By excluding nomadic societies from what he took as legal culture because of his preoccupation with centrally organized territorial states, Hegel once again found it straightforward to categorize the traditional societies of the Americas as uncivilized.

Territorial knowledge for Hegel had a second feature. This arose from the fact that legal objectivity was a construction of legal self-consciousness. The codification of rules represented cognitive objects of the will of legal persons, whether individuals or states. Accordingly, it was not enough for a state to physically control a territory; the state had to claim a property interest in the territory. Because the legal culture of *Bildung* represented the most advanced stage of self-consciousness, according to Hegel, the invariably separate legal objectivity drove states, as authors, to occupy *terra nullius* (that is, territory belonging to no one). Although at least 11 million Indigenous people occupied North America at the time of European contact, Hegel expressed the view that such people could not be legally recognized, because they supposedly lacked the capacity to think about concepts. In particular, lacking self-consciously written laws, Indigenous peoples did not have states that could claim "radical title" (a term used today to describe the state's ownership of land) to the land.

Accordingly, the boundary between the European civilization and Indigenous traditional societies was not physical, but culturally constructed. The boundary was territorial-like rather than territorial. The state did more than physically possess territory: it owned the territory. In like vein, a legal right possessed a boundary within which a legal person could freely think, express, and act. Again, the boundary of a right was not a physical fact but a cultural construction. Legal space, not physical space, represented a right. The same could be said of a contract or of the jurisdiction of the monarch, legislature, court, or governmental agent. Even what Hegel called "world history" (or what we would call international law) protected the territorial-like legal space inside each state.

The Hierarchy of Societies

Hegel's understanding of a legal culture led to a hierarchy of societies. Each individual in a civilized society was considered a self-generating and self-conscious author. Self-consciousness measured the condition and place of a human being and a society in the European hierarchy of social progress.

More generally, much of the globe lacked any semblance of self-consciousness as represented by self-generating secular states as authors, according to Hegel. Societies, though, could progress into "advanced" stages of self-consciousness and thereby become civilized. France, England, Spain, Denmark, Sweden, Holland, and Hungary had reached such a higher stage of civilization in Hegel's time.

When Hegel turned to the Americas, however, the traditional societies lay beyond his recognition on any scale of civilization. Hegel offers no anthropological evidence, to my knowledge, about the social life of traditional societies of the Americas. European legal officials just had to make a metaphysical and epistemological "leap" from an identity with nature among individuals in traditional societies to an identity with a conceptual objectivity as in European legal culture. Settlers, religious agents, and military officers carried "the advantages of civilization" to the Americas. The problem was that Hegel conceived the Indigenous inhabitants as individuals living close to nature and, therefore, without any semblance of the *Bildung*. *Bildung*, again, embodied the ethos of a civilization.

Although Africans and Asians were described as possessing a lower category of legal culture and therefore of civilization, they could, with self-education, emerge into civilized societies, according to Hegel. The Indigenous traditional societies of the Americas, however, remained entirely outside the capacity to form a legal culture. Their social life had to be totally dissolved into the European legal culture. Law only began when its peoples and rulers were sufficiently self-conscious to enact their will in writing and to reflect about the concepts signified by the writing. Traditional societies, lacking any of the indicia of patriarchal state-centric institutions and concepts as laws, did not have any laws or legal structure (or at least, laws as Hegel understood them). They felt bonded to nature, outside any legal recognition as being capable of owning property, entering into contracts and treaties, legislating written laws, punishing offenders, or even possessing "a community." Hegel therefore described them as "pre-legal" and "pre-historical." They were just a "mass" of atomistic individuals.

Interestingly, this hierarchy, presupposed and constructed by Hegel's sense of a legal culture, recognized legal persons in terms of a bloodline or *sanguinis*.[6] One's bloodline determined whether one was a national of this or that state. Only nationals possessed legal rights vis-à-vis her or his state. *Sanguinis* reinforced the hierarchy of societies because the inhabitants of a colony lacked legal personhood if they lacked the politically dominant bloodline of the colonial state. Conversely, military and bureaucratic officials who possessed the bloodline of the colonial state, remained nationals of a colonized society (this was so, for example, until the postwar British empire began to shrink). The dark moments of European legal culture—racial segregation, biological experimentation, Nazism, indefinite internment, apartheid, and ethnic atrocities—have taken *jus sanguinis* for legal justification. *Jus sanguinis*, reaching its ultimate consequence in the citizenship laws of European states, ironically transformed *Bildung* into institutional racism. I say "ironically" because Hegel aspired to privilege a legal culture characterized by the quest for self-consciousness. And yet, because this very quest left the Indigenous inhabitants of the Americas before law and before history, such inhabitants remained in nature and therefore external to the *Bildung* of European legal culture.

One might well ask of Hegel, "what were his anthropological sources for his categorization of the indigenous inhabitants of the Americas?" To be sure, one has to wait for over a century before anthropology took hold as a necessary study of the stranger to the European legal culture. The absence of anthropological evidence or even the absence of travels on Hegel's part (the latter being something he could ill afford), however, reinforces my argument. Hegel's hierarchization of societies is not of his own making. He elaborates an exclusionary perspective toward the Indigenous inhabitants that he shared with other European and American jurists and judges of his day.[7] Lacking a centralized state with a pyramidal structure of offices, and lacking written laws along with the other indicia of a legal culture, American and British courts also excluded the legal orders of the Indigenous Americans as uncivilized and savage.[8]

To take the leading constitutional and international law precedent of *Campbell v. Hall* (1774), the "pagans" of traditional societies had to be subject to "one state or the other."[9] The territorial claim of title to all land under its suzerainty authorized the European state to "exterminate them" if they refused to recognize the state's claim of title to the land.[10] Hegel's approach was not peculiar to himself (or to Kant). His approach manifested assumptions that one can trace through the writings of the early modern jurists (Conklin 2012, 2001, 73–170). Since Greek and Roman literature was the mainstay of the education of such jurists, Hegel's assumptions can also be traced most certainly to Roman law (Conklin 2010). Hegel's sources associated civilization with the "legal culture" much as briefly outlined above. Hegel's legal philosophy represented a legal culture that excluded a consideration of the Indigenous social and legal life from the start of "law."

The Leap

Against the background of Hegel's sense of a legal culture, he insisted that it could only begin after individuals organized according to the indicia of a legal culture of *Bildung*. The jurist, historian, and philosopher had to "leap" from the world of nature into a world of self-conscious authors. He considered the state as the ultimate such author. A deep rupture was believed to separate an unwritten and bodily transmitted social life of individuals in a traditional society from a legal culture where self-consciously authored scripts signified concepts and where the concepts, in turn, categorized social experiences. With such a leap, concepts replaced the animalistic passions of the individuals on the Americas. Again, Hegel was not alone in this regard.

Self-consciously posited laws and institutions were the mark of civil society (Hegel 1975b, 250). This was so because codification represented concepts about how one ought to act. Being humanly constructed, the rules/concepts governed and controlled the otherwise uncontrollable bodily desires of rulers and ruled alike. Even justice could only take shape *after* the leap from the uncivilized world into the European legal culture (Hegel 1975a, 124). Until that point, one would live a fragmented and "sensuous" existence driven by passions of the body rather than by thinking about concepts (1975a, 184). One's bodily actions would remain immediate with nature.

Justice, then, only took form *after* the leap from the alleged uncivilized world (Hegel 1975a, 124). That is, the customs of the traditional societies of North America simply could not be just because, for Hegel as much as our contemporary analytic jurists (Conklin 2000b), justice originated after the leap from nature into a state-centric legal structure. Such a leap was possible only once inhabitants had begun to reflect about a self-consciously conceived legal objectivity represented by writing in the form of statutes and treaties. However, with this presupposed leap into a modern legal culture, some societies failed to progress to higher and higher levels of civilization. Other societies might retract back to the "primitive" customs characteristic of a traditional society. Chronologically *after the leap* from pre-civilization, a "gray" area would intercede between the "developing" (the contemporary term) and a "developed" (again, the contemporary term) legal structure.

This "necessary" leap was elaborated in the subsequent nineteenth-century European and American juristic scholarship (Anghie 2004, 39–114). The leap historically reached its apex with the breakup of the Austro-

Hungarian Empire. The League of Nations' *Covenant* reflected the leap by highlighting formally equal sovereign states as the only legal persons in the international community. The League's *Covenant* also stated that some societies remained in a pre-legal condition, and as such, they had to be left under "the tutelage" (the term of the *Covenant*) until they eventually leapt into civilization. States were legally bound to contracts or treaties with other states, but not with Indigenous parties.[11]

The self-image of the European jurists as representing civilization just could not address the nature of law in the diverse and complex legal structures of the traditional societies. To the contrary, only the will of states could be binding. The leap permeated the domestic and international legal culture to the point that the newfound state of Canada authorized residential schools which were believed to offer the opportunity to "educate" children of Indigenous inhabitants into the *Bildung* of European legal consciousness. Millions of inhabitants of the globe have been left stateless as a consequence of the legal culture of European civilization.[12] Without being recognized as legal persons by states, their legal and social insecurity has remained profound.

The Absence of a Legal Culture in the Americas

One can now appreciate the social consequences of the leap. The leap simply left the unwritten customs and rituals of traditional societies of the Americas as legally unrecognizable, and without recognizable states, the Indigenous social life of the Americas could not be protected against outside intruders such as Europeans. A state and its laws represented an act of self-conscious willing. But Indigenous inhabitants, unlike the Europeans, were "obviously unintelligent individuals with little capacity for education." They were "like unenlightened children, living from one day to the next, and untouched by higher thoughts and aspirations" (Hegel 1975a, 164,165). Only those individuals who could think about concepts could be active, Hegel tells us. Lacking a propensity to reflect about concepts, Hegel believed, the Indigenous peoples of the Americas were "mild" and "passive." The "dullest savages," Hegel posited, were "the Pecherais and Eskimos" (Hegel 1971, 393Z 45). "It is true," he advises, "that in some parts of America at the time of its discovery, a pretty considerable civilization was to be found" (1971, 393Z 45). Hegel adds that "this was not comparable with European culture and disappeared with the original inhabitants.... The natives of America are, therefore, clearly not in a position to maintain themselves in the face of the Europeans. The latter will begin a new culture over there on the soil they have conquered from the natives" (1971, 393Z 45). Let us identify why Hegel considered the Americas as lacking a legal culture.

For one thing, without a consciousness about the world as separate from self-reflective subjects, Indigenous inhabitants could not combat nor overcome European superiority by virtue of its capacity to think, according to Hegel (1975a, 163). Only if the inhabitants leapt from nature into the European legal culture would they begin to possess laws. Until then, they were "culturally inferior nations" to the "more advanced nations which have gone through more intensive cultural development" (163).

The Indigenous inhabitants of the Americas, in sum, lacked Hegel's sense of a legal culture needed for such cultural development. They were immediate with nature (Hegel 1975a, 177). They socially related with one another through the passions of their bodies and through the stories and myths of nature's control over their social lives. As Hegel lectures in 1817–18, "all simply did their duty, without moral consternation and without the vanity of claiming to know better. There was simple consciousness that the laws *were*" (1817b 126).

Unwritten laws were said to be all-controlling, and Indigenous Americans felt immediate with customs (Hegel 1991a, 211A). Customs constituted "a second nature." Accordingly, Hegel considered traditional societies "lawless" (1975a, 177). They lacked any capacity for *Bildung*, in contrast with the Indigenous Africans who were said to possess strong wills. The European legal culture would inevitably dominate the traditional societies of the Americas. Hegel could categorize them as "passive" and "docile," lacking in intellectual curiosity, unfamiliar with formal education, physically weak, spiritually and sexually impotent, and a dying race.[13] My point is that Hegel's racial categories, which have been the object of recent scholarly commentary, followed from the radical rupture between pre-legality and legality.[14] In sum, the Indigenous traditional societies of the Americas remained stuck in a pre-legal world, signifying that they had to be transformed by education and, if necessary, by state violence.

The Indigenous inhabitants of the Americas were said to lack self-reflection about mediating concepts between themselves and nature (Hegel 1822/23, 151; 1991a, 211A). As Hegel lectured, "some of them have visited Europe, but they are obviously unintelligent individuals with little capacity for education. Their inferiority on all respects, even in stature, can be seen in every particular" (1975a, 164).Without a capacity to reflect about concepts, their acts were arbitrary, violent, blind, irrational, and formless. Revenge rather than punishment characterized their deeds (Hegel 1991a, 102). One could only be punished for violating concepts or self-consciously posited laws (Hegel 1817/18b, 104). With revenge, one was driven by biological motives without the constraints of acts of intellectualization (Hegel 1991a, 211A). A sense of blameworthiness and even a sense of right or wrong were lacking (Hegel 1824/25, 177). Bodily impulses had, for millennia, been attributed to nature. One acted because nature so dictated. Indigenous societies were guided by such biological drives in contrast to the European legal culture that Hegel identified. Indeed, he goes so far as to liken the absence of self-consciousness among the Indigenous inhabitants of the Americas to animals. In this respect, Hegel's description of the pre-legal world was shared by Lucretius, Cicero, and Seneca (Conklin 2010, 449–504).[15] Although racism is often associated with the Enlightenment, the exclusionary character of a legal culture can be traced to the Romans and Greeks (Conklin 2012, 2001).

As for Hegel, he distinguished two elements of experience: the physical and the spiritual. Animals were driven by physical needs, and human beings by spiritual needs (Hegel 1991a, 11A; 190A; 1975a, 39; 49). Only human beings could think about concepts. By such thinking, one came to appreciate that one was separate from the objectivity of nature. The distinction between animals and humans presupposed that each human being, unlike an animal, was driven by a desire to become self-conscious (Hegel 1991a, 260). Without a thinking legal culture, biological drives would reign supreme, according to Hegel. As such, desires would be unlimited. "Savagery and unfreedom" would thereby be characterized in social relations (Hegel 1991a, 194R; 1991b, para. 24A2). The Indigenous North Americans, lacking a European legal culture, did not have the capacity to mediate biological drives with concepts. That is, they lacked discrete wills, and because of this, they were at one with nature. There was no separation of individual and nature. Nature controlled their lives by acts of disease, starvation, storms, and wars. In Hegel's words, "after the creation of the natural universe, man appears on the scene as the antithesis of nature; he is the being who raises himself up into a second world" (1975a, 44). The second world is the objectivity of consciousness. Much like one might have experienced in learning about Euclidean geometry, a structure of legal concepts would "follow its own course" (Hegel 1991b, para. 24A2). The Indigenous "savages" of the Americas could not appreciate the importance of concepts in their respective life-worlds.

Once one became conscious of a separation of the individual from nature, the objectivity of nature shifted into the objectivity of consciousness.

Written laws, being concepts, manifested such a consciousness. This human capacity to think about concepts was possible because (Hegel believed), unlike animals, human beings possessed languages. Once one had a language, one could think (1975a, 39).

Thus, Hegel's own structure of legal consciousness pre-censored the traditional societies of the Americas as pre-legal and therefore "savage." A "civilized" society was characterized by the signification of concepts as laws. The concepts were rules. A "savage" society remained in a condition more appropriate for animals, he asserted. Hegel explained that "as soon as man emerges from nature, he stands in opposition to nature" (1975a, 177). Because a thinking being recognized that she or he was separate from nature, nature could no longer be attributed as the cause of all harm. Once one recognized that she or he was separate from nature, however, this consciousness alone did not ensure that one was civilized: "he is still at the first stage of his development: he is dominated by passion, and is nothing more than a savage" (Hegel 1975a, 177). What was necessary was that the "savage" should construct a legal objectivity. Such a humanly constructed objectivity would displace nature and the biological drives of the "savage." Although Hegel argued that the state was a mere passing moment of self-consciousness, it best represented a higher-ordered objectivity of legal consciousness in his day. A stateless community, such as a traditional society in the Americas, remained outside such objectivity.

The Alleged Absence of a Social Community

To take a second point, Hegel found it difficult to describe the Indigenous Americans as constituting a community. A community, to be one, had to be the object of self-reflecting individuals who would recognize each other as self-reflecting. Shared concepts of objectivity of consciousness constituted such a community. A community, then, was embodied in an ethos that has been described as a "reflective *Sittlichkeit*" rather than a "primitive *Sittlichkeit*." From Hegel's standpoint, it was impossible to talk about Indigenous inhabitants of the Americas as sharing a community. A reflective community could not exist for individuals who lacked the intellectual curiosity to know the concepts represented by codes and mediating institutions such as courts, legislatures, a bureaucracy, and a monarch. As noted above, Hegel believed Indigenous peoples of the Americas lacked the capacity to think and act through such mediating concepts and institutions. They lacked the capacity for self-reflection, and therefore they lacked any social consciousness "of communal existence without which no state can exist" (Hegel

1975a, 165). Without centralized institutions to author the will of the social whole, the inhabitants of the Americas were an undifferentiated mass of "savage hordes,"[16] "physically and spiritually impotent," and passively controlled by nature.[17]

When one reflected about concepts, the thinker no longer felt immediate with her or his biological drives and nature, according to Hegel. One became a legal subject of objectivity. The subject could now be recognized as a legal person with rights and duties. Concepts mediated between the immediate identity of an Indigenous inhabitant with nature on the one hand and the European legal objectivity "out there" separate from the individual on the other. The separation of the subject from the objectivity of consciousness, in turn, marked the freedom of the individual. The reflective legal person was consciously free to act independent of objectivity, whether of nature or of legal consciousness. The thinking capacity transformed the biological needs of nature into social needs of consciousness (Hegel 1991a, 194).

Hegel's self-reflecting human beings were not the same as Kant's. Kant's legal persons were located in an idealized world of a priori concepts. Such concepts were emptied of social-cultural assumptions of a phenomenal world. Rules and maxims, universal inside their boundaries, were purged of social-cultural contingencies. Hegel is very critical of Kant's preoccupation with a priori concepts in a *noumenal* world. Instead, for him, legal persons are immersed in socially and historically contingent phenomena. This explains why Hegel privileged the ethos as determinative of the obligatory character of a discrete coded law. Human action remained in the phenomenal world. Shared concepts in such a phenomenal world would make for an ethos. As such, a community would exist whose members recognized one another as self-originary and self-reflecting subjects and where the products of such self-reflecting individuals embodied with social relationships. Such socially contingent thought could thereby be rendered concrete. Abstractions of thinking individuals become immersed in a reflective social ethos (Hegel 1991a, 192).

Freedom, then, involved the reflection about the constructed objectivity of legal consciousness immersed in an ethos. As Hegel puts it, freedom is linked with the spiritual drive to reflect about the external world (1991a, 194R). The "savages" of the Americas lacked freedom because their actions did not yet manifest this spiritual drive to reflect about the objectivity of consciousness. As Hegel stated, "we do have information concerning America and its culture, especially as it developed in Mexico and Peru, but only to the effect that it was a purely natural culture which had to perish as soon as the spirit [of European culture] approached it.... For after the Europeans had landed there, the natives were gradually destroyed by the breath of European activity" (1975a, 163). The legal person reflected about his own role in the production of legal objectivity. Precisely because the Indigenous inhabitants of the Americas lacked the recognition of their separation from the objectivity of nature, the "civilized" peoples of Europe possessed an ethical obligation to uplift them into civilization—to "educate them," to assimilate them into acceptance of European institutions, to preach to them, to teach them, and to institutionalize European legal culture.

In sum, the bonding of members of a (European) civilized society was the product of reflection about concepts. The subject *intentionally* and reflectively bonded with society as an objectivity of legal consciousness (Hegel 1991a, 94). By doing so, the legal person, as a subject of legal objectivity, would access a higher stage of civilization. So too, justice and goodness would only become possible after the individual had become self-conscious of her or his relation with others. Most importantly, Hegel expected that legislators and thinking individuals would evaluate the social-cultural content of coded rules. In particular, such discrete laws would only be obligatory if their social-cultural content manifested a reciprocal social recognition of individuals toward one another as thinking beings. At that point, the content of laws would manifest ethicality.

Lawlessness

A third feature of Hegel's legal philosophy worked to exclude Indigenous inhabitants of the Americas from Hegel's civilization. Lacking self-reflection, the "savage hordes" were said to lack the capacity to reflect about concepts and therefore, to construct a state. A state was considered an object of the self-consciousness of human beings. Much like a self-conscious autonomous legal person, a state acted as a subject opposed to another objectivity: namely, an international legal objectivity separate from state members (Conklin 2008, 270–98). Hegel called this objectivity "world history"; today, we would call it public international law. Just as the state constrained the human subject inside the territorial border of the state, the international legal order constrained and guided the actions of authors/states. States became legal subjects of the international legal objectivity.

In contrast, traditional societies were said to lack law. Their customs were categorized as pre-legal because their unwritten customs, rituals, stories, and myths were excluded from the writing authored by a state. Their customs were unwritten and unstated; they lacked the expression of self-reflective authors. Members of a traditional society felt bonded with customs; they followed them without reflecting about their content or even whether they were self-consciously authored as acts of intellectualization. They lacked picture thoughts or mediating concepts *about* the customs, according to Hegel.

The Alleged Social Progress

The above factors suggest this point. By studying a society in terms of its level of development of legal self-consciousness, Hegel believed that he could hierarchize societies throughout the globe and throughout history. Before individuals and their societies became self-conscious, there was no law, no justice, and no culture. Outside such a vertical social/ethical hierarchy, as noted above, there were the Indigenous peoples. The Indigenous American inhabitants lacked form to intellectually join one individual with another and to join one traditional society with another. A state, as Kant argued, was such an empty form (although, for Hegel, the laws of such a form were only binding if the content of the form recognized the reciprocal recognition of individual subjects). At this point, one may well appreciate the importance of social and ethical progress according to Hegel: "it is important that we should recognize that the development of the spirit is a form of progress" (1975a, 125). Hegel continually wrote about "development," "gradual progression," "progress," "a higher plane," and "culturally inferior nations." Progress was "immanent" from within the social-cultural ethos. This contrasted with understanding "progress" as if it could be posited "out there" by some written constitution (Hegel 1975a, 131). Progress began when "the savage hordes," driven by animalistic instincts and ends, became self-conscious. One could only understand the early stages of something in the light of its *telos* in something more developed. Civilized European states, being more "developed," therefore had an ethical obligation to "uplift" the inhabitants of primordial societies into higher stages of social development.

Hegel's legal philosophy suggests that one must read a society backward from where it is today to where it began. The beginning, though, occurs after inhabitants have leapt into their self-conscious separation from nature. If a nation took the form of a sovereign state, the nation progressed toward a higher-ordered level of civilization (Hegel 1991a, 351). Ethnic nations were treated as barbaric if they were "less advanced" than the higher-ordered, self-reflective societies. Even barbarism had different stages of progress: cattle-raising peoples might regard huntsmen as barbaric, agricultural peoples might regard both huntsmen and cattle-raising peoples as barbaric. Since customs shared the immediacy that characterized the natural being, unwritten norms marked a lower stage of progress, while acts of representation characterized a higher legal order. The role of legal philosophy was to recognize the stage of civilization that the legal consciousness of a particular society presupposed.

This "ethical" and historical progress toward higher and higher levels of self-consciousness, not toward the sovereign state per se, marked the "conquering march of the world spirit" (Hegel 1975a, 63). Such a spirit expressed "the divine process which is a graduated progression" (64). Hegel also described this movement of self-consciousness as the "march of God" of which the state was the dominant moment in his day (1991a, 258A; 1975a, 112). The state was just one higher form of development from the natural forms of "docile" "unintelligent" "savages" (the Indigenous inhabitants of the Americas), a "savage horde" (Mongols), restorative invaders (Teutonic barbarians of Rome), a traditional society (Antigone's), family (the family in civil society), despotism in the form of a state (Cicero's Rome), and civil society (possessive individualism). The intellectualization that constructed objectivity carried "uncivilized" peoples into civilization signified by authored and written "laws." This all happened at the likely erasure of the legal *ethoi* of the Indigenous inhabitants of the Americas.

Conclusion

Hegel's highlights of a legal culture—*Bildung*, writing, legislative authors, the state, the separation of governmental jurisdictions, and territorial knowledge and a hierarchy of societies—are familiar to jurists today (Conklin 2011a). We also know enough about the social life of the pre-contact traditional societies to appreciate that Hegel had re-conceptualized their own particular *ethoi*. He did so to make them fit into his starting-point of the leap. The traditional societies certainly had laws, although Hegel did not and could not recognize them as binding in what he conceived as the legal culture of a civilized society. The laws certainly had *ethoi*, although hardly Hegel's sense of an ethos as *Bildung*. The Indigenous customs were unwritten, being signified and transferred from generation to generation through gestural languages, although Hegel did not recognize such because of his association of language with writing. Indigenous languages appealed to stories and myths rather than to concepts (although, to be sure, myths and stories certainly permeated the legal culture of civilization). Higher education was experienced through the extended family and one's elders rather than in the universities of *Bildung*. Meaning was gestural rather than cognitive (Conklin 1999, 2011a, 25–31). A child was educated through festive celebrations, rituals, dances, and play of the experiential body (Huizinga 1955, 76–88). Social rituals exalted nature because nature was so important to the very survival of the community of Indigenous inhabitants.

Hegel's distinction between intellectual passivity and thinking beings, his distinction between biology and thinking, and the difference between immediacy with nature and immediacy with a reflective legal objectivity: these differences all marked the possibility of social progress as he pictured it. Hegel believed that the Indigenous inhabitants of the Americas were at one with nature. Since nature was believed to be all-controlling of human action, the Indigenous inhabitant was thereby considered intellectually docile, mild, and passive, humble and "obsequious[ly] submissive" in the face of "degradation" (Hegel 1975a, 164). The Indigenous inhabitants of the Americas were situated outside even the lowest structure of civilized societies.

Even today, what is taken as a pre-civilized society has been considered anthropologically, phenomenologically and analytically, prior to the civilized society. The state-centric legal objectivity excludes the pre-legal stateless social life. We have colonized others, schooled their children, assimilated them into our state-centric legal order, interned them, and killed them in order to institutionalize what we have taken as a higher stage of ethicality. Once the Europeans became civilized, they had an ethical duty to educate and elevate the Indigenous inhabitants into civilization. Colonialism and post-colonialism just seemed "natural" to the higher ordered societies that had progressed into civilization.

Built into Hegel's belief about European civilization, then, was the exclusion of societies that had failed to progress to what he felt were higher and higher levels of civilization. An untranslatable gap pierced the relationship of the civilized European legal culture and the Indigenous inhabitants of the Americas. For most societies, it was always possible to leap into a civilized condition. Only a society that had emerged into the condition of civilization could make a judgment about the stage of civilization in which Indigenous inhabitants found themselves. They could not assess and evaluate their own stage of consciousness and, therefore, of civilization.

The legal culture of European civilization required a leap into civilization. This priority remains an important feature of contemporary legal philosophy (Conklin 2001, 2011a, 2011b). Questions thus come to the fore even for the contemporary self-conscious "civilized" jurist. Why did Hegel begin a social theory about the importance of the state without a state? Why were the Indigenous inhabitants stuck in a pre-legal condition that left them outside legal protection unless they became "like the European civilization"? Why was a state-centric European society at a higher stage of social progress than a stateless society such as Hegel characterized of the Indigenous inhabitants of the Americas? Once Indigenous inhabitants became "civilized" into legal culture, could they return to their former pre-legal society, or were they invariably destined to remain civilized and alienated from their own *ethoi*? Such issues remain with jurists today.

Hegel was right on one point, however. His pre-legal world of traditional societies remained a concept signified by the legal culture of European civilization. This being so, Hegel was entrapped in his own image of *Bildung* as self-consciousness. This image pre-censored the voices of the Indigenous inhabitants of the Americas without a hearing among jurists. Hegel's image of legal culture remains our own, two hundred years later, because we lawyers tragically share with Hegel the legal culture of European civilization.

Notes

1 See generally, Kant (1997); Harvey (2000, 532–36; 2011, 267–84); Bernasconi (1979; 1998; 2000; 2001; 2003; 2007); Buck-Morss (2000; 2009); Hoffheimer (2001), Eze (1997); Serequeberhan (1979).

2 For an examination of Hegel's racial categories, however, see Hoffheimer (2001).

3 This notion is elaborated in Conklin (2008, 27–29).

4 I have retrieved such shapes from Conklin (2008).

5 *Guerin v. The Queen* [1984] 2 SCR 335; 13 DLR (4th) 321.

6 Today, nationality according to *sanguinis* is traced to the relation of an individual to the nationality of the parents (often the male parent). The problems of such a view are examined in Conklin (forthcoming 2014).

7 See Anghie (2004, 39–114); B. Williams (2004, 20–39). Indeed, even in our own day, a leading Anglo-American jurist, H.L.A. Hart, has written that the leap (he calls it a "step") is necessary as a matter of "faith" (1994, 94, 170).

8 *Campbell v. Hall,* [1774] 1 Cowp. 204 at 210, 212; 98 E.R. 1045 at 1049, 1050; [1774] Lofft 655; *The Antelope,* 23 US (10 Wheaton) 5 [1825]; *Johnson and Graham's Lease v. M'Intosh,* [1823] 8 Wheaton 543, 21 US 240; *Cherokee Nation v. State of Georgia,* [1831] 30 US 1 at 17. Also see the documentation in Williams (1990, 227–32, 235–38); Ferguson (2011, 103–40); Pagden (1986, 1–12); Asad (2002, 133–39); Hill (1996, 7–13).

9 *Campbell v. Hall,* [1774] 1 Cowp. 204 at 212; 98 E.R. 1045 at 1049.

10 *Campbell v. Hall*, [1774] 1 Cowp. 204 at 209–210; 98 E.R. 1045 at 1048.

11 *R. v. Vincent*, [1993] 12 OR (3d) 427 (CA), at 437a, 437h, 440c–h (CA).

12 See generally Conklin (forthcoming 2014), Chapter 3.

13 Hoffheimer (2001) documents Hegel's views of the Indigenous Americans being the lowest territorial group with reference to European civilization.

14 Hegel distinguishes between pre-legality and civilization throughout the *Philosophy of Right* (75A, 78–79, 107A, 330, 349–360) and in his *Lectures on the Philosophy of History*.

15 For an example of the Epicurean view, see Lucretius, *De Rerum Natura*, Book 5, esp. lines 1446, 1157. For an example of the Stoic view see Seneca, *Epistulae Morales*, vol. 2, letter 76.9–10; vol. 3, letter 124.13–14.

16 See esp. Luce Irigaray, "The Necessity for Sexate Rights," in *The Irigaray Reader*, 198–203.

17 They were barbarians who, in turn, were described as dull, open to "solitary brooding," clumsy, not in control of one's actions, driven by habit, and lazy (Hegel 1991a, 197A; cf. Conklin 1999).

References

Albers, Patricia C. 1996. "Changing Patterns of Ethnicity in the Northeastern Plains." In *History, Power and Identity: Ethnogenesis in the Americas, 1492–1992*, edited by Jonathan D. Hill, 90–118. Iowa City: University of Iowa Press.

Anghie, Antony. 2004. *Imperialism, Sovereignty and the Making of International Law*. Cambridge: Cambridge University Press.

Asad, Talal. 2002. "From the History of Colonial Anthropology to the Anthropology of Western Hegemony." In *The Anthropology of Politics: A Reader in Ethnography, Theory and Critique*, edited by Joan Vincent, 133–39. Cornwall: Blackwell.

Bernasconi, Robert. 2001. "Who Invented the Concept of Race? Kant's Role in the Enlightenment Construction of Race." In *Race*, edited by Robert Bernasconi, 1–36. Malden, MA: Blackwell.

———. 1997. "African Philosophy's Challenge to Continental Philosophy." In *Postcolonial African Philosophy: A Critical Reader*, edited by Emmanuel Chukwudi Eze, 183–344. Oxford: Blackwell.

———. 1998. "Hegel at the Court of the Ashanti." In *Hegel after Derrida*, edited by Stuart Barnett, 41–63. London & New York: Routledge.

———. 2000. "With What Must the Philosophy of World History Begin? On the Racial Basis of Hegel's Eurocentrism." *Nineteenth-Century Contexts* 22: 171–201.

———. 2003. "With What Must the History of Philosophy Begin? Hegel's Role in the Debate on the Place of India within the History of Philosophy." In *Hegel's History of Philosophy: New Interpretations,* edited by David A. Duquette, 35–49. Albany: State University of New York Press.

———. 2007. "The Return of Africa: Hegel and the Question of the Racial Identity of the Egyptians." In *Identity and Difference: Studies in Hegel's Logic, Philosophy of Spirit, and Politics,* edited by Philip T. Grier, 201–16. Albany: State University of New York Press.

Buck-Morss, Susan. 2000. "Hegel and Haiti." *Critical Inquiry* 26: 821–65.

———. 2009. *Hegel, Haiti, and Universal History.* Pittsburgh: University of Pittsburg Press.

Conklin, William. 1999. "Legal Modernity and Early Amerindian Laws." In *60 maal recht en 1 maal wijn: Rechtssociologie, Sociale Problemen en Justitieel Beleid,* edited by F. Van Loon, 115–28. Leuven: Acco.

———. 2001. *The Invisible Origins of Legal Positivism: A Re-Reading of a Tradition.* Dordrecht, Netherlands: Kluwer Academic Publishers.

———. 2008. *Hegel's Laws: The Legitimacy of a Modern Legal Order.* Stanford: Stanford University Press.

———. 2010. "The Myth of Primordialism in Cicero's Sense of *Jus Gentium.*" *Leiden Journal of International Law* 23: 479–506.

———. 2011a. *Le savoir oublié de l'expérience des lois.* Trans. Basil Kingstone. Quebec: Laval University Press.

———. 2011b. "The Ghosts of Cemetery Road: Two Forgotten Indigenous Women and the Crisis of Analytical Jurisprudence." *Australian Feminist Law Journal* 35: 3–21.

———. 2012. "The Exclusionary Character of the Early Modern International Community." *Nordic Journal of International Law* 81: 133–73.

———. Forthcoming 2014. *Statelessness: The Enigma of an International Community.* Oxford: Hart.

Eze, Emmanuel Chukwudi. 1997. "The Color of Reason: The Idea of 'Race' in Kant's *Anthropology.*" In Eze, *Postcolonial African Philosophy: A Critical Reader,* 103–40.

Ferguson, Niall. 2011. *Civilization: The West and the Rest.* New York: Penguin.

Foucault, Michel. 1984. "What Is an Author?" In *The Foucault Reader,* edited by Paul Rabinow, 101–20. New York: Random House.

Hart, H.L.A. 1994 [1961]. *Concept of Law.* 2nd ed. Oxford: Clarendon.

Harvey, David. 2000. "Cosmopolitanism and the Banality of Geographical Evils." *Public Culture* 12: 529–64.

———. 2011. "Cosmopolitanism in the *Anthropology* and *Geography.*" In *Reading Kant's Geography,* edited by Stuart Elden and Eduardo Mendieta, 267–84. Albany: State University of New York Press.

Hegel, Georg Wilhelm Friedrich. 1817/18a [2002]. Lectures Supplement in *Philosophy of Right.* Trans. Alan White. Newburyport, MA: Focus Philosophical Library.

———. 1817/18b. *Lectures on Natural Right and Political Science.* Trans. J. Michael Stewart and Peter C. Hodgson. Berkeley: University of California Press.

———. 1824/25 [2002]. Lectures Supplement in *Philosophy of Right.* Trans. Alan White. Newburyport, MA: Focus Philosophical Library.

———. 1971 [1930]. *Hegel's Philosophy of Mind: Part Three of the Encyclopaedia of the Philosophical Sciences.* Trans. William Wallace with the *Zusätze* in Bouman's text (1845). *Zusätze.* Trans. by A.V. Miller (with foreword by J.N. Findlay). Oxford: Clarendon Press.

———. 1975a. [1822, 1828, 1830]. *Lectures on the Philosophy of World History: Introduction.* Trans. N.B. Nisbet. Cambridge: Cambridge University Press.

———. 1975b. *Philosophy of Fine Art.* Vol. 1. Trans. F.B.P. Ormaston. New York: Hacker.

———. 1991a [1821]. *Elements of the Philosophy of Right.* Ed. Allen W. Wood. Trans. H.B. Nisbet. Cambridge: Cambridge University Press.

———. 1991b. [1817, 1826, 1830]. *Encyclopaedia of Logic.* Part 1 of the *Encyclopaedia of Philosophical Sciences* with the *Zusätze.* Trans. T.F. Geraets, W.A. Suchting, and H.S. Harris. Indianapolis, IN: Hackett Publishing.

———. 2002 [1822/23]. Lectures in *Philosophy of Right.* Trans. Alan White. Newburyport, MA: Focus Philosophical Library, Supplement.

Hill, Jonathan D. 1996. Introduction. *History, Power and Identity: Ethnogenesis in the Americas, 1492–1992,* edited by Jonathan D. Hill, 7–13. Iowa City: University of Iowa Press.

Hobbes, Thomas. 1968 [1651]. *Leviathan.* Ed. and intro. C.B. Macpherson. London: Penguin.

Hoffheimer, Michael H. 2001. "Hegel, Race, Genocide." *Southern Journal of Philosophy* 39: 35–62.

Huizinga, J. 1955. *Homo Ludens: A Study of the Play-Element in Culture.* Boston: Beacon Press.

Von Humboldt, Wilhelm. 1994 [1836, 1836–40]. *On Language: The Diversity of Human Language-Structure and Its Influence on the Mental Development of Mankind.* Trans. Peter Heath. Intro. Hans Aarsleff. Cambridge: Cambridge University Press.

Luce Irigaray. 1991. "The Necessity for Sexate Rights." In *The Irigaray Reader,* edited by Margaret Whitfrid. Oxford: Blackwell.

Kant, Immanuel. 1997 [1785]. "Review of Herder's *Ideas on the Philosophy of the History of Mankind.*" In *Race and the Enlightenment: A Reader*, edited by Emmanuel Chukwudi Eze, 65–70. Malden, MA: Blackwell.

———. 2000 [1777]. "Of the Different Human Races." In *The Idea of Race*, edited by Robert Bernasconi and Tommy L. Lott, 8–22. Indianapolis, IL: Hackett.

Levy, David J. 2003. "Ethos and Ethnos: An Introduction to Eric Vogelin's *Critique of European Racism.*" In *Race and Racism in Continental Philosophy*, edited by Robert Bernasconi with Sybol Cook, 98–114. Bloomington: Indiana University Press.

Lucretius. 1959. *De Rerum Natura.* Trans. W.H.D. Rouse. Cambridge, MA: Harvard University Press.

Pagden, Anthony.1986 [1982]. *The Fall of Natural Man: The American Indian and the Origins of Comparative Ethnology.* Cambridge: Cambridge University Press.

Seneca. 1953. *Epistulae Morales.* 3 vols. Trans. Richard M. Gummere. Cambridge, MA: Harvard University Press.

Serequeberhan, Tsenay. 1997. "The Critique of Eurocentrism and the Practice of African Philosophy." In Eze, *Postcolonial African Philosophy: A Critical Reader*, 141–61.

Schmitt, Carl. 2006 [1950, 1974]. *The* Nomos *of the Earth in the International Law of the* Jus Publicum Europaeum. New York: Telos.

Williams, Bernard. 2004. *Truth and Truthfulness: An Essay in Geneology.* Princeton, NJ: Princeton University Press.

Williams, Robert A. 1990. *The American Indian in Western Legal Thought: The Discourses of Conquest.* New York: Oxford University Press.

Chapter 4

Retrospective, Myth, and the Colonial Question: Twentieth-Century Europe as the Other in World History

David B. MacDonald

As the twentieth century drew to a close, retrospectives entered into fashion, be they boxed set or abridged, chronological descriptions, or *fin de siècle* memoirs.[1] Written by some of the period's leading historians and political scientists, these attempted, by and large, to portray the twentieth century as the most atrocious in human history in terms of totalizing ideologies, bloodshed, terror, and mass death. While providing useful coverage of twentieth-century events, retrospectives had a tendency to downplay or ignore conflict and conquest in earlier centuries. The nineteenth century emerged as an age of moral values, hope, progress, and enlightenment—an era squandered only from the First World War onward, leading inexorably to Auschwitz, Vietnam, Cambodia, and Yugoslavia.

In this chapter I seek to explore how and why the twentieth century has been cast as the most atrocious. I also problematize the creation of a nineteenth-century foil, a moral opposite and other that has often been used to create a false before-and-after portrayal of historical events. Historian Will Durant calculated that there has been a period of only twenty-nine years in all of human history during which no warfare was in progress somewhere in the world (Hynes 1998, xi). Yet a form of historical amnesia seems to pervade Western scholarship, whereby the twentieth century emerges as decisive break from the past, an anomaly—or "very unpleasant surprise" (Glover 1999, 3).

Previous centuries, however, were hardly ideal—either for Europeans or their colonial subjects. Colonialism in earlier centuries saw large percentages of Indigenous peoples killed—there were more examples of successfully implemented genocide in the eighteenth and nineteenth centuries than afterward. Without downplaying the reality of twentieth-century horrors (or their death totals), there needs to be space for resurrecting the past. This chapter will critically examine twentieth-century retrospectives, contrasting them with recent critiques of colonialism in the nineteenth century and before. I critique *fin de siècle* Eurocentric scholarship for deliberately ignoring many of the negative aspects of Western history, even reconstructing *time* in such a way as to privilege European history and events over those of other continents and peoples. This underlines the trend, as Chakrabarty has noted, of putting "Europe first, the rest of the world later" (2000).

Approaching History: Conflicting Perspectives

How history is approached is often as important as the events themselves. Hayden White has critiqued the idea that histories or retrospectives are authentic representations of actual events, with only "certain rhetorical flourishes or poetic effects" to distract readers from the truth of what they are reading (1987, x, 24). Rather, White argues that all forms of historical narrative, be they "annals," "chronicles," or "history proper" (according to his taxonomy), are subject to a process of "narrativising." Here historians try to create a story from the "real events" of history, complete with a beginning and an end, and some type of moral lesson. As White argues, the biases, desires, and fantasies of the historian cannot be considered separate from the events they are describing. Which events are chosen and how they are presented will depend on a number of very personal factors, expressed through the "narrativising" process (White 1987, 4).

This argument about "narrativising" was later raised by Campbell, in his alternative reading of the first Gulf War. He describes how policy-makers, historians, and others interpret events and craft a "story" with an "ordered plot," "cast of characters," "attributable motivations," and "lessons for the future" (Campbell 1993, 7, 26–27). Historical accounts are often little more than one interpretation and organization of a myriad of events, arranged according to the bias and ideals of the "narrator." White and Campbell both laudably attempt to examine the method by which a series of chronological events eventually emerge as a closed historical juncture, with a beginning and an end and a series of moral lessons of good and evil. Through such a reading, retrospectives on the twentieth century involve a set of judgments, normative redefinitions of the past, and prescriptions for the future. We learn lessons from them: "Don't follow charismatic leaders"; "Beware of totalizing ideologies"; "Democracy is the best defence against violence and bloodshed"; and so on. Retrospectives tell us where we went wrong and why. Finding an "other" or a foil in the nineteenth century provides a useful contrast if we are to moralize about twentieth-century depravity.

Indeed, "facts" as we know them are not always givens, nor are a historian's motivations always obvious. While motives may be relatively benign, historians can exclude much, in their need for concision, or due to their ignorance of some aspects of history. Perhaps more likely is historians' desire to have their histories fit into a neat framework, conferring their own view of the world. Roberts' *The Twentieth Century* offers a good example of such a process in action. In his introduction, Roberts adopts a mixture of apology and defiance when he argues, "the history of the twentieth century has therefore to be approached with (what is sometimes deplored) a 'Eurocentric' stance. In many ways, the world actually was centred on Europe when the twentieth century began. Much of that century's story is of how and why that ceased to be true before it ended" (1999, 38). Here, European history takes precedence because the world was "centred on it"—non-European history is devalued and marginalized before the book even begins.

Creating a New Twentieth Century

In coming to terms with twentieth-century "narratives," it is useful to look at how time can be reinterpreted in light of an author's personal viewpoint. For some, writing history is little more than "measuring an endless piece of string with a ruler." Centuries are arbitrary inventions, "just a distance between two chosen points" (Roberts 1999, 3). For others, centuries are defined by wars, revolutions, and other major transformations that encapsulate the mood or overall feel of a century and come to symbolize it. Thus emerges the concept of "long" and "short" centuries. Lukacs' "short century" is but seventy-five years in length—running from 1914 to 1989 (1993, 1), as are those of Grenville and Hobsbawm (Grenville 1994, 1).

For Lukacs as for others, time and its division into centuries is purely a European affair, established primarily by military victories and defeats. The "real" nineteenth century begins only after Napoleon's defeat at Waterloo, in 1815, and ends with the First World War, a century of ninety-nine years. The eighteenth century is 126 years long, beginning with "the world wars between England and France" and ending with Waterloo. The 101-year seventeenth century begins with the defeat of the Spanish Armada in 1588 and closes with the rise of France as England's chief enemy in 1689 (Lukacs 1993, 1–2). But such demarcations depend on individual choice. Grenville offers alternatives: a nineteenth century starting with the French Revolution of 1789, with the beginnings of the twentieth century in 1871 (with German unification) or 1890 (with the beginnings of German *Weltpolitik*) (1994, 1). Such divisions are as inherently Eurocentric as their authors. After all, the First World War had little direct impact in Asia, Africa, or Latin America. Similarly, the collapse of Communism in 1989 had significantly greater repercussions within Europe than outside it. We can also criticize the short century's reductionism—it becomes little more than the clash between Communism and liberal democracy (Ponting 1998, 4).

Hobsbawm's short century epitomizes such criticisms. His is effectively encapsulated by the rise and fall of Soviet Communism, which, he asserts, "forms a coherent historical period" (Hobsbawm 1994, 5). However, like Lukacs and Grenville, personal motivations, such as his long-term affiliations with Communism, have much to do with his choice of dates (Conquest 2000, 10–11). In these cases, White's narrativity is obvious—even the division of centuries owes much to the motivations and desires of the individual historian.

The Twentieth Century as Squandered Utopia

The most prevalent portrayal of the twentieth century is one of squandered legacy—the belief that the wonders of the nineteenth century were forever tarnished by the horrors of technology, war, and totalizing ideologies. In *The Age of Extremes* the twentieth century emerges as the worst in human history, "not only because it was without doubt the most murderous century of which we have record, both by the scale, frequency and length of warfare which filled it ... but also by the unparalleled scale of the human catastrophes it produced, from the greatest famines in history to systemic genocide" (Hobsbawm 1994, 13). Glover's *Humanity: A Moral History of the 20th Century* advances essentially the same view. He too sees the century as one of dashed expectations:

> At the start of the century there was optimism, coming from the Enlightenment that the spread of a humane and scientific outlook would lead to the fading away, not only of war, but also of other forms of cruelty and barbarism. They would fill the chamber of horrors in the museum of our primitive past. In light of these expectations, the century of Hitler, Stalin, Pol Pot, and Saddam Hussein was likely to be a surprise. Volcanoes thought extinct turned out not to be. (1999, 6)

Similar portrayals can be found throughout this body of contemporary literature. Gilbert's *A History of the Twentieth Century* opens with the following statement: "The twentieth century has witnessed some of humanity's greatest achievements and some of its worst excesses" (1997, 1). Howard and Louis' *Oxford History* portrays the century's beginning as a "paradoxical combination of hope and fear." There was hope for a "new Golden Age" of "scientific discoveries and technological developments." Nevertheless, "fear arose from the apparent disintegration of traditional values and social structures, both secular and religious ... and from the prospect that the world was therefore confronting a future in which only the strongest and the most ruthless would survive" (Howard and Louis 1998, xix).

Violence is often premised on the irrationality of ideology in the twentieth century, and the abandonment of Christianity and its moral precepts. Furet commented that, "in the nineteenth century, History replaces God as the all powerful force in the destiny of men, but only in the twentieth century do we see the political madness caused by this substitution" (qtd. in Finkielkraut 1998, 63). For Brzezinski, Nazism and Communism tried to "usurp the role of the world's great religions"—but produced fanaticism and "megadeaths" instead (1995, 34). For Coker, Nazism was based on "an irrational ideology," one which was "deeply antagonistic to the values of the Enlightenment" (1998, 169).

For many retrospectives, a focus on the First and Second World Wars is an obvious starting point. Popular consensus in the literature suggests that the First World War inaugurates the "short" century through its surprising mix of death and destruction, setting the stage for further conflict as the century progresses. Hobsbawm states that one of the four reasons for the violence of the twentieth century was "the limitless sacrifices which governments imposed on their own men as they drove them into the holocaust of Verdun and Ypres," and that this "set a sinister precedent, if only for imposing even more unlimited massacres on the enemy" (1997, 256–57). Technology also plays a crucial role. It allows war to escalate beyond belief, and in Finkielkraut's words, sets off an "endless chain" that leads to the Russian revolution, the rise of Stalin and Hitler, the Cold War, and so on (2000, 69–70). The twentieth century is thus an "endless conflict" requiring "total mobilization," "total war," and "total victory," a new and startling break with the past (Finkielkraut 2000, 72).

For others, the Second World War is the nodal point and defining event of the twentieth century. Lukacs is a particularly strong adherent of this idea. For him, "much of the twentieth century before 1940–41 led up to Hitler." As well, "so much of the rest of the century, from 1941 on, was the consequence of the Second World War that he alone had begun and that was dominated by his presence until the end" (Lukacs 1993, 9). Howard and Louis similarly advance the Second World War as "the pivotal event of the century." The emergence of an "American century"; the decline of Europe and its old imperial system, and the rise of ideological conflict during the Cold War figure as little more than a denouement (Howard and Louis 1998, xxi).

While wars figure as high-water marks in the grim history of the twentieth century, they do not encapsulate the totality of the century's horrors. One must also rely on utilitarian appraisals using statistics and quantitative analysis. In 1993, Brzezinski dissected the century in terms of "megadeaths"—death tolls over ten to the power of six. This includes the two world wars and roughly thirty civil wars with at least ten thousand casualties each. In these cases, civilians suffered the majority of deaths and injuries. Totalitarian ideologies, bent on creating "coercive utopias" are for Brzezinski a unique feature of the twentieth century, as is the invention of genocide—specifically the idea of mass killing unrelated to traditional war aims (1995, 8–9). Brzezinski calculates that some sixty million alone died in failed attempts to create Communist utopias in the Soviet Union, China, and Cambodia. The total number of casualties for the twentieth century is between 167 and 175 million dead—a result, Brzezinski posits, of "politically motivated carnage" (1995, 11–18). A more recent update by the Carnegie Commission adds another four million casualties since 1989—and includes conflicts in the Gulf, the Horn of Africa, and the Balkans (Jacoby 1999, 168).

What Brzezinski, Hobsbawm, and Glover share is the belief that raw data or quantitative analysis provide the best gauge of a given century's horror. For utilitarian philosophers, the higher the death totals, the worse the century. Judgments of good and evil are reducible to a comparison between the numbers of people killed in any given situation. Such a belief allowed Glover to posit in an earlier work, "when we think soberly about the worst hypothetical choice in the world, it is hard not to conclude that a Nazi society, including the extermination camps, would be less terrible than a major nuclear war." At the same time, Glover offers another scenario where nuclear war would in fact be the lesser of two evils: "If you construct an imaginary case in which the *only* way to stop the leaders of a country releasing a virus that will kill everybody on earth is to wage nuclear war, I will agree that in those circumstances nuclear war would be justifiable" (2000, 262).

The key issue here is high numbers. The relative horror of an event or potential event is measured largely by the numbers of people killed (and perhaps tortured); morality lies in the minimization of death and suffering.

High casualty rates—when added to the rise of dictatorships, irrational ideologies, technological warfare, and the collapse of Enlightenment narratives and Christian morality—produce a century that is seemingly unique in its atrociousness. Or do they?

Colonialism and Imperialism

The mere exercise of promoting the twentieth century as the worst in history necessarily involves some level of wilful blindness. In order to create a form of dramatic contrast between then and now, the past is presented in glowing colours, involving what Edward Said has called a "blotting out of knowledge" (qtd. in Stannard 1992, 14).

Western and other crimes go back centuries. Stannard's *American Holocaust* was one of the first books to promote earlier eras as qualitatively and quantitatively worse than the more recent past. Writing in 1992, Stannard advanced that the average rate of depopulation in the Americas since 1492 has been between 90 and 98 per cent, due to a combination of "firestorms of microbial pestilence *and* purposeful genocide" (1992, xii). Caused by a mixture of disease, slave labour, massacre, and forced resettlement, the death toll from continual orgies of violence was fixed at roughly 100 million people, making the destruction of the American Indians "far and away, the most massive act of genocide in the history of the world" (1992, x).

As well, we need to consider that Spanish crimes in the Americas also reflect events that took place in Spain at the time, from the final defeat of the Moors to the expulsion of the Jews, as Enrique Dussell and Walter Mignolo both discuss (Dussell 1995; Mignolo 1995; 2005). Colonial terror continued in various forms, under various empires, for almost five centuries. The Spanish were responsible for the deaths of tens of millions of Indigenous peoples, followed by the British during the sixteenth century and after, who continued the wholesale slaughter of them. The torch was then passed to the United States in the eighteenth century.

Shelley Wright invited us to see that twentieth-century horrors like the Holocaust hardly constitute "a great chasm dividing us irrevocably from our brutal past. It is a very thin line. We have crossed it many times." The difference between the pre- and post-Holocaust world is not that the world has necessarily become any more violent or evil. Rather, the Holocaust has forced us to "understand that the violence of ethnic tribalism is not confined to Africa, or Asia, or the Middle East, or the cities of Eastern Europe—it is here, at home—We are the Savage" (Wright 2001, 18–19).

The Nineteenth Century as Pristine

The nineteenth century is portrayed as the era when the ideals of the Enlightenment were put into practice, namely: "a universal system of ... rules and standards of moral behaviour, embodied in the institutions of states dedicated to rational progress of humanity" (Hobsbawm 1997, 254). It is also described as a peaceful century, because there were no major wars in Europe until 1914 (1994, 22). Hobsbawm's "long nineteenth century" is relatively mild, since it "seemed, and actually was, a period of almost unbroken material, intellectual *and moral* progress" (13). Violence was uncommon, and events such as the Irish Republican bombing of Westminster Hall, and the pogroms of Russian Jews were, "small, almost negligible by the standards of modern massacre." As well, "the dead were counted in dozens, not hundreds, let alone millions" (13). For Brzezinski, there is no doubt that "the twentieth century was born in hope. It dawned in a relatively benign setting, [with] ... a relatively prolonged spell of peace" (1995, 3). While we are presented with the Crimean War, the Franco-Prussian War, and the Russo-Japanese War of 1905, each is dismissed with a banal revisionism. Crimea had "no major geopolitical repercussions," while the other two are cast in an almost positive light, since they "signalled the emergence on the world scene of Germany and Japan respectively, as new potential major actors" (Brzezinksi 1995, 3).

One detects a similar outlook with Glover's first chapter in *Humanity*, entitled "Never Such Innocence Again." He too describes "one hundred years of largely unbroken European peace," making it "plausible to think that the human race was growing out of its warlike past" (Glover 2000, 3). The early twentieth century marked, he argues, a belief in moral progress, with "human viciousness and barbarism in retreat" (2000, 1). Lukacs' nineteenth century is distinguished by "the absence of world war"—thus accounting for its prosperity and progressiveness (1993, 2). For Howard and Louis, the nineteenth century emerges as a Golden Age, with the end of the century marking "the dawn of a new and happier age in the history of mankind," an age dominated by science and technology, trade, finance, and growing military power (1998, 3).

In the search for a contrast and foil, much of this literature elides the negative realities of colonialism, at best dealing with them in a cursory and superficial fashion. Peace in Europe implies ipso facto that Europeans are peaceful and rational by nature. The application of this idea with regards to colonialism renders a skewed portrait of events. For Howard and Louis, colonialism in Africa and Asia lead to an "almost unquestioned belief in the cultural and indeed racial superiority of the 'white' races over the rest of mankind" (1998, 3–5). This state of affairs was not necessarily negative, however, since "this belief was usually combined with a sense of obligation to bring the blessings of 'civilization' to 'backward' peoples; an obligation combined with one very much older, to spread the Christian gospel among the heathen" (Howard and Louis 1998, 5). A healthy dose of paternalism, it seems, gives colonialism carte blanche.

Colonialism is also excused on the grounds that it had few negative long-term effects. Howard and Louis argue that "even where Western imperialism seemed most triumphant, indigenous cultures remained largely intact, making no concession to the conqueror other than what was strictly necessary." It is only in the twentieth century that "Western communications, trade, and technology" undermined "traditional lifestyles"—a trend that also affected Europe (Howard and Louis 1998, 6). Here, colonialism emerges as relatively benign—a shallow and easily rectified form of exploitation. Things change only in the twentieth century, a time when everybody—irrespective of race—shares the same sense of dislocation.

Roberts argues that despite famines and attacks by raiders or conquerors, "old ways" could be resumed. We are to believe that "the warp and weft of daily life and the way people lived through it hardly changes much in predominantly agricultural and pastoral societies and the acceptance of occasional disaster was part of that" (Roberts 1999, 29). For groups that didn't survive—too bad. Roberts describes them as being "at a stage of achievement low enough to be called Neolithic if not Paleolithic, and ... very vulnerable" (1999, 90–102). There is a strong and distasteful sense of historical inevitability here, with certain groups being fated to die out once they were confronted with Western civilizations.

On balance, colonialism and its close cousin imperialism emerge as both positive and negative forces. Imperialism introduces education, technology, Western medicine, and Christianity. It also introduces organization and new concepts of identity (Roberts 1999, 98–99). Genocide, terror, economic exploitation, and other features do not seem important enough to merit condemnation—they are par for the course—byproducts of the colonial experience. Criticism of imperialism, argues Roberts, often centres on the "diatribe" (Roberts 1999, 83). By establishing a hegemonic discourse about the twentieth century as the worst, Roberts, Gilbert, Howard, Hobsbawm, and others have to distort earlier periods of history—excising the "dark side" of the nineteenth century. However, it is only by coming to terms with the nineteenth century and its associated colonial horrors that we can better understand the violence of the twentieth century—a century when the outrages perpetrated in Africa, Asia, and elsewhere came back to haunt the countries of Europe.

Darkness from the Past

Colonialism should and must be counted as an aspect of European degeneracy, and as a potential precedent for later dehumanization, racism, and warfare. In *Death and Deliverance*, Burleigh described the long and arduous training process of ss killers during Germany's euthanasia programs in the 1930s (Burleigh 1994). Browning's *Ordinary Men* similarly describes how killers were created rather than born (1993). Both authors emphasize that the ability to dehumanize an enemy, to destroy life with unmitigated cruelty, had to be learned. And not everyone could assimilate these lessons. So it was with European states coming into the twentieth century. Those who cut their teeth on the Boxer rebellion, or raped the Congo of its human and natural resources, those who had exterminated the Tasmanian Aboriginals or mowed down the Western Canadian Métis with Gatling guns were not the peace-loving, morally progressive peoples we believe them to be.

An alternative view of the twentieth century, and a plausible one, is to see it as a continuation of the past. "Communism and Nazism," after all, "had their origins deep in nineteenth century history" (Ponting 1998, 9, 18–19). Racism, ethno-nationalism, eugenics, phrenology, and social Darwinism— all are rooted in nineteenth-century racial science and social theory. Little about these ideologies was new or particularly innovative. The innovation lay in the transplantation of colonial violence to the European context. As Grenville describes, "since the mid-nineteenth century the Europeans had avoided fighting each other for empire, since the cost of war between them would have been of quite a different order" (1994, 5). Grenville's analysis touches perhaps on the real reason for stability in Europe—the projection of Western aggression onto outside countries, aggression that was "crudely proven by his [the colonizer's] capacity to conquer other peoples more numerous than the invading European armies" (1994, 5).

Such retrospectives provide a more balanced coverage of the twentieth century than others, since they actually look for the roots of aggression in earlier times, rather than seeing 1914 as a complete break from the past. For those truly looking at nineteenth-century precedents, there is little in the twentieth century that is a surprise. In earlier centuries, a greater *percentage* of people died in European colonies than at any time in the twentieth century, even if the absolute numbers were lower. Arguably, more groups were the victims of successful genocide in the eighteenth and nineteenth centuries than afterward, despite superior technology and communication. Writing during the 1980s and 1990s, historians and journalists like Tatz, Stannard, and Hochschild have been pushing for recognition of Indigenous genocides in Australia, the Americas, Africa, and the Asian subcontinent.

I have briefly touched on Stannard's work, which blames Spanish, British, and settler authorities from bringing about what he feels is the largest genocide in world history (1992, x, 128–29,222–23). This follows and precedes a growing literature on colonial crimes in the Americas, including the works of Todorov, Thornton, Sale, and Churchill. Much of this builds on the pioneering work of Richard Drinnon, who thoughtfully laid out the case for genocide in his *Facing West: The Metaphysics of Indian-hating and Empire-building* (1980).

Hochschild's *King Leopold's Ghost* explores the horrific legacies of Belgian colonialism in the Congo, from the foundation of the colony in the 1880s, to the death of the Belgian king in 1910. He delivers a damning critique of colonialism, positing that Belgium's rule in the Congo brought about the deaths of some ten million Congolese Africans (50 per cent of the population), through massacre, disease, forced relocation, and slave labour. While the apogee of the killing occurred from 1890 to 1910, straddling the twentieth century, the Congo genocide was nevertheless a pure product of nineteenth-century colonialism (Hochschild 1999, 225–33). Implicit here was the belief that European countries had the right to exploit Africa to the fullest, particularly if great profits could be gained, in this case from the forced cultivation of rubber. Much of this work is a gripping tale of intrigue and duplicity, with King Leopold taking centre stage, emerging as an ungainly, strutting, conniving pedophile who succeeds in carving out his kingdom, then maintains and enhances it with deliberate care.

Hochschild's narrative style is full of battles between good and evil—bloodthirsty Belgian soldiers and company officials versus human rights workers and foreign observers. However, Leopold is not alone in his ruthless methods. Hochschild notes that other colonial empires followed relatively the same course of action. Rubber production in French West Africa, Portuguese Angola, and the German Camaroons followed a similar trajectory, with the percentages of dead in these regions also approaching 50 per cent (Hochschild 1999, 280). More recent work by LeCour Grandmaison traces links between the mentality and techniques that inspired nineteenth-century French colonialism in Africa and the Holocaust (2005).

While involving much lower casualty figures, the genocide of the Australian Aborigines during the eighteenth and nineteenth centuries has provoked considerable research in recent years. As Tatz has argued, British colonialism was responsible for the deaths of some 95 per cent of the Aboriginal population in Australia, and for the complete extermination of the Tasmanian Aborigines. Here, the original population were much lower than in the Americas or in the Congo, totalling somewhere between 250,000 and 750,000 at the time of Captain James Cook's arrival in 1788. Whatever the earlier figures, by the 1911 there were less than 31,000 Aborigines alive (Tatz 1999, 6–8). Using the 1948 UN *Genocide Convention*, specifically Article II as a reference, Tatz cites Australia with at least three acts of genocide (1999, 6).

Tatz's monograph is a step by step, region by region study of how and why genocide was carried out from the eighteenth to the early twentieth century. The work of Tatz and others recently encouraged the Australian government to issue an apology for its past mistreatment of its Indigenous populations, who until 1965 had no right to vote or hold a passport. A 1997 *National Inquiry* acknowledged that the Australian government had "knowingly committed genocide through the forcible transfer of children, as a matter of official policy, not just yesteryear but as recently as the 1970s" (Tatz 1999, 33). The recognition of an Australian genocide has inaugurated a series of "History Wars" in Australia as to how that country's history should be understood and represented.

While studies of Indigenous genocides and colonial oppression are arguably becoming a growth industry, the tragic impact of two centuries of British rule in India has been underexplored in recent times. Davis' *Late Victorian Holocausts* provides another recent account, although he raises the total numbers of dead to thirty million overall, based on statistics from *The Lancet* (2001, 7–8). While Brzezinski is content to blame ideology and dictators for megadeaths, he has yet to apply his model to earlier colonial periods. Forays into the past present us with new challenges. We are forced to consider the twentieth century not just as one of change and transformation, but also as a time of evolution and inherited moral corruption from the past. Should we acknowledge the reality of past atrocities, history is neither a surprise nor a break from the past. A forum is opened where debate and discussion over the past can come forth.

Dissecting the Twentieth Century

If there have been horrors in previous centuries every bit as bad as those in the twentieth, why then do current retrospectives elide the realities of the past? I offer six key reasons of potentially many more, for why previous centuries have not been deemed worthy of comparison but should be:

(1) Twentieth-century violence is condemned as irrational, versus the rationality and profit-oriented motives of colonialism.

Retrospectives of the twentieth century often focus on the irrationality of violence, and the rapid, unexpected, but inevitable escalation of warfare. It is almost tautological to say that the madness or bestiality of the twentieth century consisted in an abandonment of earlier values and norms. The old order was seemingly rational, moral, and Christian—the new order, with its "arrogantly irrational goals," its moral nihilism, and its totalitarian ideologies, was not.

However, in condemning the new order as an abandonment of the old, the nineteenth century emerges as a time of rationality, morality, and idealism, as does colonialism. In the nineteenth century, J.A. Hobson and Karl Marx would condemn colonialism as oppressive, but would similarly see the rationality behind it: establishing and expanding markets, while bringing about trade monopolies in lesser developed regions. Greed and the quest for profit were and still are seen as inherently rational—as was the quest for exclusive control over regional trade. As Nicholson describes the logic behind this process, "an obvious way of trying to reduce the risks on investment was to take political control of the area it was in ... imperialism developed to defend and promote economic activity" (1998, 71–72).

Nostalgia for nineteenth-century liberal democracy and free trade often ignores the highly exploitative nature of these systems. For example, the bleeding of India in the eighteenth and nineteenth centuries gave Britain the raw materials and later the markets to fuel its industrial revolution, something for which, Nehru ironically remarked, "Bengal can take pride." Describing British rule as little more than a "gold lust," Nehru saw the "liquidation of the artisan class" as directly attributable to the suppression of Indian domestic manufacturing in favour of British imports. This led to the deaths of "tens of millions" of people (Nehru 1990, 209–11).

Killing in order to clear land for settlement, or killing and enslavement as a byproduct of industrialization, urbanization, cultivation, or other aspects of modernity, all emerge as essentially rational but regrettable aspects of the forward march of "the history of commerce." Coker has cleverly compared "Westernization" in the colonies with nihilism in the West. Both for him perform the same function—they break down traditional cultures and destroy self-respect (Coker 1998, 158). As more studies expose the irrationality and brutality of colonialism, our previous conceptions of it will necessarily change.

(2) The development of the mass media and the globalization of information allows us to know about twentieth-century atrocities. However, such access to information was not available in earlier centuries, leading to a false impression that "no news is good news."

Northrop Frye argued several decades ago that "man has doubtless always experienced time in the same way, dragged backward from the receding past into an unknown future. But the quickening of the pace of news, with telegraph and submarine cable, helped to dramatize a sense of the world in visible motion, with every day bringing new scenes and episodes of a passing show" (1967, 31). The evolution of mass media allows us to know much more about the world than ever before. But with this knowledge comes obligations, as Ignatieff has argued. We have become more attuned to what he calls the "the needs of strangers"—and these needs can include protection from cruelty and harm. Graphic images from around the world allow people to empathize with one another, reinforcing a sense of global responsibility. The increased demand for humanitarian intervention in such trouble spots as Rwanda, Bosnia, Kosovo, Darfur, and Syria is proof of this phenomenon (Ignatieff 1998).

(3) We expect people to live today, and we have a belief in human equality. It is difficult to understand how attitudes could have been otherwise in previous centuries.

With international conventions on human rights and genocide, there is at least a hope that nations will conform to some moral standard of behaviour, and treat their citizens with equal fairness. However, conceptions of universal rights and equality are new—largely a reaction to the two world wars. Before the last century, when colonialism ran riot throughout much of the world, most Indigenous inhabitants were not considered full persons. The 1788 doctrine of *terra nullius*, for example, declared Australia to be "a land empty but for fauna and flora." Aborigines were denied the status of being considered humans until the mid-twentieth century (Tatz 1999, 7). Theories of superior and inferior religions, civilizations, and races were crucial in the development of colonialism, and such a sense of superiority legitimated a litany of colonial atrocities: land theft, enslavement, deliberate spreading of disease, and massacre.

As Nicholson argues, "one hundred years ago, the idea that people of all races and both sexes had equal rights was accepted only by a minority" (1998, 194). Singer adds that "racist assumptions shared by most Europeans at the turn of century are now totally unacceptable, at least in public life" (1979, 14). With an evolving sense of morality and equality comes a lack of understanding of past conceptions of inequality. While we might expect the Interahamwe or Arkan's Tigers to slaughter their enemies with impunity, we don't expect Western leaders to be overtly racist or bloodthirsty. The projection of twentieth-century norms on an understanding of past leaders and their motivations obscures the reality of the racial attitudes of earlier epochs.

(4) Personifying evil is something more common to the twentieth century than earlier periods. We need to be aware that the lack of an evil dictator or totalizing ideology does not detract from the horrors of an event.

Discussions of twentieth-century evil often involve the personification of it—in the policies, ideology, or personal traits of Adolf Hitler, Joseph Stalin, or Mao Zedong, for example. While such personification is possible for twentieth-century atrocity, earlier instances of genocide and suffering are much harder to personify in one man or one ideology. Historical characters such as Genghis Khan or Napoleon Bonaparte were the exceptions rather than the rule.

Earlier periods of history were not so simple to understand. Genocide and terror could take place over generations, and often did. With few interested lobby groups or photojournalists to hide from, no international conventions to uphold, and no television cameras to avoid, pre-twentieth-century killers could afford to take their time. They could be systematic or not, and they could choose a variety of methods: disease, army massacres, settler militia patrols, bounties, slave labour, or whatever means deemed appropriate. In some countries like Australia and the United States, large numbers of settlers were seemingly eager to do their part in the killing of Indigenous peoples, who at any rate were denied the status of being fully human. Governments sometimes, but not always, condoned atrocities. The victims of genocide were an inconvenience, a troublesome eyesore, often dying because they stood in the path of so-called progress and civilization.

Discussions of past genocides must reject the twentieth-century need for figureheads and stereotypes. As Tatz argues, people today have a particular image in mind when they think of genocide, conditioned by the standards of Hitler or Stalin. For many, the success of a genocide accusation of genocide depends on the structure and "look" of the state involved,

> Australians understand only the stereotypical or traditional scenes of historical or present-day slaughter. For them, genocide connotes either the bulldozed corpses at Belsen or the serried rows of Cambodian skulls, the panga-wielding Hutu in pursuit of Tutsi victims or the ethnic cleansing in the former Yugoslavia. As Australians see it, patently we cannot be connected to, or with, the stereotypes of Swastika-wearing ss psychopaths, or crazed black tribal Africans. (Tatz 1999, 2)

In Tatz's definition of genocide, intent is not even necessary, as long as there are sufficient casualties and a high enough percentage of the target population killed (1999, 36). Helen Fein similarly advances that genocide can be the result of "sustained purposeful action by a perpetrator to physically destroy a collectivity directly or indirectly" (qtd. in Chalk 1994, 49). In the Australian case, there does not have to be a Hitler-like figure for genocide to have occurred.

A common element of these critiques is their structuralist outlook. Tony Barta has argued for "a conception of genocide which embraces *relations* of destruction and removes from the word the emphasis on policy and intention which brought it into being" (Nicholson 1998, 137). Here it is the system, but not any specific policies or actors, which brings about genocide. One could also adopt Nicholson's distinction between "somatic violence" and "structural violence"—somatic being the intentional killing of individuals through war or mass murder. Conversely, structural violence "happens when people die because of the activities of other human beings even though they did not intend to kill them as such" (Nicholson 1998, 137).

(5) The inability or lack of interest in statistically quantifying the suffering or deaths of non-European groups. No quantum of suffering has been done for the nineteenth or earlier centuries in terms of "megadeaths."

In the twentieth century, "before" and "after" population statistics (however imprecise) make it relatively easy to estimate the numbers of dead in conflict. Population losses during the Holocaust, ditto those in Cambodia and Rwanda, can be quantified reasonably accurately, even if there is disagreement about specifics. While there is often some covering up of death totals, as in Stalinist Russia or Maoist China, we still have a good idea of how many people died, and when. For political scientists obsessed with quantifying precise totals or calculating precise numbers of "megadeaths," the imprecision of previous centuries can be frustrating, leading to a rejection of the reality of past horrors.

While the number of wars in the nineteenth century can be ascertained (Henderson and Tucker 2001, 317–38), casualty rates are not always obvious—especially for non-European combatants. Colonialism often produces slow and steady casualty rates comparable to losses in low- to medium-intensity conflict. Researchers looking into past genocides must content themselves with ranges of numbers, rather than precise totals. Tatz, for example, has no accurate figures for the Aboriginal population before Cook's voyages. The range of pre-conquest figures varies from 250,000 to 750,000, even though we know that by 1924 only 31,000 remained. Researchers into the Bengal famine must content themselves with a rough estimate of ten million casualties. Even the total deaths for the 1943 Famine are expressed as a range. As Keay puts it, "famine fatalities are notoriously unreliable" (2001, 504). Hochschild is in the same boat. To reach his figure of ten million, he has relied on a 1919 official Belgian government commission, which concluded that the population had been "reduced by half." However, it was only in 1924 that the first proper census was taken, which gave a figure of ten million survivors (Hochschild 1999, 233).

Stannard's research has also involved a rejection of older, less accurate population totals. These estimates, based on the work of Kroeber and the "Berkeley School" put the total population of the Americas at less than fifteen million (with only one million in North America). Stannard therefore privileges Borah and Dobyns, both of whom put the pre-conquest population of the Americas at well over 100 million. However, even these are dismissed as an underestimation—for him, "all estimates to date have been too low." In general, Stannard argues that as archaeological investigation becomes more sophisticated, it will be easier for "previous 'invisible' population loss," to be discovered (1992, 267–68). Clearly, we will never know precisely how many people perished as a result of colonialism, nor will we ever have completely accurate totals for evaluating population size before European conquest. Nevertheless, there may be anywhere from twenty to seventy million Indigenous casualties in the nineteenth century as a direct result of colonialism in Africa, the Americas, Asia, and the Antipodes.

(6) Wilful blindness, and a lack of desire to tarnish the past can prevent rigorous examination of the negative aspects of colonialism.

Anthony Smith has written much on myths of the Golden Age, something which pervades Western—and indeed—all cultures to one extent or another. Positive myths about a nation's past help to both "define the historic culture community," while endowing it with a "particular energy and power" (Smith 1983, 152). History, argues Smith, forms a "repository or quarry from which materials may be selected in the construction and invention of nations" (1997, 37). Further, a nation's "immortality" is based on its ability to "unfold a glorious past, a golden age of saints and heroes, to give meaning to its promise of restoration and dignity" (Smith 1983, 153–54). The desire to preserve a pure and unadulterated sense of national history might be responsible for much of the wilful blindness we see in twentieth-century retrospectives.

All nations wish to preserve a positive sense of their own history. While Blake's "Jerusalem" might be embarrassingly dated for some, a sense of empire as a positive endeavour remains in many historical accounts. As Paxman has argued in *The English*, there is a certain nostalgia for the forgotten "Breed"—those who created and maintained the British empire. Such men were presented as "Fearless and philistine, safe in taxis and invaluable in shipwrecks ... the embodiment of the ruling class, men you could send to the ends of the earth and know that they would dominate the natives firmly but fairly, their needs no more than the occasional months-old copy of *The Times* and a tin of their favourite pipe tobacco" (Paxman 1998, 177).

Most nations have a tendency to gloss over their past, to diminish the negative aspects of their history in the service of national mythology. The twentieth-century retrospective is but one example of this process is motion. We are thus left with Howard and Louis' promise that "Indigenous cultures remained largely intact," even after centuries of colonial exploitation (Gilbert 1997, 14–15). We also have Brzezinski's hopeful analysis that atrocities in the past were rarely "a matter of sustained policy" (1995, 5). Perhaps America and Australia's Indigenous peoples would disagree. Protecting his conception of a European Golden Age, Roberts had this to say: "The dark side of the balance sheet of empire has so often been set out that there is mercifully no need for further elaboration on the many wickednesses it contains" (1999, 90). The key word here is "mercifully"—suggesting that in commemorating the negative legacies of colonialism, we deride the self-esteem of the colonisers, destroying the portrait historians are trying to paint.

Conclusions

In the final analysis, the nineteenth century and those preceding it allow us to see the twentieth century as an evolution and application of earlier forms of behaviour. Our century was not in every sense a break with earlier periods, but was in many respects a continuation of it. While it is much harder to quantify, personify, and document the evils of the past, this does not meant that atrocity, violence, and abject terror did not exist. What we remember and commemorate about the twentieth century, the events we enshrine and pass down to our children will be based on the previous century as the worst ever—the best of times and the worst of times.

Fortunately, perhaps, retrospectives carry their own in-built obsolescence. In his analysis of Russian history after 1989, Hobsbawm argued that Cold War–era analyses written in the West, compiled by the piecing together snippets of information from the Soviet Union, were now of little use. With the opening up of the Russian archives we now have almost full access to the "truth" of what happened during Communism's history. Because of increased information, he argues, "an enormous mass of literature that appeared during this time will now have to be junked, whatever its ingenuity in using fragmentary sources and the plausibility of its guesswork. We just won't need it anymore. These books will now provide insight into the historiography of the Soviet era, not its history per se" (Hobsbawm 1997, 243). The same can and may well be said about twentieth-century chronologies in the not-so-distant future. What emerges from these retrospectives, and a new era of genocide studies, is that there are two very different ideas about previous centuries, and their significance in world history, one which privileges the twentieth century, and another which resurrects the past as an important focus of study.

Notes

1 A version of this chapter was previously published as "Imagining the Twentieth Century: Retrospective, Myth, and the Colonial Question," in 2007, *POR-TAL: Journal of Multidisciplinary International Studies*, 4 (1): 1–27. See more at http://davidbmacdonald.com/?q=publications#sthash.sCnmEBIx.dpuf.

References

Browning, C. 1993. *Ordinary Men: Reserve Police Battalion 101 and the Final Solution in Poland*. New York: HarperCollins.

Brzezinksi, Z. 1995. *Out of Control: Global Turmoil on the Eve of the 21st Century*. New York: Touchstone.

Buckley-Zistel, S. 2006, "Remembering to Forget: Chosen Amnesia as a Strategy for Local Coexistence in Post-Genocide Rwanda." *Africa* 76 (2): 131–50.

Burleigh, M. 1994. *Death and Deliverance: 'Euthenasia' in Germany 1900–1945*. Cambridge: Cambridge University Press.

Campbell, D. 1993. *Politics without Principle: Sovereignty, Ethics and the Narratives of the Gulf War*. Boulder, CO: Lynne Rienner.

Chakrabarty, D. 2000. *Provincializing Europe: Postcolonial Thought and Historical Difference*. Princeton: Princeton University Press.

Chalk, F. 1994. "Redefining Genocide." In *Genocide: Conceptual and Historical Dimensions*, edited by G. Andropoulos, 47–63. Philadelphia: University of Pennsylvania Press.

Chomsky, N. 1993. *Year 501: The Conquest Continues*. Boston: South End Press.

Coker, C. 1998. *Twilight of the West*. London: Westview.

Conquest, R. 2000. *Reflections on a Ravaged Century*. New York: W.W. Norton.

Davis, M. 2001. *Late Victorian Holocausts*. London: Verso.

Drinnon, R. 1980. *Facing West: The Metaphysics of Indian-hating and Empire-building*. Minneapolis: University of Minnesota Press.

Dussel, E. 1995. *The Invention of the Americas: Eclipse of "the Other" and the Myth of Modernity*. New York: Continuum.

Finkielkraut, A. 1998. *The Future of a Negation: Reflections on the Question of Genocide*. Translated by Mary Byrd Kelly. Lincoln, NB: University of Nebraska Press.

———. 2000. *In the Name of Humanity: Reflections on the Twentieth Century*. New York: Columbia University Press.

Frye, N. 1967. *The Modern Century: The Whidden Lectures 1967*. Toronto: Oxford University Press.

Gilbert, M. 1997. *A History of the Twentieth Century*. Vol. 1, *1900–1933*. London: HarperCollins.

Glover, J. 1990. *Causing Death and Saving Lives*. London: Penguin.

———. 1999. *Humanity: A Moral History of the Twentieth Century*. London: Jonathan Cape.

Grenville, J.A.S. 1994. *A History of the World in the Twentieth Century*. Cambridge: Harvard University Press.

Henderson, E., and R. Tucker. 2001. "Clear and Present Strangers: The Clash of Civilizations and International Conflict." *International Studies Quarterly* June: 317–38.

Hobsbawm, E.1994. *Age of Extremes: The Short Twentieth Century 1914–1991*. London: Penguin.

———. 1997. *On History*. London: Weidenfeld & Nicolson.

Hochschild, A. 1999. *King Leopold's Ghost: A Story of Greed, Terror and Heroism in Colonial Africa*. London: Macmillan.

Howard, M., and W.R. Louis, eds. 1998. *The Oxford History of the Twentieth Century*. Oxford: Oxford University Press.

Hynes, S. 1998. *The Soldier's Tale: Bearing Witness to Modern War*. London: Pimlico.

Ignatieff, M. 1998. *The Warrior's Honour*. London: Chatto and Windus.

———. 2001. *Virtual War: Kosovo and Beyond*. London: Vintage.

Jacoby, R. 1999. *The End of Utopia: Politics and Culture in an Age of Apathy*. New York: Basic Books.

Judah, T. 1997. *The Serbs: History, Myth and the Destruction of Yugoslavia*. New Haven, CT: Yale University Press.

Keay, J. 2001. *India: A History*. London: Grove.

LeCour Grandmainson, O. 2005. *Coloniser, Exterminer: Sur la guerre et l'État colonial*. Paris: Fayard.

Lukacs, J. 1993. *The End of the Twentieth Century and the end of the Modern Age*. New York: Ticknor & Fields.

Malcolm, N. 1998. *Kosovo: A Short History*. London: Macmillan.

Margaret, S. 2005. *Reckoning with the Past: Teaching History in Northern Ireland*. Lanham, MD: Lexington Books.

Marriott, J.A.R. 1930. *The Eastern Question: An Historical Study in European Diplomacy*. Oxford: Clarendon Press.

Mignolo, W. 1995. *The Darker Side of the Renaissance: Literacy, Territoriality, and Colonization*. Ann Arbor: University of Michigan Press.

———. 2005. *The Idea of Latin America*. Malden, MA: Blackwell.

Mullerson, R. 1997. *Human Rights Diplomacy*. London: Routledge.

Nehru, J. 1990. *The Discovery of India*. New York: Oxford University Press.

Nicholson, M. 1998. *International Relations: A Concise Introduction*. London: MacMillan.

Paxman, J. 1998. *The English: The Portrait of a People*. London: Michael Joseph.

Ponting, C. 1998. *The 20th Century: A World History*. New York: Henry Holt.

Roberts, J.M. 1999. *The Twentieth Century: The History of the World, 1901 to 2000*. New York: Penguin Viking.

Singer, P. 1979. *Practical Ethics*. Cambridge: Cambridge University Press.

Smith, A. 1983. *Theories of Nationalism*. New York: Holmes & Meier.

———. 1997. "The 'Golden Age' and National Revival." In *Myths and Nationhood*, edited by G. Hosking and G. Schöpflin, 36–59. London: C. Hurst and Co.

Stannard, D. 1992. *American Holocaust: The Conquest of the New World*. London: Oxford University Press.

Steiner, G. 1972. *In Blue Beard's Castle: Some Notes on the Redefinition of Culture.* New Haven, CT: Yale University Press.

Tatz, C. 1999. *Genocide in Australia.* AIATSIS Research Discussion Paper No. 8, Canberra.

Todorov, T. 1984. *The Conquest of America: The Quest for the Other.* New York: Harper & Row.

White, H. 1987. *The Content of the Form: Narrative Discourse and Historical Representation.* Baltimore, MD: Johns Hopkins University Press.

Wiesel, E. 1960. *Night.* New York: Avon Books.

Wright, S. 2001. *International Human Rights, Decolonization and Globalization: Becoming Human.* New York: Routledge.

Chapter 5

Gender Equality Identity in Europe: The Role of the EU

Kimberly Earles

Introduction

Gender equality between women and men is uneven across the continent of Europe. Many southern European countries, as well as many of the newer European Union (EU) member states, such as Malta and Hungary, lag far behind the Scandinavian gender equality pioneers, but no country has been successful in achieving substantive equality. While one could argue that the EU has been interested in the issue of gender equality, particularly within the labour market, from its inception,[1] it is only in the past two decades that the issue has been placed higher on the political agenda. In addition, the EU has expanded the scope of its gender equality policy beyond the labour market to include social and political issues such as violence against women, female poverty, work–life balance, parental leave, and women in decision-making positions. In terms of political representation, the EU has taken up the cause of promoting more women within the European Parliament and within the national legislatures of the twenty-eight EU member states. In this chapter, I argue that the increase in women in decision-making positions in the European Commission and the European Parliament since the early 1990s,[2] combined with the accession of Sweden and Finland into the EU in 1995, and the interplay between internal EU factors and external factors, such as the UN Beijing Women's Conference in 1995, have contributed to the current situation where the EU is working toward the creation of a European gender equality identity related to citizenship rights as well as equal opportunities in the economic, political, and social spheres. I will analyze this new focus on gender equality as a "European identity" in terms of women in decision-making positions within EU institutions, the numerous gender equality bodies and agencies that have emerged within the EU in recent years, the influence of the Scandinavian member states on the EU's gender equality policy, the expanded scope of this policy, the adoption of gender mainstreaming, and finally in terms of outcomes from an increasing number of EU directives on issues of gender equality, to concrete policy outcomes for women and men living within the boundaries of the EU.

This anthology addresses questions of European identity, both in terms of how Europe views itself and how those outside of Europe perceive it. My contribution is to analyze the current project undertaken by the EU to construct itself as a collective on the path to achieving gender equality. The EU fully acknowledges that its member states have not yet achieved gender equality, and that much inequality still exists in the realms of economic, political, and social life. However, in recent years the EU has placed more emphasis on achieving gender equality through its many agencies, programs, and policies. Whether or not more equality has actually been achieved due to the EU's efforts is a separate question, to be addressed later in this chapter. A more intriguing point is how the EU is trying to construct itself as a leader in efforts to combat gender inequality (Elman 2007). This relates to the argument in MacDonald's chapter about the historical construction of Europe as relatively peaceful during the nineteenth century and marred by violence during the twentieth century, discounting the horrors perpetrated by European imperialists in the earlier century. MacDonald's case and the case of gender equality identity in the EU both demonstrate an attempt to construct a particular image of Europe internally and externally. In its most recent Equality Strategy (2011–2015), the European Commission reiterates that "equality is one of five values on which the [EU] is founded," and in the foreword, Viviane Reding, Vice-President of Justice, Fundamental Rights and Citizenship, states "gender equality is more than just a slogan; it is our social and economic responsibility" (European Commission 2011). Despite its limitations, the EU has provided a more favourable venue for equality issues than most member states (Roth 2008). Kimberly Morgan (2008) argues that gender equality has become a regular feature of European policy debates, mentioned in the majority of EU speeches and reports. Thus, the EU has worked hard to portray an image of not only caring about, but also taking action against, gender inequality.

Women's Representation in EU Institutions

As Table 5.1 illustrates, since the first European Parliament (EP) elections, women's representation within the EP has more than doubled from 16.6 per cent in 1979 to 34.8 per cent in 2009. And today there are nine female Commissioners out of a total of twenty-eight, with women now comprising 32 per cent of the European Commission. In addition, a woman, Catherine Ashton, fills one of the two new high-level EU positions created by the Lisbon Treaty—High Representative for Foreign Affairs and Security.[3] The EP leads the other EU institutions in terms of women's representation among senior officials and administrators, with women accounting for more than 40 per cent of such positions, compared to 23.4 per cent in the EU overall (European Commission Directorate-General for Employment, Social Affairs and Equal Opportunities 2010). This increase in women in decision-making positions at the EU level has led to mobilization around a variety of gender equality issues in recent years. However, this is not to say that gender equality was not a priority for some in earlier years.

The term "critical mass" is important when analyzing the situation of the European Union, and particularly the EP. The concept of critical mass is the idea that once women constituted a certain percentage (usually believed to be about 30 per cent) of parliament, they would be able to work

Table 5.1 Proportion of Women in the European Parliament, 1979–present

Year	Women as % of all MEPs*	Change from previous election (%)
1979	16.6	
1984	17.7	+1.1
1989	19.3	+1.6
1994	25.9	+6.6
1999	30.3	+4.4
2004	30.2	-0.1
2009	34.8	+4.6

Source: European Parliament Directorate-General for Personnel's Equality and Diversity Unit 2011.

*Members of the European Parliament (MEPs)

together to implement positive policy changes for women and gender equality. For a long time the problem with critical mass theory was that there were few, if any, real-world examples of women constituting such a high proportion of parliamentary seats, so testing the hypothesis was difficult or impossible. The theory of critical mass is based on the idea that a small minority of women in parliament is unlikely to make change, as each woman must conform to the male-dominated system in order to get elected and, once elected, in order to have her voice heard. Thus, the argument is the more women there are in parliament, the more the political culture is likely to change and the easier it will be for women to act "as women" and "for women" to place gender equality on the political agenda. In her study of Scandinavian politics, Drude Dahlerup (1988) did notice changes in social conventions and political discourse as the number of women increased in parliament. More women in politics also can lead to an increase in the number of women in powerful political positions, such as ministers and prime ministers. This, too, can change the landscape of how politics is conducted and what issues are given priority. Here there are links to Markovits' chapter about the inclusion of racial and ethnic minorities into North American sports leagues in increasing numbers as both players and fans, which, he argues, has led to a situation where racism has become socially taboo at such sporting events. Markovits also argues that the increasing presence of women as spectators at American sporting events has led to a decrease in the acceptability of violence there. Thus, increased diversity within a sphere can change the culture of that sphere, whether it is sports or politics.

While in recent years the concept of critical mass has come under criticism from many feminists who argue that a magical threshold of women in politics does not automatically lead to change or better policies for women, the concept still holds value when examining the case of the EU.[4] Here, women's representation within the EP and the Commission began to increase rapidly in the 1990s, at the same time that gender equality became a higher priority for the EU in terms of the number of directives adopted, the expanded scope of gender equality policy to include traditionally excluded issues—such as violence against women, the gendered division of labour in the home, and the implementation of gender mainstreaming. While the increased representation of women alone was not the sole cause of this change, it certainly was one crucial element among many, including the accession of Sweden and Finland to the EU in 1995, and the interplay between internal EU factors and external factors, such as the UN Beijing Women's Conference in 1995.

Writing more than twenty years ago, Elizabeth Vallance (1988) argued that the impact of women Members of the European Parliament (MEPs) on the EU's gender equality policy was neither direct nor unambiguous. Vallance argued that many factors were needed to create a favourable environment for gender equality issues, including the increasing number of women representatives, but also timing, favourable economic conditions, political will, and individual actors. However, in the end she does concede that women MEPs have played a significant role in the development of the EU's gender equality policy, even prior to their reaching a critical mass. Catherine Hoskyns (1996) picked up on Vallance's idea of the importance of individual actors when she argued that "lone women" have played an important role in developing the EU's gender equality policy; she also argued that "supported women," or women who are part of networks both within and outside of the formal system, are also beginning to play an important role in the EP when it comes to gender equality.

When looking at the early development of the EU's gender equality policy in the 1960s and 1970s, individual women did play a crucial role before women's numbers increased substantially in the EP or in the Commission. One woman who is mentioned time and again is Eliane Vogel-Polsky, a Belgian lawyer who argued for a strong definition of Article 119, representing Gabrielle Defrenne in her case before the European Court of Justice (Hoskyns 1996, Ellina 2003, Morgan 2008). Defrenne, an air hostess forced to resign due to her age, is often mentioned as an important figure in the early development of the EU's gender equality policy. Vogel-Polsky was also involved in another important case in Belgium, where she contended that pensions constitute "deferred pay" or a "social salary," using Article 119 of the Treaty of Rome. The outcome of these court cases were the EU's first three gender equality directives: the 1975 Equal Pay Directive, the 1976 Equal Treatment Directive, and the 1978 Social Security Directive. With the addition of the 1986 Occupational Social Security Directive, they formed the basis of the EU's gender equality policy until the 1990s.

Other individual actors significant to the early development of the EU's gender equality policy include Evelyne Sullerot, a French sociologist, and Jacqueline Nonon, a French official within the Commission. Sullerot produced a report on women's employment across the EU, highlighting comparisons and trends across the member states (Hoskyns 1996), which was important in the drafting of the 1975 Equal Pay Directive (EPD). Nonon was involved with Sullerot's report and the drafting of the Equal Treatment Directive (ETD). In preparing the ETD, Nonon created an ad hoc group on women's work to consult with—the group was comprised of eighteen representatives from the member states who met four times during 1974 to exchange and compare information. This led Nonon to be appointed as the first head of the Women's Bureau (later renamed the Equal Opportunities Unit) set up in the European Commission's Directorate-General of Employment, Social Affairs and Inclusion in 1976. Thus, the significance of individual women, and networks of women, can be seen in the creation of the EU's first two gender equality directives, the EPD and the ETD.

During the late 1970s and early 1980s there was a growing awareness of gender equality issues at the EU level, which has provided the foundation for the EU's current gender equality policy. For example, the Manchester conference, held in May 1980, was launched to build upon the existing directives and establish firmer links between the new gender equality agencies popping up at the member state and EU levels. This led to a resolution coming from the women MEPs who attended the conference which was debated and adopted in the EP in February 1981, and that had considerable influence on EU policy-making during the 1980s. In 1982 there was a second conference in Bonn that resulted in the Women's Bureau providing funding to the Centre for Research on European Women (CREW) to coordinate women's organizations across the EU. In addition, Odile Quintin, head of the Women's Bureau from 1982 through 1990, was a key actor during the 1980s, encouraging coordination among women's networks, and coming up with proposals[5] for new EU directives in the area of gender equality (Hoskyns 1996).[6] While the 1980s were not a particularly fruitful time for EU directives in the area of gender equality, it was a time for raising awareness on a number of gender issues, such as sexual slavery, reproduction, and sexual harassment at work through international meetings and conferences like the UN conferences in 1980 and 1985 (Hoskyns 1996). Another important development which occurred in the 1980s that would lay the foundation for future change was the adoption of the Charter of the Fundamental Social Rights of Workers in 1989, which included a commitment to measures helping parents reconcile work and family life (Morgan 2008).

In terms of the influence of women MEPs, writing in the 1980s, Elizabeth Vallance and Elizabeth Davies (1986) argued that many women MEPs felt a sense of solidarity and cooperation on women's issues that crossed party lines. For example, in a November 1981 session of the EP, a spontaneous group of women MEPs emerged to discuss issues such as prostitution, military service for women, and cohabitation laws (Vallance and Davies 1986). Chrystalla A. Ellina argues that from the mid-1990s there was intense development of the EU's gender equality policy, "suggesting ... a new period of punctuation" (2003, 40). In the early 2000s, Jane Freedman conducted surveys and interviews with female MEPs as the basis for her article "Women in the European Parliament" (2002), and found that female MEPs felt that there was a far higher level of solidarity among women in the EP that spanned across political parties and ideologies. The majority of female MEPs interviewed believed their presence in the parliament helped to put women's rights on the agenda. In the end, Freedman(2002) concluded that the EP has a critical mass of women members, as the majority of female MEPs have a strong connection to women's rights and feel they can make a difference in terms of EU policy. Ruth and Simon Henig (2001) argue that women MEPs have exercised a great deal of influence by working across national and party boundaries, particularly through the Committee on Women's Rights and Gender Equality.

In terms of explaining why there are more women in the EP than in most European national parliaments, Freedman (2002) found that female MEPs felt that there was a critical mass in the EP because there were far less institutional constraints there than in any national parliament. Willy Beauvallet and Sébastien Michon add "gender ... seems to be a positive characteristic in the political competition" at the European level (2008, 11). Freedman argues that because the EP has traditionally not been perceived as "an effective centre of political power" (2002, 179), women face less competition from men when it comes to candidacy. She goes on to argue that the political culture of the EP includes more gender equality than exists within the political culture of most member states. In fact, the EU as a whole prides itself on consensus when possible, and the EP also values consensus and cooperation over the traditional adversarial style of many national legislatures (Freedman 2002).[7] In addition, because the EP is a relatively new institution (as an elected parliament) there is no long tradition of male hegemony for women to break through (Vallance and Davies 1986).[8] This relates to Markovits' discussion of "counter-cosmopolitanism," where challengers and newcomers are often met with ridicule and harsh, even violent, reactions. Because the European Parliament does not have a long history of entrenched male dominance, women have been welcomed into the institution more readily, as they do not constitute the same threat to entrenched identities at the EU level that they do at the national level of the member states.

In addition to women's increased representation in the top decision-making positions of the institutions of the EU, there are also an increasing number of EU bodies concerned with issues of gender equality in recent years. In addition to the European Parliament's Committee on Women's Rights and Gender Equality which has been around since 1979, there is now an Equality and Diversity Unit within the EP's Directorate-General for Personnel, and a High-Level Group on Gender Equality and Diversity within the EP. Within the Commission there is an Advisory Committee on Equal Opportunities for Women and Men, a European Network of Women in Decision-Making in Politics and the Economy, a Group of Commissioners on Fundamental Rights, Non-Discrimination and Equal Opportunities, an Inter-Service Group on Gender Equality, a High-Level Group on Gender Mainstreaming, an Advisory Committee on Women and Rural Areas, and a number of other expert groups or advisory bodies on issues such as women and science, gender equality in development cooperation, women's entrepreneurship, and human trafficking. In addition, there are autonomous EU agencies such as the European Institute for Gender Equality (EIGE),[9] which is not directly linked to any EU institution, and there have been a number of temporary groups over the years, such as Females in Front, which was created by a group of female MEPs in 2008 to lobby for at least one woman to be appointed to one of the four top EU positions in 2009. A number of these groups are based on women working together across political parties/ ideologies and across member states, toward the advancement of gender equality within the EU as a whole. This was made possible by the increase in women's representation within the European Parliament and the European Commission, beginning in the early 1990s.

The EP's Committee on Women's Rights and Gender Equality (FEMM) first met in 1979, immediately following the first EP direct elections. FEMM originated from an ad hoc Committee on Women's Rights and Equal Opportunities and, over time, has become the key body for advancing gender equality and issues of women's rights in the EP, focusing a great deal of attention on enhancing women's political participation. The High-Level Group on Gender Equality and Diversity within the EP was established in 2004, and tasked with promoting and implementing gender mainstreaming within the EP's activities, structures, and bodies (European Parliament Directorate-General for Personnel's Equality and Diversity Unit 2011). It is composed of MEPs cooperating across party and ideological lines, and EP staff all working together toward a common goal.

The European Commission's Advisory Committee on Equal Opportunities for Women and Men was established in 1981, and is comprised of representatives from the member states, European social partners, and various non-governmental organizations (NGOs)—it assists the Commission in formulating its gender equality policy (European Commission Directorate-General for Employment, Social Affairs and Inclusion, "Gender Equality" 2011b). A number of other Commission agencies were created in response to the adoption of gender mainstreaming in the mid-1990s, which I will discuss in greater detail below. For example, the Inter-Service Group on Gender Equality was formed in 1996 to bring together representatives from all of the Commission's services responsible for gender equality to develop a gender mainstreaming approach in all EU policies. There is also a High-Level Group on Gender Mainstreaming, created in 2001, chaired by the Commission and composed of representatives responsible for gender mainstreaming in each member state. Many of the expert groups and advisory committees focusing on specific topics were created in the late 1990s and early 2000s and usually meet once or twice a year, but often produce opinions and reports for the Commission on their specific topic (European Commission Directorate-General for Employment, Social Affairs and Equal Opportunities 2006). Since 2007, the Commission also relies on two external networks of experts in formulating its gender equality policy—the European Commission's Expert Group on Gender and Employment, and the European Network of Experts on Gender Equality, Social Inclusion, Health and Long Term Care. Both networks prepare two thematic reports each year and support the Commission's work in the area of gender equality (European Commission Directorate-General for Employment, Social Affairs and Inclusion, "Network of experts" 2011d).

In addition to establishing a European Network of Women in Decision-Making in Politics and the Economy in 2008, the European Commission has also recently established a database on women and men in decision-making positions within politics, public administration, the judiciary, and the economy. This database provides reliable statistics that can be used to "monitor the current situation and trends through time" (European Commission Directorate-General for Employment, Social Affairs and Inclusion, "Database" 2011a). The database also keeps track of women's representation in the national parliaments of EU member states; as of autumn 2010, women accounted for 24 per cent of the members of these national parliaments, much lower than the nearly 35 per cent in the European Parliament (European Commission Directorate-General for Employment, Social Affairs and Inclusion 2011).

In recent years, the EU has also been pushing for better gender representation within the corporate world, with the European Commission Directorate-General for Employment, Social Affairs and Equal Opportunities releasing a report in 2010 entitled "More Women in Senior Positions: Key to Economic Stability and Growth." In the report, the Commission argues "a good gender balance at all levels can be beneficial to business," but points out that "more efforts are needed to encourage women entrepreneurs" and to encourage women into the fields of science, research, and development (2010, 6). The report argues for the use of role models, mentors, networks, and even quotas to address the gender gap in the corporate world. In addition, recently the EP adopted a non-binding recommendation advising businesses within the EU to hire more women to their executive boards. If voluntary measures do not see the appropriate gains, the EP has recommended that the European Commission table legislation to make the quotas binding (Pop 2011).[10]

The Influence of Sweden and Finland Post-1995

After years of resistance to joining the EU, in 1995 Sweden, Finland, and Austria became EU member states. In particular Finland and Sweden, countries with a historic commitment to gender equality, have had a great deal of influence on the EU's gender equality policy since their entry into the union. For example, Swedish Commissioner Anita Gradin and Finnish Commissioner Erkki Liikanen pushed for the establishment of a Group of Commissioners on Equal Opportunities immediately upon entering the European Commission in 1995. Jacques Santer, president of the Commission at the time, agreed to appoint and chair the group, composed of himself, Gradin, Liikanen, Padraig Flynn of Ireland, and Monika Wulf-Mathies of Germany. The group came into being at the same time as the Commission was drafting its Fourth Action Program on Equal Opportunities for Women and Men (1996–2000), where gender mainstreaming figured as the single most important element (Pollack and Hafner-Burton 2000). As Anne Havnør argues (2000), the group played an important role in the Commission's commitment to gender mainstreaming, particularly in areas such as employment policy, Structural Funds and research. Ellina (2003) notes that the Scandinavian countries insisted on gender mainstreaming as an EU priority leading into the 1995 UN Beijing Conference on Women. Thus, the impact of the accession of Sweden and Finland on the EU's gender equality policy was immediate, but also sustained.

Since joining the EU, Sweden and Finland have pushed for more gender equality in a number of areas. Silke Roth (2008) argues that Euro-skeptic women who feared joining the EU would negatively impact Swedish gender equality were the reason Sweden focused on exporting its gender equality policies to the EU once a member. Erika Björklund (2007) argues that Sweden, in particular, raises the issue of gender equality in consultation groups and in EU negotiations. In 2009 Margot Wallström[11] (Swedish), vice-president of the Commission, launched a debate about women and politics on the Commission's web forum "Debate Europe," which was linked to the 2009 EP elections and International Women's Day (European Women's Lobby, "50/50 Campaign for Democracy" 2011). In addition, Henig and Henig argue that Sweden and Finland have campaigned vigorously in the Council of Ministers, the Commission, and the EP on a broad range of equality issues since they have become members of the EU (2001). During their terms holding the presidency of the Council of the European Union, Sweden and Finland have prioritized issues of gender equality, leading to agreement on an EU definition of sexual trafficking in 2001 (Björklund 2007), the inclusion of gender equality targets in the European Employment Strategy, the 2002 Directive on Equal Treatment in Employment (Swedish Presidency 2001), and the finalization of the creation of the European Institute on Gender Equality (Finnish Presidency 2006). As Ellina argued, "the Scandinavian experience could directly influence all EU institutions" (2003, 42).

Expanded Scope of EU Gender Equality Policy

In the early years and decades of the EU, gender equality was only ever discussed in relation to the labour market. Gender equality issues outside of the scope of the strictly economic were not seen as the purview of the EU and, as such, were not discussed at the EU level. While the EU has always demonstrated some level of interest in gender equality in the labour market, even here it has expanded the scope of issues that it addresses. As mentioned above, the EP recently came out in favour of legal quotas for corporate executive jobs if voluntary action proves to be insufficient. Also, after a decade of struggle and negotiation, the EU adopted the Parental Leave Directive in 1996, and included the issue of reconciliation of work and family life as a priority area in the 2006–2010 Roadmap for Gender Equality. In addition, following the 2006–2010 Roadmap, the European Commission's Directorate-General for Employment, Social Affairs and Equal Opportunities' Advisory Committee on Equal Opportunities for Women and Men (2010) recommended that the Commission encourage member states to develop a more egalitarian family and social model, and a new model of labour and employment relations; it also recommended that the Commission and member states work together to fulfill the Barcelona targets on child care, and to undertake periodic awareness-raising campaigns aimed at men. Morgan argues, "the role of the EU in work-family policy has been transformed" (2008, 37). She contends that while historically there was resistance from the member states over EU involvement in social affairs, by the early 1990s there was agreement that the EU should develop its social agenda, including policies related to the reconciliation of work and family life. Since the 1990s there have also been more EU policies and recommendations targeted specifically at changing male behaviour. The first instance of this came in a 1992 Council Recommendation on Child Care, which encouraged men to participate more in caring for children (Elman 2007). While instances of "encouragement" and "recommendations" are obviously not binding, they do demonstrate a new development in the EU's gender equality policy, which is now no longer solely targeted at women and women's labour force participation, but also at changing men's behaviour.

In recent years, the EU has also become more interested and involved in gender equality issues that could be deemed social or political, such as women's political representation (as discussed above), sexual harassment, and violence against women. Getting the EU involved in issues of sexual harassment and violence against women was not an easy task, as such issues were for a long time considered private matters, and were not viewed as being within the EU's competence. During the 1980s and 1990s, a number of studies and reports on sexual harassment lead the EU to implement nonbinding resolutions and recommendations encouraging member states to adopt measures against sexual harassment. After two decades of struggle,[12] feminists framed sexual harassment as an issue of equal treatment of working conditions, which lead to the inclusion of sexual harassment in the 2002 Equal Treatment in Employment Directive. Framing the problem as a "workplace issue" of occupational health and safety rather than one of sex discrimination proved to be more successful at the EU level. In addition, Anna Diamantopoulou, Commissioner for Employment, Social Affairs and Equal Opportunities, played a role in pushing the directive through (Zippel 2008), demonstrating once again the importance of individual women activists and decision-makers in influencing the EU's gender equality policy.

Violence against women was first mentioned in the EU in 1984 by the EP, which followed up its concerns with a report in 1986 (Elman 2007); however, the other EU institutions did not pick up the EP's concerns, and most abused women advocates were not yet focusing their attention at the EU level. By the time the EU entered into the realm of violence against women, most of the member states had already created programs to address the issue; at this point, the EU was expected to get involved by its citizens, and particularly by the women's movement (Elman 2007). Anita Gradin, Swedish Commissioner for Justice and Home Affairs, played a pivotal role in placing violence against women on the EU agenda in a way that incorporated the issue into her Justice and Home Affairs portfolio. In response to mounting criticism for not having addressed the topic, in 1996 the EU created STOP (Sexual Trafficking in Persons),[13] and the following year it created Daphne,[14] a program that provided financial assistance to the voluntary sector for initiatives to combat violence against women. These programs were linked to Justice and Home Affairs through the trafficking in women and children and the fight against international crime (Havnør 2000). The EP also designated 1999 the "European Year against Violence," raising awareness of the issue particularly through Daphne's information campaigns.

The Commission and the EP have been leading the campaign to get the EU more involved in the issue of violence against women. In 2005, the Commission adopted the Roadmap for Equality between Women and Men for 2006–2010, which included eradicating gender-based violence and trafficking as one of its six priority areas. The Commission's follow-up Equality Strategy for 2011–2015 also includes an end to gender-based violence as one of its five priority areas. Here the Commission put forward a proposal to adopt an EU-wide strategy for combating violence against women that would be the first of its kind (European Commission 2011). In 2011, the EP adopted a report entitled "Priorities and outline of a new EU policy framework to fight violence against women," that criticized the lack of coherence between member state laws on the issue of violence against women. The report calls for an EU directive on the subject to more effectively combat the issue across Europe (Party of European Socialists 2011). Thus, both the Commission and the EP are headed in the same direction of wanting an EU-level strategy to address violence against women.

In addition to expanding the scope of issues encompassed in the EU's gender equality policy, the EU has also expanded the scope of its approach to gender equality policy. As Pollack and Hafner-Burton (2000) argue, the EU has, since the 1990s, adopted three approaches to gender equality— equal treatment, positive action, and gender mainstreaming. Gender mainstreaming is the "systematic incorporation of gender issues throughout all governmental institutions and policies" (Pollack and Hafner-Burton 2000, 434). While gender mainstreaming was only discussed in the EU for the first time in 1991, by 1996 the European Commission had formally adopted it as part of its gender equality policy in a communication entitled "Incorporating Equal Opportunities for Women and Men into all Community Policies and Activities," and the following year gender mainstreaming was confirmed in the Treaty of Amsterdam. It was also the backbone of the Commission's Fourth Medium-Term Action Program on Equal Opportunities for Women and Men (1996–2000).

Pollack and Hafner-Burton (2000) explain the EU's decision to adopt gender mainstreaming as due to three factors: (1) the political opportunities offered by EU institutions to gender equality advocates, (2) the mobilizing structures, or European networks, established by gender equality advocates, and (3) the efforts of gender equality advocates to strategically frame gender mainstreaming to ensure its acceptance among EU policy-makers. The timing of the adoption is partially explained by Pollack and Hafner-Burton (2000) by the passage of the Maastricht Treaty (1993), which greatly expanded the powers of the EP, long the strongest advocate for gender equality among the EU institutions; the accession of Sweden and Finland (1995), countries with long-standing commitments to gender equality; and the UN Beijing Women's Conference (1995), where gender mainstreaming received worldwide acceptance as an approach to gender equality. In particular, Sweden and Finland had considerable experience with gender mainstreaming in their own national contexts, so they had much to offer the EU in this regard (Roth 2008).

In terms of implementation, gender mainstreaming has raised some concerns and controversies. In the beginning, there was a concern raised by many feminists that the adoption of gender mainstreaming would mean an end to positive action programs for women within the EU. And for a short time in 1998 this looked to be the case, when the EP proposed abolishing all of its committees that did not perform any legislative tasks, including the Committee on Women's Rights and Gender Equality; the European Women's Lobby and other women's organizations responded by mounting a successful campaign to defend women-specific policies and structures (Ellina 2003). In the end, the EU declared its commitment to a dual approach, which included both gender mainstreaming and positive action programs targeted specifically at women. And the Commission has taken its commitment to gender mainstreaming seriously, appointing officials to each Directorate-General to coordinate gender mainstreaming across the Commission. However, as Pollack and Hafner-Burton point out, "despite these considerable strides," (2000, 446) by 2000 it was obvious that there remained serious obstacles to the commission's gender mainstreaming approach, from lack of gender awareness among EU officials to insufficient funding for training, to the overwhelming dominance of male officials at the highest level of the bureaucracy, to the need to develop new instruments and procedures. As a result, progress has been uneven across issue areas. However, one could argue that the institutionalization of gender training that comes with gender mainstreaming has potential for consciousness-raising within the EU (Marx Ferree 2008).

Conclusions: The Impact of EU Gender Equality Policy

When looking at the EU's gender equality policy, one must recognize that only four EU directives on gender equality were adopted before 1990, while seven have been adopted since 1990. The increased emphasis on gender equality at the EU level has also resulted in a number action programs emanating from the Commission since 1982. In addition, gender equality concerns have been incorporated into the European Employment Strategy (EES) and the Europe 2020 agenda.[15] With the current amount of EU legislation, non-binding recommendations and resolutions, as well as action programs and strategies in the area of gender equality, it would appear as though the EU is on the path to achieving gender equality. But some attention must be paid to the impact of the EU's gender equality policy—what are the outcomes for the citizens of the EU? One could argue that the impact of the EU's gender equality policy has been both a direct and indirect. For example, the 1992 Pregnant Workers Directive directly influenced Portugal and the UK, which had to increase their maternity leave standards (Ellina 2003), while the 1996 Directive on Parental Leave directly influenced the expansion of parental leave policies in member states such as the Czech Republic, Estonia, Hungary, Portugal, and Spain. In addition, the EU's European Employment Strategy (Lisbon strategy) has played a role in encouraging member states to increase women's labour market participation (Kamerman and Moss 2009). Morgan (2008) agrees that the EU's Parental Leave Directive has had a direct influence on member state policies, and also asserts that other directives have influenced member states' part-time work policies, directly benefiting part-time workers in the EU, who gained improved legal protections as a result.

For those member states with a poor record on gender equality issues and policies, the EU offers an additional, supranational level for women and women's organizations to lobby for change. As Vallance (1988) argues, advocates for change have been able to point to EU initiatives and use them in their own national campaigns. Roth (2008) agrees, pointing to the EU as an important resource for those promoting gender equality within the member states and candidate countries. Candidate countries must now adopt the *acquis communautaire* in order to join the EU, and since gender mainstreaming is a part of the *acquis*, it has been used by activists within these countries to demand the establishment of gender offices or the adoption of gender equality legislation (Roth 2008). The European Women's Lobby (EWL) also provides an interesting lobbying opportunity for women's organizations within the member states. The EWL is composed of more than 2,500 organizations from across Europe, and acts to defend women's interests at the European level by providing information to EU decision-makers and promoting the participation of women's organizations at the EU level (European Women's Lobby 2011).[16]

Thus, the question remains: has the recent prioritization and development of the EU's gender equality policy, largely thanks to the critical mass of women in the EP and the Commission, the accession of Sweden and Finland, and the interplay of internal and external factors led to real improvements in gender equality within the EU? R. Amy Elman (2007) argues that the EU confers only "virtual equality," or impressive rhetoric that is disappointing in practice. She goes so far as to suggest that the biggest beneficiary of the EU's gender equality policy may be the union itself. She argues that the EU's gender equality policy did not develop from a deliberative plan, and thus the negotiations between and influence of member state governments, EU judges, bureaucrats, EU Commissioners, and activists have led to the creation of a somewhat ad hoc policy, lacking in coherence and commitment. However, Morgan (2008) tempers Elman's pessimism when she acknowledges that the rhetorical attention given to gender equality outweighs the depth of the EU's commitment, but that nonetheless the shift in discourse is a significant development for the EU's gender equality policy.

Much of the EU's involvement in the social dimension of gender equality policy has come not through directives, but through non-binding recommendations and targets agreed to through the open method of coordination (OMC). While the OMC has allowed forward movement on social issues at the EU level, it has also meant that the member states still have a great deal of power when it comes to social issues and whether or not to adhere to EU recommendations and targets. As Morgan (2008) argues, the ambiguous nature of the EU's gender equality policy leaves the member states much room for interpretation. Thus, the EU's involvement in social affairs has contributed to raising the profile of issues such as the reconciliation of work and family life in the member states, but there are definitely limitations in using "soft" measures such as the OMC in developing a coherent EU-level policy (Morgan 2008).

Following the completion of the European Commission's 2006–2010 Roadmap for Gender Equality, the Commission set up an Advisory Committee to determine the success of the roadmap and the main issues that remain to be addressed in the future. The Advisory Committee concluded that the "EU has made significant progress over the last decades in delivering greater gender equality" and it is essential that the advances made not be eroded during the economic crisis (European Commission Directorate-General for Employment Social Affairs and Equal Opportunities' Advisory Committee on Equal Opportunities for Women and Men 2010, 5). The Advisory Committee indicated that differing implementation across the EU was a major challenge in moving forward with the EU's gender equality policy; it also indicated that in order to meet ongoing challenges, the awareness and active involvement of all stakeholders must be raised, including the institutions of the EU, the member states, the national parliaments, the social partners, NGOs, and civil society.

During the 1970s and 1980s, women within the EU made strides in protecting the fledgling gender equality policy that was developing at the EU level. They created women's committees and groups within the EU institutions, they created networks of women's organizations outside of the EU, and they ensured a relationship between the two through regular meetings and the exchange of information. Building upon the early work of a handful of feminists within the EU bureaucracy, the increased numbers of women in the EP and the Commission since the 1990s has unquestionably helped to increase the profile and expand the scope of the EU's gender equality policy. The sheer volume of expert groups, networks, and committees that have been established in the EP and the Commission since the 1990s demonstrates the significance of gender equality on the EU agenda during this time, and the number of equality directives that have been adopted in recent years is promising. Certainly there remains a great deal of gender inequality within the EU, and there remains a great number of obstacles to overcome in achieving substantive equality, but the path taken by the EU in the past two decades does show an increased commitment to overcoming these obstacles.

Notes

1 As evidenced by the inclusion of the principle of equal pay in the 1957 Treaty of Rome.

2 It was in 1994 that women's representation within the European Parliament reached 25 per cent; women comprised 25 per cent of the European Commission the following year.

3 A man—Herman Van Rompuy—fills the other position, President of the European Council.

4 See the collection of articles in the "Do Women Represent Women? Rethinking the 'Critical Mass' Debate" issue of *Politics & Gender* (2006) from authors such as Sandra Grey, Manon Tremblay, Sarah Childs, and Drude Dahlerup.

5 Proposed new directives included a directive on parental leave that was not adopted until 1996, a directive on equal treatment for the self-employed campaigned for by farm women, and a directive on the protection of pregnancy, adopted in 1992 (Hoskyns 1996).

6 Other female actors important to the development of the EU's gender equality policy during the 1980s include Simon Veil, the first female President of the EP (1979–1982), and Yvette Roudy, French MEP and the first chair of the EP's Ad Hoc Committee on Women's Rights (Ellina 2003).

7 Other issues to consider when analyzing women's higher representation at the EU level include the electoral system and the adoption of gender quotas, as well as the predictability of the schedule that allows for easier planning.

8 However, it is important to remember that women still do not constitute half of the MEPs, and that struggles remain in terms of the EP committee system, where women are over-represented on committees dealing with social issues, and under-represented on committees concerned with issues such as trade, defence, and foreign affairs.

9 The idea of creating the EIGE was first proposed in 1995, but it did not come to fruition until 2007 when it was established in Brussels and then moved to its permanent home in Vilnius, Lithuania (European Institute for Gender Equality 2011c). EIGE's operating budget for the years 2007–2013 is €52.5 million (European Commission Directorate-General for Employment, Social Affairs and Inclusion, "European Institute for Gender Equality" 2011), and this money is spent on building up a comprehensive gender equality library, as well as compiling a Gender Equality Index to monitor the EU's progress in the field of gender equality. The EIGE's main priorities are gender mainstreaming, the Gender Equality Index, and the Beijing Platform for Action (European Institute for Gender Equality 2011).

10 The binding quotas proposal is based on the successful Norwegian model of 40 per cent female quotas for top corporate positions (Pop 2011).

11 Swedish Commissioner Wallström is a strong proponent of increasing women's representation within the top decision-making positions of the EU;

she has been quoted as saying "a democracy which does not make enough room for 52 per cent of the population at the decision-making table is no real democracy at all" (European Parliament 2009).

12 Sexual harassment was first introduced at the EU level in 1983 by MEPs Yvette Fuillet and Maria-Lisa Cinciari-Rodano, who initially framed the issue as "worker exploitation" (Zippel 2008).

13 In its first five years, STOP was granted €6.5 million to fund research and implement training programs for EU public officials, particularly law enforcement and migration officers. Following the 9/11 attacks, the program faded away and anti-trafficking efforts continued under AGIS, a catch-all criminal justice program.

14 With its €5 million budget per year, the Daphne program funded projects for the prevention of violence against women, children, and young people, in addition to providing support to the victims of violence. In 2008 the program was discontinued, leaving no budget for EU programs to combat violence against women (Party of European Socialists 2011).

15 Of course, both the EES and Europe 2020 agendas have been criticized for lacking teeth, as both set targets that leave the member states to come up with their own strategies to reach the targets, and there are no penalties for failing to reach them.

16 The EWL was established in 1990, and that same year the European Commission endorsed the foundation by providing a Secretariat based in Brussels, and funding. The EWL lobbies the EU on all manner of gender equality issues, from women in decision-making to issues of employment, immigration, diversity, women and the media, and violence against women; it also prepares reports, publishes an online magazine, and organizes conferences on these issues.

References

Beauvallet, Willy, and Sébastien Michon. 2008. "General Patterns of Women's Representation at the European Parliament: Did Something Change after 2004?" Paper presented at the Fourth Pan-European Conference on EU Politics, ECPR, Riga, Latvia, September 25.

Björklund, Erika. 2007. "Issue Histories Sweden: Series of Timeline of Policy Debates." QUING Project, Vienna: Institute for Human Sciences (IWM). Accessed October 5, 2011. http://www.quing.eu/files/results/ih_sweden.pdf.

Childs, Sarah. 2006. "Should Feminists Give Up on Critical Mass? A Contingent Yes." *Politics & Gender* 2: 522–30.

Dahlerup, Drude. 1988. "From a Small to a Large Minority: Women in Scandinavian Politics." *Scandinavian Political Studies* 11 (4): 275–98.

Ellina, Chrystalla. 2003. *Promoting Women's Rights: The Politics of Gender in the European Union.* New York: Routledge.

Elman, R. Amy. 2007. *Sexual Equality in an Integrated Europe.* New York: Palgrave Macmillan.

European Commission. 1996. "Incorporating Equal Opportunities for Women and Men into All Community Policies and Activities." Communication from Brussels, February 21.

———. 2011. "Strategy for Equality between Women and Men 2010–2015." Luxembourg: Publications Office of the European Union.

European Commission Directorate-General for Employment, Social Affairs and Equal Opportunities. 2006. "A Roadmap for Equality between Women and Men 2006–2010." Luxembourg: Publications Office of the European Union.

———. 2010. "More Women in Senior Positions: Key to Economic Stability and Growth." Luxembourg: Publications Office of the European Union.

European Commission Directorate-General for Employment Social Affairs and Equal Opportunities' Advisory Committee on Equal Opportunities for Women and Men. 2010. "Opinion on *The Future of Gender Equality Policy after 2010* and on the Priorities for a Possible Future Framework for Equality between Women and Men." January.

European Commission Directorate-General for Employment, Social Affairs and Inclusion. 2011a. "Database: Women & Men in Decision-making." Accessed July 20. http://ec.europa.eu/social/main.jsp?catid=764&langid=en

———. 2011b. "Gender Equality." Accessed July 20. http://ec.europa.eu/social/main.jsp?langid=en&catid=418.

———. 2011c. "European Institute for Gender Equality." Accessed July 20. http://ec.europa.eu/social/main.jsp?catid=732&langid=en.

———. 2011d. "Network of Experts." Accessed July 20. http://ec.europa.eu/social/main.jsp?catid=748&langid=en.

———. 2011e. "Women and Men in Decision-making: Highlights (First Quarter 2011)." May 24. Accessed July 20.http://ec.europa.eu/social/main.jsp?langid=en&catid=762&newsid=1031&furtherNews=yes.

European Institute for Gender Equality website. 2011. Accessed October 5. http://www.eige.europa.eu.

European Parliament. 2009. "Poll Backs More Women in Politics but Not Quotas: Tell Us Your Views." March 5. Accessed July 24, 2011. http://www.europarl.europa.eu/sides/getDoc.do?language=en&type=IM-PRESS&reference=20090302STO50555.

European Parliament Directorate-General for Personnel's Equality and Diversity Unit. 2011. "Women in the European Parliament." March 8.

European Women's Lobby. 2011. "50/50 Campaign for Democracy." Accessed July 20. http://5050campaign.wordpress.com/.

———. 2011. "Women lobby website." Accessed July 20. http://www.womenlobby.org.

Finnish Presidency. 2006. "Finland's EU Presidency." Accessed October 24, 2011. http://eu2006.fi.

Freedman, Jane. 2002. "Women in the European Parliament." *Parliamentary Affairs* 55 (1): 179–88.

Grey, Sandra. 2006. "Numbers and Beyond: The Relevance of Critical Mass in Gender Research." *Politics & Gender* 2: 492–502.

Havnør, Anne. 2000. "Partnership, Political Will and Agency—Gender Mainstreaming at the EC Level and in the Central Administration of Norway." Paper presented at the Mainstreaming Gender in European Union Public Policy workshop, University of Wisconsin–Madison, October 14–15.

Henig, Ruth, and Simon Henig. 2001. *Women and Political Power: Europe since 1945*. London: Routledge.

Hoskyns, Catherine. 1996. *Integrating Gender: Women, Law and Politics in the European Union*. London: Verso.

Kamerman, Sheila B., and Peter Moss, eds. 2009. *The Politics of Parental Leave Policies: Children, Parenting, Gender and the Labour Market*. Bristol: Policy Press.

Marx Ferree, Myra. 2008. "Framing Equality: The Politics of Race, Class, and Gender in the US, Germany, and the Expanding European Union." In *Gender Politics in the Expanding European Union: Mobilization, Inclusion, Exclusion*, edited by Silke Roth, 237–55. New York: Berghahn Books.

Morgan, Kimberly J. 2008. "Toward the Europeanization of Work-Family Policies? The Impact of the EU on Policies for Working Parents." In Roth 2008, 37–59.

Party of European Socialists. 2011. "Violence against Women: European Parliament Report Puts Pressure on Commission." April 5. Accessed July 20, 2011. http://www.pes.org/en/news/violence-against-women-european-parliament -report-puts-pressure-commission.

Pollack, Mark A., and Emilie Hafner-Burton. 2000. "Mainstreaming Gender in the European Union." *Journal of European Public Policy* 7 (3): 432–56.

Pop, Valentina. 2011. "EU Parliament Backs Female Quotas for Top Corporate Jobs." *EU Observer*, July 7. http://euobserver.com/18/32598.

Roth, Silke. 2008. "Introduction." In Roth 2008, 1–16.

Swedish Presidency. 2001. "The Swedish Presidency." Accessed October 24. http:// eu2011.se.

Tremblay, Manon. 2006. "The Substantive Representation of Women and PR: Some Reflections on the Role of Surrogate Representation and Critical Mass." *Politics & Gender* 2: 502–11.

Vallance, Elizabeth. 1988. "Do Women Make a Difference? The Impact of Women MEPs on Community Equality Policy." In *Women, Equality and Europe,* edited by Mary Buckley and Malcolm Anderson, 126–41. London: Macmillan Press.

Vallance, Elizabeth, and Elizabeth Davies. 1986. *Women of Europe: Women MEPs and Equality Policy.* Cambridge: Cambridge University Press.

Zippel, Kathrin. 2008. "Violence at Work? Framing Sexual Harassment in the European Union." In Roth 2008, 60–80.

Chapter 6

The Emptiness of European Identity and the Discourse on Turkish EU Membership

Dirk Nabers

Introduction

The European Union (EU), the grand example of every integration process in the world, has grown in size with successive waves of accessions. Denmark, Ireland, and the United Kingdom joined the original six members of the European Communities in 1973, followed by Greece in 1981, Spain and Portugal in 1986, and Austria, Finland, and Sweden in 1995. In 2004, the EU welcomed ten new countries: Cyprus, the Czech Republic, Estonia, Hungary, Latvia, Lithuania, Malta, Poland, Slovakia, and Slovenia; Bulgaria and Romania joined the union in 2007; and Croatia and Turkey began membership negotiations in 2005, with Croatia joining the EU as its twenty-eighth member in 2013.

Successive enlargement processes of this kind raise important questions about the identity around which the community, and with it the whole notion of "Europe," is constructed. Representations of identity seem to be significant as a frame of reference for international relations (IR) (Larsen 1997; Campbell 1998; Diez 1999; Brown 2001; Fuchs and Klingemann 2002; Nabers 2006; Kratochwil 2006), but identity is also constructed through foreign policy and international politics (Hansen 2006; Manners and Whitman 2003; Nabers 2009). As I will demonstrate in the course of this analysis, identity is neither stable nor undisputed, and it might not be appropriate to talk of straightforward, categorical identities. As a result, it is theoretically not obvious at all when the process of EU enlargement will come to an end. This is all the more interesting because new rounds of enlargement will stretch beyond what was originally seen as the "natural" geographical borders of the region.

On the background of these preliminary thoughts, with this analysis I seek to scrutinize ongoing constructions of regional identity in Europe as the basis for further institutionalization and institutional enlargement. Taking the works of Thomas Diez (2004) and Ole Waever (2000) and their notion of temporal othering as a starting point, I argue that once the process of accession negotiations has started, discussions of identity are expected to move from general concepts such as "freedom," "democracy," and temporal othering to more specific issues like market economy, institutional reform, and a cultural form of othering. While constructing the self relies on historical self-reflection and the creation of chains of equivalence between ingroup members, the construction of the other is shaped by antagonism and *difference*. The prospect of integrating new members into the community must thus be seen as overcoming difference. Enlargement hence depends on the stability of constructions of difference.

The analysis proceeds in five steps: Following this introduction, I will set out the ontological premises of the study, outlining a theory of identity that is characterized by the key concepts of difference, equivalence, the construction of so-called empty signifiers, and an excluded other. Subsequently, I will show how identity can be operationalized methodologically, and follow with an empirical analysis of identity constructions in the process of European Union negotiations with Turkey between 2005 and 2008, that is, the first three years of accession negotiations. The final section will sum up the results along the lines of the developed theoretical framework.

Constructing Identity

The following discussion of the concept of identity is very much indebted to new developments in post-structuralism, critical theory, and linguistics. First and foremost, it is inspired by the work of political theorists Ernesto Laclau and Chantal Mouffe. In their research, "identity" is conceptualized as an unstable and negative term, never closed in itself, ephemeral in character and relying on the constant movement of differential relationships (Laclau and Mouffe 1985, 95; Smith 1998, 87). The undecidability of structure leads to the incompleteness of identities: "the presence of some objects in the others prevents any of their identities from being fixed" (Laclau and Mouffe 1985, 104). This basic idea has been reflected in the notion of the EU's malleable and fluid external borders, leading to unclear and moving boundaries and overlapping identities (Zielonka 2000; Drulák 2006).

Laclau and Mouffe compare the concept of identity to the French linguist Ferdinand de Saussure's concept of signs, rejecting a referential theory of identity in favour of a relational account. This means that any element in a system gains significance only through its relations with other elements, rather than through essential qualities found in the elements themselves. It also implies that one element is impossible without the other; both are mutually contaminated, traces of one element are always visible in the other. Laclau and Mouffe therefore belong to a group of theorists who favour an ontology of "lack," asserting the incompleteness of any identity, as individual subjects never accomplish complete self-consciousness. A husband's identity always rests on his relationship with his wife, and vice versa. Identity remains partial; it can never be full or complete. It can therefore be established only by difference, by drawing a line between one thing and something else. In this view, all identity is relational, formed by social practices that link together a series of interrelated signifying elements. All principles and values, therefore, receive their meaning from relationships of difference and opposition (Laclau 1990, 21, 58). The subject is seen as an attempt to fill structural gaps, or subject positions, within a structure. Hence Laclau's differentiation between *identity* and *identification*, unveiling a basic ambiguity at the heart of identity (2000, 58; 1990, 60–63). The individual cannot completely identify with the subject position the discourse supplies, "but is forced into filling the structural gaps through identification" (Andersen 2003, 52).

Thus, brute material cannot be the substratum of identity either (Kratochwil 2006, 19). Instead, language[1] is constitutive in the shaping of identities. As we will see, some kind of universal reference is required to make the illusion of a European society possible. Laclau and Mouffe thus reject the notion of a harmonious and naturally bound collective entity, and maintain that dominant interpretative frameworks result from the specific dialectic relationship between what they call the *logics of equivalence* and *difference* (1985, chapter 3). The logic of equivalence constitutes the fullness of a community by linking together a variety of unfulfilled demands, such as democracy, liberal economy, and free will; difference contradicts this logic (Laclau 2005, 106; Smith 1998, 89–90). Different identities are grouped together in opposition to another camp to form a chain of equivalence. Equivalence thus highlights the effect of a perceived common "negative" or "enemy"; the demands of different social groups are articulated into a larger common movement (Critchley and Marchart 2004, 4).

If we assume that identity rests on the opposing logics of equivalence and difference, and the construction of an excluded outside, we have to emphasize the process of multiple and mutually reflective constructions in the analysis of identity politics. Furthermore, it is only by reference to an outside *other* that identity constructions of the *self* become achievable. At the centre of such a discourse, we usually find what Laclau and Mouffe call an empty signifier, which arises from the need to signify something that is both impossible but necessary at the same time. Under such logic, it was possible to construct a German in the Nazi era as worker—"Aryan"—non-Jew, et cetera. The empty signifier that symbolizes the hegemonic operation has a deeply catachrestical character; in fact, it often takes the form of a *synecdoche*, as a part comes to represent the whole (Laclau 2005, 72).

The two scholars hypothesize that the term "Europe" plays the role of an empty signifier in this analysis, with Turkey assuming the role of a possible cultural and geopolitical other. Empty signifiers are characterized by an indistinct or non-existent signified, that is, terms that can have different meanings and can thereby serve to unite disparate social movements. They have no fixed content, and can embrace an open series of demands. Its purpose "is to give a particular demand a function of universal representation—that is, to give it the value of a horizon giving coherence to the chain of equivalence and, at the same time, keeping it indefinitely open" (Laclau 1996, 57–58). To assume the role of an empty signifier, a particularity must void itself of its very particularity. An empty signifier is never completely empty; universality never completely universal—quite the contrary is true. Universality, as materialized in the form of an empty signifier, "is the symbol of a missing fullness" (Laclau 1996, 28).

Talking about "Europe" thus presupposes the construction of relations of equivalence and difference, which are not instituted outside some discursive social space, but are based on the linguistic construction of empty signifiers. If we understand that the hegemonic project is built on chains of equivalence using empty signifiers, then the identification of those signifiers becomes a first, crucial step in the analysis. As I argued above, empty signifiers are essential and central to all political processes, and must hence be identified and interpreted. The first analytical step will therefore be quantitative in nature. While Petr Drulák (2006), starts his analysis of metaphors in the discourse about European integration with an identification of his analytic units through a survey of theoretical discourses on the EU and only uses quantitative analysis as a second step, this order is reversed in my analysis.

I employed lexicometric approaches (Teubert and Čermáková 2004) to analyze the frequency and the typical co-occurrences of dominant signifiers in a specified text corpus. The goal was to define which potential empty signifiers occur with a high frequency in the whole corpus. For this purpose

I used WordSmith 5, an integrated suite of programs for looking at how words behave in texts. WordSmith offers three tools that guided the first step in my analysis: *WordList* classifies a list of all the words or word-clusters in a text, and *Concord* contextualizes any given word or phrase, making it possible to observe so called co-occurrences in a text—that is, concepts that occur more often in the environment of an empty signifier. Finally, *KeyWords* makes it possible to isolate the key words in a text, thereby enabling the researcher to analyze language patterns in large text corpora. Once I classified the central signifiers, their frequency and co-occurrences, I followed the lexicometric analysis with qualitative scrutiny. I used the *computer-assisted qualitative data analysis software* (CAQDAS) ATLAS.ti, a program that provides qualitative analysis of large bodies of textual data, to help arrange and manage the used material in a more efficient way.[2]

Identity Constructions and EU Enlargement

Puzzled by the existing difficulties in explaining international cooperation in general and EU integration in particular (Rosamond 2000, 197), IR scholars have offered numerous different theories to explain the origin and development of international institutions. In this chapter I seek to identify empty signifiers first, and the construction of chains of equivalence and difference second. An analysis of the central role of the so-called "constitutive other" will round out the empirical analysis.

Identifying Empty Signifiers

To soothe the possibly diverging identities and interests of EU members in the enlargement process over the period from 2005 to 2008, the European Commission submitted regular reports to the EU Council, which enabled the council to make decisions about the conduct of the negotiations on the basis of the accession criteria. The actual negotiations took the form of a series of inter-governmental conferences between the EU members and each of the applicant countries. For the identification of empty signifiers, key official documents made available by the EU Commission, the Council of the European Union, and the European Council between the December 2004 official declaration of EU leaders to open entry talks with Turkey have been included in the analysis; in addition, documents related to the accession negotiations (starting in October 2005) have been scrutinized. The initial step is solely based on the quantitative analysis of these texts. In contrast, the *qualitative* analysis (in the next section) rests on the examination of a number of different issue-related statements, speeches, and interviews by

EU officials and politicians from member countries in the period between 2005 and 2008.

In detail, the following documents have been evaluated for the quantitative analysis: commission enlargement strategy reports, progress and monitoring reports for each candidate country, and documents related to accession negotiations, including all statements by present EU members listed in the archive of the European Navigator, run by the *Centre Virtuel de la Connaissance sur l'Europe (Virtual Resource Centre for Knowledge about Europe, CVCE):*[3] commission communication papers; council presidency conclusions; European Parliament debates and resolutions on membership applications; speeches, statements, interviews, and articles by the EU Commissioner for Enlargement Olli Rehn since he took office in 2004. Secondary sources, such as newspaper articles and scientific work, have been excluded from the quantitative, corpus-based analysis. The number of files was reduced by including short statements by one speaker in a particular year (e.g., Olli Rehn in 2004) and yearly council conclusions in one single file. In sum, 155 files were incorporated in the analysis. The selection of these documents merely served the task of identifying central concepts of the discourse and their dominant connotations.

Altogether, 11,152 different words were used in the analyzed texts. Of all nouns, adjectives, and verbs employed, unsurprisingly, the term "European" showed the highest rate of recurrence, as it appears in "European Union"; it occurred in 154 texts (99.35 per cent of all texts), with a total frequency of 4,250. Additionally, the term "Europe" occurred 857 times (80.00 per cent of all texts). As the chosen documents are all related to the general topic of enlargement, it is not surprising that "European" is most commonly followed by "council," "union," "accession," "progress," and "enlargement." Terms like the latter three refer to what Drulák (2006) has dubbed the metaphor of the EU: "motion," signifying the fluidity and dynamic character of European integration. In that sense, as Philippe Schmitter maintains, EU institutionalization "should be recognized as the transient result of an ongoing process, rather than the definitive product of a stable equilibrium" (1996, 6).

It has to be noted here that nouns are of particular importance in the analysis of empty signifiers. Linguistic studies have widely shown that every noun affirms a difference, while at the same time denying "a universe of differences" (Currie 2004, 4). Most nouns—like dog, cat, human being, tree, house, people, nation, et cetera—reflect categories or generalizations, thereby naturalizing chains of equivalence and difference. Expressions like "Europe" allow diverse groups in a society to affiliate and identify with one another. (See table 6.1.)

Table 6.1 Nouns Used in Enlargement-related Documents

Word	Frequency	% of corpus	Texts	% of texts
European	4,250	0.97	154	99.35
Council	2,679	0.61	123	79.35
progress	1,546	0.35	117	75.48
commission	1,428	0.33	139	89.68
Turkey	1,402	0.32	97	62.58
Union	1,279	0.29	145	93.55
countries	1,252	0.29	118	76.13
member	1,207	0.28	136	87.74
accession	1,192	0.27	123	79.35
enlargement	1,038	0.24	135	87.10

Nouns not listed in Table 6.1 with a relatively high rate of recurrence are "process" (92.26 per cent of all texts), "support" (72.26 per cent), "negotiations" (70.97 per cent), "reform" (70.97 per cent), "reforms" (73.55 per cent), "security" (69.68 per cent), "efforts" (64.52 per cent), and "democracy" (58.06 per cent; the adjective "democratic" occurs in 61.29 per cent of all texts), while "freedom" (40.65 per cent) and "freedoms" (29.68 per cent) still occur in more than half of the texts if taken together.

As I will show in the next section, the dominant terms "Europe" and "European" are themselves characterized by indistinct signifieds, thus representing signifiers that have different meanings and can thereby serve to unite various actors under one label. Habitually used expressions like "accession," "progress," and "enlargement" are to a lesser extent indifferent to the content of their filling, and carry with them a certain tendency to be conflict prone. An empty signifier is, however, also never completely empty. Empty signifiers are often connected with or connoted by other terms.

During the first phase of the accession negotiations with Turkey, "modern" and "democratic" were, according to a 2007 *Eurobarometer* poll (European Commission 2007), the most suitable adjectives to denote the European Union (70 per cent in both cases), and more than half of EU citizens also believe that the EU is "protective" (57 per cent). The quantitative analysis of typical clusters used in the official discourse reflects the liberal and democratic nature of the community. The constitutionalization of the EU thus has to cohere with certain positive, pre-existing community norms. Though not explicitly dealing with the case of the EU, Laclau would probably argue that if the project of EU integration clashes with the "ensemble of sedimented practices constituting the normative framework of a certain society" (Laclau 2000, 82; see also Laclau 1990, 66), it would likely be rejected. In a very similar vein, Rittberger and Schimmelfennig (2006) maintain that the constitutionalization of democratic norms is most likely to succeed when they relate to pre-existing community norms and practices both within and beyond the community (indicating internal and external "coherence"), and when the issue has attracted public attention ("publicity"). A political project obviously has to be connected with certain political traditions that subjects identify with.

Therefore, it comes as no surprise that the dominant clusters that give "Turkey" a more specific meaning are those related to the process of negotiations with the potential new EU member: not only "negotiations with Turkey" (total frequency: 72) and "accession negotiations with Turkey" (66) but also expressions that reflect the prerequisites of Turkey's entry into the EU, such as "Turkey needs to" (16) and "Turkey has not" (14). On the basis of these preliminary findings, I will analyze the discourse about enlargement from a qualitative perspective in the next section, giving specific emphasis to the empty signifiers "European" and "Europe" and its interconnection with other frequently used expressions (see table 6.1), especially dominant characterizations of Turkey as the "other" of the EU's fluid identity.

Constructing Identity

Constructing the Self

Although "Europe" in the past always stood for diversity more than unity, and there have been significant differences in meaning across different countries and over time (Olsen 2005), constructing a European self has been unproblematic as long as it relied on the general depiction of some fundamental principles and norms. To start with, the European Community/European Union has always understood itself as existing "along the path of civilisation, progress and prosperity" (European Union 2004, Preamble). It claims the heritage of European Enlightenment. Concepts such as freedom, democracy, human rights, equality, and the rule of law structure the field and represent the only possible way for outsiders to gain membership. Ole Waever has thus contended that "Europe's 'Other' these years is Europe's own past" (2000, 279). Thomas Diez later built on this argument, maintaining that temporal othering has a self-reflexive character, as it does not represent another group as a threat but merely serves to construct the self (2004).

A clear line can indeed be drawn from the post–Second World War era to today's Europe. While the 1948 Brussels Treaty on collective defence and the 1949 Statute of the Council of Europe centre on the protection of human rights and the rule of law, restricting membership to those states that respect these values (Thomas 2006, 1193), the Constitutional Treaty characterizes Europe as a progressive "ethical project of civilization," based on the heritage of the European Enlightenment as the historical project of Christian culture (Callahan 2007). A direct relationship between the ethical and institutional basis of the European idea can be seen in the strong pursuit of rights that is encouraged by EU institutions, representing an important driving force of the enlargement process and a clear expression of EU identity constructions. This is why Karen Smith maintains that "respect for human rights is already felt to form part of the EU's international identity" (2001, 203). Visible expressions of this identity are the Court of Justice, the Commission, and the European Parliament. The Preamble of the Charter of Fundamental Rights and Freedoms, proclaimed at the Nice Summit on Institutional Reform and Enlargement in December 2000, spelled out the importance of the community values: "Conscious of its spiritual and moral heritage, the Union is founded on the indivisible, universal values of human dignity, freedom, equality and solidarity; it is based on the principles of democracy and the rule of law. It places the individual at the heart of its activities, by establishing the citizenship of the Union and by creating an area of freedom, security and justice" (qtd. in Fossum 2001, 19).

As Laclau (1996) has pointed out, a discourse can only generate a dominant interpretative framework if its "system of narration" operates as a surface of inscription for a wide variety of demands. This is especially true considering the diverse attitudes toward the idea of "Europe" among the peoples of the European Union. While, according to *Eurobarometer* polls, the economy and culture are the issues that most create a feeling of community among Europeans (European Commission 2007), and fields such as the common development of welfare states, legislation, religion, and geography fare comparatively low, even the impact of the two dominant factors is trifling, with only 27 per cent of Europeans pointing to economic and cultural issues as triggers for a collective identity. The success of collective identity representations is thus due to its abstract form. It does not necessarily have to be related to a specific substance, but has to come with some kind of positive ontic content, which in turn makes it possible to form more identifications. Understood in this way, "Europe" has to be conceptualized as a dynamic and contested discourse that takes place within the borders of an abstract but intangible system of recitation.

This system of recitation is framed by particular moral standards that have developed out of lessons drawn from history. The German government summarized the path toward membership in the EU as follows:

> The disappearance of the Iron Curtain in 1989/90 presented the countries of both eastern and western Europe with the challenge of completely redefining their relationship.... The enlargement of the EU fulfils the hope that the successful model of the EU, with its values of democracy, the rule of law, and the protection of human rights and minorities can be transferred to the countries of Central and Eastern Europe, thus ensuring lasting peace, freedom, security and political stability. (Auswärtiges Amt 2004)

With peace, freedom, security, and political stability representing the dominant connotations of the EU, Europeanization to a great extent resembles the hegemonic project put forward by Laclau and Mouffe, as it rests on the "diffusion of global prescriptions; templates and standards of universalistic rationality and validity" (Olsen 2002, 939). Once the process of accession negotiations has started, however, discussions of collective identity are expected to move from general concepts to more specific issues like market economy, institutional reform, and difference through exclusion. It is during this process that identity is likely to become contested.

Constructing the Other

Identity is status quo in that asserting one's own identity means asserting the identity of a particular other at the same time. Simultaneously, constructing a collective identity means the adoption of common values. While the EU has stabilized the identity of the self on the basis of general principles, these principles will have to be filled with substance in the actual accession negotiations with potential new members. Enlargement is a question of fit and misfit, and for the candidate country it means leaving a particular identity behind, as EU commissioner Olli Rehn makes clear with regards to Turkey in a 2004 speech before the European Parliament: "I can assure the Members of this House that the Commission remains committed to monitoring Turkey's compliance with the Copenhagen political criteria. These criteria, the fundamental values on which the European Union is based, are not subject to negotiation" (2004). As I pointed out in the quantitative analysis of the discourse, expressions like "Turkey needs to" and "we expect Turkey to" reflect this argument.[4]

Enlargement entails overcoming difference, while the terms of the rapprochement are unilaterally set by the EU. This, however, does not mean that the EU's identity remains unaffected by the ongoing interaction with the candidate country. As Daniel Thomas has shown in his historical analysis of European integration, "it was interactions with outsiders that drove political actors within the community to debate and then define what would distinguish 'us' from 'them'" (2006, 1191). Accordingly, Ian Manners and Richard Whitman (2003) have conceptualized the EU as a form of "difference engine" that continuously reconstructs the identity of the EU.

The accession negotiations with Turkey serve as a prime example to underline this argument, as that country has always triggered debate about whether Europe is a territorial, institutional, or cultural entity (Callahan 2005; McLaren 2007), and has led to different, at times contradictory, representations of self and other within the EU. Rather than being a product of Christian civilization, Turkey has a Muslim majority, and was the former centre of the Ottoman Empire. As well, Turkey's human rights record is seen as problematic from a European perspective. Although the European Union started negotiations with Turkey in 2005, within a year the EU froze negotiations in eight of thirty-five policy areas because Turkey declined to open its harbours to trade with Cyprus, who became an EU member in 2004. EU Commissioner Olli Rehn therefore habitually put pressure on Turkey by reminding Ankara that the EU would be "watching closely" to see how changes were implemented in Turkey (e.g., Rehn 2004, 2005a).

Discursive differences are at the centre of constructing Turkey as Europe's other, although direct hints at cultural assimilation are rarely stated in speeches by EU officials. References to culture are usually related to more specific problems, such as "fundamental freedoms and human rights, particularly on freedom of expression, women's rights, religious freedoms, trade union rights, cultural rights and the zero tolerance policy against torture and ill-treatment" (Rehn 2005b). In their speeches, EU officials generally do not hesitate to call Turkey a part of Europe. For instance, Commissioner Rehn states that "there is no doubt that Turkey is part of Europe and has been part of our European political project from the beginning" (2006a).

The cultural dimension is more apparent in statements made by EU members. It is this finding that leads Iver Neumann to conclude that "even though Turkey is a modern secular state, Europe still defines it in terms of Muslim other" (1999, 63). Traditionally, France displayed the greatest opposition to the project of Turkish EU membership, followed by Greece. French President Nicolas Sarkozy repeatedly said Turkey is in Asia Minor, not Europe, and has no place in the EU (AFP, 20 September 2007), while Greece declared Turkey "a threat" after Ankara's 1974 decision to invade and occupy Northern Cyprus (MOFAG 2008). It was only in 2007 that Greek Foreign Minister Dora Bakoyannis declared that "the relations of our countries have entered into a new period of dynamic development" (MOFAG 2007).

On the basis of implicitly generalizing Turkey as the other of European civilization, empty signifiers such as "Europe," "democracy," and "freedom" were filled with more specific substance after accession negotiations were initiated in 2005. The more precise character of the terms used from 2005 onward is inherent in the nature of the process: As a first step in the so-called screening process, the commission and Turkey analyzed in detail the laws and policies of the EU and compared them to existing legislation in Turkey (Rehn 2005a). According to subsequent progress reports, Turkey did too little to root out corruption, modernize its judiciary, reduce the power of the military, and increase freedom of expression (Commission of the European Communities 2006, 2007), which led Commissioner Rehn to conclude that "significant further efforts are required on fundamental freedoms and human rights, particularly on freedom of expression, women's rights, religious freedoms, trade union rights, cultural rights and the zero tolerance policy against torture and ill-treatment" (2005a). While the 2007 progress report stressed that the number of prosecutions of journalists, intellectuals, and human rights activists for expressing non-violent anti-government opinions was on the rise, and Turkey was found to be in breach of the European Convention on Human Rights in 330 cases, cultural difference was also highlighted by stressing Turkey's strategic importance as a "unique interface between the West and the Muslim world" (Commission of the European Communities 2007; Rehn 2006b).

Most significantly for the argument I have developed here, the process of filling empty signifiers with specific substance is not without political implications. Theoretically speaking, the illusion of the EU's universal homogeneity is permeated by particular meanings, and the chain of equivalences that the EU is trying to establish within its borders does not melt into a singular uniform mass. In the communicative struggle over giving Turkey a specific meaning, Britain, for example, has repeatedly backed Turkish membership in the EU (FCO 2008), emphasizing the open character of the union. To quote Denis MacShane, former British state minister for the EU, as a paradigmatic example: "Turkey is really part of Europe. I, for one, have no doubt about this. Turkey is a country with a rich culture and deep traditions. But this should be no more of a barrier to Turkey's entry to the EU than it is for Hungary or Poland or any other candidate. Part of the beauty of Europe is the fact that it is not boringly homogenous, but a mosaic of diversity" (MacShane 2004). Struggles over Turkey's specific meaning for the EU can be seen as a potential source of identity change within the EU. Prominent voices pointing at Turkey's geopolitical significance include Swedish foreign minister Carl Bildt, and former Italian foreign minister Massimo d'Alema (Bildt and d'Alema 2007), while Commissioner Rehn summarizes Turkey's importance for the EU: "As a result of its combined strategic, economic and population potential, Turkey can make a major contribution to regional and international stability. Europe needs a stable, democratic and prosperous Turkey which adopts and implements our values, our rule of law, our policies, our standards. It is in our own strategic interest" (2005a). The process of continued rapprochement between the EU and Turkey—over the declaration of Turkey as a candidate for membership in December 1999, the agreement to open entry talks with Turkey in December 2004, and the commencement of membership talks in October 2005—can be grasped only by employing a process-based concept of identity. It also shows the bounded nature of the EU as a political community, which leads Christiansen, Petito, and Tonra to portray the actual borders of the EU as "fuzzy ... because they produce interfaces or intermediate spaces between the inside and the outside of the polity" (2000, 392). Antagonism rests on heterogeneity, and "without heterogeneity, there would be no antagonism either" (Laclau 2005, 149). Because there is significant heterogeneity in any society, a "community" such as the EU has to be continuously reinvented. Empty signifiers hence appear in a new light, as they serve the task of combining heterogeneous demands in an equivalent chain. The more specific the content of empty signifiers becomes, the more likely they are to be contested. While Turkey's accession to the EU is unlikely to become imminent until 2021 or even later, the process has gained momentum. Since geographic borders are unclear, cultures are diverse, and the polity of the EU is multi-layered, it is perhaps difficult to imagine the materialization of a single pan-European identity excluding Turkey in the long run. During Slovenia's EU presidency in the first half of 2008, Dimitrij Rupel, Slovenia's foreign minister, therefore concluded that, "there is no doubt in my mind that Turkey will be a member of the EU sooner or later" (qtd. in IHT, 6 May 2008).

Even though a number of setbacks have occurred over the years—with the EU and Germany criticizing Ankara's suppression of mass demonstrations in the summer of 2013 as one of the flashpoints ("Westerwelle bestellt," 2013)—Turkey's accession has become one of the fundamental identity questions facing the European Union after 2005. A politic of intermittently and temporarily distancing itself from Turkey can be understood as a symbol of the EU's ongoing search for identity. Through repetitive acts of identification with what one perceives to be the true self, the illusion of a stable identity can be strengthened. Yet, the EU's identity remains subject to antagonism and cannot escape the illusionary quality of a homogeneous self. This illusion will set in motion a permanent struggle for closure and search for identity through identification.

Conclusion

The analysis conducted here supports the argument that identity is an unfinished enterprise, relying on constant struggles over meaning. While some authors maintain that it is uncertain whether the constitution of a European demos with a sustainable collective identity is possible at all (e.g., Fuchs and Klingemann 2002), I identify a common denominator in the discourse about different self-understandings. The self is more straightforwardly constructed than the other, but identity becomes increasingly contested when empty signifiers are filled with more specific meanings. Against this background, the shape of the EU can, in Manners and Whitman's sense, be understood to represent "an extreme version of a polity with flexible territoriality" (2003, 385). The emptiness of European identity becomes unstable as soon as it is filled with a particular substance. In the process of the union's enlargement, difference continues to exist within the EU. At this point, it is far from clear whose views will prevail. The discourse over Turkish integration into the EU has not gained a hegemonic character in Laclau and Mouffe's sense. Turkey cannot be regarded as truly existing on the outside, an excluded element that the EU expels in order to constitute itself. If it were a real outsider, all other elements standing in opposition to Turkey would be equivalent to one another in their negation of the excluded identity. Conversely, an empty signifier like "Europe" takes a stable frontier for granted; the more specific its content becomes, the higher the possibility of collapsing frontiers. Empty signifiers therefore do not express any positive content, but symbolize a fullness that is conspicuously absent. The failure to fill the empty space of identity, the breakdown of the hegemonic constellation, provides the basis for the fullness of a community as a future promise: identity-building, in consequence, resembles an open-ended hegemonic struggle.

Only if the equivalent chain is emptied from all differential relations can the totality of the system logically be achieved. As this is not the case in the reality of the EU, it is impossible to say which particular standpoint will become "universalized" in the end. The political is structured in terms of the *logic of contingency*, which rejects the assumption that the social is organized according to general laws that hold true in any case. Politics exists because structures are never complete; if a structure was fully closed, politics would have found its final designation. The impossibility of closure entails an impossibility of society, calling into question the very foundation of classical structuralism. In arguing that neither a fully constituted self, nor a complete other is impossible, the common post-structuralist argument that ultimate meanings are unattainable is reiterated here.

As the cases of France's opposition against Turkish EU membership and Britain's support for accession show, there always remains a part of society that resists symbolic integration. Germany also demonstrates similar attitudes. Society is characterized by a degree of complexity that defies homogenization. Every political process will, in consequence, be threatened by heterogeneity, which is not purely "outside" but part of a complex game of social interaction. Some speakers, be they EU officials or national representatives, supply the discourse with meaning. It is the nature of the communicative process that decides whether others will identify with these meanings. Politics has to be understood as contestation and interrogation between competing social logics. Democracy is about the competition of different groups for universal representation. In a pure binary opposition, the border between inside and outside would be immobile and the social would lose its undecidable character. As I have shown in this chapter, the reality of EU enlargement looks quite different.

A short word on alternative accounts of politics is in order: The view offered here, which is inspired by Laclau and Mouffe's work, stands in stark contrast to Jürgen Habermas' model of "deliberative democracy," most elegantly developed in his two-volume *Theory of Communicative Action* (*Theorie des Kommunikativen Handelns*; 1995a, 1995b). While both approaches claim to present a particular version of "radical democracy," avoid reducing the political process to the expression of exogenously formed interests and identities, and highlight their constitution and reconstitution through "debate in the public sphere," Laclau and Mouffe—*contra* Habermas—maintain that any final reconciliation, in terms of complete rationality, is unattainable. As Laclau writes, universality must not be misunderstood as the "expression of a necessary requirement of reason" (1996, 103–4). Consequently, Laclau, in company with Judith Butler and Slavoj Žižek, distances himself from Habermas' conjecture of universality as a premise of the speech act and his assumption that politics is constituted by rational actors (2000, 3). Any universality remains contaminated by particularity and is thus only "relative."

In that context, it is, however, necessary to note that Laclau's theory also rests on several simplifying assumptions. Most significantly, the logics of equivalence and difference at times take a stable antagonistic frontier within society for granted. My brief analysis of EU–Turkish relations in this chapter has shown that this antagonistic frontier does not exist in reality. Laclau is well aware of this obvious shortcoming, as he starts to discuss the notion of *heterogeneity* more broadly in his later work to dispose of the static assertion of a binary opposition (e.g., Laclau 2005). It is on the concept of heterogeneity that more research in IR has to be done.

To conclude, in a discourse as it is defined here, any teleological drive of the system remains elusive. While Wendt sees a world state as "inevitable" but confesses that "the speed with which this one will be realized is historically contingent" (2003, 491), I dispute an inherent finalistic logic of EU integration. Identity change is a constantly working mechanism deeply ingrained in any society, as no identity is closed in itself but is submitted to continuous displacements.

Notes

1 Laclau interprets the universal and the particular as "tools in the language games that shape contemporary politics" (1996, 48). For a critical discussion of this approach, see the section "Limits and Critique."

2 For a discussion of the merits of Atlas.ti in qualitative research and the question of how software of this kind can be made compatible with the radical constructivist, linguistic, or even post-structuralist paradigms of interpretation, see Konopásek 2008.

3 The Luxembourg-based CVCE aims at gathering and disseminating information on the European integration process. It provides digital libraries on the work of the European Union. See the website at http://www.ena.lu.

4 To quote just one example of a speech by Commissioner Rehn: "Now we expect Turkey to honour its commitments; to begin with, as mentioned in the Accession Partnership, Turkey must ensure the implementation of commitments undertaken under the Association Agreement, including the Customs union" (Rehn 2005b).

References

Andersen, Niels Åkerstrøm. 2003. *Discursive Analytical Strategies. Understanding Foucault, Koselleck, Laclau, Luhmann*. Bristol: Policy Press.

Auswärtiges Amt. 2004. *The Enlargement of the European Union*. Accessed March 10, 2006. http://www.auswaertiges-amt.de/www/en/eu_politik/vertiefung/erweiterung_html#3.

Bildt, Carl, and Massimo d'Alema. 2007. "It's time for a fresh effort," *New York Times,* August 31.

Brown, Chris. 2001. "Borders and Identity in International Political Theory." In *Identity, Borders, Orders: Rethinking International Relations Theory,* edited by Mathias Albert, David Jacobson, and Yosef Lapid, 117–36. Minneapolis: University of Minnesota Press.

Butler, Judith, Ernesto Laclau, and Slavoj Žižek. 2000. *Contingency, Hegemony, Universality. Contemporary Dialogues on the Left*. London: Verso.

Callahan, William. 2007. "Comparative Regionalism: The Logic of Governance in Europe and East Asia." In *The International Politics of EU–China Relations,* edited by David Kerr and Fei Liu, 231–58. Oxford: Oxford University Press.

Campbell, David. 1998. *Writing Security: United States Foreign Policy and the Politics of Identity,* 2nd ed. Minneapolis: University of Minnesota Press.

Christiansen, Thomas, Fabio Petito, and Ben Tonra. 2000. "Fuzzy Politics Around Fuzzy Borders: The European Union's 'Near Abroad.'" *Cooperation and Conflict* 35 (4): 389–415.

Commission of the European Communities. 2006. *Turkey 2007 Progress Report*. Brussels, 8.11.2006, SEC(2006) 1390.

Commission of the European Communities. 2007. *Turkey 2007 Progress Report*. Brussels, 6.11.2007, SEC(2007) 1436.

Critchley, Simon, and Oliver Marchart. 2004. "Introduction." *Laclau: A Critical Reader,* edited by Simon Critchley and Oliver Marchart, 1–13. London: Routledge.

Currie, Mark. 2004. *Difference*. London: Routledge.

Diez, Thomas. 1999. "Speaking 'Europe': The Politics of Integration Discourse." *Journal of European Public Policy* 6 (4): 598–619.

————. 2004. "Europe's Others and the Return of Geopolitics." *Cambridge Review of International Affairs* 17 (2): 319–35.

Drulák, Petr. 2006. "Motion, Container and Equilibrium: Metaphors in the Discourse about European Integration." *European Journal of International Relations* 12 (4): 499–531.

European Commission. 2007. *Eurobarometer 67: Public Opinion in the European Union.* Accessed 5 April, 2008. http://ec.europa.eu/public_opinion/archives/eb/eb67/eb67_en.pdf

European Union. 2004. *Treaty Establishing a Constitution for Europe.* CIG 87/2/04 REV 2. Brussels: European Union.

FCO (Foreign & Commonwealth Office). 2008. *Turkey: International Relations.* Accessed May 20, 2008. http://www.fco.gov.uk/en/about-the-fco/country -profiles/europe/turkey?profile=intRelations&pg=4

Fuchs, Dieter, and Hans-Dieter Klingemann. 2002. "Eastward Enlargement of the European Union and the Identity of Europe." In *The Enlarged European Union. Diversity and Adaption,* edited by Peter Mair and Jan Zielonka, 19–54. London: Frank Cass.

Habermas, Jürgen. 1995a. *Theorie des kommunikativen Handelns. Bd. 1: Handlungsrationalität und gesellschaftliche Rationalisierung.* Frankfurt A.M.: Suhrkamp Taschenbuch.

————. 1995b. *Theorie des kommunikativen Handelns. Bd. 2: Zur Kritik der funktionalistischen Vernunft.* Frankfurt A.M.: Suhrkamp Taschenbuch.

Hansen, Lene. 2006. *Security as Practice: Discourse Analysis and the Bosnian War.* London: Routledge.

Konopásek, Zdeněk. 2008. "Making Thinking Visible with Atlas.ti: Computer Assisted Qualitative Analysis as Textual Practices." *Forum Qualitative Social Research* 9 (2): http://www.qualitative-research.net/fqs-texte/2-08/08-2 -12-e.htm.

Kratochwil, Friedrich. 2006. "History, Action and Identity: Revisiting the 'Second' Great Debate and Assessing its Importance for Social Theory." *European Journal of International Relations* 12 (1): 5–29.

Laclau, Ernesto. 1990. *New Reflections of the Revolution of Our Time.* London: Verso.

————. 1996. *Emancipation(s).* London: Verso.

————. 2000. "Identity and Hegemony: The Role of Universality in the Constitution of Political Logics." In Butler, Laclau, and Slavoy, 2000, 44–89.

————. 2005. *On Populist Reason.* London: Verso.

Laclau, Ernesto, and Chantal Mouffe. 1985. *Hegemony and Socialist Strategy. Towards a Radical Democratic Politics.* London: Verso.

Larsen, Henrik. 1997. *Foreign Policy and Discourse Analysis: France, Britain and Europe*. London/New York: Routledge.

MacShane, Denis. 2004. "Britain and Turkey Together in Europe." Address at the University of Izmir, January 14, 2004. Accessed April 4, 2008. http://www.ena.lu/

Manners, Ian, and Richard G. Whitman. 2003. "The 'difference Engine': Constructing and Representing the International Identity of the European Union." *Journal of European Public Policy* 10 (3): 380–404.

McLaren, Lauren. 2007. "Explaining Opposition to Turkish Membership of the EU." *European Union Politics* 8 (2): 251–78.

MOFAG (Ministry of Foreign Affairs, Greece). 2007. Statements of Foreign Minister Ms. Dora Bakoyannis and her Turkish counterpart, Mr. Ali Babacan following their meeting. Accessed May 14, 2008. http://www.mfa.gr/www.mfa.gr/Articles/en-US/041207_McC1101.htm

MOFAG (Ministry of Foreign Affairs, Greece). 2008. *Turkey: Historical Background*. Accessed May 14. http://www.mfa.gr/www.mfa.gr/en-US/Policy/Geographic+Regions/South-Eastern+Europe/Turkey/History

Nabers, Dirk .2006. "Culture and Collective Action: Japan, Germany and the United States after 11 September 2001." *Cooperation and Conflict* 3: 305–26.

———. 2009. "Filling the Void of Meaning: Identity Construction in US Foreign Policy after September 11, 2001." *Foreign Policy Analysis* 2: 191–214.

Neumann, Iver B. 1999. *Uses of the Other: "The East" in European Identity Formation*. Minneapolis: University of Minnesota Press.

Olsen, Johan P. 2002. "The Many Faces of Europeanization." *Journal of Common Market Studies* 40 (5): 921–52.

———. 2005. "Unity and Diversity—European Style." ARENA *Working Papers* (WP 24/05). Accessed March 10, 2006. http://www.arena.uio.no

Rehn, Olli. 2004. "EU and Turkey on the Threshold of a New Phase." Speech presented at the European Parliament Plenary Session, Turkey debate, Strasbourg, 13 December (Speech 04/538).

———. 2005a. "Accession Negotiations with Turkey: Fulfilling the Criteria." Speech presented at the European Economic and Social Committee EU–Turkey JCC, Brussels, November 28 (Speech 05/733).

———. 2005b. "Accession Negotiations with Turkey: The Time for Celebration Is Over, Now Comes the Time for Delivery." Speech presented at the EU–Turkey Joint Parliamentary Committee, Brussels, November 23 (Speech 05/716).

———. 2006a. "Turkey's Accession Process to the EU." Lecture presented at Helsinki University, Helsinki, November 27 (Speech 06/747).

———. 2006b. "Enlargement Package 2006." Speech presented at the European Parliament, Foreign Affairs Committee, Brussels, November 21 (Speech 06/727).

Rittberger, Berthold, and Frank Schimmelfennig. 2006. "Explaining the Constitutionalization of the European Union." *Journal of European Public Policy* 13 (8): 1148–167.

Rosamond, Ben. 2000. *Theories of European Integration.* Basingstoke: Macmillan.

Schmitter, Philippe. 1996. "Examining the Present Euro-Polity with the Help of Past Theories." In *Governance in the European Union*, edited by Gary Marks et al., 121–50. London: Sage.

Smith, Anna Marie. 1998. *Laclau and Mouffe. The Radical Democratic Imaginary.* London: Routledge.

Smith, Karen. 2001. "The EU, Human Rights and Relations with Third Countries: 'Foreign Policy' with an Ethical Dimension." In *Ethics and Foreign Policy*, edited by Karen Smith and Margot Light, 185–203. Cambridge: Cambridge University Press.

Teubert, Wolfgang, and Anna Čermáková. 2004. *Corpus Linguistics. A Short Introduction.* London: Continuum.

Thomas, Daniel C. 2006. "Constitutionalization through Enlargement: The Contested Origins of the EU's Democratic Identity." *Journal of European Public Policy* 13 (8): 1190–1210.

"Turkey does not belong in Europe: Sarkozy." 2007. AFP, September 20.

Waever, Ole. 2000. "The EU as a Security Actor: Reflections from a Pessimistic Constructivist on Post-sovereign Security Orders." In *International Relations Theory and the Politics of European Integration: Power, Security and Community*, edited by Morten Kelstrup and Michael Williams, 250–94. London: Routledge.

Wendt, Alexander. 2003. "Why a World State Is Inevitable: Teleology and the Logic of Anarchy." *European Journal of International Relations* 9 (4): 491–542.

"Westerwelle bestellt türkischen Botschafter ein." 2013. *Der Tagesspiegel*, June 21.

Zielonka, Jan. 2000. "Enlargement and the Finality of European Integration." *What Kind of Constitution for What Kind of Polity? Responses to Joschka Fischer*, edited by Christian Joerges, Yves Meny, and Joseph Weiler, 151–62. San Domenico de Fiesole: European University Institute.

Section II
Memory and Identity in Europe

Diversity in the Homeland: The Changing Meaning of Transylvania in Mihail Sebastian's *The Accident*

Stephen Henighan

The Romanian writer Mihail Sebastian (1907–1945) was one of the most accomplished Central European novelists, playwrights, and literary critics of the 1930s, and his work continues to be widely read today. Although only his wartime diary was available in English until recently, his novels and plays remain in print in the major Western European and some Central and Eastern European languages, as well as in Chinese, Hindi, Bengali, and Hebrew. Here I examine Sebastian's last novel, *Accidentul* (1940), which I translated into English as *The Accident* (2011). The publication of this translation marks the first appearance of Sebastian's fiction in English.

Sebastian was born Iosif Hechter in Brăila, a town on the Danube in southeastern Romania. His parents were assimilated, non-religious Jews. At the time of Sebastian's birth, Romanian had been the only language spoken in the Hechter home for at least two generations. Like other young Romanian intellectuals who became adults in the 1920s, Sebastian felt challenged by the changes in Romania's borders and ethnic composition that resulted from the Treaties of Versailles and Trianon at the end of the First World War.

In 1920, the Treaty of Trianon had ceded Transylvania to Romania. This culturally rich region of mountains and hilltop towns, inhabited by a Romanian majority and large Hungarian and German minorities, had been governed by Austria-Hungary until the Austro-Hungarian Empire's dissolution during the First World War. The addition of Transylvania in the northwest to Wallachia and Moldavia, the two regions whose union in 1859 had created modern Romania, was matched in the south by the acquisition of the former Bulgarian territory of northern Dobrogea, and in the east by the recovery of the largely Romanian-speaking regions of Bessarabia and Bukovina from the defunct Russian and Austro-Hungarian empires respectively. These gains resulted in a Romania that had more than twice the territory and population of the pre-1914 nation. Between 1920 and 1939, for the first—and, as it would turn out, only—time in their history, nearly all Romanians were together in one country. This unexpected territorial good fortune created a cultural ebullience that inspired a vigorous search for national self-definition. However, 28 per cent of the expanded nation consisted of ethnic minorities, as opposed to 10 per cent before the First World War (King 1998, 38). The 1923 constitution, which had guaranteed equal rights for these minorities, came under ferocious attack from the far right in the 1930s. Sebastian's intellectual and creative growth is inseparable from the debates stirred up by this atmosphere.

Like his close friends the novelist and academic Mircea Eliade (1907–1986), the philosopher Emil Cioran (1911–1995), and the novelist Camil Petrescu (1894–1957), Sebastian wrote for the newspaper *Cuvântul* (*The Word*), edited by the charismatic mathematician and philosopher Nae Ionescu (1890–1940), who was a mentor and father figure to all of these young men. Under Ionescu's tutelage, Sebastian learned to argue against minority rights and in favour of an integrated *sufletul românesc* or "national soul" rooted in a mystical, Christian Orthodox conception of Romanianness and the country's landscape and history. As a young man, Sebastian defined the Romanian soul as the meeting point of the opposing currents of "fizzy Latinity" and "Slavic Christian melancholy" (Dragot 2007, 280). Like much of the country's Jewish bourgeoisie, he included himself within the circle of Romanian nationalism; where Roma, Hungarians, Germans, Ukrainians, and Bulgarians were minorities, he was not. Sebastian asserted his right to be considered pure and simply a Romanian, devoid of ethnic tags. While embroiled in a literary scandal over his Jewishness, he recounted to a fellow writer in a letter written in 1936: "my maternal great-grandfather was a banker in Bucharest in 1802. He contributed money to help the leaders of the 1848 revolution. Both of my parents, born in this country (my father in 1868), speak only Romanian and brought me up as a Romanian.... My childhood, like that of everyone of my generation, unfurled beneath the sign of care and love for my country" (Cornea 2007).

As the 1930s advanced, the Iron Guard nationalist movement with which Nae Ionescu was allied adopted an increasingly anti-Semitic stance, strongly influenced by Adolf Hitler's Germany. In spite of being an assimilated, non-religious Jew who was often uncomfortable in a Jewish social context, Sebastian (2000, 263) found himself denounced by his closest friends. In the late 1930s, anti-Semitic legislation barred him from practising law, publishing in the newspapers, writing for the stage, or continuing to occupy his desirable downtown apartment. Having been deprived of both his professional income and his residence, he was forced to move into a slum with his mother. Until 1944, they lived in extreme poverty and fear of the pogroms that resulted in the murder of nearly 500,000 Romanian Jews during the Second World War.

The Accident, Sebastian's fourth and last novel, continues to be widely read in Romania today and is available in translation in accessible paperback editions in German, French, Spanish, and Italian. *The Accident* is often read as the study of an intellectual who has lost touch with his emotions. The family background of the protagonist, Paul, is never elucidated. A hint that he might be of Jewish ancestry occurs in Chapter 11, when a business acquaintance encountered in a nightclub invites him to come to a party at "Zissu's place" (Sebastian 2011, 31), an apparent reference to the Romanian Zionist leader Abraham Zissu. Paul declines, a decision that seems to echo Sebastian's own preference for avoiding ethnic enclaves. Paul's obsession with the young painter Ann, which draws him into an exhausting journey across Europe in search of her—an act that today we might see as an extravagant form of stalking—is inseparable from the repeated lift of his shoulders that signals his indifference. Paul's emotional vacancy feeds his obsession.

Even though *The Accident* is the product of the years of Sebastian's estrangement from the friends of his youth, the solution to Paul's conundrum is one of which few contributors to *Cuvântul* would disapprove: a trip to the mountains of Transylvania. The novel originated, however, in a vision of the second female protagonist's accident in the snowy Bucharest streets—an eerie presentiment of the author's own death in 1945, when he was run down by a truck at the age of thirty-seven while hurrying to the new Workers' University to give a lecture on Honoré de Balzac. Sebastian spent his twenty-ninth birthday, October 18, 1936, in the company of Mircea Eliade. As he went out to buy champagne, "I suddenly had the picture of a road accident into which I should have liked to be drawn. I could see the first chapter with a wealth of detail so pressing that I thought that, when I got home, I would be unable to do anything other than write, as if under the command of an imperious voice" (Sebastian 2000, 94–95).

The novel that began in inspiration became an ordeal to finish. In September 1937, during a trip to Paris, Sebastian lost (or was robbed of) the suitcase that contained the only copy of his manuscript. He had to rewrite the first five chapters from memory. Given the stresses he faced as the pillars of his life as a lawyer, novelist, playwright, and journalist were demolished, it is a testament to his determination that he completed the book. Sebastian wrote much of *The Accident* in resort towns in the mountains where he retreated to take skiing lessons. He was able to afford these trips due to his press card, which granted him free travel on the nation's railways, and which he retained until 1940, after he had lost some of his other social privileges and sources of income. It is curious to think that as the clamps were being tightened on the country's Jewish community, the sunburned author was swooping down mountain slopes, then returning to his cabin to compose his romantic love story. But it may have been this separation from the repercussions of the war that spared his creativity. By the time he was writing the novel's final pages in January 1940, Sebastian was labouring under a military call-up notice (he did military service intermittently during these years) and was aware that "what is happening to the Jews now in Hitler-occupied Poland is beyond all known horrors" (2000, 267).

The Accident combines interior monologues that display in a concise way the influence of Marcel Proust—on whom Sebastian had published a book at the age of twenty-five—with the crisp, telling dialogue that he was mastering in his plays. The book's careful crafting is evident in embedded details whose relevance becomes clear many pages after they appear. In the Transylvanian scenes another pivotal element emerges: the protagonist's lyrical immersion in nature.

It is the region's natural wonders that cure Paul of the over-intellectualized "sickness" of the city. At the conclusion of his stay in the mountains, Paul expresses his incredulity that people who have been in the mountains "still believe in the things they left down below." To which Nora replies, "he who has been in the mountains is a free man" (Sebastian 2011, 240).

This theme is compatible with much European nationalist thinking of the interwar years, in which the nation's natural attributes promise an "authentic essence" that acts as an antidote to the ills of a corrupt or decadent civilization. The two female protagonists embody this pattern. While neither is native to the capital, Ann, the unscrupulously ambitious painter who tips Paul into obsession, has become a creature of the city, a prisoner of her ambition who subordinates her body to the demands of her career. Her identity as "this blond girl in boyish slacks" (2011, 72–73) underlines her estrangement from her femininity.

By contrast, Nora, whom Paul rescues from the tram accident in the snow, and who invites him to go skiing with her in Transylvania, evokes the motherland, the nation in female form. She is a teacher of French, the language that Romanian intellectuals of the day saw as the bridge to their culture's ancestral home in the Latin West. From the beginning, in spite of the fact that she has just suffered a fall from a tram, she cares for Paul in a way that is conspicuously maternal. Although sexually emancipated, Nora respects the emotional seriousness of her relationships with men, an attitude that contrasts with that of Ann, who sleeps her way to the top. This difference crystallizes in Nora's discomfort at leaving her initial encounter with Paul as a one-night stand. She is older than he, while Ann is younger. Where Ann's figure is boyish, Nora's lines are reassuringly solid. Observing her standing naked in their room in a mountain cabin, Paul notes that "her body was strong, with a slight heaviness in its long, firm lines. *Nothing adolescent here*, Paul thought, watching her" (2011, 176). The reference to adolescence may be read as a reflection on "boyish" Ann and the immature urban world she represents. Although she is famous, Ann's surname is never revealed; by contrast, Nora's last name, Munteanu, contains the word *munte*, "mountain." Her mother lives in Cernăuți, the birthplace of Mihai Eminescu, Romania's national poet. Cernăuți—which today is Cernivitsi, Ukraine—was located in Bukovina, whose reunion with the motherland in 1919 was seen by many Romanians as central to the fulfillment of the country's destiny.

If, in spite of the heavy thematic cargo they bear, these women emerge as vital, persuasive characters, it is because they were nourished by two of the most important women in Mihail Sebastian's life. Ann was almost certainly inspired by Leni Caler, an actress revered in her day with whom Sebastian had an on-again/off-again affair that lasted for almost a decade. (When *The Accident* was published, Caler's husband made an emotional phone call to tell Sebastian that he knew who Ann was based on.) Nora, on the other hand, is sometimes seen as a portrait of the painter Zoe Ricci, a supposition that can be only partly correct because Sebastian had been writing *The Accident* for over a year when he met Ricci and, six months later, became romantically involved with her. The physically slight, Italian-descended Ricci was not a maternal figure like Nora, yet Sebastian himself linked her with his character. He noted of Ricci's telling him during a romantic moment how nice it was not to be alone: "That's something Nora could have said. She actually says it, in a way. So here is life, a year later, repeating a situation in a novel" (Sebastian 2000, 161). On February 21, 1940, a few days after the novel's publication, Sebastian, finding that he, Leni Caler, and Zoe Ricci were all in the Transylvanian capital of Braşov on the same day, wrote, "as in the final chapter of *Accidentul*" (2000, 274). Nora, more of a composite than Ann—who, as the Romanian critic Paul Cernat (2007) points out, is given Zoe's profession—is a character to whom Ricci contributed; but she was not inspired by her.

The Transylvanian setting acquires layered meanings. Paul and Nora's skiing holiday may begin as a recuperative expedition into the mountains that harbour the vigorous natural world exalted by partisans of the "Romanian soul." Yet in many respects, Transylvania incarnated the contradictions that plagued Romanan nationalist discourse as the Second World War approached. Having joined Romania only in 1920, the region retained its Austro-Hungarian culture; it was home to large Hungarian and German minorities. Yet paradoxically, Transylvania had also been the point of origin of the early-nineteenth-century Transylvanian Latinist Movement that reaffirmed Romania's ties with Western Europe by converting written Romanian from the Cyrillic to the Latin alphabet. On December 1, 1918, the boundaries of modern Romania were consolidated at a massive nationalist rally held in the Transylvanian city of Alba Iulia.

After getting lost in a snowstorm during their first night in the mountains, Paul and Nora take refuge in the cabin of a Transylvanian Saxon family whose destiny provides an ironic counterpoint to that of the three characters in the central love triangle. By introducing the Grodeck family into the novel, Sebastian balances the claims of ancestral belonging with those of ethnic diversity. This tension transposes to the Transylvanian setting the clash in the author's own psyche as a nationalist whose Jewishness became an ever more unavoidable fact of his identity as the Second World War approached. The Grodecks, although fluent in Romanian, speak to one another in Saxon dialect and call local geographical features by their German names, a habit that invests the Transylvanian landscape with a dual lexicon. Allusions by the narrator reinforce this duality, for example, in Chapter XIV, where the region is referred to as "*cele şapte sate*" (Sebastian 1974, 320)—"all the seven towns"—a Romanian-language allusion to *Siebenburgen*, or "seven towns," Transylvania's original name in German. The cabin where Paul and Nora reside during their stay in the mountains is the home of artistic twenty-year-old Gunther, who suffers from a congenital heart defect, his dog Faffner, and his guardian Hagen, a dark, gloomy figure whose affair with Gunther's mother precipitated the breakup of his parents' marriage. As Gunther's father reveals on a visit to the cabin, Hagen's real name is the decidedly unromantic Klaus Schmidt, yet all the other characters refer to him by the sobriquet of the most destructive figure in Richard Wagner's *Ring Cycle*. The use of names from Wagner's trilogy appears to be more a homage to Teutonic culture than an allegory of the threat represented by Nazi Germany. The most appealing portrait is that of the dog, Faffner, who protects his master, Gunther, just as the Wagernian figure of nearly the same name—the giant Fafner, who transforms himself into a dragon—guards the treasure stolen from the gods. Yet the characters of the human figures bear only tangential resemblances to those of their Wagnerian prototypes. In the opera, Hagen, the son of a god and a human woman, is a "coldly calculating villain, consumed with envy and hate. He knows exactly what he wants and he will do whatever it takes to achieve it" (Lewsey 1997, 93). In Sebastian's novel, Hagen is a forbidding figure, defined by his intuitive accord with the flora and fauna of the mountains (he celebrates the New Year by bringing a live bear cub into the cabin). In the end, however, like the mountains, he shields young Gunther's artistic sensibility from the pressures of his family, particularly his father, Old Grodeck, who travels to the cabin to try to persuade Gunther to return to civilization and join the family logging business. In the *Ring Cycle,* Gunther is Hagen's half-brother rather than his stepson; in spite of being a king, he is "the most pathetic and unattractive" (Lewsey 1997, 84) character in the trilogy. He seeks social propriety before all else, in direct opposition to Sebastian's Gunther, who, although weak and arguably even "pathetic," flees and fears respectable society, particularly the powerful Grodeck clan, and longs to devote himself to art. As the novel progresses, the threat embodied by the rough-hewn Hagen dwindles: like the Transylvanian mountain landscape he represents, and that is instrumental in Paul's psychological cure, he becomes an ever more comforting presence.

The coexistence of the Grodecks, particularly the daunting Hagen, with the Transylvanian mountains creates dramatic tensions that express the conflict between Sebastian's nationalist intellectual roots and his awareness of belonging to an ethnic minority. Closely identified with classical music, the manifestation of German culture that Sebastian adored, Gunther Grodeck rescues Teutonic civilization from the grim images of Hitler's Germany that appear during Paul's train odyssey across Europe. Even though the portrait is ultimately tragic—Gunther suffers from an incurable disease—it establishes the positive attributes of German culture; at the same time, the Grodecks become a trope for the presence of minority groups within the most traditional precincts of Romanian life. Transylvania appears as a zone of multiplicity and mutual enrichment. The love triangle of Gunther's mother, father, and Hagen mirrors that of Paul, Ann, and Nora: in each, the unhealthy original couple is pried apart by a vigorous individual identified with the mountains. While Gunther and Hagen inhabit opposite extremes of cosseted sensitivity and feral toughness, Nora balances civilization with nature; she transmits this lesson to Paul. In the final chapters, the two triangles nearly mesh as romantic tensions develop between Gunther and Nora. The novel does not abandon the rhetorical glorification of the mountains: they dominate the final chapters, and confirm Paul's cure from his malaise. But the chauvinistic overtones, including the Wagnerian allusions, are reconciled—in part by the recasting of figures with Wagnerian names in less menacing roles—with a panorama that seems to make a desperate, almost paradoxical assertion that "national essence" and ethnic diversity *are* mutually compatible. In the scene in Chapter xv where Nora parades at the edge of the ski run with Gunther on her left and Paul on her right, she is not only reacquainting two neurotic intellectuals with nature; she is also incarnating the Romanian motherland's capacity to harmonize the country's disparate ethnic groups.

The novel's final scenes, set in Braşov, include references to Transylvania's largest minority, the Hungarians (who at this time numbered about 1.4 million in the region, compared to about 500,000 Germans [Cadzow et al. 1983, 305]). A headline in untranslated Hungarian, a language that most Romanians cannot read, both makes clear and conceals Sebastian's ultimate pessimism: *Létrejött Rómában a megegyezés!* Seeing the headline, Paul thinks "that extraordinary events might have taken place in the world during the two weeks he had spent in the mountains, and that the headline, printed in large letters, might be announcing a crucial event that would change the fate of mankind" (Sebastian 2011, 241). Once he finds newspapers he can read, Paul decides that he is mistaken: "nothing's happened. Truly nothing" (2011, 242). In fact, it is here that he makes an error. The Hungarian headline translates as "An Agreement Was Reached in Rome!" The agreement announced by the headline, reached on January 7, 1935, was the Treaty of Rome, in which the government of France made its peace with Benito Mussolini's Italy by conceding territory to Italy in Somalia and Libya, staging an economic retreat from Ethiopia, and pledging to consult with Italy before announcing a policy on Austrian independence or German rearmament (Duroselle 2004, 94–95). This capitulation of the country that incarnated Western civilization for educated Romanians of Sebastian's generation to the depredations of Fascism undermines the resolution made by Paul and Nora at the novel's close "not to let ourselves be defeated again" (2011, 243). They begin their new life unaware that the process that will lead to Europe's destruction is already underway. Sebastian's decision to insert this dark omen into the novel's conclusion, yet make it invisible to most readers, is typical of the double-edged vision he conveyed with such delicacy and humanity.

Much of the imaginative originality of *The Accident* springs from the author's attempt to hew from the ruins of the nationalist discourses of the 1930s a creative space capable of reconciling the idea of national essence with ethnic diversity, and pride in specificity with the absorption of minority experience. By creating a sympathetic German family precisely in response to the German-influenced forces that had ostracized him from the intellectual community which had been his lifelong home, and by domesticating the intimidating figure of Hagen, who embodies the mythological avatars of Nazism, Sebastian also tamed the advancing threat in imaginative form. The Romanian nation emerges triumphant from *The Accident*, capable of sustaining its cultural authenticity by recasting that authenticity in a more multifarious form. Yet as the newspaper headline at the novel's conclusion—ironically presented in one of Transylvania's minority languages—warns, in the world beyond the mountains, minorities remain marginalized and have nowhere to hide from the approaching destruction of the Second World War, which is destined to demolish the illusion that nationalism and minorities' rights can coexist and complement each other. "Do you think that skiing can save a person?" Paul asks Nora in the novel's final scene. "Can it change his life?" (Sebastian 2011, 243). The conclusion announces the answer to this question as an affirmative Yes, while the details and structure of the novel insinuate that, in fact, the answer is No.

Note

The author thanks Mária Palla for help with Hungarian and Paola Mayer for encouragement and advice on Wagnerian references.

References

Cadzow, John F., Andrew Ludanyi, and Louis J. Elteto, eds. 1983. *Transylvania. The Roots of Ethnic Conflict.* Kent, OH: Kent State University Press.

Cernat, Paul. 2007. "Intre somaţiile Istoriei şi utopia Vacanţei." *Observator Cultural* 393 (Octombrie). Accessed September 25, 2010. www.observatorcultural.ro/ Intre-somatiile-Istoriei-si-utopia-Vacantei*articleID_18472-articles_details.html.

Cornea, Paul. 2007. "Mihail Sebastian și problemă identitară in *De două mii de ani.*" *Observator Cultural* 399 (Noiembre). Accessed 24 September 2010. www .observatorcultural.ro/Mihail-Sebastian-si-problema-identitara-in-De-doua -mii-de-ani*articleID_18764-articles_details.html.

Dragot, Emanuela. 2009. "Review of Mihail Sebastian, *Ce vârsta dați acestor texte?...* (București: Editura Hasefer, 2007)." *Litere* (2009): 279–82.

Duroselle, Jean-Baptiste. 2004. *France and the Nazi Threat: The Collapse of French Diplomacy, 1932–1939.* New York: Enigma Books.

King, Charles. 1999. *The Moldovans. Romania, Russia and the Politics of Culture.* Stanford, CA: Hoover Institution Press, Stanford University.

Lewsey, Jonathan. 1997. *Who's Who and What's What in Wagner.* Aldershot: Ashgate.

Sebastian, Mihail. 1974. *Orașul cu salcîmi. Accidentul.* București: Editura Eminescu.

———. 2000. *Journal. 1935–1944.* Ed. Radu Ioanid. Trans. Patrick Camiller. Chicago: Ivan R. Dee.

———. 2011. *The Accident.* Trans. Stephen Henighan. Emeryville, ON: Biblioasis.

Chapter 8

"Rome was in ruins": Transatlantic Urbanism in Heller's *Catch-22*

Spencer Morrison

Sigmund Freud's famous tour through Rome in the opening section of *Civilization and Its Discontents* positions the reader as archaeologist uncovering the ruins, the overwritten spaces, of the Eternal City's palimpsest. Traversing both space and time, we encounter not only contemporary sites like the Coliseum and the Pantheon but also their ghostly antecedents, each site in Rome evoking within us the tourist "equipped with the most complete historical and topographical knowledge," both recognition of that space's particular history and a broader sense of the perpetual presence of the past (Freud 1962, 17). Freud jettisons his comparison of urban space's layered past to the past of the psyche because of his sense that the "destructive influences" which checker the evolution of urban space would, when trained upon the psyche, render beyond recovery traces of prior stages in its evolution; in this case, the ego that once included everything before demarcating an "interior" protected from the outer world (1962, 19). Where the analogy between urban and psychic pasts fails, then, is in the fact that while all psychic change arises as a defence against unpleasant stimuli, urban renovation can occur in a peaceful mode: "Demolitions and replacement of buildings occur in the course of the most peaceful development of a city" (1962, 19).

While in the economy of *Civilization*'s larger argument our walk with Freud serves primarily to distinguish a uniquely psychic process of preservation and evolution, it also maps a relationship between urban space and processes of deconstruction and reconstruction that sits ambivalently beside more recent formulations of how collective memory and communal identity hinge in part upon the built environment.[1] On the one hand, Freud's model of urban memory seems to trivialize the actual physical process of urban destruction by overlooking how a city's built environment accrues personal resonances, born through senses, emotions, and experiences in the minds of its users. Such resonances define what Henri Lefebvre called representational spaces, generating an individualized urban geography that aids in solidifying a sense of place and selfhood. On the other hand, while *Civilization* overlooks the harm done by spatial destruction to collective identity, it nevertheless proffers a model of spatial "reconstruction" that melds processes of physical building with those of storytelling and fabulation. Before embarking on our Roman tour, Freud notes that the human psyche exhibits its earlier stages in a way that highly evolved animal species do not: of these species, he claims that "the intermediate links have died out and are available to us only through *reconstruction*. In the realm of the mind, on the other hand, what is primitive is ... commonly preserved alongside of the transformed version" (1962, 16; emphasis mine). This reconstruction represents a form of storytelling, an imaginative imposition upon the animal here before me of outmoded forms, which anticipates the very "flight of imagination" that leads Freud to fictively reconstruct Rome's urban past from the traces of its current cityscape (1962, 18). Freud notes the physical impossibility of resurrecting extinct urban forms in his claim that "the same space cannot have two different contents," but the hypothetical visitor he guides through Rome can nevertheless imaginatively "reconstruct" these annihilated forms overtop of the structures that are their spatial tombstones (1962, 19). In many areas of the Eternal City, for instance, this visitor encounters sites entirely denuded of markers of the past, where the place of the primitive buildings "is now taken by ruins, but not by ruins of themselves but of later restorations made after fires or destruction" (1962, 17). Nevertheless, the visitor's complete topographical and historical knowledge enables her to "reconstruct" what has been lost, even in the absence of historical traces.

This process of imaginative and fabulistic "reconstruction" links sites not only across time but also in another sense, across space, and it is this particular sense of "reconstruction" (and concomitant deconstruction) that I intend to explore by making reference to Joseph Heller's famous American novel of the Second World War, *Catch-22* (1961). Freud's dismissal of the city as analogous to the psyche in its mode of historical preservation arises from his contention that the "destructive influences" that prompt psychic growth through unpleasant stimuli appear in urban space not only in times of strife and threat but in peacetime as well: "destructive influences which can be compared to causes of [psychic] illness ... are never lacking in the history of a city, even if … like London, it has hardly ever suffered from the visitations of an enemy" (1962, 19). The "fires or destruction" of ruined Rome, an exemplary site of conflict in Freud's argument, bear uncanny affinities with the peaceful, quotidian urban changes effected in London by government and commerce. Just such imaginative associations of urban renovation, renovation that links divergent spaces, renovation transpiring in both wartime and peacetime, preoccupy an individual who walks the Roman streets decades after Freud's reconstructive visit, after yet another war has wounded the city: Heller's Yossarian.

Among the most popular and critically acclaimed depictions of Europe in post–Second World War American prose, *Catch-22*, I argue, depicts war-torn Rome as a site that bears and bares key discursive and ideological contradictions of Cold War American culture. The novel tells the story of Yossarian, an American bombardier stationed on the island of Pianosa during the second half of the Second World War who, having flown all the missions asked of him when he first joined the Air Force, now simply wishes to avoid dying and get home safely. None of the men in Yossarian's squadron can ever make it home though, because their commanding officer, Colonel Cathcart, keeps raising the number of missions required for discharge from the Air Force. Yossarian no longer cares about doing his job well, but only about surviving each mission, even if this means sabotaging his own airplane or dropping bombs on the wrong targets. For roughly the first three-quarters of the novel, readers are given sketches of various characters and incidents that flesh out the absurdity of *Catch-22*'s military bureaucracy, with the novel's scrambled time scheme moving us chaotically backward and forward between different incidents. In the closing stages, however, the narration proceeds in a linear fashion, as Yossarian goes to Rome and witnesses a sequence of violence and exploitation that represents the novel's climax.

By the moment of Yossarian's Roman stroll, our readerly encounter with the ruins in *Catch-22* functions as the culmination of the novel's sustained reflection on how physical, urban destruction corrodes a communal identity that invigorates the body politic. Moreover, the climactic walk poses the question of how urban demolition and "reconstruction," both material and fictive, involve its practitioners in ethical questions of atonement, compensation, and payback. As in Freud, *Catch-22* conceives of "reconstruction" across both time and space, linking the shattered infrastructure and political community of Second World War Rome to the fraying seams of American Cold War urbanity. Within Rome's contact zone, *Catch-22* stages the intersection of devastated European metropolitan life with American forces of war and commerce. The novel projects upon this city, both demolished and reconstructed in part through American capital, anxieties about the dehumanizing tendencies of an administrative logic that abstracts both space and life from its lived actuality, subjecting them to a fearsome law that threatens their very existence. In this way, just as Heller claimed that *Catch-22* casts fears distinctly characteristic of the Cold War upon the novel's Second World War milieu, I claim that the novel's European spaces open themselves up to broader considerations not only of urban decay in postwar America but also to the relationship between modes of postwar urban "reconstruction" on both sides of the Atlantic.

This essay, then, reads *Catch-22*'s images of European city space as productively twinned reflections on the social configurations tasked with rebuilding and restructuring American and Western European polities mired in singular crises in the Second World War's wake. While the crises of Western Europe in this period require little explanation here, those of America are less well known, as the postwar period there is popularly associated with affluence and buoyant consumerism. This period also witnessed, however, the rise of a discourse of American urban crisis that subsumed, beneath a broad narrative of decline, numerous social anxieties: for instance, anxieties generated by antagonistic race and class relations, a frayed sense of civic belonging, and an eroded collective memory embodied in a deteriorating urban environment. As Robert A. Beauregard notes in *Voices of Decline: the Postwar Fate of US Cities*, "After World War II, the large industrial cities of the United States entered a period of profound collapse" to such an extent that "the proclaimed decline of large cities framed the lives of those who came of age in the last half of the twentieth century" (2003, vii, viii). America's urban crisis as framed within Cold War culture, however, betrayed international dimensions. Jane Jacobs, for instance, in her epochal *The Death and Life of Great American Cities*, likens public housing project money for East Harlem to "the generosity of a rich nation" extended as "massive aid to a deprived and backward country" (1992, 307). As Tim Clune notes, Jacobs, in her critique of American city planning, "borrows her characteristic rhetorical move from free market discourse, asking city dwellers whether they would prefer to make their own choices, or to have their choices made for them by planners" (2006, 59). In an era during which cities represented the most salient domestic barometer of American cultural and economic dynamism against a competing form of Communist political organization, domestic governmental aid to American cities takes on necessarily geopolitical importance. In American Cold War foreign policy in Europe, however, Jacobs's model of opposed camps of planners and city dwellers recedes before a more harmonized approach to international aid by which both the American state and civil society cooperatively reshape European polities. As Victoria de Grazia notes, an "impeccable synchronicity" is characterized by the manoeuvres of America's businesses, its entertainment sector, and its State and Commerce Departments during the postwar period as these actors moved "with that enthusiastic unity of purpose called the 'national interest' that was the hallmark of the Cold War consensus" (2005, 7). They worked, de Grazia argues, in tandem over the course of the twentieth century to expand practices of American-style mass consumption within European societies, but she locates the dawn of a fully fledged American "Market Empire" at the outset of the Cold War, seeing in the 1948–1951 Marshall Plan, America's plan for European reconstruction, an important "bearer of new ways of thinking about affluence" (2005, 5, 338). Heller's seminal novel arises within this ideological field as an American representation of Europe that bears the imprints of crises foreign and domestic, negotiating in its presentation of European urbanity the conflicting promises and tensions of "reconstruction" effected through both America's international aid and its model of consumer capitalism.

Catch-22 frames Second World War Europe as a "contact zone" replete with the conflicts and struggles that would attend intercultural relations between America and Western Europe in the immediate postwar period.[2] I borrow the term "contact zone" from Mary Louise Pratt, whose Imperial Eyes: Travel Writing and Transculturation defines it through a post-colonial lens as "the space of colonial encounters ... in which peoples geographically and historically separated come into contact with each other ... usually involving conditions of coercion, radical inequality, and intractable conflict" (1992, 6). Needless to say, Pratt's specific cartography of "contact zones" within nineteenth-century European travel writing differs widely from Catch-22's twentieth-century postmodernist project of satirizing and interrogating the techniques of an American military, governmental, and commercial apparatus anchored in that country's urban modernity. Insofar as Heller's novel meditates on issues of American urbanism in its representations of a ruined European urbanity open for "renovation" and "reconstruction," the broad contours of Pratt's model of "contact zone" writing obtain, just as in her samples of imperialist European travel writing, "the ways in which the periphery determines the metropolis" (1992, 6).[3] In a postwar era of unprecedented American economic and political strength in its relationships with Europe, the novel's staging of European-American intercultural "contact" allows *Catch-22* to formulate a sense of American urban identity in relation to a (ravaged and destroyed) peripheral "other" ticketed for "reconstruction"—a refashioning, repetition, and reiteration with difference—through American aid.

Rome serves as *Catch-22*'s most prominent "contact zone," a space of fearful mixture in which American representations of national identity collide with, and are elided by, those of a trenchant other. *Catch-22*'s geopolitical unconscious questions the possibility of American spatial and cultural "reconstruction" of destroyed European urban space, insisting upon the perdurability of Old Europe in the face of American foreign policy. In this regard, the old man at Nately's whore's bordello embodies an ineffaceable past that resists "reconstruction." The old man's encounter in Chapter 23 with Nately, a young soldier in Yossarian's squadron who professes eternal love for a Roman prostitute, can be read as an allegory of Cold War foreign policy, with the lascivious old man cast in the role of both tempter and prophet, "sitting in his musty blue armchair like some satanic and hedonistic deity on a throne, a stolen US Army blanket wrapped around his spindly legs to ward off a chill," his frail body sustained by pilfered American goods (Heller 2004a, 242). Nately, a scion of American bluebloods, in this encounter seems the epitome of youthful, jaunty American idealism as he boasts that "America is the strongest and most prosperous nation on earth" (2004a, 242). Amid Rome's ruins, however, Nately's nationalistic rhetoric falters as he encounters a historicity—a sense of deep time—unbeknownst to an America only recently risen to global prominence. Both Nately and the reader gain the chilling sense that Rome's ruins hold the key not only to Europe's past but also to America's future, as the old man intones that "Rome was destroyed, Greece was destroyed, Persia was destroyed, Spain was destroyed. All great countries are destroyed. Why not yours?" (2004a, 243). In the old man's indictment of American bravado, destroyed European urbanity reveals a latent and inextricable rot—a destiny of decay—at the heart of American civilization.[4] The old man in this passage embodies a long history punctuated by rises and falls that expose the vainglory of superpower imperialism. In the logic of this encounter, sheer endurance becomes a virtue that overrides the fleeting glories of momentary geopolitical power. The old man's insistence on a priceless cultural inheritance that persists against historical change echoes, on a geopolitical scale, the vision of American class relations expressed by Nately's old-money American aristocrat father, who claims that "old money is better than new money and ... the newly rich are never to be esteemed as highly as the newly poor" (2004a, 249). In this terrible realm of contact, *Catch-22* stages Old Europe's jaded intransigence toward American prosperity, as well as its potential disloyalty to the country responsible for its "reconstruction": the old man sneers to Nately that "your country will have no more loyal partisan in Italy than me—but only as long as you *remain* in Italy" (2004a, 245). Here, the *tactics* of everyday citizens, to borrow the terminology of Michel de Certeau in *The Practice of Everyday Life*, subvert the technocratic *strategies* of the planners of European reconstruction.[5]

However, it is during Yossarian's city walk through Rome in *Catch-22*'s Chapter 39, "The Eternal City," that the novel's preoccupations with modes of political community, bodily harm, just compensation, and intercultural contact come together in their most fearful form. Yossarian's journey through shattered European urbanity functions as both a tactile engagement with a city more often viewed by him through crosshairs from an airborne bomber, and an indictment of American strategies of urbanism. The novel's focalization of the night journey through Yossarian allows readers to conclude, along with the protagonist, that American-funded "reconstruction" of war-wracked Europe risks fostering a callous individualism associated in *Catch-22* with American identity. At the same time, though, Rome's ruins evoke both memories and portents; memories of a deep historicity against which the poise of Yossarian's newly hegemonic but culturally jejune country falters, and portents of Rome's possible future following American-influenced "reconstruction," imaginings of a city whose physical sites have been rebuilt, but whose sense of urban community remains lost amid a tide of foreign culture. As Yossarian enters the city, he feels the weight of a history of violence, the "chain of inherited habit that was imperiling them all," a history propagated by the very urban destruction he himself perpetrates as an American bombardier: Italian collective history and cultural identity crumble as we learn that "the Colosseum was a dilapidated shell, and the Arch of Constantine had fallen" (Heller 2004a, 406). Significantly, the old man, an embodiment of European perdurability and marker of its history has by this point died, the novel's narration insinuates, at the hands of military police versed in the language of aerial bombardment: the soldiers' "*fiery* and malicious exhilaration" complements their "sanctimonious, ruthless sense of right and dedication" (2004a, 408; emphasis mine). The old woman's description of her partner's death elides the boundary between bodily and urban wreckage: "Something broke in here," she claims, a statement that could describe just as aptly Rome's destroyed buildings as the old man's destroyed body. It is no coincidence that later in Yossarian's walk he witnesses, outside the "Ministry of Public Affairs," "a drunken lady ... backed up against one of the fluted Corinthian columns by a drunken young soldier" who ignores her pleas to stop, for this climactic chapter of *Catch-22* depicts the intertwined destruction of bodies, laws, and "Public Affairs" in European urban space under the weight of American interventions (Heller 2004a, 414). In Yossarian's nighttime walk we see, in its most visceral form, the imbrication of body politics and politicized bodies in which *Catch-22* locates not only the evident violence of an American military-commercial complex associated with American urbanism but also possible avenues for the rehabilitation of that urbanism.

What characterizes the code of Catch-22 itself is its absence of textuality, its existence as an unwritten other[6] that represents the obverse of juridical law: "Catch-22 did not exist, [Yossarian] was positive of that, but it made no difference. What did matter was that everyone thought it existed, and that was much worse, for there was no object or text to ridicule or refute, to ... rip to shreds" (2004a, 409). In this way, Catch-22, the unmediated violence of its execution laid bare in Rome's state of urban emergency, reveals itself as law's zero degree, as the other that lies behind and energizes the application of written law in the symbolic realm. Law's unwritten other becomes most starkly legible to Yossarian through the urban signifiers of annihilated buildings and wounded bodies. While the nightmarish scene of Yossarian's walk has often been characterized as his descent to a mythic underworld that precedes his moment of revelatory insight at chapter's end,[7] Heller's Rome nevertheless retains an essential worldliness in a passage crucial to understanding *Catch-22*'s geopolitical unconscious, the stakes it invests in relations between American and European modes of urbanity. Upon witnessing a destitute mother and child shivering in the rain, their homes presumably destroyed, Yossarian likens the inequalities of Roman urban space under a wartime state of emergency to urban life in his own land:

> What a lousy earth! He wondered how many people were destitute that same night even in his own prosperous country, how many homes were shanties, how many husbands were drunk and wives socked, and how many children were bullied, abused or abandoned. How many families hungered for food they could not afford to buy? How many hearts were broken? How many suicides would take place that same night, how many people would go insane? How many cockroaches and landlords would triumph? How many winners were losers, successes failures, rich men poor men? How many wise guys were stupid? How

many happy endings were unhappy endings? How many honest men were liars, brave men cowards, loyal men traitors, how many sainted men were corrupt, how many people in positions of trust had sold their souls to blackguards for petty cash, how many had never had souls? How many straight-and-narrow paths were crooked paths? How many best families were worst families and how many good people were bad people? When you added them all up and then subtracted, you might be left with only the children, and perhaps with Albert Einstein and an old violinist or sculptor somewhere. (Heller 2004a, 412–13)

Here, ruined Rome mirrors the urbanity of Yossarian's America, reflecting the class divisions that become so noticeable in a crowded cityscape, but also unveiling a sordid reality that belies public spectacle. Rome's mirror, for instance, reveals American "wise guys" as "stupid" and "sainted men" as "corrupt," bequeathing to Yossarian (and, by extension, to *Catch-22*'s audience) through the city's fragmented physical environment and brutishly exploitative encounters a sense that all class relations—even those "in his own prosperous country"—rely upon a sheer power whose rawest form instantiates itself in the law with force but without content that is Catch-22. To be sure, the inequalities portrayed in this passage are primarily economic (for instance, in descriptions of "families [who] hungered for food they could not afford to buy" and of "rich men" who are really "poor men"), largely overlooking inequalities of race and gender (the latter of which appears only in passing in a description of "wives socked" by drunken husbands). That Yossarian foregrounds class inequalities in his imaginative linkage of shattered Rome to urban America implicates a manipulative and violent international capitalism fed by American mass market consumerism in Rome's—and America's—urban deterioration. If the Lacanian mirror presents a fantasy of wholeness that is actually absent from the viewing subject, Rome as a mirror of American urbanity presents a grim reality of fragmentation that, Yossarian suggests, is actually present in American cities. The length of this catalogue of discrimination, abuse, and deception, as well as the anaphora by which it becomes one of the novel's gravest passages, suggests that if we are to read Yossarian's walk through "The Eternal City" as *Catch-22*'s climactic moment of discovery and revelation, the tenor of this climax cannot be adequately explained without an awareness of how the novel imaginatively overlays one mode of urbanity upon another, disclosing through Rome's urban destruction the grim status of American city space. In Yossarian's ruminations on this wounded European city, the fall of buildings raises the curtain on American urban rot.[8]

Conceiving of *Catch-22*'s Rome as a "mirror" does not entail understanding American urbanism as merely its static reflection, however. Rather, in displaying brutalism that subtends the economic disparities and spatial segregations of American cities, this destroyed Rome reveals present fissures in America's body politic but also—insofar as any ruin invokes an imaginative "reconstruction" on the part of its viewer, an act that imagines both past spatial forms and potential future reconstructions—suggests possible avenues for rehabilitating American urban space, for healing the fissures. The depredations Yossarian imagines as he gazes upon Rome's ruins suggest the need for economic, governmental, and spatial orders attuned to human vulnerability—to the finitude of the woundable (and killable and exploitable) human body—in ways that America's technocratic and ruthlessly violent military or its exploitative mode of capitalism are not.

It is precisely this sense of human frailty, of the concomitant necessity for compassion in engaging another human that Yossarian acquires near novel's end as he reads the "message" in the wounded body of the American gunner in his plane, Snowden: "Man was matter.... Drop him out a window and he'll fall. Set fire to him and he'll burn. Bury him and he'll rot, like other kinds of garbage. The spirit gone, man is garbage" (Heller 2004a, 440). Snowden's "message" expresses a universalism that levels distinctions between bodies on a global scale: all bodies, no matter which side of the bomb line they occupy, are mere killable matter. Yet, *Catch-22* tempers this universalism by portraying asymmetries of international geopolitical power and wealth that impede fellowship across nations rooted in bodily finitude. This is to say, then, that a "community" rooted in finitude can emerge in America as an alternative to *Catch-22*'s nefarious technocratic military-commercial complex, just as it can emerge in ruined Rome, but that these respective communities remain, in the novel's narration of intercultural interactions, irreconcilable to one another. To understand Rome as an urban mirror for American city life, therefore, is to read into its cityscape properties of the heterotopic mirror described in Michel Foucault's essay "Of Other Spaces":

> From the standpoint of the mirror I discover my absence from the place where I am since I see myself over there. Starting from this gaze that is, as it were, directed toward me, from the ground of this virtual space that is on the other side of the glass, I come back toward myself; I begin to direct my eyes toward myself and to reconstitute myself where I am. The mirror functions as a heterotopia in this respect: it makes this place that I occupy at the moment when I look

at myself in the glass at once absolutely real, connected with all the space that surrounds it, and absolutely unreal, since in order to be perceived it has to pass through this virtual point which is over there. (1986, 24)

Foucault's heterotopic mirror brings together all the other places it holds in juxtaposition, but nevertheless generates a sense of discrete selfhood—the reconstituted self in the mirror—for the viewing subject. In the space of wounded Rome, a space traversed and shaped by the novel's destructive military-commercial complex, the European city becomes a mirror that juxtaposes Roman urbanity to American urbanity while nevertheless holding them apart, intimating an insurmountable difference between American soldiers and Roman urbanites rooted in geopolitical and economic relations.

Yossarian's final and culminating encounter with woundable life in the chapter entitled "The Eternal City" illustrates the tension in *Catch-22*'s presentation of intercultural and geopolitical relations between a universalism based in human mortality, and an intractable separateness based in power relations that continuously differentiates Americans like Yossarian from the European urbanites whose cities they have destroyed and, in the postwar period of *Catch-22*'s composition, are now helping to reconstruct. After Yossarian's comrade Aarfy throws Michaela, a maid in their apartment, out a window, Yossarian confronts her defenestrated corpse:

> Her dead body was still lying on the pavement when Yossarian arrived and pushed his way politely through the circle of solemn neighbours with dim lanterns, who glared with venom as they shrank away from him and pointed up bitterly toward the second-floor windows in their private, grim, accusing conversations. Yossarian's heart pounded with fright and horror at the pitiful, ominous, gory spectacle of the broken corpse. (Heller 2004a, 417)

The fact that the body "still" lies on the pavement upon Yossarian's arrival allows readers to imagine the scene that immediately precedes his intrusion: an unbroken circle of destitute Roman urbanites brought together before Michaela's dead body. By coming together before the supreme example of human bodily frailty, these urbanites resemble the sort of "community" envisioned by Jean-Luc Nancy in *The Inoperative Community*, who argues that "it is through death that the community reveals itself" (1991, 14). For Nancy, true community requires its subjects to abandon notions of a transcendent immanence or essence that binds them together; rather, the inoperative community, which he poses in opposition to the immanent communities of Fascism, consists of a "resistance to immanence," a "communication of finitude" between subjects so that community becomes "a gift to be renewed and communicated ... not a work to be done or produced" (1991, 35).[9] If we see the Roman urbanites who encircle Michaela's corpse as a tenuous "community" brought together by a public spectacle of bodily finitude, Yossarian's entrance into the circle shatters this community, dispelling a sense of communication between European urbanites as "private ... conversations" ensue among them (Heller 2004a, 417). Yossarian, despite being AWOL, nevertheless retains his army uniform, a marker of an immanent or essential aspect of his identity within the ruined city. In the eyes of this fragile Roman community, then, Yossarian's uniform becomes the synecdochic marker of a broader force of violence that wracks the city, provoking their "glare[s]" (2004a, 417). Yossarian's intrusion into the circle of destitute Roman onlookers reveals *Catch-22*'s awareness of irremediable markers of cultural difference—markers given meaning by the geopolitical encounters the novel stages—that attenuate possibilities for a universalism rooted in human mortality. In *Catch-22*'s "Eternal City," geopolitical violence demarcates the boundaries of human community.

Aarfy's act of murder, however, also occasions *Catch-22*'s grimmest reflections on payback, positioning European city space as the locus of the novel's anxieties over ethical modes of compensation for acts of violence. When asked by Yossarian why he chose to rape and murder Michaela rather than simply hiring a prostitute, Aarfy brags, "I never paid for it in my life" (2004a, 418). Harkening back to earlier scenes in *Catch-22* that query the status of cash payments as just compensation for myriad wrongs, this scene stages the horrific alternative to paying: rather than pay, Aarfy rapes and murders. This alternative generates Michaela's "broken corpse," a silent (for Aarfy holds "his hand over her mouth") and forever silenced European urbanite whose death catalyzes a community inaccessible to Americans like Yossarian (Heller 2004a, 417). Aarfy never pays for "it" in either pecuniary or legal terms: he never pays prostitutes, just as he never pays a legal price for homicide.[10]

If the geopolitical unconscious of *Catch-22* has already suggested both the inadequacy of monetary payback for bodily and urban destruction and the ominous expansion of American culture that attends such payback in the form of Cold War programs like the Marshall Plan, it nevertheless suggests, despairingly, the necessity of such payback by rendering its grisly alternative in the form of Michaela's corpse. *Catch-22* queries the efficacy of American Cold War foreign policy by revealing the need for an ethical mode of payback that respects otherness as such.

Elaine Scarry's classic analysis of pain's ultimate inexpressibility, its lack of an exteriorized object, in *The Body in Pain* (1985), captures in its subtitle ("The Making and Unmaking of the World") the fulcrum upon which spatial change occurs, and what lies at this fulcrum's centre is the human (and, more specifically, the urban) body. While *Catch-22* foregrounds the unmaking of bodies and territories through a gallery of weapons including bombs, words, and commerce, it nevertheless gestures toward and meditates upon the possibility of geopolitical processes of "making." Scarry herself posits as an example of vast civilizational "making" the postwar processes of European reconstruction at the heart of which lay America's Marshall Plan: "If the period between 1939 and 1945 is conventionally identified as one of the darkest in Western civilization, then there can also be taken as one of its most luminous the period of years during which Europe was rebuilt" (1985, 178). Like Freud in *Civilization and Its Discontents* (1961), Scarry characterizes urban reconstruction as akin to fabulation, describing the Marshall Plan as an "imagining" on the part of American and European leaders of a restored Europe (1985, 178). More preoccupied with the complexities of Cold War America than with those of Second World War Europe, *Catch-22* evokes through its depictions of urban unmaking corresponding questions surrounding how to "make" and how to "reconstruct" European urbanity and community, questions that engage larger issues of how cultural communities interact, how political rhetorics are disseminated and received across national borders,[11] as well as of what conditions should attend payment from debtor to creditor. *Catch-22*'s fictive "making" of processes of urban unmaking not only harbours in its textual unconscious the question of how to revitalize shattered communities in ways that honour and preserve their heterogeneity, but also locates its reflections about community in the human body. Andreas Huyssen argues, "the modern imaginary of ruins remains conscious of the dark side of modernity" (2010, 22). Attending to wreckage bodily, architectural, ethical, and communal, *Catch-22* crystallizes a particularly American mode of Cold War ruin-gazing that mourns spatial loss while fearing its reconstructed future.

Notes

1 See, for instance, discussions in geography of the concept of urbicide, the deliberate destruction of non-militarized urban space. Two recent and exemplary books on this concept are Martin Coward's *Urbicide: The Politics*

of Urban Destruction (2009) and Robert Bevan's *The Destruction of Memory: Architecture at War* (2006). For Coward, urbicide assaults the built environment conceived of as the condition of possibility for heterogeneity. Moving beyond the mountain of scholarship on architectural monumentality, Coward's *Urbicide* asks what is significant in the destruction of prosaic urban architecture: while symbolism attends the destruction of certain iconic buildings, for what reason are non-military buildings of negligible cultural significance destroyed? Bevan, who centres his discussion much more heavily on monumental spaces than does Coward, investigates how processes of heavily politicized urban "reconstruction" can allow fictitious communal histories to be forged as new buildings arise atop the ruins of the old. My own discussion of the relationship between the built environment and notions of community owes much to these two books.

2   While I am aware that what is colloquially referred to as "Americanization" is really an intricate process of cultural creolization on both sides of the Atlantic (see Rob Kroes' *If You've Seen One, You've Seen the Mall: Europeans and American Mass Culture* [1996] for an influential version of this argument), the "Americanization" dealt with in this chapter is the type of top-down imposition of cultural values upon postwar Europe that Frances Stoner Saunders describes in *Who Paid the Piper?* (1999).

3   My argument here uses the terms "metropolis" and "periphery," traditionally associated with theories of third-world dependency and underdevelopment in tongue-in-cheek fashion, with full awareness of the postwar historical fact of Europe's own metropolitan status in relation to its imperial peripheries. What I wish to highlight with these terms, however, is the relational nature of the "metropole-periphery" model: intermediate points in a global constellation of metropoles and peripheries can be both "peripheral" to a larger metropolis and "metropolitan" to a less economically developed periphery. In this sense, then, my argument applies Pratt's metropole-periphery model in an extremely loose fashion to the relationship.

4   Urban decay features prominently throughout Heller's career—as Heller himself mentions in a 1981 interview with *Rolling Stone*, "in all my books … there's a passage on the degeneration of cities, the deterioration of law and order" ("Checking in with Joseph Heller" 1993, 229–30). This motif of American urban rot can be seen throughout Heller's oeuvre, from Bob Slocum's comment in *Something Happened* that "From sea to shining sea the country is filling with slag, shale, and used-up automobile tires.… Towns die … 'America the Beautiful' isn't," (2004c) to Bruce Gold's walk through dilapidated Coney Island in *Good as Gold*, all the way to *Closing Time*, Heller's 1994

sequel to *Catch-22*, in which Yossarian, watching panhandlers in New York City, reflects that "nowhere in his lifetime … not in wartime Rome or Pianosa or even in blasted Naples or Sicily, had he been a spectator to such atrocious squalor as he saw mounting up all around him now into an eminent domain of decay" (2004b, 484, 49). Curiously, Heller scholarship leaves the theme of urban rot in his novels almost entirely unmentioned.

5   Also noteworthy is that the old man partially blinds *Catch-22*'s clearest emblem of an American cultural spread in Europe that proceeds lawlessly and unboundedly, Major de Coverley. See, for instance, the opening pages of Chapter 13, where the old man appears as a caricature of Old Europe, his mouth "reeking with sour fumes of wine, cheese, and garlic" (2004a, 133). Significantly, Major de Coverley enters the "shattered city" in "a jeep he had obtained from somewhere," the ambiguity of the jeep's source suggestive of de Coverley's lawless practices, established earlier when readers learn that his duties include "kidnapping Italian labourers" (131). The lawless de Coverley, unidentifiable even to the army's American technocracy, nevertheless "spearhead[s] every important [American] advance fearlessly and successfully," operating in the text as a type of American rugged individualism. His blinding by the old man, then, signals the perils of European engagement for this type of individualism.

6   By "other" in this paragraph I refer to the notion of the Lacanian big Other as explained by Slavoj Žižek in *Interrogating the Real* as an external presence which "'quilts' … discourse" and "'totalizes' it from outside," instilling it with what Žižek calls a "performative" power (2005, 128).

7   The original expression of this argument is Minna Doskow's article "The Night Journey in *Catch-22*" (2009). While Doskow's argument focuses on Yossarian's education, by which he learns his "proper course of action," my reading of Yossarian's night walk emphasizes that it teaches both us and Yossarian more than Doskow suggests (e.g., the universality of the suffering depicted in this episode is associated within the novel's narrative patterns with urban space—it's no coincidence that musings on responsibility, ethics, and payback take place in a city bombed by the American Air Force) (2004a, 189).

8   In his *Voices of Decline: The Postwar Fate of US Cities*, Robert A. Beauregard notes that, in the postwar period of *Catch-22*'s composition, "Urban decline lurked behind every postwar story" of Heller's America, and that the "spread of physical decay" in American cities leant credence to a sense in public consciousness that "the modern city seemed on the verge of total collapse" (2003, 4, 151).

9 Nancy's inoperative community, then, represents the antithesis of the "camp" which Giorgio Agamben in *Homo Sacer* (1998) sees as the inescapable political structure of our age. Ana Luszczynska's article "The Opposite of the Concentration Camp: Nancy's Vision of Community" (2005) explains this contrast between inoperativity and the Fascist camp with astounding clarity. Juxtaposing Nancy's conception of community with Agamben's allows us to see more clearly how *Catch-22* articulates competing models of communal and spatial organization via representations of wounded bodies. Ian James lucidly explicates death's centrality to this type of community:

> Nancy's community is "unworked," then, insofar as it is a multiplicity of singular existences who are "in common" only on the basis of a shared mortality which cannot be subsumed into any communal project or collective identity. Their relation to death is not the communication, communion, or fusion of a subject and object. It is the exposure of each singular existence, its being-outside-of-itself, to a death that is revealed in and through the death of others. Community reveals, or rather *is*, our exposure to the unmasterable limit of death, and thus our being together outside of all identity, or work of subjectivity. (2006, 185)

10 In *Catch-22*'s Roman state of emergency, spatial divisions seem to be policed more heavily than anything else: rather than arrest Aarfy for murder, the military police arrests Yossarian for entering Rome without a pass; also, Aarfy's assertion that Michaela's dead body has "no right" to be out in the street because it is "after curfew" elevates in his own mind—and perhaps in the minds of the policemen who fail to arrest Aarfy—Michaela's public transgression over Aarfy's homicide (2004a, 418).

11 International dissemination of pro-American rhetoric, covertly funded by America's government, accelerated during the time of *Catch-22*'s composition. As Frances Stoner Saunders argues in *Who Paid the Piper? The CIA and the Cultural Cold War*, "During the height of the Cold War, the US government committed vast resources to a secret programme of cultural propaganda in Western Europe" (1999, 1). The Marshall Plan, the very program so integral to revitalizing economies, cities, and societies in Western Europe, also proved a useful resource for aiding American Cold War foreign policy interests: "Marshall Plan funds were soon being siphoned to boost the cultural struggle in the West" (26).

References

Agamben, Giorgio. 1998. *Homo Sacer: Sovereign Power and Bare Life*. Trans. Daniel Heller-Roazen. Stanford: Stanford University Press.

Beauregard, Robert A. 2003. *Voices of Decline: The Postwar Fate of US Cities*. New York: Routledge.

Bevan, Robert. 2006. *The Destruction of Memory: Architecture at War*. Chicago: Reaktion.

de Certeau, Michel. 1984. *The Practice of Everyday Life*. Trans. Steven Rendall. Berkeley: University of California Press.

Clune, Tim. 2010. *American Literature and the Free Market, 1945–2000*. New York: Cambridge University Press.

Coward, Martin. 2009. *Urbicide: The Politics of Urban Destruction*. New York: Routledge.

Doskow, Minna. 1967. "The Night Journey in Catch-22." *Twentieth Century Literature* 12 (4): 186–93.

de Grazia, Victoria. 2005. *Irresistible Empire: America's Advance through Twentieth-Century Europe*. Cambridge, MA: Belknap Press of Harvard UP.

Foucault, Michel. 1986. "Of Other Spaces." *Diacritics* 16 (1): 22–27.

Freud, Sigmund. 1961. *Civilization and Its Discontents*. Trans. James Strachey. New York: W.W. Norton.

Heller, Joseph. 1993. "Checking in with Joseph Heller." In *Conversations with Joseph Heller* edited by Adam J. Sorkin, 224–34. Jackson: University Press of Mississippi.

———. 2004a. *Catch-22*. New York: Simon & Schuster.

———. 2004b. *Closing Time*. New York: Simon & Schuster.

———. 2004c. *Something Happened*. New York: Simon & Schuster.

Huyssen, Andreas. 2010. "Authentic Ruins: Products of Modernity." In *Ruins of Modernity*, edited by Julia Hell and Andreas Schönle, 17–28. Durham, NC: Duke University Press.

Jacobs, Jane. 1992. *The Death and Life of Great American Cities*. New York: Vintage.

James, Ian. 2006. *The Fragmentary Demand: An Introduction to the Philosophy of Jean-Luc Nancy*. Stanford: Stanford University Press.

Kroes, Rob. 1996. *If You've Seen One, You've Seen the Mall: Europeans and American Mass Culture*. Urbana: University of Illinois Press.

Luszczynska, Ana. 2005. "The Opposite of the Concentration Camp: Nancy's Vision of Community." CR: *The New Centennial Review* 5 (3): 167–205.

Nancy, Jean-Luc. 1991. *The Inoperative Community*. Trans. Peter Connor. Minneapolis: University of Minnesota Press.

Pratt, Mary Louise. 1992. *Imperial Eyes: Travel Writing and Transculturation*. New York: Routledge.

Saunders, Frances Stoner. 1999. *Who Paid the Piper? The CIA and the Cultural Cold War*. London: Granta.

Scarry, Elaine. 1985. *The Body in Pain: The Making and Unmaking of the World*. Oxford: Oxford University Press.

Žižek, Slavoj. 2005. *Interrogating the Real*. London: Continuum.

Chapter 9

Postcards from Europe: Representations of (Western) Europe in Romanian Travel Writing, 1960–2010

Oana Fotache Dubălaru

Introduction: Romanian Journeys to the West—Historical Contextualization and Recent Perspectives

Starting with the modern age, Europe has been a constant reference for Romanian intellectuals. The synchronization of Romanian civilization and culture with Western European patterns has been at the centre of numerous ideological disputes against the background of Romanian society's modern development. Apparently the representations of the West varied considerably across time, and were in a complex relationship with Western depictions of Romania and Romanians.

Two historical periods stand out in this process of constructing a (national) identity in relation to the other: the one around the mid-nineteenth century (before and after the 1848 Revolution that marked the start of Romania's modernization, interpreted as Westernization); and the interwar period, when the national state consolidated its democratic values and institutions, and developed a stronger sense of cultural legitimacy (Spiridon 2009). During both these periods, intellectuals and especially the literati played a key role in establishing a sense of Europeanness among Romanians. As to the particular forms that this European consciousness embraced, one notices the dominance of the French model, to which a German cultural influence was later added (by the end of the nineteenth century) and to a lesser extent an Italian one, this motivated by common linguistic origins that helped envision a kind of singularity "among a Slavic world" (as a frequently used phrase goes). Of course these cultural models were enhanced at different times by political alliances, societal models, customs, religious beliefs, and other factors.

A persistent theme is noticeable with Romanian cultural ideologists for about a century (1830–1930)—from the Romantic writers up to modern ideologists such as the cultural critic Titu Maiorescu (1840–1917) and the literary critic and sociologist Eugen Lovinescu (1881–1943): that of the necessary synchronization with Western Europe on a societal and cultural level. At first this synchronization was understood as an import of Western models—all the way from translations to the creation of institutions and patterns of state governance. Then this process underwent a very critical phase (which coincided with the influence of the German model) when the import as such was perceived as degrading since the borrowed cultural forms did not manage to generate "content," and thus could not function properly. The cultural society "Junimea" [The Youth] led by Titu Maiorescu objected to what its members saw as very superficial adaptations of the Western institutions and manners that could only lead to inferiority and loss of genuine values in favour of second-hand perceptions of Europeanness. This was an organicist (and conservative) view that played an important part in the development of Romanian society. Its source was of course Hegelian dialectic, as Maiorescu had studied philosophy in Berlin and Giessen.

After the Great War and the unification of Transylvania with the other two Romanian historical provinces (1918), the slogan in circulation was different: not that *translation* as such was the solution, but that *creative adaptation* eventually leads to original forms ("make it new"). This idea was promoted by the most important Romanian modernist literary critic, Eugen Lovinescu. By that time, Romanian society was already modern enough to be accepted in the family of the Western states partly because the royal family was of German origin; Bucharest was then named "little Paris," Romanian intellectuals had strong connections with their Western colleagues, and the process of modernization seemed to be very advanced.

After the Second World War, all these connections and the cultural and historical legitimacy they brought with them were suddenly dropped and replaced by a "colonization" of the country by the Soviet Union. For more than fifteen long years (1947 through 1960–64), contacts with the West were scarce and strictly controlled by the Communist regime. The Romanian cultural elite were destroyed (by imprisonment, forced labour camps, social marginalization, some people's own compromises, etc.). Western Europe was no longer a travel destination; all roads led to the East, to Russia, or even China.

A Few Methodological Caveats

No wonder, then, that Europe had to be rediscovered. This process started by the middle of the sixties, with the wave of (partial) liberalization brought by Ceausescu's rule in its beginning. Everybody's hopes turned toward the West; Western Europe[1] was perceived as a validating instance since it was the depository of political, ethical, and cultural values. Being part of it could not be a legitimate claim for Romania (despite geographical and historical evidence) unless that claim was supported by self- and others' representations of this status.

In the following pages I will propose a sketch of Romania's recent cultural history from the perspective of this process of rediscovery that triggered significant changes in the structure of collective identities and representations. I chose travel writings (mainly travel diaries) as case studies for several reasons: first, they render more directly the personal, subjective experiences of this other that was Western Europe for Romanians—so they are, at least in principle, more authentic than other discourses, fictional or not (although subject to censorship as much as them). Second, the travel diary as a genre is a privileged witness of the process of self-definition and identity construction.[2] As the theorists Cornis-Pope and Neubauer wrote, "in East-Central Europe, poets and philologists were major contributors to this invention [of the nation and at the same time of its other(s)] by constructing *texts* as well as *institutions*." (2002, 13). Third, travel writings have a double nature, that of a *literary work* and of an *anthropological document*. So I will be reading them as documents of Romanian intellectual mentality representative for the time when they were written.

The five travel diaries further discussed were chosen both due to the similarities and differences among them. Differences function on various levels: the time of the travels to the West (during the sixties, seventies, eighties, and finally the nineties); the purpose of the travel and accordingly the duration of stay (study, research, academic contacts, participation in conferences, teaching Romanian language and literature abroad); the age of the traveller (early thirties to mid-forties and fifties); not least differences in education and personality. Among these five writers, we encounter a historian (Dan Berindei, born 1923), two literary critics (Eugen Simion, b. 1933, and Ioana Both, b. 1964), a literary theorist (Adrian Marino, 1921–2005), and a religious anthropologist (Teodor Baconschi, b. 1963).

A few words about their similarities: one can trace here a first distinction between diarists that travelled before and after 1989, when control of the ruling Communist party was not exercised anymore, and travelling abroad was constrained mostly by financial rather than political reasons. Most of these texts display a strong (and also traditional) fascination with French culture and with Paris as a cultural centre (even *the* cultural centre of Europe at certain times). Most travellers define their writings similarly, refusing the type of *tourist diary* and going instead for what Adrian Marino theorized as an *intellectual diary* (1976).[3] Their diaries testify to the experiences of Eastern intellectuals confronted with a different mentality and trying to find their place in a cultural and academic world quite unlike their own. So we should expect to find here an understanding of self-writing as *Bildung*, as a means of spiritual formation. Last but not least, an important criterion for this selection was the air of "family resemblance" brought by their similar way of relating to the Romanian cultural tradition of the journey to the West.

Of course "the West" and "Europe" will not be regarded here as stable and unitary entities. As Gerard Delanty writes in a widely influential book, "the idea of Europe itself as an invention has never been scrutinized"; "every age reinvented the idea of Europe in the mirror of its own identity" (1995, 1). Especially in these texts, published between 1960 and 2010, Western Europe was experienced as a place of desire more than an object of knowledge; so even when the authors pass stereotypical judgments and opinions on various issues, these are not to be read as attempts to render an idea of what Europe as a strong notion meant for them, but rather as very fragmented and partial visions of distinct aspects of European culture or civilization. I definitely share Diana Mishkova's view on this matter, that using the notion of Europe nowadays implies an awareness "both of the plurality of contents and forms, which the 'idea of Europe' spawned over time, and of the analytical objections to treating '(Western) Europe' as an entity and a coherent unit of analysis" (2008, 240).

Yet despite this diversity of perceptions regarding "Europe" (and I am equating here Europe with Western Europe, to speak from the Romanian travellers' perspective), there is one common denominator: Europe stands for the idea of modernity, and of "cultural superiority and power" (Mishkova 2008, 253).

These ideas were promoted by Western Europeans themselves since the Enlightenment (as Larry Wolff accurately points out in his *Inventing Eastern Europe*, 1994); they were reflected and gained circulation in the self-representations of Eastern Europeans since about the same time. That is how the East–West opposition took shape. Yet, as Wendy Bracewell points out in the introduction to a comprehensive anthology of East European travel writing, "these travellers' accounts complicate the image of a Europe divided neatly into East and West: neither half of the continent has ever been so monolithic and coherent as this formula implies" (2009, xiv).

Europe as an Imaginary Space: Topoi of a Cultural Encounter

This age-old opposition was still in place at the time our travels were made. According to Cornis-Pope and Neubauer, "this mental polarization was subsequently challenged by integrative-federalist projects, political unions, or cross-cultural hybrids ... that cut across the imaginary dividing line between Eastern and Western Europe. And yet, no matter how porous or chimerical, cultural oppositions have a tendency to perpetuate themselves" (2002, 23). As Michel Foucault brilliantly stated in his *L'Archéologie du Savoir* (1969), discourses are strictly conditioned by history; there are patterns of reading reality and also culture that cannot be easily replaced.

I would like to use as a starting point the idea expressed by Longworth in his *The Making of Eastern Europe. From Prehistory to Postcommunism* (1997): the historian implies—seemingly departing from the established line of thought on this issue—that Eastern Europe (and Western as well) is not an entirely arbitrary construct either.[4] He refers to the existence of a long tradition of collective representations that is responsible for the present ways of relating to the other (which is a sort of pessimistic interpretation of Edward Said's views, if you like). This also holds true for my case studies. In the introductory remarks I pointed to the mid-nineteenth-century emergence of the idea of national identity modelled after Western European prototypes. In the travelogues of the time, this emergence took the form of a sincere and almost total admiration for all things European. As important as this attitude was in the process of Romanian society's modernization, it also brought along a persistent inferiority complex (usually called *Dinicu Golescu's complex*).[5] The intellectual generations that followed responded to this perception either actively, by engaging in a process of original cultural creation, or by inventing another set of myths in return which they tried to legitimate by restoring an alternative tradition—that of folklore, rural customs, and the like, in a word, pre-modern cultural patterns.

In the interwar period, this inferiority complex is expressed by a foreign observer and then assumed by the Romanian intelligentsia: the would-be French president Raymond Poincaré who visited Romania as a lawyer defending an Austrian company. His much commented-upon phrase goes:

"Que voulez-vous, nous sommes ici aux portes de l'Orient, ou tout est pris à la légère ..." After the isolation that Romania had gone through under Communist rule in the 1950s, the reactivation of this complex by our travellers in the 1960s and after cannot surprise us. The feeling of a permanent need to legitimate one's culture in the eyes of the West is expressed in many ways by these travel diaries.

The opposition between East and West was translated by the Romanian travellers further discussed either as one between *home* versus *here*, or as that of *before* versus *now*. This is highly significant in several ways. First, *home* becomes sometimes an embarrassing reference point, an awkward heritage that one is not entirely responsible for but still has to suffer effects from; while *here* is often distanced from the traveller's conscience and perception because it is viewed as a *beyond*, as an entity that overcomes one's capacity of representation, an object of both desperate desire and resentment (the belief that Europe and the US abandoned Romania to the Communists was very popular at that time). Moreover, Romania was seen as a country stuck in its own past and struggling without much success to be recognized as part of Europe again.[6]

To illustrate the images of Western Europe, I will discuss first the representations of the European city. One thing to be noted here is that Eastern cities are valued according to their proximity in cultural terms to a kind of Western ideal metropolis—most often Paris. Thus Dan Berindei (*Drumuri în lume: 1965–1980: în vremuri de speranță și incertitudini / Rambling through the World in Times of Hope and Uncertainty: 1965–1980*, 2005) is enchanted by Belgrade and Budapest because they look more like the cities on the other side of the Iron Curtain. As for Paris itself, the myth is still in place for most of them. When arriving there for the first time, Adrian Marino writes, "I feel that I came back to a familiar landscape." That is because he had planned his trip thoroughly, since "a culture cannot be mastered but from the inside, not wandering on the streets" (*Carnete europene / European Notebooks* 1976, 40).[7] We should expect then a *livresque*, mythologized Paris, not a real place. Unfortunately this "familiar landscape" is not very welcoming to the visitor. The monuments or the paintings are warmer than the people, and the writer doesn't miss the chance to pass judgments on Gallic individualism, the death of French manners, the decadence of contemporary French culture, and the like.

Eugen Simion (*Timpul trăirii, timpul mărturisirii... Jurnal parizian / A Time to Experience, a Time to Confess. Parisian Journal*, 1977) is more tolerant and definitely has more time to construct his personal myth. He spent four years in Paris as a visiting lecturer teaching Romanian at Sorbonne University. Already serving as a guide for Romanian colleagues coming over to Paris, he notices that "Romanians feel very good in Paris. They have already known the city from their readings. When they finally arrive, they have no other curiosity than to simply recognize it" (Simion 1977, 159). Yet the same experience was overwhelming upon his arrival: the feeling of a foreign, indifferent, hostile city. While embracing this sense of familiarity with a cultural *topos*, Simion struggles at the same time to be recognized, to be more than "a mere spectator" (130) of Parisian intellectual life, as he wrote after his first visit to Roland Barthes's famous seminar at the École pratique des hautes études. In the end, his reading of the city evolves from a superficial and bookish encounter to a better understanding of his own self: "The city had received me with the hostility of its indifference and I now leave it feeling calm and serene. It revealed something in me and made me see with greater lucidity the place where I come from" (1977, 421).

There is a change of attitude with Teodor Baconschi, who had studied for his PhD at Sorbonne. His trip coincided with a significant change of paradigm: the Paris of the 1990s is already a global city, crowded by immigrants and tourists from all over the world. Here are the significant entries in his diary: "Had someone told me—3 years ago ... that I would so naturally spend a whole day *sous le parvis de Notre-Dame,* I would have said that's a fairy tale" (Baconschi, *Insula cetății: Jurnal parizian, 1991-1994/ Island of the City. Parisian Journal* 2005, 13). But later on the myth loses its force: Paris is "Americanized, McDonaldized, sick of its old glory" (25). Paris is no longer a myth for him also because it has become accessible to many: "nowadays any Romanian can stroll at will on *Boul' Mich*" (30).

As Monica Spiridon noted in her article, "Paris, *terre d'asile*: Exile, Nostalgia and Recollection" (2004), Paris has perhaps never been a "real" city for Romanian intellectuals but an imaginary construct, always refashioning itself.

For an intellectual and even more so for a writer, going to or living in Paris should imply a lot more than taking pictures or queuing in front of *Mona Lisa.* He or she will try to be part of the city's cultural life, to make contacts with like-minded people, to get whatever symbolic profit available. These Romanian travellers are no exception. Marino seems to be the most determined of them; he lives each journey "as if it were the last one" (1976, 21), which certainly affects the style of his cultural and existential contact with the city. Always running out of time, he establishes the perfect technique of reading as much as possible at the French National Library. Under these circumstances, human contacts are limited and superficial. On most of his trips to Paris, Marino's priority is to check sources and complete bibliographic research for his books; on another level, he tries to find collaborators and improve the circulation of the academic journal he was editing in Romania, *Cahiers Roumains d'Études Littéraires*. Since his funding was limited, if not scarce, he preferred to maintain a more or less closed circle of friends and acquaintances, and made the most of his library visits.

In these writers' images of Western culture there is a prevalent reaction: a clear preference for canonical, classical reference points and correspondingly, a lack of sympathy for avant-garde forms of expression. For instance, Marino visits museums of classical art and classical writers' memorial houses. On an Easter holiday he goes to see the houses of Delacroix, Balzac, and Hugo, "which I also visited in the last years" (Marino 1976, 124). He definitely prefers literary history to contemporary art and literary forms. When visiting an exhibition of Italian futurist art, he ignores the formal innovation and jumps straight to an inadequate interpretation of content and meaning: "The central idea here is the suggestion," he writes (1976, 115). Marino strongly reacts against popular French culture, but embarks on a guided boat tour on the Seine as one of the common tourists he despises; moreover, he finds the tour to be "very instructive" (117).

Both Marino and Simion react very critically to the public appearances and statements of Philippe Sollers or Roland Barthes, major figures of French literary life at the time. Public appearances look frivolous to them, displaying contradictory behaviour which they eagerly and ironically comment upon. Simion writes that Sollers is "typical for Western *intelligentzia* [*sic*], radical, politicized, determined to get involved in the social life" (1977, 28). At that time, the prevailing mode of Romanian intellectuals was one of evasion, of retreat from civic life, feebly motivated by the political circumstances of Communist dictatorship in the country. Even with Baconschi, a member of another generation, we encounter the same rejection of a non-familiar intellectual discourse: "I read in Sollers's face expression the complex of isolation of this humanist intellectual class" (2005, 34). So the same reading habits regarding otherness are perpetuated from a generation to another.

French (and Dutch, and Swiss) contemporary culture are seen by them as entertaining a direct relationship with consumer culture—and are criticized for this. Life in the West appears to be devoid of values, empty and meaningless. Superficiality and the obsession with novelty prevent Western intellectuals from focusing on their real mission, or at least that's what the

Romanians think. After he assisted in a public debate hosted by the *Tel Quel* group in a Parisian bookshop, Simion noted, "nobody spoke a word about literature or new critical methods. Slightly disappointed, I asked my neighbour: what is the topic of this debate? He answered promptly: *la masturbation de l'esprit!*" (1977, 25).

In this context, the Easterners are invested with the privileged "mission" to keep alive the humanist tradition (an attitude that measures exactly the persistence of the inferiority complex I described). Their style is characterized by a richness of erudite comments and allusions meant to prove their right to belong to this (long-gone) classical culture of the West. Marino's discourse turns melancholic when he diagnoses, in the footsteps of Spengler, the decline of the West, and then militant when he advocates the chance of the smaller (i.e., Eastern) cultures to make themselves known on the European stage as "true" inheritors of classical values.

As to the other term of the opposition, their reaction to Romanian culture is no less problematic. The difference between East and West is acutely perceived by all of them. "When compared to our neighbours, we find ourselves in a situation of clear inferiority in terms of promoting our image abroad, especially in its positive aspects," notes Berindei in a bitter tone (2005, 142–43).

The complex of belonging to a cultural periphery is to be found with Ioana Bot also, although she meets all the criteria for and actually manages to fully integrate herself in the new Swiss environment (Zürich University):

Today I have read Jean Cohen, *La structure du langage poétique*. I realize I shouldn't say that, as people might ask me how did I come to this age without reading Cohen, or about the Romanian's complex not to be left outside European culture. But Europe doesn't care about all that, my young European colleagues live happily and don't worry about reading Cohen; obviously the question comes out: who is inside and who was left aside? Paradoxically, it seems that we are always those who miss the train. (*Jurnal elveţian. În căutarea latinei pierdute/ Swiss Diary. In Search of Lost Latin*, 2004, 124–25)

Baconschi's perspective of Romanian intellectual circles is a dim one as he comes to realize how far behind they are compared to the different branches of Western science (especially those that had been marginalized by the Communist regime for decades, such as anthropology or psychoanalysis; after 1989, these "new" disciplines in the Romanian academia lacked professionals, course materials, circuits of validation, and so on).

When tailoring plans for his return to Bucharest, he finds himself in a similar situation to the 1848 generation of Romanian intellectuals: "I wonder which the priorities should be: to translate Western texts or to produce compilations?" (Baconschi 2005, 121).

Regarding the issue of Romanian culture's situation in Europe, a common sense of mission and duty is to be found with them (also reiterating the nineteenth-century reaction of the young aristocrats who returned home after studying abroad): minor cultures have to struggle to make themselves known and recognized by the others who are invested with the power to legitimatize values. An immense frustration arises when this recognition is sometimes delayed or partial. Simion is obsessed with the obstacle represented by Romanian language, which has less circulation than many other European languages and thus prevents Romanian culture from becoming "universal" (as if universality would be an essential quality of an object, not a pragmatically negotiated one).

Ioana Bot expresses in a memorable phrase this blocked communication (actually, it was not always blocked on a personal level, but on the collective one): "While I find myself in a foreign country, I am also foreign to them; the way seems to be blocked in both directions" (Bot 2004, 34). One cannot help thinking about Montesquieu's *Lettres persanes*.... Bot reiterates here, on a different level, Montesquieu's perspective embodied in his Persian character Usbek. She willingly cultivates her own strangeness as seen by her Swiss colleagues in order to be better placed for a lucid image of the other. Hers is a distant reading, although the premises for a perfect integration to the Swiss/Western intellectual milieu are all met (plurilinguism, intellectual curiosity, a vivid intelligence, etc.).

An Opposition to Deconstruct: Provisional Conclusions

What is to be done then? Should the traveller free oneself from this obsession, as Baconschi attempts? ("The West was good for me, but that was all. At least I cured myself of superior illusions," 2005, 135). Should one postulate an imaginary superiority, since the marginal is better read in and appreciates more the Western cultural tradition than Western intellectuals do themselves nowadays, as Marino states (1976, 121)?

Starting their travels to this challenging, accessible Europe with the feeling that they really deserve to be there, some of them come back with another prejudice in their luggage: that the West is somehow doomed (Spengler again!) and that it is their mission to try to save as much as possible from its heritage since they are more European than Western Europeans themselves, culturally speaking. This prejudice is less present with the younger generation, but the patterns of relating to the other established by the Romanian intellectual tradition are still functioning. Eventually the opposition is not deconstructed but perpetuated. Newer generations must attempt that.

The type of otherness that Western Europe stands for in the eyes of Romanian (and probably also Eastern European) writers is a particular one, because it does not name the dialectical match of its own identity, but is part of a projected identity with powerful affective connotations. Western Europe emerges from these travel writings as a privileged and idealized cultural space of almost mythical character, an object for various feelings like admiration, wish, complex, frustration, nostalgia.

These fragmented, sketchy, over-interpreted images of Europe represent, in fact, the opposite of a postcard in what they indirectly say about Romanians: there's too much writing for so little space and time. Packed with myths and bookish allusions, pervaded by melancholy and complexes, the travel writings I have discussed here are to a lesser extent representations of Western Europe than fragile Romanian identity constructs.

Notes

1 Often thought of as simply "Europe" throughout history.

2 For a pertinent discussion of its generic status, see David Chirico, "The Travel Narrative as a (Literary) Genre," (2008) in Bracewell and Drace-Francis, eds., vol. 2.

3 Marino was probably the most prominent figure abroad among them due to the many translations of his theoretical works into English, French, Italian, and a few other languages of circulation.

4 See especially "Introduction" in Longworth, 1997.

5 Dinicu Golescu (1777–1830) was a Wallachian boyar whose book *Însemnare a călătoriii mele / Account of My Travels* (Buda 1826) established a pattern for Romanian travel representations of Europe.

6 The themes approached by Romanian travel diaries are actually recurrent in East European travel writings, as Wendy Bracewell points out: "the discovery of European difference; tourism and the traveller; the big city; exoticism and the self" (2009, xvii). Yet the limited space of this analysis does not allow us to go into a detailed comparison, however interesting that might prove.

7 All quotations from Romanian travel diaries are my translations.

References

Baconschi, Teodor. 2005. *Insula cetății: Jurnal parizian, 1991–1994* [*Island of the City. Parisian Journal*]. Bucharest: Curtea Veche.

Berindei, Dan. 2005. *Drumuri în lume: 1965–1980: în vremuri de speranță și incertitudini* [*Rambling through the World in Times of Hope and Uncertainty: 1965–1980*]. Bucharest: Paralela 45.

Bot, Ioana. 2004. *Jurnal elvețian. În căutarea latinei pierdute* [*In Search of Lost Latin*]. Cluj-Napoca: Casa Cărții de Știință.

Bracewell, Wendy, ed. 2009. *East Looks West*. Vol. 1, *Orientations. An Anthology of East European Travel Writing, ca. 1550–2000*. Budapest: Central European University Press.

Bracewell, Wendy, and Alex Drace-Francis, eds. 2008. *East Looks West*. Vol. 2, *Under Eastern Eyes. A Comparative Introduction to East European Travel Writing on Europe*. Budapest: Central European University Press.

———. 2008. *East Looks West*. Vol. 3, *A Bibliography of East European Travel Writing on Europe*. Budapest: Central European University Press.

Cornis-Pope, Marcel, and John Neubauer. 2002. "Towards a History of the Literary Cultures in East-Central Europe: Theoretical Reflections." ACLS Occasional Paper 52.

Delanty, Gerard. 1995. *Inventing Europe*. Houndmills and London: Palgrave Macmillan.

Longworth, Philip. 1997. *The Making of Eastern Europe. From Prehistory to Postcommunism*. Houndmills and London: Palgrave Macmillan.

Marino, Adrian. 1976. *Carnete europene* [*European Notebooks*]. Cluj-Napoca: Dacia.

Mishkova, Diana. 2008. "Symbolic Geographies and Visions of Identity. A Balkan Perspective." *European Journal of Social Theory* 11 (2): 237–56.

Simion, Eugen. 1977. *Timpul trăirii, timpul mărturisirii... Jurnal parizian* [*A Time to Experience, A Time to Confess. Parisian Journal*]. Bucharest: Cartea Românească.

Spiridon, Monica. 2004. "Paris, *terre d'asile*: Exile, Nostalgia and Recollection." *Neohelicon, theme Migratio et litterae* 31: 61–69.

———. 2009. "Literature and the Symbolic Engineering of the European Self." *European Review* 17 (1): 149–59.

Wolff, Larry. 1994. *Inventing Eastern Europe: The Map of Civilization on the Mind of the Enlightenment*. Palo Alto, CA: Stanford University Press.

Chapter 10

On the Ruins of Memory in Miron Białoszewski's
A Memoir of the Warsaw Uprising

Jeannine M. Pitas

Memory is a form of fiction. Very often, it is a projection of present-day desires and beliefs about the past. At times, this type of fiction is created deliberately: perhaps recollecting the past in its full intensity would be too painful for the one remembering, or perhaps too many of the details have been forgotten. Even those who consciously strive to resist this fictionalizing process most often find, however, that they cannot do so. Looking at twentieth-century Polish writer Miron Białoszewski's *A Memoir of the Warsaw Uprising*, we see an attempt, or perhaps a compulsion, to remember the event as accurately as possible: to capture every detail, every feeling, and to immerse the reader fully into the experience as the author lived it. And yet Białoszewski himself admits that this kind of perfect, "authentic" remembrance is not possible. As Madeline Levine, who translated the Polish poet's memoir into English, comments in her introduction to the text,

> The Tolstoyan rejection of the overview in favour of the distancing achieved through individual observation assumes the integrity of the individual observer. Białoszewski undermines even this premise by questioning the validity of his own perceptions and recollections. Memory is not a simple process, and he is careful to insist repeatedly on the shakiness of his recollections. Indeed, Białoszewski is obsessed with the problems of remembering: the difficulty of fixing an event in time, the inevitable fusing of distinct memories into a single image; or, conversely, the fragmenting of a single image into several disjointed images; the near impossibility of freeing one's personal recollections from accepted interpretations and the numerous literary and cinematic depictions of a celebrated event. (1991, 16)

My intention in this essay is to examine some of the ways memory functions in Białoszewski's memoir and to speculate on their significance. After giving a brief historical introduction to the Warsaw Uprising, I seek to show the ways it was later adopted into Poland's collective memory as a sort of grand narrative of the national myth. I then suggest that Białoszewski's narrative, which was very controversial when originally published in Poland, poses a challenge to that myth. Instead of deifying (and reifying) the historical event, it seeks to reveal it as exhaustively and accurately as possible. The situation still is not this simple, however, for we soon see that this attempt at honest remembrance becomes quite difficult for Białoszewski. Time, space, and even personal identity become shapeless and fused in a constantly changing realm of destruction and creation. Some memories inevitably get buried under the rubble. Under these traumatic circumstances, the attempt to remember becomes as much an uncontrollable, even compulsive, process driven by the need for healing as it is a conscious strategy of resistance against totalizing, reifying metanarratives that would seek to use the past instrumentally in pursuit of current political aims. I suggest that Białoszewski's narrative is both of these at once, ultimately standing as both a war memorial and a ruin. It is a memorial because on the one hand, it has been purposefully created in the aftermath of a tragic event with the intention of preserving the memory of lives lost. On the other hand, it is a ruin, the fragmented remains of an experience scooped up from the rubble. Białoszewski has written about his memories of the event in the most honest way he can. Paradoxically, by recognizing the elusive nature of memory and the impossibility of telling the full, veritable story of the Warsaw Uprising as he lived it, Białoszewski manages to produce a deeply authentic account of this event.

Making a Myth: The Commemoration of the Warsaw Uprising

The Warsaw Uprising began on August 1, 1944, at a crucial stage of the Second World War. By this time the Nazis were significantly weakened; the Allies had gained air supremacy, and Soviet forces, who were marching toward Germany from the East, had almost reached Warsaw. At this point, the Polish underground "Armja Krajowa" (Home Army) decided to start a rebellion in Warsaw against the occupying Nazi forces. Their primary goal was to secure Poland's independence and to try to prevent it from being subjected to a Communist regime after the war (Ensink 2003b, 12). Having already witnessed the failed uprising in the Warsaw Ghetto in 1943, the Polish Home Army thought that they stood a strong chance of defeating the

Nazis in their weakened state and that they would be able to rely on Ally support. In the end, however, no such support came. Although the Home Army had asked the London-based Polish government in exile for permission before starting the uprising, they had not communicated with the Soviet forces who, in turn, did not allow the Western Allies to send planes with food, arms, or ammunition. Although the fighting was successful during the first few weeks of the uprising, it soon became clear that the Polish forces were destined to lose. After their surrender on 2 October, the Germans deported 80,000 citizens from Warsaw and embarked on a systematic destruction of the city's remaining infrastructure. By this time, 16,000 Polish soldiers, 26,000 German soldiers, and 150,000 civilians had lost their lives (Ensink 2003b, 13).

Fifty years later, on 1 August, 1994, Lech Wałesa, then the president of Poland, led a ceremony to commemorate the uprising in Warsaw's Krasinski Square. Analyzing the speeches given by world leaders from Poland, Germany, France, Britain, Russia, the United States, Canada, and other nations, Titus Ensink and Christoph Sauer point out the common rhetorical features of each. These include a narrative style, the use of eulogy praising the Poles for their bravery, and a focus on values, suggesting that the ideals that led to the uprising are still relevant today. They conclude that "the speeches contribute to a political discourse, which enables the participants to have words and symbols at their disposal which one can refer to (political) 'normality' and to political values and goals. Such support of political thinking and debating is the main impact of the rhetoric use of epideictic speech" (2003a, 30). The use of "praise and blame" language serves to contextualize the event in terms of larger beliefs and ideals and can then be used for various political ends. Ensink and Sauer also mention that a public commemoration "is almost always based on a procedure of selection: the choice of a specific actualization implies that other possibilities consciously are *not* realized" (2003b, 7). In other words, a commemoration involves speech and silence, remembrance and forgetting. While multiple, competing narratives exist around any event, those engaged in the commemoration choose which aspects of the event they want to accentuate, which narratives to propagate, and which ones to cast aside. In this way, an event such as the Warsaw Uprising is transformed into an object with a certain use value; it is a historical event that is being recreated in the present in a different form in order to serve current political needs. This phenomenon is certainly not unique; as Maurice Halbwachs suggests in his study of collective memory, "every group ... immobilizes time in one way and imposes on its members the illusion that, in a given duration of a constantly changing world, certain zones have acquired a relative stability and balance in which nothing essential is altered" (1980, 126). The question, then, is just whose needs are the commemoration of the Warsaw Uprising serving? What is the advantage of turning a tragic event into a public narrative? Titus and Ensink suggest that the fiftieth anniversary commemoration of this event had much more to do with the political situation in Poland in 1994—as a former Soviet satellite country making the transition to democracy—than it did with the historical event itself.

Looking specifically at Lech Wałesa's speech, Dariusz Gałasinski argues that the president "invokes the myth of Poland as the Messiah of nations, and even brings the myth to a culmination point by representing the Uprising as its redemption" (2003, 41). Wałesa claims that the uprising, though a military failure for Poland, was in fact a moral victory. This type of attitude is nothing new for Poland; it has its roots in Polish Romanticism, which flowered during the late eighteenth century when the country lost its independence to Prussia, Russia, and Austria. During the nineteenth century, several uprisings were organized against the partitioning powers, and while each one was a military failure, these rebellions served to muster up a greater sense of nationalism during this time and to encourage the hope that Poland would one day regain its freedom. Romantic poets such as Adam Mickiewicz and Juliusz Slowacki established a myth of Poland as a Christ-like nation whose suffering and patriotism would redeem the other nations (Gałasinski 2003, 43). Gałasinski suggests that this myth has been invoked again and again throughout Poland's history, for example during the Solidarity anti-Communist movement of the 1980s (43). Referring to the Warsaw Uprising, Wałesa represents Poland as a romantic hero acting alone without any friends or allies. For instance, he mentions that while John F. Kennedy famously announced "Ich bin ein Berliner" [I am a Berliner], no one stood up to say, "I am a Varsovian" (Gałasinski 2003, 45). He depicts Poland as completely defenceless, ignored by the outside world in its time of difficulty, its heroic efforts later unrecognized as it was left behind the Iron Curtain. In this sense, he invokes what literary scholar Aleida Assman describes as the "distinction" of cultural memory: to invoke the past as a means of solidifying a nation's identity and difference from other nations (2011, 129).

Gałasinski also takes note of the strong language of Wałesa's speech. "I trust Warsaw's experience will not be repeated. I trust that at the threshold of the third millennium, such hideous betrayal will not happen again," says

Wałesa (2003, 46). Similarly, "The city ... was murdered with premedita-tion. Finished after capitulation. It was buried in this land, like its defenders' bones" (49). The highly charged diction of a phrase like "hideous betrayal" and the city's personification as an innocent victim of a murder serves to solidify Poland's status as a lone, sacrificial lamb among nations. Although this "betrayal" and "murder" are not attributed to any particular agents, the implicit references are clear. For Gałasinski, the significance of this dramatic rhetoric is that it plays on its audience's sentiments and desire for heroism. "Wałesa provides the country, which in 1994 was stricken by economic hardship, a moment of symbolic glamour," he says. "More impor-tantly, it is the glamour of its most beloved myth" (51). We might suggest that Wałesa reads the uprising in terms of what Northrop Frye would call "typology": the idea that "despite apparent confusion, even chaos, in hu-man events, nevertheless those events are going somewhere and indicating something" (1982, 81). In his study of the Bible, Frye suggests that it was written to be read in terms of corresponding "types" in which a certain nar-rative or metaphor from the past can be understood as prefiguring a related "antitype" in the present. To understand this we need only look at the Gos-pel of Matthew, in which most of Christ's words and actions are presented as fulfillments of Old Testament prophecies. Here, Wałesa interprets the Warsaw Uprising in similar terms, viewing it as a "type" that can be under-stood in terms of other structurally similar events in Poland's history. By situating the uprising in the context of the larger Polish myth, Wałesa man-ages to distract the people from their country's current difficulties and thus to ensure his own continued popularity. Thus, the commemoration of the Warsaw Uprising becomes a tool of power to maintain and advance its own interests.

A Collection of Moments: An Alternative to Myth-making

Written twenty years after the event, Białoszewski's narrative reveals itself to be quite different from what we have seen in Wałesa's commemorative speech. He states very explicitly that he will not stand to see the event made part of the Polish myth. Białoszewski suggests that at the time of the upris-ing, the rest of Poland was completely removed from what was going on in Warsaw; even though the entire nation was torn apart by war, this specific event concerned only Warsaw and its inhabitants: "Warsaw was not Poland; Poland lived her own life. For Poland, the most important thing about War-saw was that it was burning" (1991, 68). This statement can be interpreted as a form of resistance against those who strive to claim the uprising as part of the nation's messianic, Romantic narrative. During the nineteenth century, when Poland was erased from the political map of Europe by the partitioning powers of Prussia, Russia, and Austria, many Polish rebellions were referred to not by place, but by periods of time, such as the November Uprising and the January Uprising against Russia. Białoszewski mentions he always imagined that the rebellion that began in August 1944 would go down as the "August Uprising." He then concludes, however, that since Warsaw was an isolated "state of exception" during this time, the event belongs to Warsaw alone. "Warsaw was not Poland, and so the uprising remained the Warsaw Uprising" (1991, 68). "Poland" as a whole did not suffer through this event and could never hope to understand it, and any attempts to incorporate it into a nationalistic grand narrative would arouse suspicion in those who had actually experienced it.

Most of Białoszewski's efforts to undermine the patriotic narrative are, however, much more subtle than this. His first recollection of the uprising is of no wider concern than his own immediate surroundings. "August 1 is Sunflower Day.… Why that association with sunflowers? Because that's when they're in full bloom and even beginning to fade already, because that's when they are ripening.… And because at that time I was more naïve and sentimental; I hadn't been made cunning yet; because the times themselves were also naïve, primitive, rather carefree, romantic, conspiratorial, wartime" (1991, 19). "Carefree" and "romantic" are not words that immediately come to most people's minds at the thought of war. Here, they tell us something important about Białoszewski's relationship to his surroundings during the war. Wartime seems carefree to him because, at age twenty-two, he is also carefree, as disengaged as possible from the political reality that surrounds him. Having heard artillery fire for the first time at age seventeen when the Nazis first invaded Poland, he has now become accustomed to it; the Nazi presence in his society has become part of the everyday scenery of the city. When the uprising begins, his thoughts are far from national patriotism; he is thinking only of the errands he has to run (his mother has sent him to get bread), an impending meeting with a colleague from the secret university where he studies Polish language and literature, and a date that he has planned for the evening. The casual, detached tone with which he relates the events—"it seems to me I didn't go the way I should have because they were rounding up people"(1991, 20)—reveals the familiarity of the war scenario; after five years, this climate of fear, danger, and violence has become an accepted part of everyday life. It is for this reason that the only accurate way to describe the Uprising is in terms of this same everyday life and experience:

All of this is like one prolonged hallucination. A terribly banal tale. But it suits me. It fits what I felt then. Because you didn't have to be a poet to have things multiplying in your head. If I write very little about my impressions. And everything is in ordinary language, as if nothing happened. Or if I hardly ever look inside myself, or seem to be superficial. It is only because it can't be done any other way. After all, that is how we experienced things. And, generally speaking, that is the only device, not an artificially constructed one, but the only natural device. To convey all of this. For twenty years I could not write about this. Although I wanted to very much. I would talk. About the uprising. To so many people. All sorts of people. So many times. And all along I was thinking was that I must somehow describe the uprising, somehow or other describe it. And I didn't even know that those twenty years of talking (I have been talking about it for twenty years because it is the greatest experience of my life, a closed experience), precisely that talking, is the only way to describe the uprising. (1991, 52)

The telling of the tale is "superficial" because he does not reflect on the events as he is telling them. While he often reflects on the process of recollection, just as he is doing in this excerpt, he does not comment on the events that occurred, choosing instead to relate them as he remembers them. He is convinced, however, that this is the only way to describe the uprising. Simple historical narratives that speak of military manoeuvres but not of individual lives fail to convey the depth of the experience. Long lists of the deceased likewise fail. Indeed, any narrative that strives to be comprehensive and continuous will ultimately be unable to relate the experience of the event. As Halbwachs points out, when trying to recollect the past, one finds that it can be hard to know which memories are really our own and which belong to others; likewise, when bringing together these fragmented stories, we wonder about the gaps between our knowledge and that of others: "What we take for empty space is, in reality, only a somewhat vague area that our thought avoids because so few traces remain. As soon as a precise path to our past is indicated, we see these traces emerge, we link them together, and we see them grow in depth and unity. These traces did exist, therefore, but they were more marked in others' memory than in our own" (1980, 76). Seeking to bring order to these traces, Białoszewski advocates a narrative that simply talks: not a politician's rhetoric, not an orderly, well-planned speech, but the digressive, unfocused chatter of a bus passenger talking to his seatmate, a bar customer talking to the waitress, or perhaps a psychoanalytic patient undergoing free association. However, while Białoszewski's description of talking about the uprising seems to suggest a rhizome-like openness, it is interesting that he refers to it as a closed experience. The fact that it is closed leads us to think that no matter how much or for how long Białoszewski continues to talk about the uprising, he will always be talking in circles. "Closed" suggests an experience that was contained in a specific place and time, not to be repeated and not necessarily having anything to do with the other aspects of one's life. It also suggests that it is finished and cannot be brought to life. In this way it is like a ruin: we can observe it, contemplate it, and try to imagine the whole of which it was once a part, but we cannot recuperate its original state. This is nevertheless exactly what Białoszewski sets out to do in this memoir.

In order to better understand Białoszewski's narrative strategy, I have chosen to take a look at "The Theory of Moments," a chapter of Henri LeFebvre's *Critique of Everyday Life*. At the beginning with this chapter, LeFebvre deals with the question of representation. He gives the example of the word "love." To what does the word, which is nothing more than an arbitrary sign, correspond? He argues that the Platonic, idealistic theory that "love" corresponds to some higher entity, some set, universal model, is untenable; however, the empiricist idea that the word signifies a completely arbitrary set of states and situations unrelated to each other is equally untenable, for it implies a situation in which communication could become impossible as each individual might interpret "love" as having completely different meanings (LeFebvre 2008, 341). He argues that despite all the tricks of language and changes of meaning, "something" remains that allows us to realize that we are talking about the same concept. This "something" is how he defines a moment, and I would like to propose that it is the same "something" which makes the Warsaw Uprising a "closed experience" and informs Białoszewski's own fragmentary account of this event.

There is an inherent tension in LeFebvre's idea of a moment, for on the one hand it is indeed ephemeral and transitory; it is the fleeting instant in which some communicative recognition of the other, some face-to-face contact with the Logos, is temporarily achieved. On the other hand, LeFebvre suggests that the moment can imply a certain amount of duration. The past of which we are speaking might be a day, a week, a month, or several years. But while the actual length of time may vary, what matters is the way we approach that slice of time, how we view it in the present. He suggests that, in some form or another, a moment asks to be preserved.

In order for us to better understand what constitutes a moment and what distinguishes it from any other activity, LeFebvre offers us a set of criteria. First, he says that a moment is constituted by a choice. While love and playfulness may be very closely intertwined, he says, love becomes love when it chooses to take itself seriously, when it chooses to "constitute its moment" and manifest itself clearly (2008, 345). The next criterion for a moment is that it should have a specific duration, a beginning and an end, its own history, and that it inevitably exhausts its potential. LeFebvre then adds that a moment has form and content, that it follows certain rules in time and space, but that its circumstantial reality gives it urgency. Finally, every moment becomes an absolute, a game in which all stakes are bet on winning and, for this brief instant, nothing outside the game matters (346). He goes on to say that because of this very intensity, the moment is doomed to "fail" in that it cannot sustain its force. It burns itself out; the "tragic" must inevitably return to the "everyday." And yet the moment remains very closely tied to everyday reality:

> The moment cannot be defined by the everyday or within it, but nor can it be defined by what is exceptional and external to the everyday. It gives the everyday a certain shape, but taken per se and extrapolated from that context, that shape is empty. The moment imposes order on the chaos of ambiguity, but taken per se this order is ineffectual and pointless. The moment does not appear simply anywhere, at just any time. It is a festival, it is a marvel, but it is not a miracle. It has its motives, and without those motives it will not intervene in the everyday. Festival only makes sense when its brilliance lights up the sad hinterland of everyday dullness, and when it uses up, in one single moment, all it has patiently and soberly accumulated. (LeFebvre 2008, 356)

The moment contains both the tragic and the trivial; it is their unification. It is an interesting concept to think of when we consider Białoszewski's account of the Warsaw Uprising, in which the tragic and trivial are so closely linked that at times it is difficult to distinguish one from the other. Another interesting idea of LeFebvre's is that of the moment's evanescence; it cannot be sustained, and there is a return to ordinariness. This very everyday life, however, provides "the native soil in which the moment germinates and takes root" (2008, 357).

Looking at Białoszewski's narrative strategy, we see that he displays a need and desire to capture every detail of the uprising. A totalized image is not enough; he prefers the fragmented, miniscule images that reveal, in the words of Wisława Szymborska, "the time of insects rather than the time of stars" (1998, 215). Rather than seeking to step outside the system and view it from the airplane window of time and distance, he strives to remain on the ground, completely embedded in the reality he is describing. It is not possible, however, for Białoszewski to sustain this perspective throughout the entire text. He describes an event, person, place, or situation for as long as it holds his attention, illustrating it in as much detail as possible, and then drops it in order to focus on something else. This is partially due to the stress and instability of the situation, in which buildings are constantly being destroyed and the once-familiar landscape is made unfamiliar. At the same time, his constant vacillation between descriptive objects is also due to the twenty years that elapsed from the time of the uprising to the writing of the memoir—and indeed the act of writing itself—preventing Białoszewski from relating a story more reflective of his immediate experience. Throughout the text, he weaves back and forth between the perspective of a young man living through the uprising and a mature one telling the tale years later. The effect of this vacillation is a narrative that is simultaneously a coherent whole and a fragmented series of impressions. We might argue that the *Memoir* is completely devoid of plot; one could open the text to any page, read any passage, and get a sensation of life during the uprising as experienced by Białoszewski. Conversely, the disjointed nature of the text, the way in which the narrator immerses us in the description of one scene only to abandon it, ruminates over the difficulties of remembering, and then starts talking about something else, certainly places some strain on the reader. We may ask, what is the point? Just what is it that Białoszewski is trying to say? As he has said, however, the only way to describe the uprising is to talk about it, interspersing air raids with chicken noodle soup. This was, after all, the war as he and thousands of other civilians had lived it.

Preservation and Expulsion

There are two possible readings of Białoszewski's attempt to embed us in the specific moments and everyday realities of the uprising. One is that he is aiming for preservation; the other is that he is undergoing a process of self-therapy or even exorcism, seeking to excavate the events and expunge them from his memory. On the one hand, Białoszewski attempts to preserve the memories of the uprising as accurately as possible so as to resist the impulse toward a totalizing narrative that would reify the event and fail to recognize the individual experiences and lives preserved and lost in that moment. He seeks to describe the experience in as raw and unmediated terms as he possibly can, drawing the reader into the LeFebvrian moment as it unfolds. On the other hand, the urgency with which Białoszewski writes, the frustration with which he expresses his inability to remember every person and place and portray the experience without stepping outside it, complicates the issue of his intentions. Why is he so concerned about excavating every detail from his memory? One cannot help but think that this urge to unravel everything related to the uprising is necessary to his personal process of healing. Of course, these two ideas are not mutually exclusive. Białoszewski's writing is "therapeutic" in the sense that it is amenable to a process of personal healing and also an active, dynamic process of questioning the static "theory" of grand narratives. In talking about the uprising, Białoszewski simultaneously relieves himself of the burdens and also solidifies them for the reader, who must then, to a certain extent, assume them. Instead of assimilating a historical narrative to his own experience, the reader is overwhelmed by that reality in a way that echoes Białoszewski's own experience.

One interesting element of Białoszewski's style that reveals the tension between preservation and forgetting is the changing of verb tenses throughout. Although the narrative is largely told in past tense, from the point of view of the middle-aged narrator looking back on the events, we see that it is suddenly interrupted by present-tense narration. This rupture occurs spontaneously and unexpectedly in moments when the narrative seems to escape the author's control. Throughout the story of the uprising, the narrator arrives at several points where he suddenly becomes immersed in the situation; instead of describing it from the distanced perspective of a middle-aged man recollecting his youth, he finds that all of the memories return suddenly, and he is thrown back into the scene he is describing. The act of recounting the event forces him to relive it and immerses the reader into it; we are compelled to become participants rather than mere spectators.

Many (though not all) of these ruptures occur in moments of urgent danger. One of these takes place toward the beginning of the narrative, when Białoszewski first becomes actively involved with the uprising by helping to dig trenches. He recalls the sight of a man scrambling to pick up the spilled cigarettes from a kiosk overturned to form part of the barricade; although onlookers shout at him for his behaviour—"Hey, mister, at such a time!"—Białoszewski shares the man's sentiments. Switching suddenly from the past-tense narration of recollection to the present-tense narration of immediacy, Białoszewski informs us,

> I am picked to be a helper. I am ashamed to refuse. But I wish for an air raid right at that moment, so that others will have to do it instead of me. And there is one. Quickly, quietly. They fly over. Already the bombs are falling!

So the men with the wheelbarrows just drop them, the German corpses sail into the trenches, into the excavations, strike the pipes, the cables and remain somewhere deep down there. With the result that some people had to dig them out afterwards, but by then it was other people who had to do it. After the bombs. I ran two houses away. As fast as I could. (1991, 26)

It is striking that, at the most crucial instant, Białoszewski's narration switches from past to present. When asked to assume an active role in the uprising, the narrator feels that his reality has become destabilized, and suddenly he goes from relating the story of that moment to actually reliving it. He is compelled to relate it as if it were happening in the present moment, and the reader is drawn into the space of danger right along with him. Once the immediate threat has passed, the narration returns to past tense, and both Białoszewski and the reader are released from the immediate sense of danger.

The same happens when Białoszewski describes the intensification of the uprising as the German offensive increases. A long past-tense narration about the years leading up to the war is interrupted by a sudden cry which is told without any reference to verb tense at all: "At someone's cry, 'Planes!' we rush to a cellar.... A crush. Panic. Prayer. Explosions. The rumbling, bursting of bombs. Groans and fear. Again they fly low. An explosion, they're already bombing the front, we crouch down. Nearby an old woman beats her breast, 'Sacred Heart of Jesus, have mercy on us'" (1991, 31). The use of verbs in the participle form suggests an experience that is immediate. The narration continues in the present tense as, once the threat has passed, the people go out to the street and find the corpses. Then, seeing a school that has been bombed, Białoszewski returns to past tense narration with a memory of a Christmas pageant he saw in that same school during which the curtain was accidentally torn and the costumed children, embarrassed at being seen by the audience, huddled together and started squealing. That innocent squealing provides a terrifying juxtaposition to the confusion and disruption of the current scene. A memory of the innocent past heightens the terror of the present moment; at the same time, the current situation recasts the memory of that earlier experience in a new, tragic light. In this moment, Białoszewski loses control of the narrative; he is no longer trying to lend immediacy to the description; instead, the memory overtakes him, and he is compelled to relate it to us.

The other occasion where present-tense narration is used is when the mature Białoszewski comments on his frustration over his inability to remember certain moments or events. After narrating the moment when he carried a wounded man through the street on a stretcher, he suddenly becomes frustrated by his own inability to recall whether or not there were pigeons at the scene: "It seems either there weren't any pigeons by then or they were kept so they wouldn't fly about; or perhaps they really were there and did fly up and wheel around and it was only the cornices and window frames which had produced the smoke and dust. But the reason I don't trust my memory is that most likely I didn't know what was what at the time, because it has seemed the same at other times and other places" (1991, 36). While the presence or absence of pigeons at the scene may seem insignificant for the content of Białoszewski's narrative, to him it is extremely significant. He sees it as his responsibility to articulate every detail of the event, even the minutest. For him, this is the only way to create an honest narrative. Initially, it appears that this use of present tense narrative serves a different function than in the previous cases where he is uncontrollably and unexpectedly drawn into the past moment. Here, it seems that he is deliberately trying to capture the singularity of the event in order to prevent the details from getting erased by the overarching narrative. However, he finds that he cannot do so completely, for his memories of that specific event get confused with memories from other events; he cannot be certain that all of his memories pertain to the experience of the uprising. This lack of certainty frustrates Białoszewski, and I would like to argue that this need for specificity can also be viewed as another sign of the narrator's traumatic experience of loss and displacement. It is important to remember that amid the destruction of the uprising, familiar places became completely unfamiliar. Białoszewski's incessant mention of proper names, his identification of streets and buildings reveals his desire for familiarity, for some sort of permanence when all of the everyday places previously taken for granted have been ruined. Thus, the need for specificity stems not only from a conscious desire to relate the uprising authentically for his readers, but also from his personal trauma. As he remembers the past, the sense of displacement, confusion, and loss returns, and he is compelled to recreate it for the reader:

We run. Barefoot. Along Ogrodowa Street. A barricade. We squeeze past. To Solna. Something's burning. Explosions. Beams are sailing through the air. Noise. They fall into the fire. With a thud. We dash along Solna. To Elektoralna. A barricade. We squeeze through. Onwards. Along Elektoralna. To Bank Square (where Dzierzynski Square is today, only smaller and triangular). Something's burning on the right. An entire house in a single flame. We race past. Somewhere beyond Orla Street a whole house is on fire on the left. Actually, it's being consumed by flames. There are hardly any ceilings left. Or walls. Just one huge fire about three stories high. Again the beams groan, collapse. It's hot. That's probably the Office of Weights and Measures. Night. It's quieter here. Maybe the attack is letting up? (1991, 39)

The mention of proper names is essential both for the young man who is fleeing through the rubble and for the older one who is relating the story twenty years later. In the moment of the attack, when the whole landscape is being transformed into a pile of ruins, the search for familiar places becomes a means of survival: both physical survival, as he tries to orient himself strategically so as to avoid the attackers and find momentary safety, and also existential survival, as he hangs on to some aspects of the familiar surroundings he knew before the uprising that might provide some momentary comfort, some sense of rootedness in a landscape where all has been uprooted. Meanwhile, for the memoirist relating the tale, it becomes necessary to preserve, in as much detail possible, the city as he knew it. For the great narratives of the Warsaw Uprising, it is completely insignificant that Bank Square has been replaced by the smaller, triangular Dzierzynski Square. For Białoszewski, however, this is extremely significant. The great patriotic narratives of the uprising do not include street names and offices of weights and measures, just as they do not include the trolley car driver and his girlfriend making love in the underground shelter, the parents singing to their daughter Basia, the Dominican nuns who gave him soup, and all the other anonymous people who make their entrances and exits throughout Białoszewski's narrative. He includes them because he needs to include them, because they are what allowed him, and other individuals, to find their way through the destruction and to survive. For Białoszewski, these seemingly insignificant faces and places are the principal things worth commemorating. At the same time, in a world where familiar landmarks have been made unfamiliar, this specificity becomes another means of survival.

Chopping Space and Time: Specificity as a Means of Preservation

Throughout the narrative, we get the sense that space, time, and human identity are all being destroyed. As buildings are ruined, space is simultaneously defamiliarized and homogenized. In its strange, undifferentiated state, it becomes more and more difficult for Białoszewski to navigate the city. Around the thirteenth day of the uprising, "There were still streets. It was incredibly strange how distant everything was then. Although now it is four times larger than it was then, Warsaw has never seemed so large and complicated, so endless. Space was chopped up" (1991, 63). We get the impression that Warsaw is being transformed into a kind of archaeological dig in which objects from the past are dug up and presented on a level plane without distinctions or hierarchies:

> Rain gutters, brackets of sheet metal hung from holes in the balconies, or from nothing at all. They swayed. Clanged. Banged. Thin, empty inside— what one had thought of as a cornice, a wall, marble. Warsaw was betraying all of her secrets. Since it was she who betrayed them there is no reason to hide the fact. She was already disintegrating. Sinking. She had been sinking for one hundred years. Two hundred. Three hundred. And more. Everything showed. From top to bottom. From the Mazovian princes. Up to us. And back again. (1991, 107)

Białoszewski tells us that Warsaw was already sinking before the war, but this slow disintegration was hidden behind cornices and walls. Now that they have been destroyed, we see the city's secrets revealed; all elements of the city's history have been brought together on a level plane. We also see that in this setting of complete danger and instability, even ruins can be subjected to further ruination. When he finds out that the ruins have been bombed three times, he says that he was completely shocked: "Because the conversation had started with me saying precisely that they probably wouldn't bother to bomb ruins. So now I didn't want to believe it. Because we were beginning to count on the ruins as a safer place. That's fate for you" (1991, 92). Even ruins can be subject to further ruination; the few fragments that remain and provide some point of reference, some degree of familiarity, can be destroyed completely. This shock at the destruction of ruins parallels Białoszewski's tremendous fear of losing the memories of the uprising and his need to preserve the ruins of memory as ruins. Ultimately, ruins become the main force that provides an alternative discourse to the grand narratives of collective memory.

Along with the disintegration and confusion of space comes a disintegration and confusion of time. Białoszewski tells us,

> We worried about the immediate needs of bare subsistence, about what touched our skins and, even worse, the threat from the Vistula and, even worse, from the sky. Memory has forced the rest back. It is difficult to say "memories" in the strict sense of the word. Because there are memories from the day before yesterday. And memories from an hour ago. Memories

from Wola and others fresh from Mostowa Street. They're all muddled. Intertwined. With possibilities, with what might have been. Against the background of what was happening. (1991, 49)

Just as space becomes chopped up and undifferentiated, so time becomes confused. Memories of different times and places become distorted, and it is always possible to imagine memories that never actually occurred. Finally, we see that just as space and time become flattened, so do the subjectivities and identities of individual people. The difference between civilians and partisans becomes blurred. Toward the end of August, nearly a month into the uprising, Białoszewski is reunited with his family in Śródmieście, near the Home Army Headquarters. He says to his friend Halina that he has thought about joining the uprising as a partisan. "I've thought about it," says Halina. "But really," he replies. "If you want we can join; it really doesn't make any difference" (1991, 147). Why does it not make any difference? Because the partisans have nearly run out of weapons? Because Warsaw has been so destroyed that it is clear there is no hope of winning? Because there is hardly any difference between partisans and civilians? I would argue that it points again to the non-differentiation that has become of Warsaw; on the one hand, every place, person, and event is extremely significant; on the other, since all are equally significant, the ultimate result is that nothing is more important than anything else. And yet, Białoszewski becomes extremely frustrated with himself for those people whom his memory has allowed him to lose in the crowd:

I'm having problems with the sequence of events between August 12 and August 18. I know that for my readers it's not exactly important what happened when. But they shouldn't be surprised. It is important for me; the precision of dates and places ... is my way of holding onto the grand design. I have also realized that in spite of myself I may mix up or lose my various distant, more distant and sometimes not quite so distant personae. But that's how it was. People lost each other as suddenly as they found each other. They'd be close for quite some time. Then others became close. Suddenly these became lost and other new people became important. That was common.... Everyone was always flitting about, as happens (at any case) at such hours of death; people couldn't find a place for themselves. The people from one cellar went to the one next door, and the people from next door went over to the first.... Because anywhere else was better. And if it entered someone's mind that it was all the same anywhere, that didn't help at all. (1991, 67)

The idea of people "flitting about" forms quite a contrast with Wałesa's image of young heroes fighting to the death. Time, space, and personal identity are all laid out on the same level, but the image is not one-dimensional. While Wałesa's depiction of the Warsaw Uprising reduces it to a few facts, places, dates, and names, Białoszewski tries to give us *all* the facts, dates, places, and names in the context of the personal lived experience of the people who inhabited those places and lived through those experiences. And he becomes extremely frustrated when he discovers that he cannot do so. They are trying to recognize familiar places amid the destruction. "It was pitiful!" he exclaims. "We went on. To the other side of Ujadowskie. Past Ujadowskie.... I'm not sure if we were there only then. That time. But that shock, realizing what it was, what will remain with me till the end of my life. To have mistaken Aleje Ujazdowskie for a lousy back alley!" (1991, 191). I would suggest, however, that this very frustration stands as evidence of the honesty of Białoszewski's narrative. It would be much easier to reduce the individual lives lost in the uprising to cold statistics and the destroyed buildings to sites on a historical map. By reflecting on the difficulty of remembering, Białoszewski shows us that memory is just as subject to destruction and ruin as are buildings and streets, and that perhaps the only way to preserve the past is, paradoxically, to admit to the impossibility of such preservation.

In Aleida Assman's work on memory, we see a distinction between the concept of the archive—a place where the past is reconstructed in accordance with present-day technological capacities and culture interests—and the idea of waste, which accumulates "outside the archive." and lives on "from one generation to the next in a no-man's land between presence and absence" (2011, 13). While Assman acknowledges that "the border between archive and refuse is a very flexible one," Białoszewski suggests that this border may not exist at all—his work is, in a sense, simultaneously archive and waste. He knows that the only thing he can offer us is a narrative of his memories, and that this narrative will be nothing more than a form of fiction—just like Wałesa's narrative or the romanticized account of the uprising depicted in a book such as the historian Norman Davies' *Rising '44*. And while Białoszewski cannot resist these Romantic tendencies entirely—indeed, the whole compulsion to tell his tale might be interpreted as a form of nostalgia—he approaches the experience with a self-reflexivity that other accounts lack. "I'm playing the wise man unnecessarily," he says toward the end of his memoir. "Long ago others created history out of this, made deductions from it, and proclaimed them. And it is known. I am speaking of this for myself—a layman. And for others—also laymen. To the extent that we can speak because we were there. Laymen and non-laymen. All condemned together to a single history" (1991, 206). What Białoszewski means by "laymen and non-laymen" is unclear. We can interpret it as referring to those "ordinary" civilians who sought to maintain some remnant of everyday life during the uprising as opposed to the Home Army partisans. Or, we can interpret it as meaning the difference between "ordinary" voices like Białoszewski's and those of "non-laymen" who ultimately summed up the total of individual experiences as a single history. Thus we see that Białoszewski recognizes that the names, places, and significant dates of the uprising are ultimately lost when woven together into the overarching narrative. Through his incessant, digressive talking, however, he manages to preserve them in the only way that they can be preserved—as the fragmented ruins of experience.

References

Assman, Aleida. 2011. *Cultural Memory and Western Civilization: Functions, Media, Archives.* New York: Cambridge University Press.

Białoszewski, Miron. 1991. *A Memoir of the Warsaw Uprising.* Trans. Madeline Levine. Chicago: Northwestern University Press.

Ensink, Titus, and Christoph Sauer. 2003a. "A Discourse Analytic Approach to the Commemorative Speeches about the Warsaw Uprising." In *The Art of Commemoration*, edited by Titus Ensink and Christoph Sauer, 19–40. Philadelphia: John Benjamins Publishing.

———. 2003b. "Facing the Past: the Commemoration of the Warsaw Uprising on the Occasion of its Fiftieth Anniversary." In Ensink and Sauer 2003b, 1–18.

Frye, Northrop. 1982. *The Great Code: The Bible and Literature.* New York: Harcourt Brace Johanovich.

Gałasinski, Dariusz. 2003. "The Messianic Warsaw: Mythological Framings of Political Discourse in the Address by Lech Wałesa." In Ensink and Sauer 2003, 41–56.

Halbwachs, Maurice. 1980. *The Collective Memory.* Trans. Francis J. Ditter, Jr., and Vida Yazdi Ditter. New York: Harper and Row.

LeFebvre, Henri. 2008. "The Theory of Moments." In *The Critique of Everyday Life*, Vol. 2, *Foundations for a Sociology of the Everyday.* Trans. John Moore. New York: Verso.

Szymborska, Wisława. 1998. *Poems New and Collected.* Trans. from the Polish by Stanislaw Barańczak and Clare Cavanaugh. Toronto: Harcourt.

Section III
Geography and **Cartography**

Chapter 11

The Dynamics of European Identity: Maps, Bodies, Views

Fernando Clara

The term "identity" when applied to an entity as nebulous and unspecifiable as that seemingly indicated by the lexeme "Europe," is of course a mystification. For "Europe" has never existed anywhere except in discourse, which is to say, in the talk and writing of visionaries and scoundrels seeking an alibi for a civilization whose principal historical attribute has been an impulsion to universal hegemony and the need to destroy what it cannot dominate, assimilate or consume as if by right divine. (White 2004, 67)

Europe: Identity—Identities

Written by a North American historian and published in a volume of essays entitled *Europe and the Other and Europe as the Other* (Stråth 2004), the above passage is interesting in several ways, one of them being that it projects a vision of Europe considerably different from the one usually found within Europe itself, at least during the second half of the twentieth century. One would be tempted to say that Edgar Morin was probably right when, faced with the proverbial difficulties of defining Europe, he repeatedly noted in his *Penser l'Europe* that "Il est difficile de percevoir l'Europe depuis l'Europe.... Il est également difficile de concevoir l'Europe d'un point particulier de l'Europe.... Il est surtout difficile de penser l'Europe depuis l'Europe" ["It is difficult to perceive Europe from Europe.... It is also difficult to conceive Europe from a particular point in Europe.... It is, above all, difficult to think about Europe from Europe"] (1987, 24–25).[1] Distance in space, according to Morin, appears to make a difference, for Europe does indeed have different contours when seen from the other side of the Atlantic.

On one hand, the criticism implicit in White's sentence affronts much of the usual European ways of thinking about Europe. On the other hand, however, one cannot help noticing that by questioning the use of the word "identity" as applied to "Europe," by emphasizing the artificiality of the "mystification" of Europe, or the fuzzy character of the lexeme and its non-existence outside the domain of "discourse" (thus exposing its alleged fundamental *immateriality*), the author merely echoes the well-known ambiguities, contradictions, and paradoxes that play a central role in the European discourse on European identity.

Considered solely from this last point of view, White's passage loses a good part of its provocative tone to become an almost classical or typical (and to some extent also trivial) observation on a geographically ambiguous and conceptually fuzzy "Europe," an observation that could actually have been taken from any of the innumerable handbooks or essays on the "History of the Idea of Europe."

If it is true that "the geographical label 'Europe' is [definitely] a term of embarrassment [for Europeans because] it gives the illusion of uniformity where at first sight only difference is visible" (Luhmann 1994, 65), it is also worth noting that the "embarrassment" caused by these alleged definitory impossibilities, along with the supposed non-existence of Europe outside the scope of discourse, contrast blatantly with its hyper-existence as an "idea," a "concept," a "notion," or even a "theory" (Dainotto 2007), that is, as an immaterial singular entity. But what about Europe's *materiality*? That is, what about the existence of the Europe that has been materialized throughout space and time in its representations, in its "impulsion to universal hegemony and the need to destroy what it cannot dominate, assimilate, or consume" (to use White's provocative words)? What are the products of its "hegemony," "assimilation," "consumption," and "destruction," and where are they to be found? Do they also reflect Europe's identity? A strategic change of viewpoint seems to be necessary in order to try to overcome some of the blind spots and tautologies that recurrently flood the discourse on the "Idea of Europe." As a possible solution to the never-ending story of Europe's identity quest, or more simply as an ingenious detour to avoid the somehow chronic dead ends of the debates, the plural "identities," when applied to Europe, produces a change of perspective that has been enriching the discussion for the past two decades in a number of ways.

Much of the success of this "plural" perspective is based on the more or less obvious fact that what we are used to calling "Europe" appears indeed to be a "family of cultures" (Smith 1992, 97), a conglomerate of national, cultural, and linguistic identities that exists despite the attempts, since the second half of the twentieth century, to push Europe toward political and economic union. Yet, we are not only *what we are*: far from being static, even when conceived on an individual or personal level, "identity" is simultaneously a *product* and a *process*. It is the product of a complex process that develops and constantly redefines itself along the axis of time: we *are* and at the same time we *are not what* we *were*. Furthermore, we keep forgetting who and how we were, and keep reinventing ourselves through documents, pictures, or stories "which simultaneously record a certain apparent continuity and emphasize its loss from memory" (Anderson 1991, 204). And that means that, besides being "plural" from a synchronic perspective (in the sense that we play different roles in different spaces, contexts, or environments), we are certainly also "plural" from a diachronic perspective, something that we evidently tend to forget.

Does this also happen with Europe? Are there many Europes in the past that we tend to overlook? And how would these forgotten Europes of the past, still available through documents, pictures, or stories help us make the lexeme "Europe" less "nebulous and unspecifiable" and its identity-building process more visible? I believe the answer to these questions calls for a different approach from the one that is focused on—and sometimes overwhelmed by—Europe's cultural, national, and linguistic diversity. A *time-binding* approach that gives due emphasis to the "plural" Europes in the past, their differences, similarities, and above all their evolution timeline, is now needed in order to complete and (to a certain extent) correct the first one.

In this chapter I will apply this time-binding approach to a set of old maps of Europe, which I think can very clearly illustrate this complex process of European identity-building. Perhaps more than any other records of European history or any other documents directly related to European identity, maps are cultural artifacts that seem particularly adequate to meet this task because of their double nature: they show something while showing themselves (Boehm 2007, 19), that is, they materialize "Europe" by presenting a picture of it and they are at the same time products of a European vision of Europe's identity. Out of these representations of European space, we will, therefore, be able to read Europe *in time* (Schlögel 2006), and that means unveiling the dynamics, agents, tensions, and interactions that play an important part in Europe's identity-building process.

Maps, Bodies, Views

Of course, the "map is not the territory" (Korzybski 1933, 750).[2] Like words, maps are discourses, texts (Bracke et al. 2007; Harley 2001), ways of communicating and understanding space (Rogoff 2000; Sick 2003), ways of world-making (Goodman 1978) and dominating the world (Akerman 2009; Harley 1988, 1989; Huggan 1989; Rabasa 1985; Stone 1988) or even ways of lying about the world (Monmonier 1991). In short, maps are

> cultural-technical constructs of image, text and number.... They demonstrate not only what people have recognized, but also what and especially how they thought and believed. They are therefore not only pure image utensils, but they construct areas, project rooms, creating knowledge and territories. They illustrate religious, political, and philosophical concepts as well as mental experiments and fictions. (Velminski 2006, 225)

The cartography of Europe thus comprises a series of "discourses" on Europe that materialize forms and produce visual iconic entities that project, divide, differentiate, dissect, rank, and order the European space, providing it with a rich and colourful pictorial existence.

From a geopolitical point of view, the map today plays an undoubtedly important role in the building of collective identities, both at global (supranational, continental) and local levels (e.g., national). At a global level, it is worth recalling in this context the "map wars," that is, the (sometimes) polemic disputes about politically correct (and scientifically more accurate) alternatives to the common flat Eurocentric Mercator projection, from the Gall-Peters projection, which above all intends to correct distortions in the area and size of the continents represented, to the Upside-Down World Maps (or Reversed World Maps), with South at the top and North at the bottom, until finally, the more curious Australian "McArthur's Universal Corrective Map of the World," a variant of a Reversed World Map that has Australia centred at its top. In all of these cases the scientific discourse about size, position, and orientation of the maps and continents is clearly over-flooded with political attitudes and ideological values.[3] At a local (national) level, the fact that representation of the territory can be seen as "the real 'body' of the nation according to nationalist iconography" (Cairo 2006, 367) and the map as "the perfect symbol of the state" (Monmonier 1991, 88) comes as no surprise. The map is definitely *not* the territory. Or at least, not *only* the territory, for it is much more than that when it finds itself iconified and transposed to political and cultural settings. As "an image for representing political authority" (Biggs 1999, 390) the map acquires a new iconic life, becoming simultaneously overloaded with meaning, values, and symbolic functions. In a context of strong geopolitical metaphorization like this, the questions that need to be answered, as far as Europe is concerned, seem fairly obvious: how does this process of metaphorization operate at a European level? What are the meanings, values, and symbolic functions conveyed by maps of Europe? Are these also "the perfect symbols" of its identity, its "real 'body,'" as it happens with many national states? What is the role of cartography in defining Europe's identity?[4]

Three variations of a well-known anthropomorphic map of Europe, dating from the mid- and late sixteenth century, may prove to be helpful in answering at least some of these questions.[5]

The first one is taken from the work that chiefly popularized this image in sixteenth-century Europe—Sebastian Münster's *Cosmographiæ Universalis*. (See figure 11.1.) The second map is a variation by Heinrich Bünting and was published in his *Itinerarium Sacræ Scripturæ* by the end of the sixteenth century. (See figure 11.2.) And finally the original engraving, by Johannes Putsch (Bucius), that appeared 1537 in Paris, with the title "Carte de l'Europe en forme de femme couronnée." (See figure 11.3.)

Figure 11.1 Europa Regina (Sebastian Münster)

Of these maps one could possibly say—borrowing the words of Aristotle's *Poetics* (1451*a-b*)—that they are more universal, "more philosophical and a higher thing" (precisely due to their poetic licence) than those produced by sixteenth-century scientific geographical discourse (such as Mercator, Ortelius, or Waldseemüller—to name only a few of the most renowned cartographers of that time). In this case, Geography becomes *literally* the "eye of History."[6]

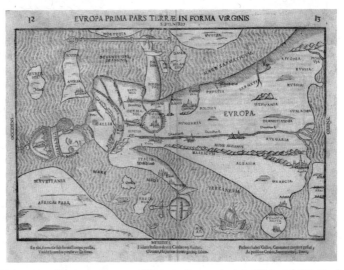

Figure 11.2 Europa prima pars Terræ in forma virginis (Heinrich Bünting)

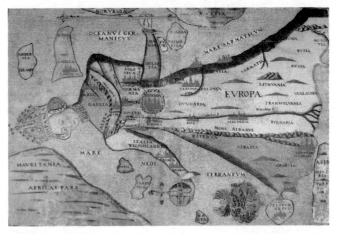

Figure 11.3 Carte de l'Europe en forme de femme couronnée (Johannes Putsch)

On one hand, it is important to note that these images reproduce a self-complacent European world view that was, by that time, beginning to become trivial. Indeed, in the prefaces of the numerous and very popular collections of voyages and travels published in Europe during the seventeenth and eighteenth centuries, it would not be too hard to find similar imperial visions, as a passage from one of these introductory essays, attributed to John Locke, plainly demonstrates:

> the empire of Europe is now extended to the utmost bounds of the earth where several of its nations have conquests and colonies. These and many more are the advantages drawn from the labours of those who expose themselves to the dangers of the vast ocean, and of unknown nations; which those who sit still at home abundantly reap in every kind: and the relation of one traveller is an incentive to stir up another to imitate him; whilst the rest of mankind, in their accounts without stirring a foot, compass the earth and seas, visit all countries, and converse with all nations. (1704, lxix)

But on the other hand, these maps also reflect and at the same time establish an inner European order that cannot be here overlooked. The images are clearly intended to be read from a complex intersection of horizontal and vertical axes that constitute their main guidelines. The anthropomorphically outlined Europe begins in the West (the head bearing an imperial crown) and ends in the East. This is the main visualization axis, from left to right, the axis where the image's meaning is produced. Both arms of the figure hold symbols of power (an orb in the South and a sceptre in the North), which are relatively secondary to the centre (head and trunk) of the whole body. The centre, the "heart" of Europe, where both axes intersect each other, is significantly marked by a circle or a golden coin: it is Bohemia.

The question of the centre is by no means a matter of less significance as far as maps are concerned, and deserves therefore some attention. Most of the aforementioned essays that deal with these three maps (see note 5) tend to favour a political interpretation of their common core, Bohemia being the centre of the Habsburg Empire and the map a display of the power of that empire; others prefer to emphasize the fact that its creator (Johannes Putsch) was from Bohemia and deliberately placed his homeland at the centre of the picture. Though the political interpretation seems to make much more sense in this case, considering the epoch and the circumstances under which the picture was drawn and popularized it would probably be more productive, in this context, to confront this Bohemian centre of

Europe with the centre of another contemporary well-known map, the one Heinrich Bünting published in the same work where his "Europa prima pars Terræ in forma virginis" (fig. 11.2) appeared. This other image, an allegorical world map entitled "Die gantze Welt in einem Kleberblatt/Welches ist der Stadt Hannover meines lieben Vaterlandes Wapen" ["The whole world in a clover leaf, which is the coat of arms of the city of Hannover my beloved fatherland"], places Jerusalem in a similar circle, at the centre of a clover leaf, which is formed by three leaflets, each one representing Asia, Africa, and Europe.[7] Now, the fact that Bohemia occupies the place of Jerusalem in the anthropomorphic European maps reproduced above announces a significant shift from medieval cartography (where a typically central position was reserved for the Holy City) and at the same time bears witness to an already ongoing important process of secularization of power and society.

Whether because of Europe's apparent self-satisfied and hegemonic attitude over the rest of the world or because of its newly found corporeal identity and secular centre, or even because of the way the internal differentiations (of countries, regions, and powers) are symbolically displayed as "head," "trunk," and "members" of the same body, the fact is that the hierarchical structure of European power at the time, the structure of Europe's identity, could hardly be more clearly drawn.

The *Europa triumphans* (Werner 2009) that these maps proudly present, this new European body order-identity lasts until approximately the mid-eighteenth century. Its origins, apart from the more local political contexts that made these cartographical personifications possible, should certainly be traced back to the complex anthropological set of problems arisen by the contacts, encounters, and confrontations with the recently discovered non-European other. Redefining itself in the eyes of the other in a typical process of identity formation and development, Europe (re)discovers, (re)invents, and (re)builds itself within this relationship. In doing so, however, Europe carries over to its own body-territory the hierarchical structure of a bipolar logic (top/bottom, up/down, dominant/dominated) that characterized its unequal relation with the non-European, which means this newborn Europe that had just learned to cast its imperial eyes over the rest of the world, was at the same time beginning to try out some kind of a colonial, hierarchical perspective on itself. In other words, the non-European other was the difference that made a difference, also within the European space. And while the anthropological questions and motivations underlying this *Europa triumphans* may well be diluted by the more powerful and explicit hegemonic discourse that emerges from these images, it is important to note that they should not, however, be put aside or forgotten, as they constitute the very conditions of production of the maps.

By the mid-seventeenth century, a map designed by the prolific Dutch cartographer Willem Blaeu makes the emerging differences within the European space much clearer in a hybrid image that combines a scientific, geographic depiction of Europe's territory along with images of its inhabitants in typical national clothing and views of Europe's most important cities (similar maps were also available for Asia, America, and Africa). As a whole, the image inevitably recalls Martin Waldseemüller's "Carta Itineraria Europæ" (1520), with its ornamental heraldic border surrounding the map, but the depicted European territory is now presented in a much more accurate Mercator projection with North at the top (whereas Waldseemüller's showed an inverted map of Europe). (See figure 11.4.)

Despite the fact that a political, geographic image of the territory now takes the place of the female European body, the whole map still owes much of its conception to the former allegorical images. In fact, the body doesn't disappear at all, it significantly multiplies itself, becomes plural and at the same time differentiated. Enclosing the central map, on both the left/West and right/East sides, are now two sets of pre-ethnographical tableaux with pairs of national figures in a social, convivial pose. These sets have what

Figure 11.4 Europa recens descripta (Willem Janszoon Blaeu)

appears to be a clear geographical North–South (or top–bottom) order: the West set, for instance, has the English at the top, then the French, followed by the Belgians, the Spaniards, and the Venetians at the bottom. The set of scenes with images of European cities at the top is rather curious in the hybrid order that it establishes: Rome is at the centre, but the usual West–East geographical guideline seems to be somehow inverted, Lisbon being the first city depicted on the East-most side, followed by Toledo, London, and Paris. On the West, the first image represents Amsterdam (where Blaeu lived and worked), immediately followed by Prague, Constantinopolis, and Venice. As in Waldseemüller's "Carta Intineraria," Europe is majestically surrounded by its grandeur, but instead of an ornamental heraldic border representing the magnificence of its princes and monarchs, there are now prospects of its most important metropolitan achievements and tableaux of the agents of these achievements, its bourgeois inhabitants, presences that clearly point to a shift within the inner structure of European power. Europe's territory may again be at the centre of this self-celebrating hybrid transitional image, where parts of Africa and Asia are still visible (as in the *Europa Regina* images), but one cannot help noticing that its territory is now divided by lines that mark political frontiers, that its bodies and spaces have become plural and differentiated, and that there seem to be relevant changes in the orientation of the main vertical and horizontal axis of the picture.

A "Brief Description of the Peoples to be found in Europe and their Characteristics," dated 1720/1730 still reproduces the basic cosmographical order popularized by Münster, but it also goes a step beyond and stereo-typically emphasizes the hierarchy of differences and values that divide the Europeans. (See figure 11.5.) It is worth noting that the line that guides the viewer's eyes cosmologically mimics the apparent movement of the sun in the sky (as indeed the very colour of the sky in the background suggests), having on its eastern obscure edge—the "end" of Europe—the "Turkish or Greek" and on its beginning, in the West, the "Spaniard." But instead of a body and mapped territory, there is now a table of characteristics, customs, traditions,[8] and several different bodies that seem to share little (if anything at all). If one considers that this table still celebrates Europe, then it must be added that it now celebrates Europe's *differences*.

This kind of cosmological vision is also found in the immense produc-tion of geographical and historical writings on Europe (descriptions, trav-els, statistics, etc.) published during the eighteenth century, the structure of which generally followed the same horizontal West–East guideline, the

Figure 11.5 Kurze Beschreibung der in Europa Befintlichen Völcker Und Ihren Aigenschaften

first volumes or chapters dealing with the Iberian Peninsula and the last one with Greece (or sometimes vice versa). The table of contents of Samuel Pufendorf's very successful *Einleitung zu der Historie der vornehmsten Reiche und Staaten* [*Introduction to the History of the Principal Kingdoms and States of Europe*], a book first published in Frankfurt in 1682 that was immediately translated into English and French, and reprinted several times throughout the first half of the eighteenth century, provides a good example of the way this perspective is deeply rooted in the mindset of the period: the twelve chapters of the book basically follow the order of the picture above, reproduced with only a few minor exceptions (Spain and Portugal are handled separately, only the main Central European States are considered, and "Turkey or Greece" are not covered in the book, which ends with a chapter on the Pope). These West–East ordered lists are evidently the remains of the sixteenth-century image of an *Europa triumphans*, an organic, imperial, united Europe like the ones Münster or Bünting gave to print, but as the differences between the elements of the lists are punctuated it becomes clear that the underlying cosmological vision wouldn't last much longer. Differences would soon become *inequalities* (Rousseau 1755) and inequalities would inevitably lead to *conflicts*. A *Europa deplorans* was already on its way.[9]

   And indeed, a century and a half later, Europe was not only considerably different, but in some aspects even unrecognizable. The "Nouvelle Carte d'Europe Dressée Pour 1870" (an engraving by Paul Hadol, published around 1870 in Paris and popularized all over Europe) could well be an example (among others) for pointing out the striking transformations that the European space and identity had undergone. (See figure 11.6.) The picture now focuses exclusively on Europe (Africa vanishes from the frame and with it the non-European other, that is, the counterpart of Europe's identity). The differences between Europeans that we saw before from a pre-ethnographical, anthropological point of view have been accentuated and degraded, becoming conflicts. Above all, the former main horizontal axis (East–West) that gave Münster's Europe a meaning, a body, and an identity has almost completely disappeared.

The allegorical, satirical map is vertically oriented, which means that the North–South (top/bottom) axis is now the central axis. Moreover, all the figures are in a more or less vertical position, with only two important exceptions at the extremes: Spain and the Asiatic part of Turkey. Metaphorically, one would say that from Putsch, Münster, and Hünting to Hadol,

Figure 11.6 Nouvelle Carte d'Europe Dressée Pour 1870 (Paul Hadol)

Europe assumes an upright position. The North/top part now takes up its dominance; the southern East and West extremities significantly lie down smoking, a lethargic position and attitude that undoubtedly recalls or refers to the former main horizontal guideline axis. The peripheral South is thus turned into a decadent place where the old European order could, from then on, be staged or even revisited, some kind of a live museum of Europe's former imperial identity, a space devoted to the past and now inhabited by an indolent, backward people. To put it in the plain words of a nineteenth-century British traveller: "The effects of climate are felt in regular gradation as you proceed southward to the Alps or Pyrenees, and thence into the Italian or Spanish Peninsula, and across the Mediterranean into Africa—lazy, lazier, laziest!" (Hughes 1847, I: 11). The clockwise rotation this allegorical map presents makes it evident that a fundamental displacement of the European axes of power and knowledge had taken place. Europe had radically changed.

In fact, one cannot stress enough that the European identity process seems strongly determined, perhaps since its beginnings, by a hegemonic logic crystalized by Francis Bacon in his emblematical aphorism "Scientia potentia est" (which dates significantly from the late sixteenth century), a logic also explicitly echoed in Hayden White's earlier observation on Europe's "impulsion to universal hegemony and the need to destroy what it cannot dominate, assimilate, or consume as if by right divine."

This "impulsion to universal hegemony" is twofold: besides acting externally (in the way Europe replicates or clones itself as a colony outside Europe), it also acts internally (in the way the hierarchical structures of power and knowledge are established and rearranged within the European framework). Hadol's "Carte d'Europe" focuses precisely these internal "impulsions," as do many of the contemporary discourses on Europe's "union of diversity" (e.g., Kraus 2008) that seek—and fail[10]—to dissolve the differences produced by a hierarchy of values, knowledge, and power which dates back to the eighteenth century and would be intensified throughout the following centuries by European nationalisms. This displacement, from a West-centred European space to a North-centred one reflects, then, a fundamental shift in Europe's identity structure that takes place with progressive intensity during the eighteenth, nineteenth, and twentieth centuries. Whatever Europe may be now, it is certainly a product of this major displacement.

European Identity Revisited

I have tried to show that the dynamics of European identity cannot be defined solely in terms of the usual "unity in diversity" (or vice versa), nor can it be fully grasped by the underlying ideas of inter- or multiculturalism. These maps, and above all the evolution and dynamics they present, show that plurality or diversity in Europe are not confined to space, culture, or nation. There are certainly many Europes in the present, but there were also many different Europes in the past. They are all products of a dynamic and complex process of identity-building that has been at the centre of my analysis. From this perspective, Europe doesn't appear to be (nor should it be seen as) a special case of identity. In fact, the ambiguities, paradoxes, and antagonisms that debates about European identity usually bring up are not that different nor distant from the ones discussed at individual or community levels. They are the consequences of what Kant described as the "ungesellige Gelligkeit der Menschen" ["unsocial sociality of man"], that is, "den Hang derselben in Gesellschaft zu treten, der doch mit einem durchgängigen Widerstande, welcher diese Gesellschaft beständig zu trennen droht, verbunden ist" ["a tendency to enter the social state combined with a perpetual resistance to that tendency which is continually threatening to dissolve it"] (Kant 1784, 392).

The appearance of the body (*Europa Regina*) clearly signals the emergence of a self. The body conveys and at the same time produces a European identity. As this identity develops, it becomes more complex. When it questions itself as an identity, thus achieving self-consciousness, the internal differences and conflicts tend to assume more visibility and importance.

These allegorical maps and figures are hence discourses that bear witness to the process of formation and development of European identity: they tell stories (Hassan 2005) and at the same time they stage History. Presenting themselves as self-conscious fictions, they produce an interesting effect, analogous to that of the double negation: they definitely are more accurate and complete, they say more about the object they're describing and displaying than their counterpart scientific discourses of Geography or History.

Furthermore, the first set of maps from the late sixteenth century show that the non-European other plays a central role in the process of European identity-building, a role that hasn't been emphasized enough in the past, and still is not today (Hansen 2002). To some extent, one could say that it is precisely the non-European other that triggers the process of European identity-building. From that moment on, both non-European *and* European change.

It is important to stress that this is a *two-way process* evolving from discovery to exploration and then colonization: the colonizer may well dominate and transform the colonized, but the colonizer is also transformed through its domination as well as through the dominated (the same goes, of course, for the discovery and exploration stages). The analyzed maps clearly illustrate the impact of this process on the dominator. While the first set of images (figs. 11.1 to 11.3) celebrates the self for its discovery, the second set (figs. 11.4 and 11.5) already shows signs of a different type of inner-European relations, where the *differences*, rather than the organic unity, are punctuated. Differences were soon to be seen as *inequalities*, and these would quickly turn into *conflicts* (fig. 11.6). The non-European other that had triggered Europe's identity-building triggered its implosion, as well.

Finally, considering the evolution of the European identity landscape here tentatively outlined, there is one last remark that still must be made concerning White's passage quoted at the beginning: if it is indeed true that Europe's "principal historical attribute has been an impulsion to universal hegemony and the need to destroy what it cannot dominate, assimilate, or consume," it should likewise be added that this "principal attribute" also applies to Europe itself, to its own territory and people. For the History of Europe itself is admittedly full of material evidence of this "need to destroy what it cannot dominate, assimilate, or consume."

Notes

1   Unless otherwise noted, this and all subsequent translations are my own.
2   See also Bateson's and Crampton's remarks on Korzybski's well-known statement (Bateson 1970; Crampton 2001).
3   Significantly, it is the map (as an icon), not the territory that is the object of these disputes. See Monmonier (2004) and Snyder (1993) among others, for details.
4   Even though I am dealing with objects that represent space, I do not intend here to get back into the much-debated issues of Europe's territory, geography, and boundaries. The question here is therefore not so much a matter of defining or delimiting European space, but rather one of analyzing the changes and dynamics that the representations of European space have undergone from the mid-sixteenth century to the late nineteenth century in the hope that some conclusions can be drawn regarding Europe's identity formation and development.
5   The three maps that follow have a complex and, to a great extent, common history. For details on their first (and subsequent) editions or on the cultural

political context of their emergence and popularization in Europe see, among many others, Benthien (2007), Bracke (2007), Deswarte (2002), Heijden (2001), Schmale (2000), or Werner (2009).

6 The metaphor is used by Abraham Ortelius in the preface of his *Theatrum Orbis Terrarum* (1570) to emphasize the important part played by Geography in the understanding of History (see details in Rabasa 1985).

7 On this particular map see Heijden (2001) and Kohl (2008), among others.

8 The left column of the table lists a series of characteristics that range from "customs," "nature and character," "science," "love," "diseases," or "how they spend time," to "their life's end."

9 Cf. Werner (2009). A map drawn by Hendrik Kloekhoff printed in Haarlem around 1790 by François Bohn, and entitled *Europa. Volgens de nieuwste verdeeling* [*Europe. According to the newest classification*], transforms the young imperial Europe into a homely middle-aged housewife (see the reproduction in Bennholdt-Thomsen and Guzzoni 1999, 23).

10 Among others, Anthony D. Smith sees the quest for a Europe "united in diversity" as inevitably condemned to failure because of the circular arguments that it involves: "cultural differences between the nations of Europe persist because of the lack of a strong central authority able to unify and homogenize the peoples of Europe, while the lack of such a centralized and unifying authority can be largely attributed to the depth of these cultural and historical differences" (1993, 133).

References

Akerman, James R., ed. 2009. *The Imperial Map: Cartography and the Mastery of Empire*. Chicago: Chicago University Press.

Anderson, Benedict. 1991. *Imagined Communities. Reflections on the Origin and Spread of Nationalism*. Rev. ed. London: Verso.

Barker, Francis, Peter Hulme, Margaret Iversen, and Diana Loxley, eds. 1985. *Europe and Its Others*. Proceedings of the Essex Conference on the Sociology of Literature, July 1984. 2 vols. Colchester: University of Essex.

Bateson, Gregory. 1970. "Form, Substance and Difference." *General Semantics Bulletin* 37: 5–13.

Bennholdt-Thomsen, Anke, and Alfredo Guzzoni. 1999. *Analecta Hölderliniana: Zur Hermetik des Spätwerks*. Würzburg: Königshausen & Neumann.

Benthien, Claudia. 2007. "Europeia: Mythos und Allegorie in der Frühen Neuzeit." In *Akten des XI. Internationalen Germanistenkongresses Paris 2005*, edited by Jean-Marie Valentin, vol. 12, 21–32. Bd. 12 (Europadiskurse in der deutschen

Literatur und Literaturwissenschaft, betreut von Claudia Benthien, Paul Michael Lützeler und Anne-Marie Saint-Gille). Bern: Peter Lang.

Biggs, Michael. 1999. "Putting the State on the Map: Cartography, Territory, and European State Formation." *Comparative Studies in Society and History* 41 (2): 374–405.

Boehm, Gottfried. 2007. *Wie Bilder Sinn erzeugen. Die Macht des Zeigens.* Berlin: Berlin University Press.

Bracke, Wouter, Lisette Danckaert, Caroline De Candt, and Marguerite Silvestre, dir. 2007. *Formatting Europe, Mapping a Continent. Dix siècles de cartes d'Europe dans les collections de la Bibliothèque royale de Belgique.* Bruxelles: Biliothèque Royale de Belgique.

Cairo, Heriberto. 2006. "'Portugal is not a Small Country': Maps and Propaganda in the Salazar Regime." *Geopolitics* 11 (3): 367–95.

Crampton, Jeremy W. 2001. "Maps as Social Constructions: Power, Communication and Visualization." *Progress in Human Geography* 25 (2): 235–52.

Dainotto, Roberto M. 2007. *Europe (in Theory).* Durham, NC: Duke University Press.

Deswarte, Sylvie. 2002. "Le Portugal et la Mediterranée. Histoires Mythiques et Images Cartographiques." *Arquivos do Centro Cultural Calouste Gulbenkian* 43: 97–147. Lisbon: Fundação Calouste Gulbenkian.

Goodman, Nelson. 1978. *Ways of Worldmaking.* Indianapolis, IN: Hackett.

Hansen, Peo. 2002. "European Integration, European Identity and the Colonial Connection." *European Journal of Social Theory* 5 (4): 483–98.

Harley, J. Brian. 1988. "Maps, Knowledge, and Power." In *The Iconography of Landscape: Essays on the Symbolic Representation, Design and Use of Past Environments,* edited by Denis Cosgrove and Stephen Daniels, 277–312. Cambridge, CT: Cambridge University Press.

———. 1989. "Deconstructing the Map." *Cartographica: International Journal for Geographic Information and Geovisualization* 26 (2): 1–20.

———. 2001. *The New Nature of Maps: Essays in the History of Cartography.* Baltimore: John Hopkins University Press.

Hassan, Ihab. 2005. "Maps and Stories: A Brief Meditation." *Georgia Review* 59 (4): 751–63.

van der Heijden, Henk. 2001. "Heinrich Büntings Itinerarium Sacrae Scripturae, 1581: ein Kapitel der biblischen Geographie." *Cartographica Helvetica* 23–24: 5–14.

Huggan, Graham. 1989. "Decolonizing the Map: Post-Colonialism, Post-Structuralism and the Cartographic Connection." *ARIEL: A Review of International English Literature* 20 (4):115–31.

Hughes, Terence McMahon. 1847. *An Overland Journey to Lisbon at the Close of 1846: With a Picture of the Actual State of Spain and Portugal.* 2 vols. London: Henry Colburn.

Kant, Immanuel. 1784. "Idee zu einer allgemeinen Geschichte in weltbürgerlicher Absicht." *Berlinische Monatsschrift* 4: 385–411.

Kohl, Karl-Heinz. 2008. "Allegorien der drei Erdteile und die Entdeckung Amerikas." *Berlin-Brandenburgische Akademie der Wissenschaften, Berichte und Abhandlungen* 14: 25–49.

Korzybski, Alfred. 1933. "A Non-Aristotelian System and Its Necessity for Rigour in Mathematics and Physics." In *Science and Sanity. An Introduction to Non-Aristotelian Systems and General Semantics,* 747–61. Lakeville, CT: International Non-Aristotelian Library Publishing.

Kraus, Peter A. 2008. *A Union of Diversity. Language, Identity and Polity-Building in Europe.* Cambridge, CT: Cambridge University Press.

Locke, John. 1704. "An Introductory Discourse containing the Whole History of Navigation from its Original to this time." In *A Collection of Voyages and Travels, some Now First Printed from Original Manuscripts. Others translated out of foreign languages, and now first published in English.* Vol. 1, ix–c. London: printed for Awnsham and John Churchill.

Luhmann, Niklas. 1994. "European rationality." In *Culture and Creativity,* edited by Gillian Robinson and John Rundell, 65–83. London: Routledge.

Monmonier, Mark. 1991. *How to Lie with Maps.* Chicago: University of Chicago Press.

———. 2004. *Rhumb Lines and Map Wars: A Social History of the Mercator Projection.* Chicago: University of Chicago Press.

Morin, Edgar. 1987. *Penser l'Europe.* Paris: Gallimard.

Pufendorf, Samuel. 1682. *Einleitung zu der Historie der vornehmsten Reiche und Staaten, so itziger Zeit in Europa sich befinden.* Frankfurt am Main: Knoch.

Rabasa, Jose. 1985. "Allegories of the Atlas." In Barker et al., 1985, I: 1–16.

Rogoff, Irit. 2000. *Terra Infirma. Geography's Visual Culture.* London: Routledge.

Rousseau, Jean-Jacques. 1755. *Discours sur l'origine et les fondements de l'inégalité parmi les hommes.* Amsterdam: Marc Michel Rey.

Schlögel, Karl. 2006. *Im Raume lesen wir die Zeit. Über Zivilisationsgeschichte und Geopolitik.* Frankfurt am Main: Fischer.

Schmale, Wolfgang. 2000. "Europa—die Weibliche Form." *L'Homme. Zeitschrift für feministische Geschichtswissenschaft* 11 (2): 211–33.

Sick, Andrea. 2003. *Kartenmuster. Bilder und Wissenschaft in der Kartografie.* Ph.D. Diss., Unviersität Hamburg.

Smith, Anthony D. 1992. "National Identity and the Idea of European Unity." *International Affairs* 68 (1): 55–76.

———. 1993. "A Europe of Nations. Or the Nation of Europe?" *Journal of Peace Research* 30 (2): 129–35.

Snyder, John P. 1993. *Flattening the Earth: Two Thousand Years of Map Projections.* Chicago: University of Chicago Press.

Stanzel, Frank Karl. 1997. *Europäer. Ein imagologischer Essay.* Heidelberg: Carl Winter.

Stone, Jeffrey C. 1988. "Imperialism, Colonialism and Cartography." *Transactions of the Institute of British Geographers: New Series* 13 (1): 57–64.

Stråth, Bo, ed. 2004. *Europe and the Other and Europe as the Other.* Brussels: Peter Lang.

Velminski, Wladimir. 2006. "Mysterien der Kartographie" In *Visuelle Argumentationen. Die Mysterien der Repräsentation und die Berechenbarkeit der Welt,* edited by H. Bredekamp and P. Schneider, 225–52. München: Wilhelm Fink.

Werner, Elke Anna. 2009. "Triumphierende Europa—Klagende Europa. Zur visuellen Konstruktion europäischer Selbstbilder in der Frühen Neuzeit." In *Europa- Stier und Sternenkranz: Von der Union mit Zeus zum Staatenverbund,* edited by Roland Alexander Issler and Almut-Barbara Renger, 241–60. Göttingen: Bonn University Press, Vandenhoeck & Ruprecht.

White, Hayden. 2004. "The Discourse of Europe and the Search for a European Identity." In Stråth 2004, 67–86.

Wintle, Michael. 2004. *Europa and the Bull, Europe, and European Studies. Visual Images as Historical Source Material.* Amsterdam: Vossiuspers UvA.

Chapter 12

Neighbourhood Identity and the Larger World: Emir Kusturica's *Underground*

Gordana Yovanovich

Mikhail Bakhtin's notion of *carnivalesque laughter*[1] and his concept of polyphony can help viewers understand Kusturica's complex and controversial film. Made during the destruction of Yugoslavia, and based on Dušan Kovačević's novel *Once Upon a Time There Was a Country*, the film *Underground* (1995) tells a local story in international cinematographic language; Kusturica's directing skills have been compared favourably to those of Federico Fellini. While the level of artistic skill in the making of the film is high, and at the level of the story there is an intricate dialogical relation between characters, at the level of the plot, as in other carnivalesque films (such as *Mardi Gras: Made in China*), numerous stories are about raw, startling celebration, where excess and transgression define everyday life. Kusturica's highlighting of a "re-creative" dimension of carnivalesque exaggeration has been seen by Slavoj Žižek as "the reverse racism which celebrates the exotic authenticity of the Balkan Other, as in the notion of Serbs who, in contrast to inhibited, anemic Western Europeans, still exhibit a prodigious lust for life" (2000, 5). I argue that the interplay of local and global in the film, more than reversing the dominant paradigm of (cold and boring) civilized West and (exotic and alive) primitive other, leads the viewer to question the world view of binary oppositions like good guys and bad guys, promoted by dominant (Hollywood) culture. I further argue that the film's highlighting of neighbourhood identities and local ways of life is not a form of nationalism but rather is a simple recognition that marginalized cultures survive because they have their own ways of gaining agency. Kusturica also shows that when local cultures are destroyed, ordinary people become "wasted humans" (Bauman 2004, 41) like Ivan in the film, who will seek justice.

Underground is the last film in the history of Yugoslavian moviemaking made in an attempt to save Yugoslavia from local and international devastation.[2] It is an intricate commentary on the destruction of a state and national identity, and on construction of new "imagined community," as Benedict Anderson would say. Sean Homer rightly observes that the film is a "critique of Tito's Yugoslavia and the film industry's role in reconstructing history and national mythologies" (2009, 7), but it is also a montage of the country beyond Tito's time. The obvious theatricality and exaggerated performances in *Underground* are a means of subverting the established order and questioning the ways of having or gaining agency in a chaotic world driven by different local and global forces. In the complexity of relationships and the development of repetitive history, community performances such as music at weddings, improvisations, and carnivalesque laughter play an important role as identity makers, particularly as a small, marginalized nation contends with rising global insecurities.

The film begins with a local exaggerated Balkan/primitive macho celebration in the late hours of the night, followed by documentary clips of the different receptions locals gave on the morning of the "civilized" German invasion of Maribor, Zagreb, and Belgrade in 1941. The film ends with a local celebration, preceded by scenes in which global UN peacekeeping "Blue Helmets" are moving refugees of the wars of the 1990s, and participating in the arms trade that fuels the global restructuring of nations. In recent history, as at the beginning of the Second World War, national and international, local and global struggles are intertwined because, as Susan Woodward points out (1995), there were two key factors that contributed to the breakup of Yugoslavia. First was the fundamental shift in the international order with the end of the Cold War that saw Yugoslavia lose its strategic geopolitical position mediating between the East and the West, as well as its role in the Non-Aligned Movement. The second factor which contributed to the breakup of the country was the global financial crisis and economic recession of the mid-1970s and early 1980s.

In the general trend of shifting identities, the destruction of a multiethnic Yugoslavian community opened up new possibilities of identity-building: first, to become a part of the European Union, as promoted—but also heavily conditioned—by the EU and the international community, and second, to revert back to ethnic or neighbourhood identities that could mean a return to traditional nationalism. Kusturica's personal choices made both during and after the making of *Underground* offer yet another option that meshes the local and the global, with local cultural ways being recognized as fountains of empowerment. Kusturica's return to his religious origins,[3] his return from France, and the establishment of "Kustendorf," a cultural centre and an international music and film festival in his newly created ethno village in Mokra Gora in Serbia, have given him a place where he can, as he says, "dream of an open place with cultural diversity which stands up to globalization" (Kusturica, July 2004). In this connection with the local environment, Aboriginal culture, and primeval energies, he offers the international community and local people a place where they are able to create an alternate culture.

Underground is a film that participates in both the destruction and the creation of a new local identity. Kusturica's appearance at the end of the film as a character purchasing arms from Marko, an opportunistic Communist turned new capitalist, can be interpreted as his admission of guilt in the destruction of Yugoslavia. "You need me," Marko tells Kusturica, as they set the price for weapons with the UN "Blue Helmets" in the background. Goran Gocić's observation that the space for political cinema in the West was very limited, but "non-Western film-makers or writers could always score points on their liberal (anti-Communist, anti-fundamentalist, human rights and so on) engagement" (2001, 21) suggests that artists and filmmakers were financially supported by patrons who used them in order to provoke changes in the Communist bloc and gain profits from such changes. *Underground* is, as Sean Homer suggests, a "critique of Tito's Yugoslavia" (Homer 2009), just as Kusturica's earlier film, *When Father Was Away on Business* (1985) is a criticism of Communist intolerance after Yugoslavia's 1948 secession from the USSR. Both of these films were awarded the Golden Palm at the Cannes Film Festival in the years of their respective releases. Twice awarding the same filmmaker for his criticism of Communist practices by such important European institution is a statement that certainly contributed to the opening up of Eastern Europe. On the one hand the opening up of the system was positive, but on the other, it did not bring artists and ordinary citizens the change they had hoped for.

The complete destruction of the Yugoslavian nation was certainly more than the Yugoslav artist had bargained for. Kusturica and his family embody Yugoslavia, and it was neither in his nor the great majority's interest to destroy a multi-ethnic and multicultural nation. He was born in 1954 in Sarajevo into a Bosnian Muslim atheist family. His wife, Maja, is the child of a Bosnian Serb and a Slovene-Croat, making their children, Stribor and Dunja, Slovene-Croat-Bosnian-Muslim Serbs. Yugoslavia was the best "home" for this family and many others like it, including families that were not ethnically mixed. In the age of public opinion, however, and as artists promoted change, not enough care was taken to examine potential dangers in dealing with local imperfections of the Communist system.

Dina Iordanova agrees with Andrew Horton that, "Kusturica's versatile background gives him a strong communicative power and provides a wide access to his idiosyncratic Yugoslav stories because he purposefully uses elements that are familiar to domestic viewers, but also cinematographic language which is familiar to international audiences, thus speaking simultaneously to local and international audiences by sending out these little signals in the forms of 'nods' and 'make-overs'" (2002, 150). In the film, Yugoslavian national stories are told in Serbian from a primarily local perspective, and from the point of view of an ordinary individual who is defined by his suburban neighbourhood values. Elemental energies are presented through makeovers and other avant-garde tropes from world cinema. The artistic hybridization in Kusturica's film is comparable to the integration and re-articulation of regional myths and African spirits with sophisticated European structural and formal literary innovations in the Latin American Boom of the 1960s and 1970s.[4] Like the Latin American Boom writers, Kusturica emphasizes in an exaggerated fashion the so-called primitive empowering energy capable of creating alternate realities.

Primitive Balkan ways of life, portrayed through sophisticated cinematographic techniques and situations, challenge Hollywood's categorization of "good guys and bad guys." Blacky, one of the main characters, is portrayed as a typical Serbian trigger-happy nationalist. He is also recognizable, however, as a comical character straight out of a silent film era slapstick comedy as he cuts live electrical wires with his bare teeth, or blows himself up in the trunk with a grenade like a Warner Brothers' Looney Tunes cartoon hero. Kusturica also subverts the classic Hollywood love triangle by colouring it with original erotic scenes. Iordanova rightly observes that Kusturica's artistic contribution is not evident in the invention of new techniques, but in the unique and energetic combination of the existing cinematographic stock. Familiar scene structures and cinematographic repertoire are used to connect the international audience to Kusturica's unusual love story. In the local love triangle, Marko takes advantage of Blacky, and they both take advantage of Natalia, who in her turn uses both of them for her own gains. But they are neither good nor bad guys. Instead, the international familiar language of "good and bad guys" gains a new local flavour and a "third dimension," as Homi Bhabha would say.

It is not accidental that, due to her financial needs and her political and historical circumstances, Natalia has three lovers: Blacky, a good-hearted but irrational nationalist, a foreigner named Franz who promises her a better financial future and an opening into the world, and Marko, a political opportunist and skilful player whose cleverness and social position make Natalia tolerate his manipulations. In her relationships with these three lovers, she embodies her region of the world, pulled and shaped by the same forces that pull and shape her: irrational nationalism, skilful opportunism, and foreign intervention. Any simplification of this complex interrelation, a reduction to a classic good and bad guys world view, would lead to misrepresentation.

The Western world view of binary oppositions: civilized/primitive, good/bad, progressive/archaic, love/hate does not hold, as Natalia both loves her men and at the same time "cannot stand them," as she declares in a drunken confession. The absence of a monolithic world view is also evident in the fact that Blacky and Marko drink together and indulge in a similar form of madness, but are otherwise two very different Balkan men. Marko is a freebooter who is able to succeed because he exploits Blacky's generosity, his popular appeal, and his readiness to fight for his country in defence of his people. Conversely, Blacky is a positive figure who comforts unfortunate people like Natalia's sick brother and the developmentally delayed Ivan, but he is also a fool because his unquestioned devotion to his *kum* (his buddy) Marko prevents him from seeing that Marko's disregard for law and morality is not the same as his own patriotic defiance.

The complexity in Kusturica's film has elicited different reactions. Despite the international critical acclaim for *Underground*, French promoters of globalization Alain Finkielkraut and Bernard Henry Lévy condemned the film for its Serbian nationalism. In the Balkans, reactions have been diametrically opposed. Impressed by the film, Goran Gocić argues that it portrays "the bliss of living" (2001, 4) that keeps people alive. As Gocić observes, "the situation [in the former Yugoslavia] at times grew so desperate that often sticking to the simplest pleasures of life and the extreme humour remained the only way out"(6). Other Serbian intellectuals, particularly in Belgrade, have been insulted by the film because, in their view, it reinstates stereotypes and prejudices about the Balkans. "Rejecting the worldwide success of Kusturica's films and Bregović's music is *de rigeur* for many Balkan intellectuals" (2002, 15), Dušan Bjelić writes. Slovenian philosopher Slavoj Žižek believes that *Underground* portrays "a mythical Balkans shot for the Western gaze," adding that "it's a film that internalized the Western notion of a crazy nation, where war is simply our nature."[5] While the portrayal of extravagance and exaggeration could certainly be seen as a reinstatement of Balkan stereotypes, this, I am arguing, is not the primary goal of the film.

While not exactly clowns and dwarfs, fools or buffoons, Kusturica's characters do belong to this family and produce through their spontaneity and impulsive behaviour the very same effects as their medieval precursors: they create "triumphant hilarity," as Bakhtin would say, which subverts the seriousness of the established order. All Kusturica's characters have elements of madness or developmental delay, but Blacky is probably the maddest of them all. He is, as mentioned earlier, a character straight out of a silent era slapstick comedy, exemplified when he forces his way on the stage in the middle of Natalia's performance and ties her to himself with a rope, carrying her off the stage as if it were a part of a play. Marko is equally mad when he plays a doctor who rescues Blacky in the trunk. Meanwhile, Blacky, the cartoon hero, blows himself up in the trunk with a grenade. These and numerous other examples of humorous madness provide entertainment, but they are also a way of coping with local tragedy, as laughter has re-creative qualities and is a way to defy misfortune, Joseph Meeker point out. "Comedy is a celebration, a ritual renewal of biological warfare as it persists *in spite of any reasons* there may be for feeling metaphysical despair" (Meeker 1974, 24). At the artistic level, or at the level of reception, laughter causes the audience to lower their guard, as Julio Cortázar explains, in order to consider a different view of the world. Some, it is true, do not make this step and see only the typical and the obvious.

Briefly, *Underground* is an allegory of a half-century in the life of Communist Yugoslavia, which is portrayed as a manipulated, backward cellar used mainly for producing weapons. The story of the people in the underground cellar is a tragic one, yet it is lived as a performance at a carnival. The film begins with Marko and Blacky's drunken ride through the red-light district of Belgrade, accompanied by Goran Bregović's blasting ethno-music piece called "Kalashnikov." It is played by a *trubači*, or Balkan brass orchestra, made up of a big drum and brass instruments played at a manic tempo. These orchestras were introduced to the country in the nineteenth century by Austrian military bands. While brass music is popular primarily with elderly people in central Europe, in Serbia *trubači* have a youthful following because of the music's fast beat and loudness. Carried away by the musical madness, Marko and Blacky fire their pistols in a nonchalant fashion and extravagantly throw money around, introducing an exaggerated Balkan style of life. Their foolishness is primitive and irresponsible, but they are simply having fun. Their Balkan primitivism and extravagant joy are sharply contrasted with the documentary footage of the German bombing of Belgrade on April 6, 1941. The unexpected juxtaposition of the "primitive" South and the "civilized" West that bombs Belgrade and leaves Ivan the Zookeeper's animals maimed and confused creates discomfort for the audience and asks them to critically view the story in the film.

While the juxtaposition between "macho" fun and the German bombing of civilians questions the meaning of "civilized," and "primitive," the notion of the local and primitive is explored through Marko and Blacky, two friends who behave in a similar irrational fashion, but with an important difference. The difference between these two Balkan men has not been sufficiently emphasized, yet it is very important in the film. Marko is Blacky's buddy, but he is an opportunist who exploits Blacky's generosity and his readiness to fight for his country. While Blacky has a good heart, he is guilty of his association with pretenders like Marko who lead him and his people into the cellar where they are exploited for decades. Blacky and Marko's exaggerated, irrational behaviour serves to subvert the seriousness of fifty years of Communist myth, but more importantly it shows that the people were not harmed as much by Communism and Tito as they were by manipulators and cronies like Marko. Using similar visual effects to those from *Forrest Gump,* the acclaimed 1994 American epic comedy-drama-romance film based on the 1986 novel of the same name by Winston Groom, Kusturica incorporates Marko into archived footage of Tito's speeches by having him shake Tito's hand at the end of the president's public performance. He also has Tito delivering party speeches reminiscent of the political rhetoric of that time in which he glorifies Blacky, who supposedly died in defence of Communist ideals.

The juxtaposition of Marko's celebration of Blacky's supposed heroic death with scenes from the cellar where deceived people and their nationalist leader (Blacky) produce weapons for Marko's profit questions Tito's time, but the story and questioning do not end there. The film portrays not so much Tito as it does his cronies and opportunists like Marko who, when Tito dies, double their profits by selling arms in the illegal international arms trade overseen by UN troops. Kusturica himself appears in this scene as a witness and a co-participant.

The inclusion of the documentary footage of Tito's funeral in the film, showing presidents and dignitaries from around the world paying tribute to the man who led the Non-Aligned Movement, links the outside world to the local drama as foreign leaders are seen in the same opportunistic light as Marko. At Tito's funeral, in addition to Leonid Brezhnev and other Eastern European leaders, we see members of the Non-Aligned Movement and leaders of national liberation struggles such as Yasser Arafat, who benefited from this movement. The camera focuses on Margaret Thatcher along with members of the British Royal family, and the heads of the major Western powers paying tribute to Tito at his funeral. Opportunistic like Marko, the West participated in the creation of Yugoslavia because it was beneficial to all of them. But after Tito's and Brezhnev's death the game changed, and they became outspoken critics of the man they praised and honoured during the Cold War. Marko also criticizes a post-Tito Yugoslavia and departs for the West to return later in a Mercedes, obviously making even greater profits through the new arms trade than he did during Tito's time.

As French philosopher Alain Badiou argues in his *Ethics: An Essay on the Understanding of Evil* in 2001, "we are at the beginning of a new era ... [which] has been massively marked by the collapse of the USSR—a major historical settling of accounts [*une échénce historique majeure*]—and consequently, a new period of American hegemony" (2001, 120). After the collapse of the USSR, no country paid as high a price for the "settling of the accounts" as did Yugoslavia. While Germany was the first to prematurely recognize independent Croatia and Slovenia, the US led the way in the recognition of Bosnia and Herzegovina, and intervened in the independence of Kosovo with its bombing of Belgrade, which Noam Chomsky called "the new military humanism" (1999). The US "humanitarian" military campaign which, according to Chomsky, has become a distinctive feature of that nation's foreign policy in recent years—regardless of the fact that there is scant evidence in human history of wars fought out of a sense of compassion—is comparable to Marko's "humanitarian" concern for his friend Blacky and the people he keeps in the cellar through manipulation.

Would the destiny of the former Yugoslavia be different if there were no foreign interventions? Kusturica seems to believe that at the local level, people have their rules of engagement, and their "new primitive" way of living that is not unproblematic. However, problems at the local level are manageable according to local rules. In his youth, Kusturica became a member of the *New Primitivs* movement, which originated in the 1980s in Sarajevo, because he believed in the right to self-determination. Art critic Nermina Zildžo explains that, "the main principle of SNP (Sarajevo New Primitivs) is the exploration of identity—an attempt to explain one's self in one's own words, through one's own, un-imposed prism. It manifests itself in: an alleged anti-intellectualism;[6] [and] the use of local iconic and lexical properties" (1990).

While *Underground* exaggerates and distorts political reality in Rabelaisian, grotesque medieval fashion in order to ridicule political reality and question the established order, the film also highlights re-creative features in the primitive Balkan makeup such as ethno-music, the "bliss of living," and above all the local history of survival. Songs such as "Kalashnikov" and "Mesečina" (or "Moonlight"), composed by Goran Bregović are not repeated as background music in the film but as an insertion of energy that drives both the characters and the film. Their repetition also brings together and juxtaposes past and present, as well as fictional and historical moments to be viewed in a new light. The words in "Moonshine" describe the general catastrophe looming over characters; the music's crescendo, however, and the attitude of those who sing it defy despair:

> There is no more sun,
> There is no more moon,
> You are no more, I am no more.
> There is nothing more ... oh
> Darkness of war has covered us,
> Darkness has covered us ... oh.
> And I wonder, my dear:
> What will happen to us?
> Moonshine, moonlight and it is not midnight ... oh-oh, oh-oh.
> Sun is shining, sun is shining and it is not noon ... oh-oh, oh-oh.
> From above, light breaks through....
> No one knows, no one knows,
> No one knows, no one knows,
> No one knows what is shining.

(Bregović 1995)

As this popular 1990s song suggests, the irrational and mysterious elements in life can defy even the darkest moments of war. The popular songs and ethno-music emphasized in the film carry positive, life-giving energy which takes the singing characters out of their horror. To portray the "bliss of living," Kusturica has Blacky, Marko, and Natalia spinning around the central axis of the camera accompanied by *trubači* playing at full blast faster and faster, until everything culminates into a happy-sounding madness. As Blacky, Marko, and Natalia sing "Moonshine" with their heads together accompanied by a gypsy band performing on a spinning wheel rotating more and more quickly, they create a feeling of togetherness that also helps them to survive the war madness. Their madness is a "festive madness," as Bakhtin would say, a communal madness with re-creative potential that was lost in the nineteenth century. In *Rabelais and His World*, Bakhtin explains how "the regenerative" aspect of play and laughter was gradually lost in Western culture, and how the madness lost its positive spirit in the Romantic grotesque and acquired a somber, tragic aspect of individual isolation (1968, 37). However, while it was lost in the written culture, it has survived in folk songs and rituals of local communities that Kusturica recognizes here and incorporates into his highly sophisticated film. The film director is rational and analytical in one way to recognize the seriousness of the situation his characters live in, but at the same time he also recognizes the irrational, festive side preserved in local culture. Kusturica's affirmation of the joys of life while portraying an awful war leads Gocić to conclude that this makes the filmmaker "stand out as a master of the tragic-comic" (2001, 6).

There are a number of other examples that Kusturica uses to show how hardship and need sharpen the instinct for survival and make people resourceful. When, for example, light is needed for the birth of Blacky's son in the cellar, people ingeniously lift up a bicycle and peddle it in the air to produce electrical energy. They also live as if they were not in a cellar. Jovan grows up normally despite being in the underground, because he is loved and cared for by his father and particularly his grandfather. We see the celebration of his third birthday in the underground. When, during the ceremony, his father Blacky lights a candle to remember his late wife who died at Jovan's birth, he expresses his sorrow through a song "Stani, stani Ibar vodo"[7] that encapsulates his pain, but in the song he also asks the river Ibar to take him away to a city where a young maiden is waiting for him. As the song transforms pain into hope, the celebration of a child's birthday also brings joy to the cellar.

Local rituals continue to give meaning to their lives in the underground cellar as Jovan grows up and falls in love with a girl from his neighbourhood. Their wedding, the next family and community celebration, is again filled with music, singing, and drinking. The festive madness in this community finally leads the people out of their cellar and out of the deceptions of Tito's time. It is during the wedding that madness reaches its peak. In the confusion, the monkey fires a cannon that breaks down a wall, opening up the world for them. Yet, instead of victory and freedom, the local people exit to find the war of the 1990s, which is a local war again with foreign influences. As characters are separated and the local community is broken, individuals like Ivan find themselves as refugees in Germany and other European countries, unable to function without their extended families. In the larger globalized world, local forces have no place and the regenerative powers of local culture are lost.

Local neighbourhood or extended family values and local forms of empowerment are portrayed in Kusturica's other films, such as *Do You Remember Dolly Bell* (1981, recipient of the Golden Lion) and *When Father Was Away on Business* (1985, recipient of the Golden Palm). The films portray imperfect local stories in which characters still have room to act, and even to win. In his interview with Bouineau, Kusturica explains that he is interested in local stories because "the family possesses a mythical dimension … [and] is the core of drama" (Iordanova 1993, 71). By family he means both the nuclear and especially the extended family, or the neighbourhood. In a local milieu, characters can find some justice. As American scholar Carlin Barton explains in her 2001 book *Roman Honor: The Fire in the Bones*, Rome had no central peacekeeping force, but the republic survived and flourished for so many centuries because it had a shared public sense of honour and shame. Those who did not behave according to the rules of the game lost their honour through public disapproval: "There was no one so poor or so despised that they could not repay aristocratic abuse with gossip and slander. Even the humblest could hiss you at the games or piss on your statue," Barton writes (2001, 23). Hence, the honour culture allowed the poor and the marginalized, women included, to express their feelings and to protest discrimination. In *Underground,* when Blacky discovers that his best friend Marko is attempting to seduce his bride Natalia at their wedding, Blacky forces Marko to carry him on his back walking on his hands and knees while braying like a mule. Natalia, the character who raises the main questions of justice in the film, also forces Marko to carry her on his back in the same fashion. Marko is a powerful political figure, but he can still be publicly degraded and shamed, and partial justice can be found in the local culture, crazy as it may appear.

Living in the world where the will of the stronger or more manipulative prevails, Natalia knows that an individual's agency comes from his or her ability to quickly adjust to the flow of events. She is exploited by the two men, but she also exploits them, achieving a sense of balance and justice in their local world. She knows, for example, that Marko is an opportunist, but is impressed by his skilfulness she tells him, "you lie so beautifully," confirming Marko's thesis that underneath "we are all at least a little liars." Such a statement, and the recognition that manipulation and desire for profit are widespread, challenges the Hollywood notion of good and bad guys. When Natalia learns how unscrupulous Marko is in his exploitation of people in the cellar, she asks if he is "afraid of God." Marko's answer, "have you been lacking anything?" makes her understand that she and many people like her have been co-participating in his world of corruption, despite the fact that they are basically good people.

Dina Iordanova writes that Western viewers find it difficult to accept Kusturica's "one-dimensional portrayal of women" and his, as Rayns says, "misogyny" evident, for example, at the beginning of *Underground* in the disturbing image where Marko plants a carnation in the prostitute's fat behind (Rayns 1996, 530). Female critics also complain about Kusturica's "reinforcement of a disturbing status quo in gender relations that require critical examination" (Iordanova 2002, 32). According to Iordanova, Kusturica's women can be divided into several categories ranging from the mainstay of domesticity (a housewife who grumbles over her husband's philandering but nonetheless shines his shoes and cooks large breakfasts to cure his hangovers), the opportunistic beauty, the blond object of desire (whose top priority is to marry a well-positioned man), and the virginal bride (a static icon with primary visual functions) (2002, 32). In *Underground,* Blacky's wife is a woman belonging to the first category because when he returns early in the morning from his drunken masculine fun, she scolds him but also makes him eggs and sausages for breakfast, irons his shirt, and shines his shoes. The domestic woman, however, plays a minor role in *Underground*, unlike the major one she has in *Do You Remember Dolly Bell* and *When Father Was Away on Business*. In these films, Kusturica does not examine critically the traditional female role, and he can be criticized for this. Yet one should recognize that in his examination of the local world, he does give domestic women credit for keeping the family together and for preserving life, as Gabriel García Márquez recognizes in *One Hundred Years of Solitude*. In his 1982 Nobel lecture, the Columbian writer complained, "it is only natural that they insist on measuring us with the yardstick they use for themselves, forgetting that the ravages of life are not the same for all, and that the quest for our own identity is just as arduous and bloody for us as it is for them. The interpretation of our reality through patterns not our own serves only to make us more unknown, even less free, even more solitary" (García Márquez 2007, 207–11).

Natalia is a women of the third category, the blond object of desire whose top priority is to marry a well-positioned man, as Iordanova says. Like women of this type, she gains her agency through sexuality. However she also uses her intelligence and is by no means passive. She is who she is because the outside pressures are such that, as a poor woman with an invalid brother to care for, she has to use whatever resources she has at her disposal to survive. At the local level, she is able to deal with the two men, who use physical force to pressure her to marry them. Encouraged by drinking and music at Jovan's wedding, she has enough courage to tell them that she cannot stand to look at them when she is sober. She dances around the tank barrel, clearly a phallic symbol, to publicly shame Marko. She also repeatedly smashes first Marko but also Blacky with a long wooden board as she spins with the musicians on the spinning wheel. In the incident before the wedding when she discovers how corrupt Marko is, her moral superiority is expressed through the position in her and Marko's sexual act. The director has her sitting on Marko's shoulders high above him, while Marko performs oral sex on her. In local culture, in which a man's honour is closely linked to sexuality, Natalia is not only in a superior *physical* position, but also a moral one. Kusturica uses a scene showing the sexual pleasures and madness of a Communist official to break the ceiling of the cellar, an event that reveals to the people the Communist deception. The system breaks from within and, if left to deal with the new situation by themselves, people like Natalia may have been able to a find solution for themselves.

In the local story, Natalia finds her own ways to stand up to oppressive forces. Just before the walls of the cellar are broken and the local situation becomes a part of a larger world, Natalia gets the upper hand with her men. At Jovan's wedding she settles her accounts with the Communist/opportunist Marko and the nationalist Blacky. She forces Marko to carry her on his back around the workshop, repeating the scene from the first wedding in which Blacky forces Marko to do the same. Using local honour culture and her skills, she reaches a South European form of justice, which is awkward but less chaotic and overpowering than when the cellar is broken and people are let loose into the outside world. What follows is nothing but destruction, aimlessness, and suffering.

Ivan, Marko's lame and stuttering brother, who appears at key moments at the beginning and at the end of the film, plays an important role in the rendering of the local story. The international as well as the local audiences feel for this type of ordinary man who cares for his animals in the Belgrade zoo. He and people like him are the real casualties of political and economic corruption and foreign interventions. Taken out of their local culture and neighbourhood relations, as Ivan is taken to Germany at the end of the film, ordinary people become, as Zigmunt Bauman says, "human waste." In their local milieu, however, they have a function and the love of their neighbours, which may not be much for the "global elite," but for them it is life and dignity.

Ivan also plays an important role when he kills his corrupt brother Marko. His subsequent suicide by hanging in the church and his later reappearance in the film are reminiscent of the death and resurrection of Christ. The ending of the film takes the audience from the historical level to the mythical one, or to the level of magical realism. The audience is told that, "This story has no end" because, one concludes from the preceding developments in the film, the local culture has a history of inventive survival and will go on. Reality is meshed with desire, collective memory that "once upon a time there was a country (Yugoslavia)," and with instinct for survival and enjoyment of life. Consequently, Blacky hears his drowned son's voice and jumps into the Danube river from which all of the characters return, led by a herd of cows. The scene alludes to animals and humans coming out of Noah's Ark after the biblical flood. The characters then continue their celebration of Jovan's interrupted wedding, this time with his dead mother Vera present, and Natalie again in her red dress, still flirting with Marko and Blacky, while the *trubači* play the same songs at full blast: the local culture endures.

Critics have interpreted the final scene, in which the small piece of land with all of the characters on it breaks off and drifts down the Danube, as a final "utopian gesture of Yugo-nostalgia," as Sean Homer says. The film does end with a feeling of nostalgia for the country that once was; however, the theme of hope and survival amid manipulation and destruction is more prominent. As he portrays manipulation and corruption at the local level, as well as alluding to "humanitarian" foreign intervention, Kusturica recognizes local values such as the irrational "bliss of living," the ability to invent or be flexible, and the ability to care for one's family or a group of friends as life-giving and life-sustaining cultural aspects that keep local communities and ordinary people from becoming "human waste." With this, Kusturica does not revert back to romanticism, but invites his audience to reflect on the relationship of the global and the local, and to question if Homi Bhabha's "third dimension" is always a happy marriage of the local and the global.

Notes

1   Mikhail Bakhtin explains in his *Rabelais and His World* (1968) that in the Middle Ages and Renaissance, comic aspects of life were presented through the clown, the fool, and the dwarf, and that the overall tone of the performance was not ridicule and mockery but a combination of celebration and subversion. Distortion was merely a way to expose the weaknesses and the imperfections of the ruling class. The transformed or reshaped reality is grotesque, but in its essence it is positive and re-creative. Bakhtin further explains that "the regenerative" aspect of play and laughter has gradually been lost in the development of Western culture. In the behaviour of the clown, masks, dwarfs, and other folk-grotesque beings of medieval times, Bakhtin recognizes a form of madness, but it is a "festive madness" (1968, 39) that functions as a gay parody of the narrow seriousness of official truth and reason. This madness loses its positive spirit in the Romantic grotesque and acquires a somber, tragic aspect of individual isolation: "It became, as it were, an individual carnival, marked by a vivid sense of isolation. Laughter was cut down to cold humour, irony, sarcasm. It ceased to be a joyful and triumphant hilarity" (37).

2   The film was made in co-production among companies from the Federal Republic of Yugoslavia, France, Germany, and Hungary.

3   On Đurđevdan (St. George's Day) in 2005, Kusturica was baptized into the Serbian Orthodox Church as Nemanja Kusturica in Savina monastery near Herceg Novi, Montenegro. To his critics who considered this the final betrayal of his Bosnian Muslim roots, he replied that, "My father was an atheist and he always described himself as a Serb. Okay, maybe we were Muslim for 250 years, but we were Orthodox before that and deep down we were always Serbs, religion cannot change that. We only became Muslims to survive the Turks."

4   Literature appears to be of particular importance to Kusturica. His early films were adapted from literary sources, and in later ones he used loose associations with literary works. In addition to his close relationship to works by Yugoslavian Nobel laureate Ivo Andric, Kusturica identifies Gabriel Garcia Marquez's novel *One Hundred Years of Solitude* as a source of inspiration for *Gypsis*, even though no concrete elements of Marquez's work were brought into the film. Other authors Kusturica has mentioned who have influenced his work include Carlos Fuentes, Jorge Luis Borges, Julio Cortázar, and Mario Vargas Llosa.

5   Žižek also sees the portrayal of Balkan stereotypes of reckless extravagance and violent gloom as "the reverse racism which celebrates the exotic authen-

ticity of the Balkan Other, as in the notion of Serbs who, in contrast to inhibited, anemic Western Europeans, still exhibit a prodigious lust for life—this last form of racism plays a crucial role in the success of Emir Kusturica's films in the West" (2000, 5).

6 It is ironic that Kusturica and Sarajevo New Primitivs advocated anti-intellectualism and that the intellectualism of Slavoj Žižek set the tone for the wider reception of the film by many on the Western European Left. Echoing the pretentious rhetoric of the Communist speeches, Žižek wrote that *Underground* is "the libidinal economy of ethic slaughter in Bosnia: the pseudo-Bataillean trance of excessive expenditure, the continuous mad rhythm of drinking-eating-singing-fornicating" (Žižek 1997).

7 Stani, stani, Ibar vodo, Ibar vodo, kuda žuriš tako? I ja imam jade svoje, jade svoje, meni nije lako.

Ponesi me ti sa sobom, ti sa sobom, do Kraljeva grada.Tamo mene čeka jedna, čeka jedna devojčica mlada.

References

Badiou, Alain. 2001. *Ethics: An Essay on the Understanding of Evil*. Translated by Peter Hallward. London: Verso.

Bakhtin, Mikhail. 1968. *Rabelais and His World*. Translated by Helene Iswolsky. Cambridge: MIT Press.

Barton, Carlin. 2001. *Roman Honor: The Fire in the Bones*. Berkeley: University of California Press.

Bauman, Zygmunt, and Benedetto Vecchi. *Identity*. 2004. Cambridge: Polity Press.

Bjelić, Dušan I. 2002. "Introduction: Blowing Up the 'Bridge.'" In *Balkan as Metaphor: Between Globalization and Fragmentation*, edited by Dušan I. Bjelić and Obrad Savić. Cambridge: MIT Press.

Bouineau, Jean-Marc. 1993. *Le petit libre de Emir Kusturica*. Carches: Sparoruge.

Chomsky, Noam. 1999. *The New Military Humanism: Lessons from Kosovo*. Monroe, ME: Common Courage Press.

García Márquez, Gabriel. 2007. "The Solitude of Latin America." (Nobel Prize acceptance speech.) Trans. Richard Cardwell. In Bernard McGuirk and Richard Cardwell, eds., *Gabriel García Márquez: New Readings*. New York: Cambridge University Press.

Gocić, Goran. 2001. *Notes from Underground: the Cinema of Emir Kusturica*. London: Wallflower Press.

Homer, Sean. 2009. "Retrieving Emir Kusturica's *Underground* as a Critique of Ethnic Nationalism." Accessed http://www.ejumpcut.org/archive/jc51.2009/Kusterica/index.html

Iordanova, Dina. 2002. *Emir Kusturica*. London: British Film Institute.

Kusturica, Emil. "Kstendorf." www.kustu.com

Kusturica, Emir, dir. 1995. *Underground* (*Podzemlje* in Serbian). Screenplay by Dušan Kovačević.

Meeker, Joseph. 1974. *The Comedy of Survival: Studies in Literary Ecology*. New York: Scribner.

Rama, Angel. 1982. "El boom en perspectiva." *La novela en América Latina. Panoramas 1920–1980*. [Bogota] Procultura: Instituto de Cultura.

Rayns, Tony. 1996. "Underground." *Sight and Sound*. March.

Woodward, Susan. 1995. *Balkan Tragedy: Chaos and Dissolution after the Cold War*. Washington, DC: Brookings Institution.

Zildžo, Nermina. 1990. "Sjećam se…." In exhibition catalogue "Sarajevo New Primitivs." Sarajevo: Art Gallery of Bosnia-Herzegovina, March.

Žižek, Slavoj. 1997. "Underground, or Ethnic Cleansing as a Continuation of Poetry by Other Means." *Inter-Communication* 18. www.nntticc.or.jp/pub/ic_mag/ico18/intercity/zizek_E.html.

———. 2000. *The Fragile Absolute, or Why Is the Christian Legacy Worth Fighting For?* New York: Verso.

Chapter 13

Italian Food on Foreign Tables:
Giacomo Castelvetro's Exile

Mary-Michelle DeCoste

Italian food existed before Italy itself. Cut off from the rest of Europe by both the Alps and the sea, a peninsula fragmented into states with shifting borders and various forms of government, Italy did not exist as a unified country until 1861. Already by the second half of the fifteenth century, however, culinary texts defined an "Italy" characterized by particular foods and food practices. These early texts favour ingredients and approaches common throughout the peninsula rather than focusing on the regional differences fetishized by modern writing on Italian food. The notion of an Italian cuisine circulated both within and outside of Italy, and indeed Italian cooks were praised throughout Europe during the Renaissance.

This Italian supremacy gradually ceded to new ways of cooking and eating developed in France in the seventeenth century. Giacomo Castelvetro, nephew of the better-known Ludovico, was born in Modena on March 25, 1546, and died in London in 1616, having been exiled from Italy by Venetian Counter-Reformation authorities for distributing anti-Counter-Reformation pamphlets. He thus lived during this last period of Italian culinary renown before the rise of French cuisine. His *Brieve Racconto di tutte le Radici, di tutte l'Herbe, et di tutti i Frutti che crudi o cotti in Italia si mangiano* (translated as *The Fruits, Herbs, and Vegetables of Italy*) of 1614, dedicated to Lucy, the Countess of Bedford, contains descriptions of and instructions for growing a wide variety of fruits, vegetables, herbs, and nuts eaten in Italy, and explains how to prepare them for the table; many of these foods were unknown or little known in England at the time. Castelvetro wrote this little book primarily to secure a patron, and he pitched it to Lucy by intertwining subjects he knew to be of mutual interest: Italian language and culture (Italian was quite chic in England at this time, and Lucy spoke and wrote it well) and gardening.

Castelvetro also knew that Lucy was sympathetic to his religious beliefs, and punctuating the descriptions of Italian fruits and vegetables are a number of remarks disparaging the papist practices of Italy. As Paola Ottolenghi writes in her book on Castelvetro, the author relates with patrons and would-be patrons "as an exile and thus as a professional observer, closed within the bitter limits of a double restriction: flight from the Inquisition and the necessity of service...." (1982, 25; my translation). As Ottolenghi writes elsewhere in her book, however, "Castelvetro never cuts himself off from the motherland, neither culturally nor emotionally" (6; my translation). My aim here is to demonstrate the way in which Castelvetro combines the "double restriction" of flight from the Inquisition and the necessity of service with the irresistible pull he feels to share his love and knowledge of Italian fruits and vegetables and how best to eat them. Castelvetro uses descriptions of Italian food to articulate a national identity coloured by the exile's longing for home. At the same time, he connects his love of Italian fruits and vegetables with his love of language and his Protestant religious convictions. While the linking of food and national and religious identity is certainly not unique to Castelvetro, his particularly clever presentation is special. Castelvetro deploys his discourse on food to create a national and a religious identity based in part on a protest of the religion of his homeland and in praise of that of his adopted country. He must separate Italian food from Italian religion, creating new associations that allow him to identify himself as a Protestant who is still very Italian.

My reading of Castelvetro's text draws on the work of anthropologists and cultural historians such as Peter Bishop, who writes, "diet's relationship to cultural identity ... [is] on a par with language in terms of cultural definition" (1991, 3). The parallel between diet and language drawn by Bishop is particularly interesting to me here, because these are the two loci of Italianness privileged by Castelvetro, who, besides being a gardening enthusiast, was also a publisher of Italian books in England and an Italian language tutor. Although Bishop's claim is certainly not self-evident to many historians and anthropologists, Castelvetro quite clearly considers food grown in Italy and prepared according to Italian customs to be an important part of Italian culture and his own identity as an Italian. For example, in discussing the fruits and vegetables that Italians eat instead of meat when the weather is very hot, he says, "in avere in tal tempo frutti rinfrescativi e buoni non cediamo a niuna generazione del mondo" (1988, 23) ("of all nations in the world, we take pride of place in our profusion of good, refreshing fruit in the summertime") (77).[1] To cite another example, of melons gown in Italy he writes, "E credami pur qualsivoglia Oltramontano, dal Provenzale e dallo Spagnuolo in fuori, che quantunque con molto studio venga for fatto d'averne nelle loro contrade alcuni un poco buoni, non hanno per ciò qual grande odore che s'hanno i nostri" (28) ("believe me, none of the foreign melons have the fragrance that ours have, not even those of Provence or Spain, for all the care and trouble they take to produce even just a few fairly good varieties") (88).

Indeed, Castelvetro privileges the ability to recognize what is delicious, to prepare it for the table, and to savour it above all other indicators of Italianness. He contrasts this ability of Italians to the ignorance of other countries, particularly England and Germany. These two countries are important to Castelvetro, England as his adopted home and Germany as the birthplace of Protestantism, his promotion of which was the cause of his exile. In his discussion of how to properly prepare a salad, for example, Castelvetro criticizes both the English and the Germans for ruining salad in different ways. Indeed, he says that many cooks "oltramontani" ("from the other side of the Alps") do not know how to properly prepare a salad. He accuses the Germans in particular of wanting to please the eye with their method of preparing a salad, whereas, as Castelvetro points out, "noi Italici abbiam più riguardo di piacere a monna bocca" ("we Italians would much rather feast the palate than the eye") (65). He cites an Italian "legge insalatesca" ("Sacred Law of Salads") as the rule of thumb for making salad: "Insalata ben salata, poco aceto e ben oliata" ("Salt the salad quite a lot, then generous oil put in the pot, and vinegar, but just a jot") (68), and he says that "chi contro a così giusto comandamento pecca è degno di non mangiar mai buona insalata" ("and whosoever transgresses this benign commandment is condemned never to enjoy a decent salad in their life").

Castelvetro's nostalgia and pride are mixed with anger in the opening and closing sections of the book, in which he makes his strongest anti-Counter-Reformation statements. I would like to examine these two sections of the book, because it is here that Castelvetro most artfully weaves together his concerns about food and language with religion. After the dedication to Lucy, the text proper begins with praise of England, called by Castelvetro "questa nobile nazione" ("this noble country"):

Più volte meco medesimo pensando e sottilmente considerando quante cose al vivere umano giovevoli questa nobile nazione da una cinquanta anni in qua s'abbia apparato a seminare e a mangiare dal concorso di molti popoli rifuggiti in questo sicuro asilo per ischermirsi e per salvarsi da' rabbiosi morsi della crudele et empia Inquisizione romanesca, le quali erano prima da quella come cattive a mangiare sprezzate e come nocive alla salute de' corpi loro aborrite.

[I often reflect upon the variety of good things to grow and eat which have been introduced into this noble country over the past fifty years by the vast influx of so many refugees into this safe asylum seeking to shield and save themselves from the vicious attacks of the cruel and evil Roman Inquisition, things previously rejected as inedible or abhorred as damaging to physical health.] (49)

Castelvetro is considering here what the English have learned to grow and eat from foreigners, specifically the "molti popoli rifuggiti" ("many refugees"). Castelvetro is himself one of these refugees, considered by Counter-Reformation officials to be poisonous to the people of Italy, exiled for his distribution of anti-Counter-Reformation pamphlets. England he calls "questo sicuro asilo" ("this safe asylum"), and it is there that people like him can hope to be saved from the Inquisition's "rabbiosi morsi" ("vicious attacks," literally, "rabid bites," a notable expression in this book about gardening and eating). In Castelvetro's discourse, the Inquisitors become predatory consumers and the "popoli rifuggiti" are the would-be prey. Castelvetro then describes the English as eaters who, in their ignorance, reject good things to eat as "nocive alla salute de' corpi loro." And he does oppose them to each other, but they are alike in that they are both what Castelvetro is not: English and Catholic. More important for my argument here is the implied conflation of the things to be eaten by the Inquisitors and the English: the "popoli rifuggiti" and the fruits and vegetables of Italy. Both are hypothetical meals only, because the refugees are only bitten, and the fruits and vegetables are, in this opening sentence, rejected by the English as unhealthy. Yet by drawing a parallel between refugees, Italian and other, and the fruits and vegetables of the lands they are fleeing, Castelvetro proposes that these fruits and vegetables are of privileged importance as indicators of nationality.

It is this ignorance of Italian produce on the part of the English that motivates Castelvetro to write this book:

Queste considerazioni adunque han mosso me a cercar di porre per iscritto (al meglio mi saprò ricordare) non solo il nome di tutte quelle radici, di tutte quelle erbe e di tutti que' frutti, che nella civile Italia si mangino, ma ancora di mostrare come, per trovare le predette cose buone si vogliono cuocere, e in compagnia di che, crude, s'usino a mangiare, acciò che, per falta di questo, non s'astengan più da seminarle né da mangiarle.

[These considerations have thus moved me to try to write down (as well as I can remember) not only the names of all the roots, greens, and fruits eaten in civilized Italy, but also to show how to cook them so that they taste good, and, if they are eaten raw, with what they should be eaten, so that the English will no longer refrain from growing and eating them for want of knowledge.]

Here Castelvetro lays out his project to educate the reader about Italian fruits and vegetables with one caveat: "as well as I can remember." With these words, Castelvetro reminds the reader that he is an exile, that he is recalling things from his past, and that his memory may be imperfect. He then relates exactly what it is he hopes to remember: not just the names of the fruits and vegetables eaten in Italy, but also how they are cooked, or, if eaten raw, what is eaten with them.

Castelvetro is strangely absent from his own discourse: in this passage, the only verb in the first person is *saprò* (I will know): literally, "as well as I will know how to remember," giving this word additional weight. This little phrase sets the tone of the book, which is as much a gardening manual and cookbook as it is a memoir—the memoir of an exile who dares not hope to see his homeland again. Castelvetro's memories of the foods of his homeland are so intense that he says on more than one occasion "che a scriverlo mi fa venir l'acqua in bocca" ("writing it makes my mouth water"). In these moments, the exile's longing for his homeland has a physical manifestation, like hunger.

In the final episode of the book, Castelvetro finds himself in Germany to learn "l'assai malagevole lingua di quella nobil contrada" ("the very cumbersome language of that noble nation"). He is invited to dine at the home of a lord of the village, where he meets a baron who had recently returned from Italy. The baron asks him to explain why the noblemen of that otherwise most noble country walk about their estates following pigs. Castelvetro immediately realizes that the baron had witnessed a truffle hunt, and he begins to laugh. The baron takes offence until Castelvetro explains to him that these noblemen go about the countryside in the company of a servant who holds a rope attached to a pig's leg. When the pig finds a truffle, which Castelvetro here calls a "rar' frutto" ("rare fruit") by snuffling along the ground, the servant pulls him back so that the nobleman might uncover it.

Castelvetro explains, "per piacer egli oltre a modo tal frutto a' nostri gentiluomini, prendon piacere grande d'andarlo a quella guisa cercando" ("because this fruit is so pleasing to our noblemen, they take great pleasure in going thus to seek it"). The baron then asks what fruit could be so delicious as to warrant such an intensive search. Castelvetro replies, "egli è senza dubbio una qualità di fongo, che non mai fuori della terra apparisce, e chiamansi tartufi" ("it is without doubt a kind of mushroom that never appears above the earth, and it's called a truffle"). The baron is very surprised to hear this, because, as Castelvetro points out to the reader, the name of this fruit is "non molto lungi da questo altro suo 'tertifle,' che nella favella nostra 'diavolo' si viene a dire" ("not much different than the German 'tertifle,' which in our language means 'devil'"). So the baron replies, "Deh, buon Dio, e qual gusto trovate voi altri in mangiare così fatta bestia?" ("Oh, good God! What pleasure do you find in eating such a beast?"), to which Castelvetro says, "Oh, volesse Iddio che al presente un tal diavolo noi qui ci avessimo, perché io mi rendo ben certo che quella e tutti questi signori non pur buono il troverebbono, ma che ancora se ne leccherebbon le dita" ("Oh, I wish to God we had such a devil here today, because I'm sure that all these gentlemen would find it not just good, but enough to make them lick their fingers!").

I read Castelvetro's recounting of his introduction to and subsequent friendship with the German nobleman as a statement of religious belief, one more subtle than that with which the book opens. The German's confusion stems from a linguistic misunderstanding, which Castelvetro, both a teacher and a student of language, must have found particularly amusing. Castelvetro's retelling of this confusion can be read as a condemnation of the Catholic doctrine of transubstantiation, the belief that the bread and wine of Holy Communion actually become the body and blood of Christ. In Castelvetro's story, it is the body of the devil rather than the body of Christ that is to be eaten. The truffle is "a kind of mushroom that never appears above the earth," and as such it has an infernal quality about it. The truffle is also closely related to the pig, as the Italian noblemen would be unable to find it without that animal. The German calls the truffle "such a beast" and Castelvetro replies by calling it "such a devil." Castelvetro thus creates the opposite of holy food in the bestial, infernal truffle.

The truffle is also, however, very delicious—enough, according to Castelvetro, to make men lick their fingers. Castelvetro rejects the idea that food must become something other than what it is, that bread must become the body of Christ, for it to be "heavenly." Castelvetro is later asked by the baron to dine at his castle, which the exile describes as being "sovra la cima d'un ameno monticello" ("at the top of a lovely little hill"), and they laugh about the German's mistake. It is important that this story takes place in Germany, and that Castelvetro's dinner companion is German, Germany being the birthplace of the Reformation. Thus it is through food that Castelvetro marries what is best about Italy, Germany, and, through the dedication of his book, England. The German's castle on a hilltop becomes a symbol of earthly paradise, excellently prepared (Italian) food, and good (German, Protestant) company being the principal attributes of this paradise. By bringing the cuisine of his homeland to the birthplace of his religion, Castelvetro marries what is, to him, the best of both countries.

Note

1 This and all subsequent translations into English of Castelvetro's work are according to the author but based on Giacomo Castelvetro's *The Fruits, Herbs and Vegetables of Italy*, trans. Gillian Riley (London: Viking, 1989).

References

Bishop, Peter. 1991. "Constable Country: Diet, Landscape and National Identity." *Landscape Research* 16: 31–36.

Castelvetro, Giacomo. 1988. *Brieve Racconto di tutte le Radici, di tutte l'Herbe, et di tutti i Frutti che crudi o cotti in Italia si mangiano*. Edited by Emilio Faccioli. Mantova: Gianluigi Arcari.

———. 1989. *The Fruits, Herbs and Vegetables of Italy*. Trans. Gillian Riley. London: Viking.

Ottolenghi, Paola. 1982. *Giacopo Castelvetro, esule modenese nell'Inghilterra di Shakespeare: spiritualità riformata e orientamenti di cultura nella sua opera*. Pisa: ETS.

Section IV
Visual Culture and **Fashion**

Chapter 14

Mediterranean Seafarings: Pelagic Encounters of Otherness in Contemporary Italian Cinema

Elena Benelli

The sea is History.
—*Derek Walcott 1986, 364*

For the last thirty years, immigration in Italy has been viewed as a problem, handled as an emergency, and defined by the Italian mass media in very negative terms. In a recent study that analyzed how immigrants are defined in Italian newspapers, two sociologists from the University of Bologna, Giuseppe Sciortino and Asher Colombo, noticed that for the Italian press, the public discourse on and around immigration became of crucial importance for the entire social life of the country because "foreign residents in Italy have long been a key element in national self-definition" (Sciortino and Colombo 2004, 97). Their study spans a period of three decades, and it highlights the fact that the Italian media "led the way, preceding the experience and often even the awareness of the presence of immigrants" in the country (95).[1] The construction of the immigrant other has been based solely on a binary opposition between Italians and immigrants, and the public discourse has clearly given in to "the progressive codification of a distinction among different types of foreigners, the gradual institutionalizing of a distinction between 'foreigner' and 'immigrant,' and the establishment of relations between these conceptual oppositions and the distinctions applicable to the Italian population" (97).

According to Sciortino and Colombo, the negative shift in the perception of migrants spilled from the media into everyday language around 1989–1991, when migrants ceased to be defined by the terms "immigrants" or "foreign workers" employed to indicate someone who moved to Italy either to live or to work, and instead were identified solely as *extracomunitari*,[2] a pejorative expression with a strong negative connotation used to indicate someone whose origin is outside the European community, and in the news is associated with criminality, as if being a migrant is synonymous with being a criminal.[3]

Two present-day surveys, one from the Italian Caritas dated October 2009, and one from Transatlantic Trends dated October 2010, clearly confirm and highlight this widespread belief in Italian public opinion: in the first study, six out of ten Italians were convinced immigration has a direct link with criminality, while in the second survey "there was a lack of distinction among Italians when asked about their perceptions of legal versus illegal immigrants; 56 per cent of Italians now believe that legal immigrants increase crime in society, the highest of all countries surveyed, and a 24 per cent increase from the 2009 survey" (Transatlantic Trends 2010). The statistics back up the generalized uneasiness Italians feel toward multiculturalism, to the point that the then-Italian *Presidente del consiglio* Mr. Silvio Berlusconi could irrationally affirm without consequences that Italy should not become, ever, a multi-ethnic society.[4]

Italian political discourse, fuelled by Mr. Berlusconi's Party of Freedom and his good ally the Northern League, an overtly xenophobic and far-right political movement founded and directed by Umberto Bossi (the Minister of Reform at the time, whose name was stamped on the latest immigration law), has been propelled by a "a right-wing legislature that coldly moves forward, pressing for additional borders and frontiers, surveillances and controls" (Bouchard 2010, 116), making it extremely difficult even for regular migrants to work and live in Italy.[5]

The legal procedures of differentiation between regular immigrants and *extracomunitari* have been brilliantly defined by Yosefa Loshitzky as "screening strangers":

> The idea of "screening" migrants, of differentiating between the "indigenous" population and desired and undesired migrants, is still influenced by popular and racist myths according to which immigrants bring disease and pollution to the body of the nation (and the continent) and therefore need to be screened and contained. The process of screening practiced by the "host" society (which very often is more hostile than hospitable) is to screen the "good immigrant" and expel the "bad" to the literal and metaphorical "dumping grounds" of "the rest" of the world. (2010, 2)

Italy has been engaged in this process on the political level; however, alternative discourses and narratives coming from literature, cinema, and the arts have started to challenge stereotypical images of migrants, removing them from the sensationalist press and resituating them in complex historical and cultural dimensions. Italian cinema, which has greatly contributed to the articulation of Italian national identity in the last century, has become increasingly interested in narrating the "preoccupation with the integration, or not, of non-Italians into Italian society" (Wood 2005, 145).[6]

Several filmmakers are engaged in creating new alternative narratives that are "in search of lines of flight embracing the new within the old and searching for possible mediations, transformations and more egalitarian visions" (Ponzanesi 2005, 270). The films, as Enrica Capussotti pointed out, are

> made on low budgets, often self-funded or supported by public money, involving the participation of friends and "non"-professional actors, and the use of digital technology to keep costs down. The distribution of these films has been supported by public institutions or limited to a few copies at film festivals and cinema d'essay (networks of theatres that promote authorial and/or experimental cinema). (2009, 58)[7]

Therefore, this kind of film is screened by a public that is usually either politically or ethically engaged in a hospitable reception of migrants, and it is not destined for a large audience as a blockbuster.

The interest in the representation of migration in Italian cinema has not been only thematic but stylistic as well. Sandra Ponzanesi described this new way of telling migrants' stories in Italian cinema as one that "puts forward different narratives and new stylistic modes that confront spectators with their racial and gendered biases by making them uncomfortable with their own assumption and, thereby, othering them from their dominant position" (2005, 270). The cinematic re-articulation of otherness offers the audience new alternative visual representations of migrancy, destabilizing their hegemonic fixed location as well as contrasting the discourse coming from the media and the state, engaging with these social issues in an innovative way.

In the three films I analyze here, I will focus on one particular space, central to the visual representation and fundamental for the construction of the encounter with the other: the Mediterranean Sea, the most important natural border of Italy, "a liquid frontier separating the rich north … from the poor south" (King 2001, 8), the symbolic, often dramatic fluid threshold for migrants arriving to the Italian shores. As Capussotti rightfully noted, "the 'Mediterranean' as a trope, as a cultural area, as a repertoire of stereotypical identities and experiences, as a cultural battleground and as a space of critique of hegemonic forms of national and Eurocentric modernity is a fundamental constituent of current representations of migrants and intercultural identities" (2009, 58). It is important to note that these films employ the images of the Mediterranean as the only possible place in which the encounter with the other, in the twofold sense of meeting and confrontation, is possible.[8] For this reason, the Mediterranean should be considered and interpreted not so much as a frontier but as Iain Chambers suggests throughout his works, as

> the linguistic, literary, and cultural evidence of a hybrid inheritance, composed in lengthy processes of creolization that produce a critical constellation [of the Mediterranean], which is irreducible to any single national, nationalistic, provincial, or local explanation…. This other Mediterranean emerges in significantly sharp focus in the figure of today's (illegal) migrant who carries within herself the complex inheritance of a *colonial* past, crossed with the longstanding historical processes that make the modern world the site of perpetual mobility and migration. (2010, 10)

The Mediterranean Sea is present as a trope in the narration and also as a sort of *deus ex machina*: its centrality forces the characters to face the other and to confront, adjust, or rethink their identities. As Aine O'Healy rightfully noted, in Italian migration cinema, "though each narrative ends differently, all suggest the possibility of existential transformation in the fluid, transitional space of the Mediterranean Sea. While the stability of national identities and ethnic affiliations is cast into doubt in these films, a provisional fraternity becomes available to the Italian character through his encounter with other Mediterranean travelers embarked on a similar voyage" (2010, 8–9).[9]

I have to add that it is not only a fraternal sentiment which becomes apparent during the encounter but, given its ambiguous status, the opposite emotion emerges as well: a strong sense of hostility and conflict is thus also explored throughout the narration.[10] This is to underline the fact that if the sea is important as a *locus* to meet the other because it provides the characters with the needed freedom from traditions and society unavailable on solid ground, it is also a place where cultural and personal perturbations are taking place, and both fear and hate can arise.

The first groundbreaking Italian film on migration is Gianni Amelio's, *Lamerica* (1994), a film that for Derek Duncan "set the terms for subsequent, albeit unresolved, discussions of migration in Italian cinema" (Duncan 2008, 205). It was filmed during the years of the first massive *sbarchi*,[11] and it inaugurated the cinematic and often traumatic encounter with the other in Italian cinema, while being a response "to the radical changes Italy went through in the wake of 1989: the fall of state communism, the opening of borders between Eastern and Western Europe, the triumph of liberal capitalism, and the emergence of a new subject in the European political landscape—the Eastern European migrant worker" (Parvulescu 2010, 50). The sea, shown at the beginning in "an Istituto Luce newsreel from April 1939 that shows the arrival of the Italian troops in the harbor of Durrës (Durazzo in Italian) on the occasion of the annexation of Albania" (Zambenedetti 2006, 109), and at the end as the ship is preparing to leave the Albanian shore for its desperate trip to Italy fully packed with people, is reinstating its twofold historical role: as the space to be crossed in order to conquer a foreign country (the forgotten Italian colonialism), and as the space to be travelled upon in order to either go back home or to the promised land, an imagined Italy that vaguely resembles the myth of the Americas reached by many Italian immigrants only fifty years before.[12]

The history of Gino (Enrico Lo Verso), a young entrepreneur who arrives to Albania to colonize it economically[13] by opening a shoe factory, finds himself in the middle of the turmoil of the Albanian transition accompanied by Spiro, a presumed Albanian (who in reality is an old Italian soldier forgotten in Albania after the Second World War, supposed to act as the president of the new Italian company). Now facing the estranged other (Spiro is incapable of taking care of himself and shows signs of dementia), and the others (the Albanians he encounters during his trip), Gino has to find a way to go back to Italy as a *sans papier*, and the only way he can do this is by embarking in an old wreck of a ship with hundreds of other migrants looking for a brighter future. As Mary Wood explained, "by stripping its Italian protagonist, Gino, of his passport and belongings, and putting the camera in his subjective viewpoint as he becomes one of the hopeful *clandestini* trying to get to Italy, the film forces an identification with the position of the Albanian 'Other'" (2005, 150). This narrative technique defined by Genette as "internal focalization" (1976, 264), is subsequently used in the two other films I will analyze and, as a cinematic technique, it forces the audience to adopt the protagonist's point of view on the world while at the same time screening the strangers on the screen.

It is only by crossing the sea, and only while at sea, that Gino will fully grasp through his I/eye the process of becoming other from himself. He has lost everything and his appearance has transformed: he has slowly metamorphosed both into an Albanian and a migrant. His identity is slowly dissolved, and "initially, his relative prosperity makes him stand out physically. Yet as he gradually loses his place as a privileged foreigner, he is effectively racialized by the circumstances in which he finds himself. As the film goes on, he looks less and less Italian as he loses the trappings of affluence, and in his beleaguered condition becomes physically indistinguishable from the Albanians" (Duncan 2008, 205).

When he finally embarks on the shipwreck, as Alberto Zambenedetti noticed, "Gianni Amelio forces viewers to align with them, to look through their eyes" (2006, 109) by the means of a montage of the faces of the Albanian immigrants who "look into the camera, thus returning the condescending gaze of the Italian spectator and rejecting the objectification of the cinematographic eye" (110). Amelio is consciously closing the circle started with the images of the Fascist documentary shown at the beginning. Gino's understanding of the *damnés de la terre,* albeit brief, become finally possible only while travelling with them at sea, unveiling his humanity.

In *Lamerica*, the sea, defined by Iain Chambers as "the site for an experiment in a different form of history writing, and, as such, an experiment in language and representation" (2004, 425) links spaces (Italy and Albania, both in the present and in the past), histories (Italy and its own colonial past through Albania), and languages (Italian, Albanian, and Sicilian). In doing so, Duncan argues that "rather than asserting with any confidence a unified and coherent version of national identity, the film is more accurately understood as a text in which identity is labile and porous with respect to spatial, temporal, and racial boundaries" (2008, 205). In other words, it sets the precedent for re-attributing a central importance to the sea because it guarantees a double-edged transit while enabling the re-elaboration of boundaries.

Two other more recent films question and explore the imaginary space of the construction of Italian national identity while at sea. The two films are *Quando sei nato non puoi più nasconderti* (*When you are born you can no longer hide*, 2005) by Marco Tullio Giordana, and *Io, l'altro* (*Me, The Other,* 2007) by the Tunisian first-time filmmaker, journalist, and writer Mohsen Melliti, who has been living in Italy for the last twenty years.

In *Quando sei nato,* Giordana tells the story of an Italian teenager, Sandro, from a wealthy family who lives in the northern city of Brescia. The film focuses entirely on the teenager's point of view of the world: the audience follows the evolution of Sandro's I/eye that corresponds with the portion of reality they are able to see, and therefore be affected by with the camera, when he traverses spaces and experiences otherness after unexpectedly falling into the water in the middle of the Mediterranean.

In *Io, l'altro,* Melliti questions whether it is ever possible to know who the other really is: two fishermen and old friends, a Sicilian named Giuseppe and a Tunisian named Yousef, fish around Sicily in both Italian and Tunisian waters, trying to escape the control of the Sicilian Mafia. They share their lives, jobs, time on Giuseppe's boat, and the same name in its Italian and Arabic forms. One is Catholic, the other Muslim. They are constructed as totally specular, belonging to the opposite sides of the Mediterranean: Italy and Tunisia.

Almost the entire film is shot on the boat at sea where Giuseppe hears over the radio that a terrorist named Yousef is wanted by the international police because of his participation in the attack on Madrid March 11, 2004. Raul Bova plays Giuseppe, the Sicilian fisherman, while Yousef is played by Giuseppe Martorana, both Italian actors. The employment of an Italian actor to portray a non-Italian character calls into question the dynamics of Italian society, as Gregory Pell underlined: "as the extradiegetic Sicilian portrays the diegetic Tunisian, the audience is forced to question how much physiognomy contributes to the categorization of identity and the profiling of would-be terrorists and criminals" (2010, 199). This visual strategy obliges the audience to re-examine their own prejudices and imagined perceptions of Italian-ness (as it happened with Gino's transformation in *Lamerica*). Pell pointed out that "the lack of distinction between the third world and southern Italy is fused onto Martorana's Yousef (through the diegesis as well as through the actor's extra-diegetic identity). Through the overlapping of the two levels, Yousef and Martorana are two inseparable halves of one man who is both southern Italian and Tunisian" (2010, 200). In some short sequences of *Quando sei nato,* we can retrace the actor who plays a small role as an immigrant smuggler. His presence and character links us again to the issues of internal migrations and racism in Italy. The fact that the *scafisti* (human smugglers) are southerners is depicting the stereotyped image of people from the south of Italy.[14]

The other-ing process is a common visual procedure in all films. All characters will have to become the other at some point in the narration.

When young Sandro falls into the water and wakes up on an old shipwreck surrounded by people he has never seen before, he is forced to hide his identity, has to deny he can speak Italian, and becomes somebody else: one young migrant among others coming from different countries, all packed on an old wrecked motorboat in the middle of the Mediterranean, all looking for a better life while risking it in the hands of two men with heavy southern accents. The camera moves as Sandro's gaze moves, and all he (and the audience) can see are tired, dirty, emaciated, harsh, and unfamiliar faces. The two pilots are even worse: uneducated and violent, they portray a suffering humanity where victims and persecutors are similar in their pain. These sequences are very powerful, and shift the focalization of the audience inside Sandro's gaze.

Giuseppe and Yousef share a common fate: both poor, they want to make a better living. Giuseppe is less educated and travelled than Yousef, but being part of the dominant culture and in charge of his own boat, he finds himself in a hegemonic position. In the middle of the sea, Giuseppe is suddenly influenced by the Italian radio's newscast: after hearing the terrorist's description, he starts perceiving his old Tunisian friend as the irreconcilable other. He convinces himself that Yousef is indeed the man Interpol is looking for, calling into question his friend's identity and their friendship.[15] The power of the media, even in a remote location, overwhelms Giuseppe's imagination. The radio is an ambivalent *medium* because through the newscast, it gives voice to a terrorized society but, at the same time, it becomes a site of hybridization when it plays both Italian and Arabic music. As Faleschini Lerner rightfully wrote, it can also be a site of contamination because "switching from Arabic pop music to Italian melodic songs, to RAI newscasts, it incarnates the intersection of languages and cultural perspectives that the liquid surface of the Mediterranean makes possible" (2010, 16–17). Music played over the radio performs the missing dialogue between the two friends and the two cultures. Iain Chambers and Lidia Curti draw attention to the role of music in contemporary culture because "sounds exceed the limits of structured politics and unilateral reasoning," and music

> means to challenge and disturb the historical and cultural mappings we have inherited. It also means to undo the consensual chronologies of "progress" and their linear accumulation of meaning. Such maps, in this case of musical geography—the simultaneous bringing into sound and the sounding out of the historical and cultural terrain being traversed as the Mediterranean becomes a sonic sea—are to be considered not merely as historical and cultural

documents, but also as composing an irreverent or undisciplined critical language, suspended and sustained in the sound itself. (Chambers and Curti 2008, 391)

The Mediterranean plays a central role in the topography of both films, but in a contrasting way: Sandro travels on an unexpected initiatory journey toward Greece on the boat of his father's friend but falls into the water. For him, travelling becomes the trigger to learn a new way of going far from his house, his family, and his country. As Trinh T. Minh-ha explained, "in traveling, one is a being-for-other, but also a being-with-other. The seer is seen while s/he sees. To see and to be seen constitute the double approach of identity: the presence to oneself is at once impossible and immediate ... traveling allows one to see things different to what they are, differently from how one has seen them, and differently from what one is" (1994, 23).

Sandro will be able to cross the invisible borders of the Mediterranean to meet himself disguised as an other, the migrants, the others. The sea represents a smooth space, where according to Deleuze and Guattari, "one 'distributes' oneself in the open space, according to frequencies and in the course of one's crossing" (1987, 481). Sandro distributes his identity in this open fluid space, simultaneously getting rid of all preconceptions. On the smooth surface of the water, where no barrier exists, he finds an improvised passage: the meeting with the other is possible only at sea, in an open space without borders or frontiers, where he is defenceless and therefore open to a new dialogue.

Conversely, the space of the sea will work for Giuseppe in the opposite way, because while travelling at sea without any fixed point of reference on the open water, he loses contact with reality and can't fix his gaze on anyone but his friend. The entire relationship between Giuseppe and Yousef embodies the cultural hybridity of the Mediterranean, and reminds the audience of its different traditions, cultures, religions, and languages, all shared in the open space of the sea. The smooth space of the Mediterranean progress as "an intricate site of encounters and currents, involving the movement of peoples, histories, and cultures, that underlines the continual sense of historical transformation and cultural translation that makes it a site of continual transit" (Chambers 2004, 427).

The boats are converted into the actual embodiment of the imposition of histories and cultures belonging to the Mediterranean, embracing the liquidity of identity formation as well as the precariousness of borders. Iain Chambers remarked that the condition "to be at sea is to be lost, and to be in such a state is to be vulnerable to encounters that we do not necessarily control" (2004, 425). In the case of Sandro, his encounter with the migrants (and his friendship with two Romanian brothers he meets among them) will change his world forever. For Giuseppe, irresponsibly unable to confirm his doubts and foolishly incapable of communication, the confrontation with the other—his friend and now imagined enemy—will bring a tragic epilogue, a symbol of the impasse of language and truth, the abrupt end to the disastrous Pirandellian multiplication of identities he can no longer sustain. In *Lamerica*, the returning boat Gino is forced to embark on symbolically condenses two different moments in history while exemplifying the horrible conditions migrants have been forced to accept for the dream of a better life, whether the mythological land of the New World is Italy or the Americas.

Derek Duncan wrote, "historically, cinema in Italy has been seen as the cultural form in which national identity is most securely located.... Histories of Italian cinema tell a national story" (2008, 211). If we accept and agree with this definition, we should wonder what kind of national story these three films are trying to articulate. Amelio's work destabilizes historical narration and prompts Italian viewers to review the past and their memories. Giordana's oeuvre initiates an unselfish narration through Sandro's ideal but includes very unrealistic gestures (at the very end of the film, Sandro escapes from his family and finds the Romanians' sister, whom he will probably save from prostitution) as he opens up to otherness. Melliti's film conversely traces the uncertain prospect of knowing who the other really is, a critique of Italian society that is too caught up with itself (and the media) to be open for a productive dialogue. There is no hero in Melliti's film, only the struggle of two men for survival.

Pell rightfully argued that, "from the title *Io, l'altro*, it is unclear whether Giuseppe or Yousef is the other. The story is not told from one particular point of view, which suggests that the first-person prerogative is available for the taking.... They are both subject/self (citizen of the destination culture, Italy) and other (caught in the interstices of identity, be it southern marginalization or orientalist discrimination)" (2010, 198–99).

In all of these films, the Mediterranean Sea plays a crucial role; it is the place where the story can start, finish, and/or unfold: the centre of an intricate crossroad of identities, languages, and cultures still to be mapped in Italian culture through its multiple encounters with the other. It is the critical discourse toward and within Italian society that should stimulate a new cultural and political discussion in which Italy should reposition itself "re-appropriating the symbolic space of the Mediterranean not to retrieve the full historical explanation of its origins but to experience its own contingency as a cultural and historical formation adrift" (Chambers 2008, 2).

The stories narrated in Italian cinema today show, record, and archive images of migration. They articulate and address the inadequacy of Italian vocabulary in describing the changes in its society, and my hope is they will continue to bring to the fore many unresolved knots which the historical narratives of Italian society can unravel on the screen and in reality.

Notes

1 From 1969 until 2001, and the two scholars provide a subsequent periodization: 1969–81, 1982–91.

2 *Extracomunitario* means "from outside the EU," but it is wrongfully employed nowadays to define European citizens belonging to Eastern Europe, as in the case of Romanian immigrants.

3 As Marcella Delle Donne observed:

> L'immigrato è l'extracomunitario, come si legge nel titolo della legge 39/90 sull'immigrazione. Ebbene, extracomunitario è anche l'americano, il giapponese, lo svizzero, ma non è ad essi che si riferisce il titolo della legge bensì a coloro che sono extra rispetto a una comunità intesa non in senso giuridico come l'Unione Europea, bensì nel senso di comunità ideale, in cui vengono compresi tutti quelli che hanno indicatori simili in senso politico, tecnologico ed economico. Indicatori che possono essere ricompresi nella categoria civiltà, la quale segna il confine tra la comunità dei civili e la comunità di coloro che ne sono fuori, per questo extracomunitari.
>
> [The immigrant is the extracomunitario, as you can read in the title of the immigration law 39/90. But an extracomunitario is also an American, a Japanese, a Swiss, even if the law does not refer directly to them but instead to all of those who are extra/outside the community. The term community here is not used in the legal sense as within the European Union, but more in idealistic terms of an ideal community to which belong all who have a common indicator, in the political, technological, and economical sense. Indicators that can be included in the category of "civilization," that marks the border of the civilian community and those who are outside of it, the extracomunitari.] (qtd. in Pastorino 2010, 318)

All translations mine unless otherwise indicated.

4 See http://www.corriere.it/politica/09_maggio_09/maroni_immigrati
_respinti_da84e542-3ca2-11de-a760-00144f02aabc.shtml

5 According to Stefano Allievi, "the Bossi-Fini law increased the number of
irregulars in the country with the paradox of producing irregularity via the
legislation" (2010, 94). See also Norma Bouchard on the subject:

> The Bossi-Fini Law is, by all accounts, a repressive bio-political
> apparatus that transforms the immigrant into the homo sacer of
> Agamben's *State of Exception* (2005), that is to say, into the bare
> life of the bios. It mandates fingerprinting, confines immigrants
> to so-called CPTs (Centers of Temporary Permanence), and has "a
> punitive and segregationist content ... in line with the constitutional
> state sanctioned by the anti-terrorism laws" (Mellino 2006, 469).
> But the peak of Italy's ill-conceived immigration policy was reached
> with the Rome-Tripoli agreement of 2005. Signed by Berlusconi and
> Gaddafi, this agreement seeks to contain the arrival of clandestine
> immigrants coming from and through Libya by repatriating them.
> Since non-Libyan immigrants are deported to the edge of the Sahara
> and left to their own devices, the 2005 agreement has claimed
> hundreds of lives. Yet, Berlusconi shows no signs of loosening the
> grip of the repressive, anti-immigrant apparatus that has taken
> hold throughout the peninsula and its surrounding Mediterranean
> waters. He continuously dismisses the notion of a multiethnic Italy,
> despite the criticism of human rights advocates, the Vatican, and UN
> officials. (Bouchard 2010, 106)

6 The Italian cinematic industry, after a crisis in the eighties due to "the overwhelming powers of American films and their distribution network," saw a
decrease in public funding and has slowly been replaced by "the role played
by the principal television networks—the state-run RAI and Berlusconi's
Mediaset—as central production companies" (Capussotti 2009, 59). If the
European Union funded through its Mediterranean Program "transnational
artistic collaboration, assigned a specific role to migration as both an object
and as part of the filmmaker's experience" (58), in Italy, mainstream cinema,
produced by RAI or Mediaset, was not particularly eager to critically address
the role of immigrants in Italian society.

7 Capussotti adds, "filmmakers such as Matteo Garrone (*Terra di Mezzo* [1997]
and *Ospiti* [1998]) and Vincenzo Marra (*Tornando a casa* [2001]), who are
now celebrated as innovative auteurs' figures, started their careers in this

niche. Others like Francesco Munzi (*Saimir* [2004]), Paolo Vari (*Fame chimica* [2004]), Vittorio Moroni (*Le ferie di Licu* [2006]) and Marina Spada (*Come l'ombra* [2006]) are examples of those who have dealt with migration in original ways" (2009, 58). This has not helped the large distribution of Italian films on migration, because, as Capussotti noted,

> Furthermore, the screening of films about migration as well as related documentaries has been closely associated with thematic exhibitions linked to political activism and anti-racist campaigns. As a result, these films attract an audience that is best described as a socially and culturally active segment of the public, which is motivated to see films as social texts and to interpret cinema as an instrument for political and cultural action. In this context, aesthetic choices and debates would appear to occupy a marginal position. (2009, 58)

8 Aine O'Healy noted that images of migrants arriving on the shores of Italy have "attained iconic status in the national imaginary, drawing attention to the porousness of Italy's maritime boundary" (2010, 1). These iconic images resurfaced this year, when large numbers of migrants arrived on Lampedusa, a small Italian island in the Mediterranean that was unprepared to deal with such a population. O'Healy remarked also that "given the striking visual drama of the 'illegal' maritime arrivals, Italy's Mediterranean migrants have appeared repeatedly in national television reports over the years and are often sensationalized" (8), an idea I agree with. Nonetheless, it is to be remembered that the sea has become, very unfortunately, a burial site for migrants and the recovery of the memory of the losts is not addressed in the news as it should. (See O'Healy 2010.)

9 O'Healy gives a very updated list of films in which the sea is important for the narration:

> Films that introduce images of "illegal" Mediterranean crossings or clandestine arrivals on Italian shores include: *Pummarò* (dir. Michele Placido, 1990, Numero Uno International and CineEuropa 92); *Lamerica* (dir. Gianni Amelio, 1994, Mario e Vittorio Cecchi Gori, Tiger Cinematografica); *L'Articolo 2* (dir. Maurizio Zaccaro, 1994, Maurizio Nichetti and Ernesto Di Sarro, Bambú Cinema e TV Produzioni with Rete Italia); *Aprile* (dir. Nanni Moretti, 1997, Sacher Film); *I figli di Annibale* (dir. Davide Ferrario, 1998, Medusa);

Tornando a casa (dir. Vincenzo Marra, 2001, Sacher Film); *L'Italiano* (dir. Ennio De Dominicis, 2002, Andrea de Liberato and Antonio Fusco for Poetiche Cinematografiche); *Lettere al vento* (dir. Edmond Budina, 2002, Donatella Palermo for A.S.P., Dodici Dicembre, and Erafilm, Tirana); *Saimir* (dir. Francesco Munzi, 2004, Orisa); *Quando sei nato non puoi piú nasconderti* (dir. Marco Tullio Giordana, 2005, Cattleya and RAI Cinema); *L'ospite segreto* (dir. Paolo Modugno, 2003, Esse & Bi Cinematografica); *Io l'altro* (dir. Mohsen Melliti, 2006, Trees Productions); *Lettere dal Sahara* (dir. Vittorio De Seta, 2006, A.S.P./Metafilm, Donatella Palermo); *Riparo* (dir. Marco Simon Puccioni, 2006, Intelfilm, Adésif); and *Billo il Grand Dakhaar* (dir. Laura Muscardin, 2008, The Coproducers). In some of these films, the representation of the sea crossing or clandestine landing is extremely brief, whereas in others the voyage becomes a major part of the narrative. (2010, 2)

10 Hostility and hospitality are both linked sematically, as Jacques Derrida explored in his work *Of Hospitality* (1996).

11 "Landings." Immortalized in the well-known Benetton campaign by Oliviero Toscani, when a ship full of Albanese refugees approached Bari's port on August 18, 1991.

12 Duncan analyzes the scene and rightfully points out that "the re-cast newsreel footage serves a pedagogical function for the spectator as the narrative that emerges disrupts consoling fictions of the national past" (2008, 205).

13 As Duncan noted, "Throughout the film, there are suggestions of a more recent mode of colonization by Italy that does not require a military presence. The omnipresence of Italian commercial television is seen as the conduit for the delivery of, what can only seem, parodically excessive dreams of Western opulence" (2008, 205).

14 As it is well known, southern immigrants travelling to the industrial triangle of Genoa, Turin, and Milan in the sixties confronted the same problems immigrants face nowadays when arriving in Italy, and the Southern question is far from being resolved. (See Ginsborg 1990.)

15 In one scene he finds in Yousef's jacket a newspaper article on an international terrorist, but at the end he will discover that he looked at the wrong side of the paper. In reality, it was about a Tunisian football player that Yousef admired.

References

Allievi, Stefano. 2010. "Immigration and Cultural Pluralism in Italy: Multicultural-ism as a Missing Model." *Italian Culture* 28 (2): 85–103.

Bouchard, Norma. 2010. "Reading the Discourse of Multicultural Italy: Promises and Challenges of Transnational Italy in an Era of Global Migration." *Italian Culture* 28 (2): 104–20.

Capussotti, Enrica. 2009. "Moveable Identities: Migration, Subjectivity and Cin-ema in Contemporary Italy." *Modern Italy* 14 (1): 55–68.

Chambers, Iain. 2010. "Another Map, Another History, Another Modernity." *California Italian Studies Journal* 1 (1): 1–14. Accessed September 15 2010. http://escholarship.org/uc/ismrg_cisj.

———. 2004. "The Mediterranean: a Postcolonial Sea." *Third Text* 18 (5): 423–33.

Chambers, Iain, and Lidia Curti. 2008. "Migrating Modernities in the Mediterra-nean." *Postcolonial Studies* 11 (4): 387–99.

Deleuze, Gilles, and Felix Guattari. 1987. *A Thousand Plateaus. Capitalism and Schizophrenia.* Translated by Brian Massumi. Minneapolis: University of Min-nesota Press.

Derrida, Jacques, and Anne Dufourmantelle. 2000. *Of Hospitality.* Trans. Rachel Bowlby. Palo Alto, CA: Stanford University Press.

Duncan, Derek. 2008. "Italy's Postcolonial Cinema and Its Histories of Represen-tation." *Italian Studies* 63 (2): 195–211.

Faleschini Lerner, Giovanna. 2010. "From the Other Side of the Mediterranean: Hospitality in Italian Migration Cinema." *California Italian Studies Journal* 1:1–19. Accessed September 15, 2010. http://escholarship.org/uc/ismrg_cisj.

Genette, Gérard. 1976. *Figure III.* Torino: Einaudi.

Ginsborg, Paul. 1990. *A History of Contemporary Italy. Society and Politics 1943–1988.* London: Penguin.

———. 1996. *L'Italia del Tempo Presente. Famiglia, Società Civile, Stato 1980–1996.* Torino: Einaudi.

King, Russell. 2001. "The Troubled Passage: Migration and New Cultural Encoun-ters in Southern Europe." In *The Mediterranean Passage,* edited by Russell King, 1–21. Liverpool: Liverpool University Press.

Loshitzky, Yosefa. 2010. *Screening Strangers: Migration and Diaspora in Contempo-rary European Cinema.* Bloomington, IN: Indiana University Press.

Minh-ha, Trinh. 1994. "Other Myself/My Other Self." In *Travellers' Tales: Nar-ratives of Home and Displacement,* edited by George Robertson, 9–28. New York: Routledge.

O'Healy, Aine. 2010. "Mediterranean Passages: Abjection and Belonging in Contemporary Italian Cinema." *California Italian Studies Journal* 1 (1): 1–19. Accessed September 15, 2010. http://escholarship.org/uc/ismrg_cisj.

Parvulescu, Costantin. 2010. "Inside the Beast's Cage: Gianni Amelio's *Lamerica* and the Dilemmas of Post 1989 Leftist Cinema." *Italian Culture* 28 (1): 50–67.

Pastorino, Gloria. 2010. "Death by Water? Constructing the 'Other' in Melliti's *Io, l'Altro*." In *From Terrone to Extracomunitario: New Manifestations of Racism in Contemporary Italian Cinema,* edited by Grace Russo Bullaro, 308–40. Leicester: Troubador Publishing.

Pell, Gregory. 2010. "*Terroni Di Mezzo*: Dangerous Physiognomies." In Russo Bullaro 2010, 178–218.

Ponzanesi, Sandra. 2005. "Outlandish Cinema: Screening the Other in Italy." In *Migrant Cartographies. New Cultural and Literary Spaces in Post-Colonial Europe,* edited by Daniela Merolla and Sandra Ponzanesi, 267–80. Oxford: Lexington Books.

Transatlantic Trends: Immigration Key Findings. 2010. Ordered by the German Marshall Fund of the United States, the Lynde and Harry Bradley Foundation, the Compagnia di San Paolo, and the Barrow Cadbury Trust. Accessed February 21, 2011. http://trends.gmfus.org/?page_id=3035.

Sciortino, Giuseppe, and Asher Colombo. 2004. "The Flows and the Flood: The Public Discourse on Immigration in Italy, 1969–2001." *Journal of Modern Italian Studies* 9 (1): 94–113.

Walcott, Derek. 1986. *Collected Poems: 1948–1984.* New York: Farrar, Straus & Giroux.

Wood, Mary P. 2005. *Italian Cinema.* Oxford: Berg Publishers.

Zambenedetti, Alberto. 2006. "Multiculturalism in New Italian Cinema." *Studies in European Cinema* 3 (2): 105–16.

Chapter 15

Euro Chic: Fashion's Bread & Butter

Susan Ingram

"Sociality is the capacity of being several things at once."
–G.H. Mead

The slogan for the Bread & Butter trade fair in the summer of 2009 was "Bread & Butter is coming home!"—meaning that it was leaving Barcelona, where it had been based for four seasons, and moving back to Berlin, where it had taken place from 2003 to 2005, after which it held back-to-back events in both Barcelona and Berlin. Starting out in 2001 in Cologne with a concept for "an innovative trade fair event for the progressive, contemporary clothing culture," Bread & Butter originally ran bi-annually as a parallel event to Cologne's *Herrenmodewoche* (Men's Fashion Week) / InterJeans, and its immediate success encouraged organizers to become more ambitious and more involved in the branding battles that cities now wage mercilessly for coveted "world" or "global" city status.[1] Building on previous work done on Berlin's success in mobilizing fashion to brand itself (Ingram and Sark), what I am looking at in this contribution are fashion-oriented identities that get coded "European" and the role that fashion trade shows have played in this process. Because trade shows cater to and are exclusively for industry representatives, they allow us to look further behind the scenes than we can, for example, with fashion shows. Bread & Butter's feeling "at home" in Berlin directs us to a key characteristic of the kind of European identity that fashion trade shows live off of parasitically and which they also help to create: namely, a kind of sophisticated slumming. After first showing how this kind of Jekyll/Hyde ("we're so very respectable, we're so very not respectable") mechanism works in the case of Bread & Butter, I then turn to the Premium trade show that also premiered in Berlin in 2003 and demonstrate that even in what initially appears to be a more straightfor-wardly elite-oriented show, one can also discover the seductively ambiva-lent high-low nature of Euro Chic that makes it seem like the best of both, and therefore all possible, worlds.

That fashion trade shows—like the fashion shows and fashion industry they cater to—are based on the principle of exclusivity is evident not only in their registration and ID procedures but also in the name of Bread & Butter's main sponsor partner: *vente-privee*. Headquartered in Paris since starting up in 2001, *vente-privee* has grown into one of the leaders of the European e-commerce industry. As one can see from its advertising in the Bread & Butter Tradeshow Guide, which prominently occupies the last two pages of the guide and therefore invites being literally ripped off, it is proud to be number one in Europe, and even spells out "number one" in a way that looks European, using French in an otherwise English-language context. Additionally, in its online press kit, *vente-privee* boasts of having "more than 10 million subscribed members *in Europe*" and "over 38 million products sold through 2,500 sales *in Europe*" (my emphasis), underscoring the field it identifies with and sees itself operating in. Many of the more than 1,200 designer brands *vente-privee* sells in limited two- to four-day runs are also present at Bread & Butter; to take a random example, the four brands that happened to have sales on *vente privee* on the day I was working on this part of this project (July 19, 2010)—Diesel, DKNY Jeans, Moschino, and Lonsdale of London—were also all in the last Bread & Butter Brand bible.

The exclusivity of the fashion trade can therefore be seen to be tempered by inclusivity in terms of style. Bread & Butter may identify itself in its pro-motional materials as "an international specialist trade fair for Street and Urban Wear," but it also claims that it "represents a marketing and commu-nication platform for brands, labels and designers from the areas of Denim, Sportswear, Street Fashion, Function Wear and Casual Dressed Up"—even its "dressed up" category is casual. This tendency is also evident in both Bread & Butter's and Premium's choice of location. Bread & Butter started off in a derelict, crumbling factory in Spandau on the outskirts of the city before moving to an old hangar at Tempelhof airport, while Premium pre-miered in a conversation-worthy section of an underground U-Bahn tun-nel beneath Potsdamer Platz that was no longer being used, before moving to the centrally located former postal freight depot at Gleisdreieck. These converted transportation sites operate in the same inclusive key as denim and sneakers, evoking image-based mediated fantasies of travel and escape for what Tobias Rapp has termed the "Easyjetset."

For high fashion to take its cues from the streets is, of course, nothing new or exciting. What is of relevance for the topic of fashion and European identity is the way one stream of this tendency tends to get coded European. A satirical example that pinpoints this stream with great precision can be found in Ralph Martin's 2009 book, *Ein Amerikaner in Berlin: Wie ein New Yorker lernte, die Deutschen zu lieben* (*An American in Berlin: How a New Yorker Learned to Love the Germans*). Detailing his attempts to adopt his metrosexual, white-scarfed, New York sartorial sensibilities for Berlin's Prenzlauer Berg, Martin describes an unsuccessful shopping experience as follows:

> My friend Annie in New York knew of a boutique in Mitte that was, as she put it, the "non plus ultra" of Berlin fashion. When I finally found the ad-dress, it looked like the boutique was hidden behind an unmarked metal door in a back courtyard. I pressed the metal door open and followed a ce-ment staircase downstairs into a small, dark basement, which was only illu-minated by a purple neon bulb. The walls were painted black, if there were any at all. Behind the counter stood a tall youth with large, black-rimmed glasses and a black zip-up sweatshirt. He had his hood up so that his face seemed to float in space. He ignored me while I groped my way through the store looking for clothes. Finally I found something: a long board made of unfinished wood. On top of it lay a sweatshirt and a pair of sneakers. I bent over and attempted to see something in the purple light. The sweatshirt seemed to be grey, with a blindingly white fleecy lining. After I had stared at the price tag for some time, the floating face with the glasses said in English: "300 Euros…. It's hand-made," said the boy. I held it to the purple light. If I had had a sewing machine, I could have made something like that myself. (Martin 2009, 50–52)

The store Martin describes so evocatively but does not name actually ex-ists. It is called Apartment (http://www.apartmentberlin.de) and, indeed, a sweatshirt/ sneaker combination there can easily set you back 1,000 euros.

The faux-inclusivity of Apartment's kind of understated, high-quality fashion gets coded as European in a particular matrix of imaginary re-lations: first, as edgier and less conservative than equally understated, high-quality Asian styles; second, as the opposite of the faux-exclusivity of

American outlet stores, where one pays as little as possible for bourgeois designer labels like Ralph Lauren that are intended to evoke exclusive, country manor lifestyles; third, as a mode of Europeanness rejecting the opulent formality of real aristocrats that celebrities turn to in order to lend special occasions the requisite solemnity; and finally fourth, as a tasteful yet still streetwise alternative to the flashy bling-encrusted urban wear associated with visible minority youth, who in the global imaginary stereotypically inhabit the streets and render them dangerously desirable.

It is crucial to remember that we are here in the connotative realm of imaginaries and image creation that branders and other forms of advertising and marketing specialists work hard to manipulate to their companies' advantage. I would not want to be misunderstood as claiming that Europeans don't wear Ralph Lauren or bling. The point I wish to make is a subtler one, because the looks that fashion trade shows promote subtly play with more general and stereotypical tendencies. As we know from Ien Ang's *On Not Speaking Chinese*, the mother tongue of the Asian woman in the black leather jacket on the Brand Bible homepage could well be Dutch or German, just as the bald gentleman behind her could well speak Japanese or Arabic. What matters for Bread & Butter, and the reason this image appears on its home page, is the ambivalence in their images: it is not individual items like scarves or coats that give them the air of Europeans, but rather a sophisticated kind of casual that makes it clear one still has both standards and style.

If we turn now to the more exclusive trade show, Premium, whose name embodies its aspirations to provide "a contemporary trade platform for choice collections, international newcomers and *exclusive* trend products" (http://www.premiumexhibitions.com/press/; my emphasis), we find an interestingly similar array of inclusive images and styles, with an emphasis on denim and sneakers. Premium attributes its success, which has been considerable—it started out in 2003 with 70 exhibitors and 3,500 visitors, and in January 2010 had 900 exhibitors and 42,000 visitors at its own dedicated site—to having a "brand new trade fair concept which PREMIUM ... used to define a completely new segment: Instead of focusing on marketing and booth construction," they put fashion in the foreground. "For the first time, women's and men's collections were presented together, denim shown alongside accessories and luxury labels. The aim [was] to deliver relevant content and first-hand fashion information as well as being a meeting place for the most innovative national and international collections and retailers from high-end stores worldwide" ("All About Premium" YEAR). Premium is proud of having "engaged and established new fields in the area of fashion.... But outside the fashion field too.... As, for example, with the premiere of the "Berlin Bicycle Show" in March 2010, where innovative trend bikes, city and mountain bikes, sport bikes as well as concepts of intelligent mobility (such as Pedelecs and E-bikes) were presented for the first time to professional visitors and an interested public." Other examples include GREEN LIVING, which was presented in 2007 to foster "fashion that is ecological as well as ethically correct and produced according to sustainable standards"; SEEK, which was launched in January 2009 and presents a selection of progressive designers and brands from the youth culture, music, and art segments; and the "next conference" on digital trends in Europe, which PREMIUM has been co-producing since 2010 (this year's theme was "Game Changers and [the] App Economy"). So when co-founder Anita Tillmann claims that "PREMIUM is the opposite of the mainstream—PREMIUM is focused, selective and unique!" and her partner Norbert Tillmann adds that "Fashion is like cooking—it's about taste, about ingredients, about the way it's presented. What counts in the end is the right mix and that's what PREMIUM provides!" they reinforce the strategy we've already found with Bread & Butter: namely, mobilizing "progressive" elements (whether bikes, apps, or sneakers) to temper the exclusivity that the fashion industry has traditionally cultivated in order to make it appealing to the high-rolling wannabe aristocrats among the nouveau, or more recently—"novi" classes. This tempering or balance is explicit in Premium's online promotional statement, and clarifies my earlier qualified reference to these elements as "inclusive." In the section "Everything hand-made," one finds that,

> PREMIUM guarantees this in its exclusive selection. Only those designers whose products perfectly fit the concept, profile and audience are exhibited. Because the focus should be 100% on fashion, the exhibition areas provided have a maximum size of 50 sq. meters. Each designer forgoes their own decoration, music and furnishings at the start. *Thus an ideal work environment is created with equal opportunity for all.* At PREMIUM, young Berlin designers are presented alongside established ones, national and international emerging talent alongside top stars. *Each receives the same attention.* (PREMIUM Promotional Statement; my emphasis)

Within this avowedly "exclusive" environment, then, there is operational a democratizing logic that disrupts and opens up that environment to challenges from "emerging talent" keen to push the limits of what "perfectly fits."

What makes Premium of particular interest in regard to the question of fashioning European identities is that it does not feel the need to demonstratively declare itself "European," while Bread & Butter, with its streetwear focus, feels it has to play up the Europeanness of its sponsors and competing urban locations: the theme of its first show in Barcelona was, after all, "Eurovision." Premium, conversely, takes its Europeanness in stride and declares itself "totally global" to the extent that it can make what must appear to many to be the exaggerated claim:

> A revolutionary, innovative fashion trade show has become an internationally successful enterprise. Many-faceted, progressive, and with an influence on the world of fashion that is beyond doubt: PREMIUM International Fashion Trade Show.
>
> Now as before, the exclusive trade show PREMIUM is the main focus of the PREMIUM team, and has, in the meantime, come to be considered the mainstay of Berlin Fashion Week.
>
> Worldwide, it is the only fair that puts fashion and lifestyle in the high-end segment together in this size and quality.

Premium can make this claim because it feels confident of being associated with the high-end quality associated with European products. For Premium, being European means identifying with an exclusive and tasteful lifestyle that is coveted on an international scale as the global middle classes enter social realms open to distinction. An excellent example is the current popularity in Hong Kong and mainland China of expensive red wine and the prominent location of a new red wine shop at Chek Lap Kok, Hong Kong's airport.

What is significant about the European identity that emerges from these fashion trade shows is the way it is constructed: namely, not inter-subjectively in terms of alterity (that is, in the tradition of the Euro-American modernity provincialized by post-colonial theory) but rather multiplicitously in terms of what could be seen either in Butlerian performativity, Deleuzian virtuality, Agambian potentiality, or, as I am more inclined to view it (having read Ilya Parkins' convincing article on "Building a Feminist Theory of Fashion"), Karen Barad's concept of agential realism, which, as Parkins draws attention to, "urges us to be attentive to the 'marks left on bodies'.... Those marks are material, and they issue from power-saturated discursive and material fields" (2008, 511).

For Bread & Butter, being European means identifying with a kind of both discursively and materially constructed urban culture produced by a constellation made available in certain European urban centres, and on the basis of the historical, material traces these centres contain, which are available to be converted and re-enlivened in ways that are attractive to contemporary lifestyle culture and attract a creative-oriented labour force sympathetic to the ideals communicated by aspects of the city's history. One could imagine that in a few years Stockholm, Helsinki, Glasgow, or Manchester will be in a position to tempt Bread & Butter away from Berlin, as Barcelona managed to do for a few years but was not able to maintain because its city brand, as demonstrated by the posters, does not contain the right kind of signifiers for an urban streetwear trade show. While Barcelona may have outranked Berlin in terms of the strength of its city brand on the 2008 Saffron European City Brand Barometer (http://www.citymayors .com/marketing/city-brands.html), its combination of World Heritage Site Roman, Gothic, and modernist architecture, soccer, and the Olympics was not able to create the necessary buzz for Bread & Butter's Euro Chic clientele. At the end of the day, Barcelona proved unsuccessful in keeping Bread & Butter, I would argue, because its organizers chose to ignore the manifest material traces of industrial proletarian labour in the city. Rather, they held the trade show in the Palau Nacional, which was built for the 1929 World's Fair and now houses the National Art Museum of Catalonia, and featured it on the event's poster. Berlin, on the other hand, has mobilized both its socialist and nineteenth- and twentieth-century industrial heritage to great effect, and with the support of one of the most effective city symbols: its bear.

To sum up: while Kylie Minogue may be sexy, she is not chic, let alone Euro Chic, and the decision to frame her 2003 "Slow" video against the backdrop of, first the Barcelona skyline, and then a pool scene featuring the athletic complex rebuilt for the Olympics Games, was unfortunate for the city's branding as it missed the Euro Chic mark.[2] The kind of Euro Chic identity production in question—that trade shows like Bread & Butter and Premium participate in the making and maintenance of—is a confluence of the forces that collect in the creative-industries-oriented, skimpy swimsuit-abhorring populaces that some (European) cities are able to make possible by drawing on the material traces of their histories. These identities are not defined against but rather with, and those who do engage in such identificatory practices are not encouraged to think of themselves in terms of nationality, or indeed, in terms of any one thing. It is a question of confluences of interests and elective affinities; anyone interested in belonging is welcome no matter their background, as long as they ascribe to the ideals that the image of sophisticated slumming stands for, namely a political sympathy for the proletariat possessed by those who take pride in being an anti-bourgeois class that aspires to creativity. If these identities are defined against anything, it is a particular past, insofar as they are as against Eurocentric "Great White Male" hegemony as post-colonial theorists. The Europeanness of the identities produced and promoted at these fashion trade shows is a new kind of "New Europe," with the potential to fundamentally reconfigure the way we think about who we are and how places and their histories figure in that process.

Notes

1 Material on the history of Bread & Butter is taken from its website: http://www.breadandbutter.com/winter2011-absolute/metanav/about-bb/bb-history/. Likewise, material presented later in this chapter on Premium is from its website. See under References, below.

2 Thanks to Marta Marin-Domine for sharing her insider knowledge of Barcelona with me.

References

Ang, Ien. 2001. *On Not Speaking Chinese: Living Between Asia and the West*. London: Routledge.

Ingram, Susan, and Katrina Sark. 2011. *Berliner Chic: A Locational History of Berlin Fashion*. Bristol: Intellect.

Martin, Ralph. 2009. *Ein Amerikaner in Berlin: Wie ein New Yorker lernte, die Deutschen zu lieben*. Cologne: Dumont Literatur und Kunst Verlag.

Parkins, Ilya. 2008. "Building a Feminist Theory of Fashion." *Australian Feminist Studies* 23 (58): 501–15.

PREMIUM. "All About Premium." http://www.premiumexhibitions.com/service/All_about_PREMIUM_EN.pdf

Rapp, Tobias. 2009. *Lost and Sound: Berlin, Techno und der Easyjetset*. Frankfurt: Suhrkamp Taschenbuch.

vente-privee. https://us.venteprivee.com/main/#/signin

Chapter 16

Dancing Up a Storm: Canadian Performance at · the Nazi Olympic Games (1936) and the Notion of Cultural Translation

Alla Myzelev

He (Boris Volkoff) is teaching us, stiff, starched, and inhibited as we are, that a gracious employment of the limbs is not necessarily synonymous with indecorous conduct. ("Ballets Scene" 1934)

When Russian dancer Boris Volkoff (1900–1974) came to Toronto in 1929 to participate in the Uptown Theatre's dance program, little did he know that the next time he saw Europe he would be representing Canada in the 1936 Nazi Olympic Games. That year, Germany decided to add a cultural component to the conventional Olympic repertoire of summer sports in the form of a dance competition. The Canadian Olympic Committee, chaired by Toronto businessman P.J. Mulqueen,[1] decided to designate Volkoff and his ballet school in Toronto as the Canadian entrant.[2] For the Olympic performance, Volkoff chose five dances, two of which were based on Canadian Native legends, and the other three derived from the European ballet tradition. All five dances included various cultural influences and styles, including Aboriginal dance and music, Russian choreography and interest in folk dances, and classical ballet choreography and music, which were blended together and offered to audiences in Germany and then in Canada. Olympic participation was also a key point in Volkoff's Canadian career, and made him a national dance icon almost overnight.

Volkoff brought to his performance and teaching in Canada the rich experience he had garnered while studying in Russia and touring Asia and North America. His main ideas, however, came from the Russian tradition of classical and folk-based ballet, which he implemented in Canada. Thus, he adapted his knowledge and love of both classical and folk dances to offer performances that were both entertaining and enjoyable for Toronto audiences. He used his skills of adaptation of indigenous tales and stories from Russia and Europe to create two ballets that were based on Aboriginal Canadian legends. These productions, which have hardly been discussed by scholars, present an ideal case study of the creation of culturally hybrid performances.[3] This article investigates two separate yet interdependent axes of translation. One is the adaptation of the Native dances for European audiences, and the second is Volkoff's translation of the Russian tradition of folk dancing for the Canadian and then the European stage. Using the notion of translation as discussed by Gayatri Spivak (2000, 400) this research shows that participation in cultural adaptation is not unidirectional and linear but that the process is full of nuances, misunderstandings, and reversals. There are situations when the message is corrupted or lost while nuances that were not emphasized acquire unexpected significance. In the words of Lawrence Venuti, "a translation is never quite 'faithful,' always somewhat 'free,' it never establishes an identity, always a lack and a supplement, and it can never be a transparent representation, only an interpretive information that exposes multiple and divided meanings" (1992, 8). This case study demonstrates the impossibility of "straight representation" by analyzing the circumstances surrounding the Canadian performance in Germany.

Volkoff: Translating Russian Tradition

A recent immigrant from Russia, Volkoff had studied classical ballet in Moscow, and danced with the Youth Division of the Bolshoi Theatre. In 1924, he left Soviet Russia to perform first in Shanghai and then became master and first soloist of the Stavrinaky Ballet Russe Company, a small troupe consisting mainly of Russian and Eastern European dancers that had no relation to Diaghilev's internationally renowned Ballets Russes. Volkoff travelled and performed extensively in Asia and the Far East as a solo artist and as part of various groups. By 1928, he had become one of the soloists in the Adolph Bolm Ballet Company in New York. When his American visa expired, he was forced to return to Europe, and from there he was smuggled to Canada by Bolm's Canadian acquaintances.

In Canada, Volkoff first danced and choreographed one-act ballets for the Uptown Theatre Company under the direction of Jack Arthur, which were "done with a little story which was quite clever and new to Toronto … quite different to anything that had been put on in Toronto before and definitely advanced."[4] Recognizing Volkoff's abilities and teaching talent, Arthur appointed him director of the Jack Arthur School of Ballet and

Interpretive Dance, which opened in 1929. But Volkoff's ambitions went much further than running a second-rate dancing school in a city that was not exposed to dance culture. A year later, he resigned from the Uptown Theatre and the Arthur Dance School to open his own studio, where he and his assistants taught ballet, dancing for children, and tap dance. The same year, Volkoff published a long article in the *Toronto Star* that outlined his views of ballet and dance. Probably translated from Russian—since Volkoff's English at that point was somewhat strained—the article explains the need to establish an expressive dance tradition in Canada. Diplomatically and astutely, Volkoff points out that Canadians should not shy away from this art form but welcome it as a symbol of modern refinement (Volkoff, "New Dance School in Canada" 1930).

Homesick and lonely (according to his friends), Volkoff continued to attract attention and seek performance venues for his amateur dancers. It appears he did not have to try very hard; only one year after the school was opened, his performances were being reviewed by leading Toronto newspapers. Reviewers were positive and complimentary, especially when it came to showcasing children, young female dancers, and Volkoff himself. An accomplished dancer, Volkoff consciously maintained an exotic aura about himself. According to the memoirs of his former students, when teaching he wore a white shirt with an open collar and usually kept the first two buttons undone, which showed his attractive neck and chest but was also a scandalously informal look in stuffy Toronto. Along with the shirt came black breeches, loose and tied below the knees to allow for freedom of movement. Volkoff always carried an intricately carved cane, which he did not hesitate to use to pace the dancers and emphasize rhythm. The cane was also used to tap female dancers on various body parts, for touching their bodies directly was not considered appropriate. This appearance, combined with his heavily accented and somewhat garbled English, created the image of an outsider, friendly yet strange, attractive yet foreign, civilized but not familiar. This borderline status of Volkoff was supported by his onstage persona, often performing Russian folk and national dances and other humorous and highly expressive numbers. All these attributes ensured that, even in the midst of the Great Depression, the school had enough students to survive and their recitals filled auditoriums. Most of the repertoire of the early years of the school consisted of works inspired by Russian folk dances or parts of classical ballets.[5] For example, *Sailors' Dance* (1934) allowed Volkoff to showcase his *virtuoso* tiptoe work and high jumps, while the music was a combination of part of Rimsky-Korsakov's *Snow Maiden* and

Russian folklore music. *Garmoshka* (1934) similarly showcased Volkoff and his dancers' mastery of fast folk dance combined with balletic movements.[6] Thus, in the conservative climate of post-Depression Toronto, Volkoff trod lightly to create a positive perception among his students and patrons. He also started to court one of his most talented students, Janet Baldwin (1912–1990), who came from a well-established Toronto family. Their courtship and marriage, one assumes, allowed him entrance to the higher echelons of society, and indirectly attracted the invitation to participate in the Olympic Games in Berlin.

In addition, Volkoff based his teaching and choreographic practice on the experience of his student years in Moscow. Between 1918 and 1924, in spite of the shortages of food and fuel, and the fact that Russia was at war with almost all of the European countries, the cultural scene was very vibrant. While studying classical ballet, Volkoff witnessed the revival of old ballets from the pre-revolutionary repertoire and the staging of the new ballets featuring revolutionary themes. At the same time, various private schools and informal dance circles opened their doors to students. The compositions that were created were often much more innovative than classical ballets, and included elements of sport, acrobatics, and physical education. Some of the teachers were avid followers of French dance innovator François Delsarte (1811–1871), or of the developer of eurhythmics, Émile Jaques-Dalcroze (1865–1950). Isadora Duncan opened a school of contemporary dance in Moscow in 1921 (Souritz 1995). Other practitioners sought to innovate further and to challenge the free, natural movement of Isadora Duncan to create more complex forms and a new dance technique. They attempted this in a variety of ways and through various combinations of classical ballet, Duncan's free movement, eurhythmics, folk dance, pantomime, *plastique*, acrobatics, Swedish gymnastics, sport, and physical education. Many schools, studios, circles, and workshops eventually formed small dance companies.[7]

Probably the most influential teacher in Volkoff's career was the leader of the experimental dance movement, Alexander Gorsky (1871–1924). While attending the dance school of the Bolshoi Theatre Volkoff learned from Gorsky to emphasize the plasticity of movement and corporeal expression. Gorsky revived, with different choreography, *Giselle* and *Swan Lake* (both of which Volkoff used in Canada) and was able to satisfy his choreographic fantasies with folkloric, grotesque movements, and intermingling *pas* of the classical dance with free movements of his own making. He derived inspiration from very different sources and widely used the methods of well-known dancers of the variety stage. Volkoff attempted to make each dance more emotional, demanding expression from the dancers and actors and repudiating the services of "cold, dispassionate, empty per-formers" (Mitchell 1982, 45). Therefore, his productions were characterized by a special ardour and this attracted the notice of his contemporaries.[8]

The fact that the honour of representing Canada at the Olympic Games was bestowed on the young and dynamic Volkoff was due in large degree to his growing reputation and experience abroad. It was also due to the fact that in Canada, before Volkoff, both contemporary and classical forms of dancing were, according to the press at the time, somewhat "provincial."[9] When asked to prepare for the Olympics, Volkoff was presented with a difficult choice. The main problem lay in the fact that most of the partici-pating countries—including Germany, Hungary, Poland, Sweden, Swit-zerland, Romania, and Italy—brought to the competition not only their most talented dancers who, as it transpired during the Olympic event, were professionals rather than amateurs but also had an established folk tradi-tion. Volkoff clearly understood the key ideas of the Nazi competition's preferences: "I think German tradition rich in folk culture will be shown and felt in this competition" (Volkoff, Personal Correspondence 1936). He therefore felt that he needed to produce a performance that showcased Canada as a unique, distinctive nation. Moreover, the *Internationale Tan-zwettspiele* competition called for "ballet dances, dances for the concert stage, historical and national dances."[10] Janet Volkoff remembered Volkoff insisting that works representative of Canada be incorporated into the per-formance (Baldwin n.d., 1–3). She recalled, "it was he who wanted to take a Canadian work when he went to Berlin—we have to have something from our country—this was a Russian—he was adamant about it" (Mitchell 1982, 73). Volkoff's sentiment was seconded in the press when Augustus Bridle, in one of the editorials on the upcoming Olympic competition, mused, "the Highland fling and Irish Jig are not ours and the Red River Jig has gone out of style" (Ayre 2006, 40). The only really national style Bridle proposed was Native, but how could that be used on stage? Volkoff was disappointed to discover that, despite the fact that the Canadian Aboriginal legends were well suited for adaptation to ballet, he had great difficulty in finding suit-able music for his renditions of the Indian and Inuit legends. In their turn, Canadian journalists were surprised at Volkoff's interest and perseverance in Native Canadian themes: "Mr. Volkoff claims that the Indian legends of Canada are highly suitable for ballet material and that the chief difficulty is finding suitable music for them. He regrets that young Canadian composers have not turned more extensively to the rich musical material which is available in the traditional Native dances" ("Toronto Dancers" 1936). As Christine O'Bonsawin noted, "he sought to define and interpret 'Canadian-ness' for the ballet concert stage by studying the Indian people of Canada and their legends" (2004, 5).

The final program, which was rehearsed for four and a half months, consisted of five dance pieces: *Ekstase* (Ecstasy), a larger group composition accompanied by the music of Tchaikovsky; an Inuit dance titled *Mala* performed by Pauline Sullivan; *Petit-Polka* danced by the young (only fifteen) and very capable Joan Hutchinson; *Pfau* (Peacock) danced by the group to music by Ravel; and *Mon-Ka-Ta* (Mitchell 1982, 28). The musical credits for the latter included Bartók, Satie, and Barbeau.[11] *Ecstasy* and *Peacock* were based on the European ballet tradition, and mainly showcased the mastery of Volkoff's students, while *Petit-Polka* allowed Joan Hutchinson to show her charisma and grace, and Volkoff the humour and playfulness that he was apt at translating into choreography. The two others were based on Native traditions; *Mala* on the Inuit tradition and *Mon-Ka-Ta* on Aboriginal folklore.

Mala was set to music by Sir Ernest MacMillan, and was based on an Aboriginal Canadian story recorded by the anthropologist Dr. Barlawau. It tells of how the shaman of an Inuit tribe descends to the bottom of the ocean to placate the Mother of Life. He passes through great danger and finally reaches his goal, where, after giving homage to the goddess, he restores peace between her and her disobedient children by combing her hair, which became a symbolic ritual of profound religious importance in the Inuit culture.[12] Comprising a much longer and more complex ballet consisting of two distinct parts, *Mon-Ka-Ta* tells the story of a recently widowed Native man who could not be reconciled with the fact that his wife had died. The performance starts with Mon-Ka-Ta surrounded by mourners and the wise women, and he decides to wait for three days at his wife's grave in order to follow her soul to the land of the departed. He invokes the aid of the medicine man and wise women. In the ceremony, they remind him of the taboo: not to look back, not to fall asleep, and not to touch her soul. The second part takes place in the afterlife. Just before dawn on the third day, Mon-Ka-Ta's vigil is over, and as he sees her soul rise from the grave, he follows her westward to the afterlife. On the other side, Mon-Ka-Ta sees his wife surrounded by spirits who have gathered for the round dance. His wife comes, and they sit and talk. She returns to the spirits and asks her husband to join in their dancing. However, he is so weary that he falls asleep. The next time the spirit of his wife comes to him, she appears more human and, unable to overcome his longing, Mon-Ka-Ta touches her, whereupon she falls into his arms. In his great sorrow at his failure, he finds that she has become a log (*Promenade Programme Book* 1936).

Mon-Ka-Ta was performed to music "selected from compositions by Béla Bartók (1881–1945), Eric Satie (1866–1925), and Indian folk tunes recorded by Canadian anthropologist Marius Barbeau (1883–1969)" (Ayre 1996, 39). The visual pageantry of costume selection complemented the "Indian atmosphere." As John Ayre has suggested, designer Ron McCrae "was more inspired by pan-Indian clichés than by anthropology." The headbands, inspired by Hollywood, consisted of a single vertical feather at the back and were designed for the Indian maidens, who were dressed in diaphanous nightgowns. The warriors were identically dressed in the ubiquitous Plains Indian war bonnets and quill-painted breast pieces (Ayre 1996, 37). The costumes attracted a great deal of attention in the Canadian media. Prior to the team's departure for Germany, *Toronto Star* journalist Augustus Bridle suggested that "the Olympic judges will not know whether these aboriginals are Micmacs from Nova Scotia or Swampies from Athabasca, but they will be excited by the dazzling costumes designed by Ronald McRae" (1936). A reporter from *Saturday Night* stated that "the costumes and setting of the Indian legends are of great interest" ("Toronto Dancers" 1936). To complement the vibrant and attractive costumes, the sets were incorporated into the performance. Art students from the Central Technical School created Pacific Indian masks and a Kwakiutl-style totem pole,[13] and the use of a shaman and a genuine turtle-shell rattle (provided by Barbeau) augmented the theme-driven performance. Lillian Leona Mitchell stated that "the work was a stage presentation of an Indian legend using movement created by Volkoff, but it was not the original folk dance of the North American Indian. The Indian atmosphere of the ballet had been created through the use of an Indian legend, some Indian music, costumes, masks, and setting" (1982, 35–37).

Volkoff's choice of the legend was also based on the popularity of the latter among both North American and European audiences. A version of the Orpheus legend is one of the most popular Aboriginal mythic tropes in North America.[14] The familiarity of European audiences with the story of Orpheus and his journey to the underworld helped ensure that the content would strike a chord with German audiences familiar with Christoph Willibald Gluck and Ranieri de'Calzbigi's *Orpheo ed Euridice* (1769). Volkoff attempted to translate the Native legend and other cultural elements for the

European audience. The choreographer and his group had to create a performance that would be undoubtedly Aboriginal in its costumes, scenography, and dance movements, but also European in its music and overall feel. For Volkoff, the learning curve was especially steep, since in the process he had to actually learn and understand the Native and Canadian culture himself. Volkoff was definitely not the first among contemporary dancers to recreate Native dances. Both Ted Shawn in *Xochitl* and Martha Graham in *Ceremonials* approached Native themes through modern dance. Their approach combined expressionistic style or choreography and execution, and Native costumes done mainly in the idiom of the "noble savage"; in other words, the costumes played on the stereotypes known to the audience. Volkoff had kept a review of another of Graham's ballets, *Primitive Misteries* (1931), which was based on the Aboriginal cultures of New Mexico and was reviewed positively by the press.[15] Within the Canadian context, what propelled Volkoff to choose two ballets that drew on Native traditions in order to represent contemporary Canadian culture, while the prevalent view in this country was that Native cultures were dying and had to be salvaged and preserved? How and why were the issues relating to the death of Native cultures mediated through the modern dance performances?

Orpheus and the Notion of Native Culture: from Aboriginal to Aryan

In 1884, amendments to the Indian Act formally banned traditional Native American ceremonies, consequently outlawing the proper ceremony for transfer of title and acts of succession for tribal chiefs. Under the governance of the Indian Act, all aspects of Native life, including traditional ceremonies, dances, and celebrations were regulated (Canada Statutes 1884). Through the act of regulating these cultural events, Canada found it possible to appropriate Aboriginal cultural traditions for its own use. In the subsequent decades, numerous anthropologists and folklorists spent years travelling and gathering whatever was left from what they thought was a disappearing tradition. In order to preserve and capitalize on the Aboriginal culture, artists, photographers, and moviemakers adapted some of the Native stories, images, and stereotypes and made them part of popular culture.[16] Yet, claiming this tradition as representative of the Canadian identity went beyond such adaptation to popular culture.

By the middle of the 1930s, Canadian businesspeople and government officials had become aware of the importance of national and international tourism (*Report of Proceedings* 1947). For example, in April 1934, the Hon. W.H. Dennis from Halifax brought to the attention of the Senate the importance of the tourist trade to the Canadian economy, and urged the federal government to cooperate with the provincial authorities in order to enhance its development. Senators then debated the best way to portray Canada as a distinctive tourist destination, because, as the Hon. C.P. Beaubien stated, "strangers come to a strange land to see strange things," and Canada had to entice foreign travellers to cross the border in order to see uncommon things that they could not see at home (Canadian Parliament and Senate 1934, 303). Dennis argued that "the natural attractions of the country constitute one great asset which can be sold lavishly and still be retained undiminished and unimpaired" (303). The problem was that the natural attractions of Canada, although easily translatable into the media of painting and advertisements, were much harder to turn into a compelling story for use in films or dance.

The Canadian North appears in several productions of the time, including the Hollywood Western *Rose-Marie* (1936), which takes place in Northern Quebec and represents Native people as a backward, racially and morally inferior group, and *Nanook of the North* (1922), a Canadian documentary looking at the extreme conditions of the lives of the Inuit people. Shot in the style which James Clifford has termed "salvage paradigm" or "salvage documentary," this film portrayed Inuit culture not only as vanishing other but also as peaceful and fighting for survival, and thus not posing a threat to the Canadian nationalist agenda. *Mala*, created for the Olympic competition, follows the tradition of *Nanook of the North*, showing Inuit people as preoccupied with the issue of survival. The shaman character in the ballet is preoccupied with restoring peace and guaranteeing the survival of his people by looking for the deity in the underwater world.

As I previously mentioned, it was Volkoff who insisted on including ballets based on Indigenous cultures in the Olympic performance; coming from the tradition of Russian-Slavic nationalism, he decided to use Native traditions as a meaningful symbol of the Euro-Canadian culture (Francis 1992). His inspiration for reviving these Native traditions came from his own experience of dancing in Europe. Volkoff consciously capitalized on his relative exoticism as a Russian dancer: for Canadians, he represented both the exotic otherness of Central Europe and the refined classical tradition of the European ballet.

Moreover, Volkoff was also aware of the successful use by Diaghilev's Ballets Russes' of Russian, folkloric, and Oriental themes in Western Europe and the US in ballets such as *Firebird, Scheherazade, Tamar,* and *The Rite of Spring. Prince Igor* and later, an excerpt from this ballet titled

Polovtsian Dances, were two of the staple dances of the Ballets Russes' early years. *Prince Igor* could be seen as a metaphor for relations between the European parts of Russia and the "barbarian" and "uncivilized" Asian areas. For the *Polovtsian Dances*, the Ballets Russes impresario and producer Serge Diaghilev dropped a large part of the operatic performance and concentrated on the dances in the Polovtsian camp. In a similar way to the costumes in Volkoff's *Mon-Ka-Ta*, the costumes for the Polovtsians, designed by Russian artist Nicolas Roerich, were not based on any particular tribe or group, but rather were inspired by several Asian nations living in the Russian Empire, namely the Kirgiz and the Tatars.[17]

Volkoff, in turn, choreographed *Prince Igor* for the Toronto Skating Club. In this production, *Prince Igor* reproduces the power relations between Euro-Canadian culture and Native culture, since the ballet shows the tribes of Eastern Russia as barbaric and untamed. Volkoff also followed Diaghilev's lead in showing mainly the exotic and expressive tribal dances. His interest in anthropology and musicology can be linked to the similar interests of Roerich and Alexander Borodin, the composer of *Prince Igor*. Finally, what the amateur troupe of fifteen dancers presented in Berlin was an attempt to recreate Native Canadian traditions in a place where Aboriginal culture was "imaginary." The reality of Aboriginal life, including the hardships, prostitution, and alcoholism caused by lack of work and other opportunities, obviously did not find its way onto the stage, and so yet again the "Indian other" came to represent life in an idealized [?] pre-industrial society. In the words of Dominique Brégent-Heald, "in nationalist mythology, Indians signify harmony between humans and nature, and the untouched and virgin natural land that [has come] to represent Canada's beginnings" (2007, 48).

The performance itself, its context, plot, and costumes, helped to reproduce the power relationship between mainstream Canadian culture and its Native periphery. However, my reading of the Canadian contribution to the Olympic Games would be incomplete if I did not address the question of how these performances were "translated" for the German audiences. I am using the term "translation" in the form in which it was discussed by Gayatri Spivak and social anthropologist Vincente Rafael as a two-directional process which, as Rafael notes, is an "indispensable channel of imperial conquest and occupation" (1988, 210). Volkoff and his dancers unwillingly found themselves in the position of translators, in a situation where the story of the Native people was packaged, flattened, and digested by an international audience. Looking at the giant totem pole and the colourful,

geometric costumes, one cannot help but think of the strong and muscu-
lar bodies in art deco design, and of the powerful and virile bodies of the
Ballets Russes dancers in later productions such as *Jeux,* or the Russian
Constructivist Soviet extravaganzas. If one bears in mind such influences,
the translation of the Indigenous cultural tradition becomes less of a one-
dimensional, belittling, and castrating affair, and more of a complex and
multi-directional process. For what we see in the photographs of the event
are people who are strong, powerful, and athletic, whose masks and costumes, although following an "imaginary Indian" trope, also symbolize
strength and resilience.

The story of *Mon-Ka-Ta* also suggests an attempt to interpret the power
relationship between Euro-Canadians and the Aboriginal nationals. Mon-
Ka-Ta, who pursues his wife to the underworld in order to see her again and
perhaps say a final goodbye, represents the hunter, or perhaps a scholar or
anthropologist, who constantly studies a culture in order to understand and
preserve it before it becomes an immovable wooden log. However, while
chasing and studying, waiting and wondering, Mon-Ka-Ta is also translating or reshuffling the power relations between the colonizers and the
colonized.

Inadvertently, Volkoff translated not only the traditional version of a Native folk story that supports the salvage paradigm, but also another story of
strength and of the power of beauty and the imagination, which was greatly
appreciated in Berlin. Both Canadian and German newspapers praised
the ingenuity of the Canadian performance, especially since the Canadian
troupe was the only amateur group, and yet finished in a respectable fifth
place. One of the reviewers noted that *Mala* and *Mon-Ka-Ta,* choreographed by Volkoff, were the first original dances on Canadian subject matter. Arguably, the German jury may have missed some of the delicacies of
the relationship between the Euro-Canadians and the Indigenous people.
What was not lost on German audiences, however, according to one German commentator, was "the athletic freshness and energy of the perform-
ers." "Indians in the Canadian ballet," he continues, "are vibrant and natural,
a subject for admiration and imitation for the modern man" (Oefierreidjer
et al. 1936).

Even though Aboriginals were not Aryan, there was a degree of identification with their historical plight ingrained in German cultural history.
Furthermore, Volkoff was aware of and possibly an avid reader of Karl
May's series about Winnetou, a fictional Apache chief. His scrapbooks
include a cover of one of Karl May's books translated into Russian. May's

books were not only among the most popular ever written in German history but also he was a favourite author of Hitler. Apparently, the latter even went to hear May's lecture in Vienna in 1912. For Hitler, Winnetou, the untiring fighter, was a symbol of "tactical finesse" and military cautiousness. Later, Hitler recommended the books to his generals and had special editions distributed to soldiers at the front (Hamman 1999). May portrayed his hero as a wise chief of the oppressed. Winnetou, with his white German blood brother, Old Shatterhand, has in many adventures in the Wild West to help and to liberate the Apache tribe from the American oppressors. The adventure novels follow the "noble savage" trope, and were inspired by the writings of James Fenimore Cooper and George Catlin. Thanks to Karl May, the Wild West became part of the national popular imagination in Germany. The notion of brave, innocent, and heroic Native Americans fed into perceived parallel history (Feest 2002). In German cultural mythology, the fight between various Native nations was often compared to the plight of divided Germany. It was also supposed, albeit falsely, that the Aboriginal North Americans were the descendants of Vikings, and thus both Native tribes and German ethnic groups shared the same origins as fighters and nomads. For example, in her analysis of Karl May's treatment of Indians, Lisa Barthel-Winkler (1893–1966), who during the Nazi period published novels under the pen name Barwin, in which the heroics of Indian leaders were explained by their assumed Viking ancestry concluded,

> In Winnetou, Karl May delineates the Indian drama. It is also the German drama Winnetou is the noble man of his race—he knows about the purity of the blood, the longing and the hope of his brothers, but they have to founder because they are worn down by discord.... This is Indian, this is also German. Who has grasped the meaning of the Indian drama has also grasped the meaning of the German drama. (Feest 2002, 612)

The choice of the Native legends, albeit much more lyrical, was calculated by the Canadian Olympic Committee and Volkoff to appeal to German audiences and Nazi officials alike. It was also perhaps a claim, on some level, of sharing the same origins. Cultural translations, it seems, have the uncanny ability to be reinterpreted and reconceptualized, a fact that was wonderfully demonstrated by the inclusion of these Native dances in Berlin.[18]

Dance and Art in the Olympics: Modern and Folk

Dance, along with the literary and visual arts, was often the subject of Olympic debates in the early twentieth century. One of the most active advocates of the modern Olympic movement, Baron Pierre de Coubertin, had campaigned for the inclusion of the arts in the Olympic protocol on the basis of the "ennoblement" of sports and bringing additional national glory (Stanton 2000, 6). Although visual and literary arts were included in three Olympic games prior to 1936—in 1924 in Paris, in 1928 in Amsterdam, and in 1932 in Los Angeles—dance became part of the Olympic program only in Berlin's Nazi Games. The inclusion of dance along with gold- and silver-smithing, as well as sport documentary (Hanley 2004, 134) was solicited by the German organizers mainly in order to outdo their predecessors and include areas in which Germany was strong. For Nazi Germany, the Olympics were a rare opportunity to showcase its official ideology and proclaim national strength.[19] Although none of the proposed inclusions were approved, the International Olympic Committee in Germany dispatched invitations to the most notable dancers, and all countries were encouraged to participate in the competitions. Dance as a branch of the arts was especially important for the Nazi regime because of its emphasis on the healthy, pliable body, the folk and modern dance productions with nationalistic material, and due to the popularity and understanding of dance by the middle and lower classes (Randall 2005). The most notable modern German choreographers, Rudolf von Laban (1879–1958), Mary Wingman (1886–1973), and Harald Krutzberg (1902–1968), were put in charge of organizing Olympic events. An especially important role was played by Rudolf von Laban, who choreographed the inaugural Olympic celebration that took place on the opening night of the games. Recently appointed as German Master of the Studio for Dance, he organized and coordinated the international dance competition.

By 1936, Nazi Germany had undergone a period of transformation and a tightening of its ideological message, which moved away from anything that would be even remotely considered "modern" or intellectual. Instead, the emphasis was put on the healthy Aryan body and the healthy mind of the new generation of Germans, uncomplicated by theoretical issues (Guenther 2004). Yet, at the same time, the Nazi regime was very concerned about international perceptions. Showing superiority and presenting the country as culturally advanced and industrially developed came very high on the Nazis' priority list; thus, oppositional behaviour and incongruity abounded. While Laban's grandiose event, "Spring Wind and New Joy" was prohibited by Goebbels after the dress rehearsal on the grounds that it was too intellectual (Hanley 2004, 154), Wigman's and Kreutzberg's modern dance troupes were celebrated and awarded Olympic medals. Moreover, Goebbels personally invited a prominent American dancer, Martha Graham (1894–1991), to participate. She declined the offer, explaining, "so many artists whom I respect and admire have been persecuted; have been deprived of the right to work for ridiculous and unsatisfactory reasons, that I should consider it impossible to identify myself, by accepting the invitation, with the regime that has made such things possible. In addition, some of my concert group would not be welcomed in Germany" ("German Invitation" 1936). England, France, Sweden, and Russia, the four countries which had the most remarkable dance traditions, decided not to send dancers to Berlin. Thus, the competition was dominated by folk dances from Bulgaria, Romania, India, and Croatia. Modern dance and ballet were also present. The Canadian program then presented all three genres; folk (Aboriginal and Inuit), ballet, and modern dance based on the Aboriginal theme. While the rest of the entrants were interested in showing their folklore, the Canadian troupe presented modern dance based on the folkloric theme.

As Elizabeth Hanley has demonstrated, judging the dance competition proved impossible because of the differences in genres (2004 136–37). The German organizers belonging to the Nazi party insisted that the official competition should underscore "the glory" of the highly accomplished German group. Yet Laban had assured Volkoff, upon his arrival in Berlin, that the competition would be more of a festival than a competitive Olympic event. Therefore, the Canadian group was not surprised when, during the awards ceremony, Laban stated in his address to the international participants: "One could not measure artistic achievement as in sport with a stopwatch and meter measurement, especially when such a variety of genres were incomparable, such as the folk dance and ballet" (Müller and Stöckemann 1993, 137). Thus everyone received a diploma, while Harald Krutzberg, Mary Wigman, Mia Slavenska, and the group from India received special recognition medals. Volkoff, however, claimed that the Canadians came fifth and that they were bringing home not only a diploma but also medals and a silver cup. Although the medal and the cup were not registered in the Olympic records, one of Volkoff's dancers, James Pape, later confirmed that Laban told the dancers that "if they looked at different groups he (Laban) would place them about fifth" (Ayre 1996, 12). Volkoff took this remark very seriously and soon the press at home happily repeated the story of the amateur Canadian group rating fifth among professional dancers from all over the world.

Conclusion: Volkoff and the Olympic Success

Satisfied with the Canadian Olympic performance, Volkoff was presented with the next challenge, namely how to translate his success in the Olympic competition into more press attention and more students in his adopted hometown. Immediately after the Olympic awards, Volkoff sent a wire stating that the Canadians had not only won fifth place but also were awarded the medal, a diploma, and a cup. Although, as was mentioned earlier, ultimately no places were awarded in the dance competition, Volkoff made sure that everyone in Toronto knew that the amateur Canadian group actually received fifth place among mainly professional dancers.

After the closing ceremonies, half the group returned immediately to Canada, the others staying to tour Europe, take dance classes, or both. Boris and Janet Volkoff took a short tour through Europe and then went to England, where they took classes with Kurt Jooss (1901–1979), a German exile and well-known choreographer who had moved to London after the Nazis took over Berlin. The couple stayed in London until their finances ran out, and then headed home to continue their teaching and choreographic careers. When Volkoff arrived in Toronto and resumed performances with his students, the critics were celebratory. "Canada doffs her cap to Boris Volkoff, recognizes his school as outstanding and concedes him first place in the art of teaching," one critic wrote ("Unidentified Article" 1936). The dancers who participated in the Berlin Olympics were interviewed, and all of them praised Volkoff's leadership and mastery. Jack Lemen and James Paper, two of the soloists in the Toronto contingent, told the interviewer, "when I saw the support which is given the dance in Europe by state and public and then when I thought of what Boris Volkoff had done in Toronto without any such general interest in the dance and without official support, I just marvelled [sic]" ("Volkoff Dancers Score in Germany" n.d.). The reviewers praised the Aboriginal-themed dances: "The dances … were handsomely done…. The Indian legend interpretation, Mon-Ka-Ta … was beautifully done with much more finely adjusted proportion than when it was first performed in Toronto" ("Prom Concert Season" 1936). Another journalist added, "it was splendour of bizarre costumes, imposing ensemble rhythms—to piano and tympani and impressive tableaus" ("Prom Season

Ends" n.d.). The dancers were also invited to perform at several private events, including the Advertising and Sales Club dance held at the Royal York Hotel. These were lucrative and well-paid engagements, which testify to the further financial and artistic success of the Volkoff School.

If one thinks of translation and adaptation as a tool for achieving one's goal and finding one's voice, the person who benefited from participation in the Olympics the most was, undoubtedly, Boris Volkoff, closely followed by his dancers. While translating Russian ballet's choreography, scenography, and choice of subject matter into Canadian and international performances, he earned success and popularity among the various audiences of his productions. His interest lay in the creation of a Canadian national ballet and receiving acclaim for that. This goal, together with accolades and admiration from press and dancers, was fully achieved.

Notes

1 Founded in 1909, the Canadian Olympic Committee (coc) was responsible for selecting and organizing Canadian Olympic teams, and for soliciting funds for the teams' support. Although the coc was officially a standing committee of the Amateur Athletic Union of Canada (aauc) until after the Second World War, it functioned independently under the leadership of its president, Toronto businessman Patrick J. Mulqueen, an amateur sports enthusiast and former Canadian champion rower. The coc, sometimes referred to in the press as "the good old boys," operated like an elite club, guarding its control of Canada's Olympic involvement. coc committee members prided themselves on managing an efficient Olympic organization that championed Canadian participation at the highest levels of international amateur athletic competition.

2 On the debates surrounding Canadian participation in the Nazi Olympics, see Bruce Kidd (1978) "Canadian Opposition to 1936 Olympics."

3 On hybridity see, for example, Home K. Bhabha (1994); Néstor García Canclini (1990); and Stuart Hall (1992).

4 Evelyn Geary, in interview with Lillian Mitchell, May 5, 1981. Geary was Volkoff's partner in the Uptown, and later taught in his school.

5 In this article I use classical ballet to designate performances that adhere to traditional ballet technique, which includes turn-out of the leg and pointework. It is important to note that many of Volkoff's ballets were created in the style of modern dance, which combines pointework and rigid ballet legwork with more fluid movements, floorwork, and turn-in of the leg.

6   For example, Augustus Bridle, "Volkoff and Pupils give Dance Program," and "Dancers Show Skill, Grace: Russian Touch Seen at Brilliant Performance of Volkoff Pupils."

7   On modern dance in post-revolutionary Moscow, see Elizabeth Souritz (1966); Boris Asafyev (2008); John E. Bowlt (2008); and Steven G. Marks (2003).

8   Lopunov Fedor Vasil'evich, 1966, *Shest'desat Let v Balete,* Moscow: Isskusstivo, 138 quoted in Mitchell, 127. On Gorsky's work and contemporary art, see Elizabeth Souritz, (1980, 112–37); and *Soviet Choreographers in the 1920s* (1990).

9   Many articles mention Volkoff's significance as an innovator in the Toronto dance scene. See Boris Volkoff Collection, Toronto Reference Library, Scrapbooks 1932–36, 1–50.

10 The criteria sent to the Canadian Olympic committee specified the following:

1   Each country was allowed three solo or pair dances, three groups for stage dances and three groups for other dances.

2   The groups were to consist of at least ten dancers, their numbers were not to be more than 45 minutes and not less than 15 minutes in length.

3   The solo or pair dances were not to exceed 5 minutes in length.

4   All entries were to be classified under the following headings: Ballet Dances, Dances for the Concert Stage, and Historical or National Dances. James Pope (1936).

11 Marius Barbeau (1883–1969) was not a composer but anthropologist. He was credited in the program for providing chants that he collected to create the ballets. On Barbeau's work, see Lynda Jessup, Andrew Nurse, and Gordon E. Smith, eds. (2008); and Nansi Swayze (1960).

12 "Toronto Dancers to Compete at the Olympics." See also *Boris Volkoff Ballet Program*, for a synopsis of the ballets.

13 Unfortunately the eleven-foot totem pole had to stay home since it was impossible to transport overseas.

14 On the Orpheus myth in Aboriginal North America, see Hultkrantz (1957, 25–57).

15 See the article "Martha Graham Dances New Indian Ballets." On Martha Graham and native dance, see Russell Freedman (1998, 68–70), and Julia L. Foulkes (2002).

16 For more on this issue, see Daniel Francis (1992); Brendan F.R. Edwards (2005); Moira McLoughlin (1999); and Heather Norris Nicholson, ed. (2003).

17 Russian artist and Ballets Russes designer Alexandre Benois offered the following description of the performance of Polovtsian Dances by Diaghilev's
Ballets Russes in Paris:

> Audiences revelled [*sic*] in the exuberant music by Alexander Borodin,
> with its stirring choruses, quickening pace, pounding drums and clashing
> cymbals. The energetic movements corresponded with the popular image
> of Russia as a wild place, still untamed and primitive at heart. Choreo-
> graphed by Michel Fokine, the dance steps were more imaginary than
> authentic but the costumes designed by Nicolas Roerich demonstrated his
> research into early Russian history and folk art. (Benois 1977, 299)

18 Jeffrey Staley (2002) quotes Richard Rubinstein in saying, "The link between
genocidal settler societies of the eighteenth and nineteenth centuries and
twentieth-century genocide can be discerned in Adolf Hitler's Lebensraum
program. As a young man, Hitler saw the settlement of the New World and
the concomitant elimination of North America's Indian population by white
European settlers as a model to be followed by Germany on the European
continent," Staley continues, "thus, it cannot be mere coincidence that the
Nazi historian Edgar von Schmidt-Pauli, writing 'history in such a way as to
demonstrate the inevitability of the rise of the German race and Adolf Hitler
in particular,' should elicit and edit the 1929 autobiography of Big Chief White
Horse Eagle, an Osage of dubious character, and title it, *We Indians: The
Passing of a Great Race* (Brumble, American Indian Autobiography, 152; cf.
Conrad, "Mutual Fascination," 459)."

19 For more on German interests in hosting the Olympics, see Arnd Krüger and
William Murray, eds. (2003); David Clay Large (2007); and Anton Rippon
(2006).

References

Asafyev, Boris. 2008. *Symphonic Études: Portraits of Russian Operas and Ballets.*
Lanham, MD: Scarecrow Press.

Ayre, John. 1996. "Berlin, 1936: Canadian Dancers at Hitler's Olympics." *Beaver
Magazine* (February-March): 35–42.

Ayre, John. 2006. "Boris Volkoff: the Beginnings." *Magazine of the Dance Collection* 62: 6–12.

Baldwin, Janet. "Volkoff Dances at the 1936 Olympiad Berlin." *Memories of Janet
Baldwin of the Olympics.* Transcribed by Marguerite McLean. Boris Volkoff
Collection. "Ballets Scene." 1934. *Toronto Saturday Night*, May 19.

Bhabha, Home K. 1994. *The Location of Culture.* London: Routledge.

Benois, Alexander. 1977. *Reminiscences of the Russian Ballet.* New York: Da Capo Press.

Bowlt, John E. 2008. *Moscow & St. Petersburg 1900–1920: Art, Life & Culture of the Russian Silver Age.* New York: Vendome Press.

Brégent-Heald, Dominique. 2007. "Primitive Encounters: Film and Tourism in the North American West." *Western Historical Quarterly* 38 (1): 47–68.

Bridle, Augustus. 1932. "Volkoff and Pupils give Dance Program." *Toronto Star,* May 25. Boris Volkoff Collection.

———. 1936. "Volkoff School Gives Olympic Entry Show: Finale of Dance Fantasias Is Indian Legend to Feature Canada—15 Going to Berlin." *Toronto Star,* May 28.

Canada Statutes on Indian Population. 1884. Indian Act. Chapter 27, Section 3. Ottawa, ON.

Canadian Parliament and Senate. 1934. Debates. 17th Parliament, 5th sess. April 25, 303.

Clay Large, David. 2007. *Nazi Games: The Olympics of 1936.* New York: W.W. Norton & Co.

"Dancers Show Skill, Grace: Russian Touch Seen at Brilliant Performance of Volkoff Pupils." 1932. *Toronto Star,* May.

Edwards, Brendan F.R. 2005. *Paper Talk: A History of Libraries, Print Culture, and Aboriginal Peoples in Canada before the 1960s.* Lanham, MD: Scarecrow Press.

Feest, Christian, ed. 1987. *Indians and Europe: An Interdisciplinary Collection of Essays.* Aachen: Herodot, Rader Verlag.

Foulkes, Julia L. 2002. *Modern Bodies: Dance and American Modernism from Martha Graham to Alvin Ailey.* Chapel Hill, NC: University of North Carolina Press.

Francis, Daniel. 1992. *The Imaginary Indian: The Image of the Indian in Canadian Culture.* Vancouver, BC: Arsenal Pulp Books.

Freedman, Russell. 1998. *Martha Graham: A Dancer's Life.* New York: Clarion Books.

García Canclini, Néstor. 1990. *Hybrid Cultures.* Minneapolis, MN: University of Minnesota Press.

"German Invitation Refused by Dancer." 1936. *New York Times,* March 13.

Guenther, Irene. 2004. *Nazi Chic: Fashioning Women in the Third Reich.* London: Berg.

Hall, Stuart. 1992. "New Ethnicities." In *Race, Culture and Difference,* edited by Donald James and Ali Rattansi, 252–59. London: Sage.

Hamman, Brigette. 1999, *Hitler's Vienna: A Dictator's Apprenticeship*. New York: Oxford University Press.

Hanley, Elizabeth A. 2004. "The Role of Dance in the 1936 Berlin Olympic Games: Why Competition became Festival and Art became Political." In *Cultural Relations Old and New: The Transitory Olympic Ethic. Proceedings of the Seventh International Symposium for Olympic Research*, edited by K.B. Wamsley, R.K. Barney, and S.G. Martyn. London, ON: International Centre for Olympic Studies.

Hultkrantz, Åke. 1957. *The North Indian Orpheus Tradition: A Contribution to Comparative Religion*. Stockholm: Ethnographical Museum of Sweden.

Jessup, Lynda, Andrew Nurse, and Gordon E. Smith, eds. 2008. *Around and About Marius Barbeau: Modelling Twentieth-century Culture*. Gatineau, QC: Canadian Museum of Civilization.

Kidd, Bruce. 1978. "Canadian Opposition to 1936 Olympics." *Canadian Journal of History of Sport and Physical Education* 9 (2): 20–40.

Krüger, Arnd, and William Murray, eds. 2003. *The Nazi Olympics: Sport, Politics and Appeasement in the 1930s*. Urbana: University of Illinois Press.

Marks, Steven G. 2003. *How Russia Shaped the Modern World: From Art to Anti-Semitism, Ballet to Bolshevism*. Princeton, NJ: Princeton University Press.

McLoughlin, Moira.1999. *Museums and the Representation of Native Canadians: Negotiating the Borders of Culture*. New York: Garland Pub.

Mitchell, Lillian Leona. 1982. *Boris Volkoff: Dance, Teacher, Choreographer*. Ph.D. thesis, Texas Women's University.

Murphy, Peter. 1983. "Tourism in Canada: Selected Issues and Options." Victoria, BC: Dept. of Geography, University of Victoria.

Nicholson, Heather Norris, ed. 2003. *Screening Culture: Constructing Image and Identity*. Lanham, MD: Lexington Books.

O'Bonsawin, Christine. 2004. "'An Indian Atmosphere': Indian Policy and Canadian Participation in Berlin's Internationale Tanzwettspiele." In Wamsley, Barney, and Martyn 2004, 105–114.

Oefierreidjer, Ganadier, Bolen, Dajweizer, und Glamen. 1936. *Volkoff Scrapbooks*. Boris Volkoff Collection.

Pope, James. 1936. "Artistic Dances Competition." In "Canada at the Eleventh Olympiad 1936 in Germany," *Official Report of the Canadian Olympics Committee 1933–1936*, edited by W.A. Fry. Dunnville, ON: COC.

Promenade Programme Book. 1936. October 15. Boris Volkoff Collection.

"Prom Concert Season Ends with Flourish." 1936. *Toronto Evening Telegram*, Oct. 16. "Prom Season Ends in Bales of Color." n.d. Boris Volkoff Collection.

Randall, Annie J., ed. 2005. *Music, Power, and Politics*. New York: Routledge.

Report of Proceedings. 1947. Dominion-Provincial Tourist Conference, Ottawa, 1946. Ottawa: King's Printer.

Riding, Alan. 2010. *And the Show Went on: Cultural Life in Nazi-occupied Paris.* New York: Alfred A. Knopf.

Rippon, Anton. 2006. *Hitler's Olympics: The Story of the 1936 Nazi Games.* Barnsley: Pen & Sword Military.

Robinson, Douglas. 1997. *Translation and Empire.* Manchester UK: Manchester University Press.

Souritz, Elizabeth. 1966. "Nachalo Puti: Balet Moskvi i Leningrada v 1917–1927 godach." In *Sovetskii Baletnyi Teatr 1917–1965*, edited by Vera Krasovskaia, 11–13. Moscow: Isskusstivo.

———. 1980. "Soviet Ballet of the 1920s and the Influence of Constructivism." *Soviet Union/Union Soviétique* 7 (Parts 1 and 2): 112–37.

———. 1995. "Isadora Duncan's Influence on Dance in Russia." *Dance Chronicle* 8 (2): 281–91.

Souritz, Elizabeth. 1990. *Soviet Choreographers in the 1920s.* Translated by Lynn Vission. London: Duke University Press.

Spivak, Gayatri. 2000. "The Politics of Translation." In *Translation Studies Reader*, edited by Lawrence Venuti, 397–417. London: Routledge.

Stanton, Richard. 2000. *The Forgotten Olympic Art Competitions.* Lausanne: International Olympic Committee.

Staley, Jeffrey. 2002. *Reading with a Passion: Rhetoric, Autobiography, and the American West in the Gospel of John.* London: Continuum.

Swayze, Nansi. 1960. *The Man Hunters: Jenness, Barbeau, Wintemberg.* Toronto, ON: Clarke, Irwin. "Toronto Dancers to Compete at the Olympics." 1936. *Toronto Saturday Night.* July 11. "Unidentified Newspaper Article." 1936. October 19. Boris Volkoff Collection.

Venuti, Lawrence, ed. 1992. *Rethinking Translation: Discourse, Subjectivity, Ideology.* London: Routledge.

Volkoff, Boris. 1936. Personal Correspondence. Boris Volkoff Collection, Metro Toronto Reference Library.

———. 1930. "New Dance School in Canada." *Toronto Star*, n.d. Boris Volkoff Collection. "Volkoff Dancers Score in Germany." *Toronto Star*, n.d. Boris Volkoff Collection.

Contributors

Elena Benelli is Italian Language Program Coordinator and Lecturer in Italian Studies at Concordia University in Montreal, where she teaches courses in Italian literature, feminism, cultural theory, and migrant writers. She edited, with Grace Russo-Bullaro, *Shifting and Shaping a National Identity: Transnational Writers and Pluriculturism in Italy Today* (forthcoming). She has published several articles in Italian, English, and French on migrant writers and contemporary Italian fiction and cinema in *Italian Studies in Southern Africa, Metamorphoses, Conserveries mémorielles, Quaderni di Italianistica,* and *Annali d'Italianistica,* as well as numerous book chapters. Her current research interests include postcolonial writing in Italian, migrant literature and cinema in Italy, and migrant women writers in Italy.

Sally Debra Charnow is a Professor of Modern European History at Hofstra University. She is the author of *Theatre, Politics and Markets in fin-de-siècle Paris: Staging Modernity* (2005), and "Critical Thinking: Scholarly Readings of the Diary" in *Mediating Anne Frank* (2012). She also co-edited two issues of *Radical History Review: Performance, Politics, and History* (2007), and *National Myths in the Middle East: Representations, Revisions, and Critiques* (2003). Additional articles and review essays have appeared in *Historical Refections/Reflexions Historiques, Radical History Review, French Politics, Culture & Society,* and *H-France.* Her current project focuses on the French Jewish writer Edmond Fleg and the multifaceted cultural milieu of interwar Paris. With her two children, she lives in Brooklyn, New York.

Fernando Clara is Professor at the Department of Modern Languages of the Faculty of Social and Human Sciences, New University of Lisbon, where he earned his Ph.D. in German Culture (2002) and his Habilitation in Cultural Studies (2010). His main work areas and research interests are in the fields of German, European, and Cultural Studies. His recent publications include *Worlds of Words. Travels, History, Science, Literature: Portugal in the German-speaking World 1770–1810* (2007; in Portuguese), and the co-edited volumes *Rahmenwechsel Kulturwissenschaften* (2010; in German) and *Europe in Black and White. Interdisciplinary Perspectives on Immigration, Race and Identity in the "Old Continent"* (2011).

William E. Conklin received his Ph.D. in Social and Political Thought from York University Canada and graduate degrees in Law from Columbia University and International Relations from the London School of Economics. Conklin teaches in the Faculty of Law and in the Graduate program (Philosophy) at the University of Windsor. His *Statelessness: The Enigma of an International Community* is to be published in 2014. His most recent books are *Le savoir oublié de l'expérience des lois* (trans. Basil Kingstone, 2011) and *Hegel's Laws: The Legitimacy of a Modern Legal Order* (2008). His most recent articles are "'The Preface' Hegel's Legal Philosophy, and the Critics of His Time" in Jonathan Lavery et al., *Ideas under Fire* (2013); "Derrida's Territorial Knowledge of Justice" in Ruth Buchanan et al., *Reading Modern Law* (2012); "The Peremptory Norms of the International Community" in the *European Journal of International Law* 23 (2012). Conklin has been a Visiting Professor at the University of London (Birkbeck College School of Law) and has taught at the Universities of Toronto, York, Carleton, and Ryerson. He is a Life Member of Clare Hall College, Cambridge University.

Mary-Michelle DeCoste is Associate Professor of Italian Studies at the University of Guelph. Her book on Italian epic poetry, *Hopeless Love: Boiardo, Ariosto, and Narratives of Queer Female Desire*, was published in 2009. She has published articles on Dante, Boccaccio, and Ariosto; her current research focuses on food, work, and Italian Renaissance culture.

Kimberly Earles received her Ph.D. in Political Science from York University (Toronto, Canada) in 2010 and is currently a Lecturer in Politics, Philosophy, and Economics in the Department of Interdisciplinary Arts and Sciences at the University of Washington, Tacoma. Her research interests include gender, family policy, pension policy, paid and unpaid work, women and politics, Sweden, and the European Union. Selected publications include "The Gendered Consequences of the European Union's Pensions Policy" in *Women's Studies International Forum* (2013), and "Swedish Family Policy—Continuity and Change in the Nordic Welfare State Model" in *Social Policy & Administration* (2011).

Oana Fotache Dubălaru is Associate Professor of Literary Theory at the University of Bucharest (Romania) with a Ph.D. in Literary Theory (2006). She has taught courses and published on modern literary theory, comparative literature, and exile studies. Her publications include "'Global Literature'—In Search of a Definition," in L. Papadima, D. Damrosch, and Th. D'haen, eds., *The Canonical Debate Today. Crossing Disciplinary and Cultural Boundaries* (2011); *Divanul criticii. Discursuri asupra metodei în critica românească postbelică* [*Discourses on Method in Postwar Romanian Literary Criticism*], (2009); and she was co-editor with Anca Băicoianu of the anthology *Teoria literaturii. Orientări în teoria și critica literară contemporană* [*Literary Theory. Directions in Contemporary Literary Theory and Criticism*] (2005). She was a postdoctoral fellow of the University of Cluj, Romania (2011–2012).

Stephen Henighan is Professor of Hispanic Studies at the University of Guelph. He is the author of more than a dozen books, including the novel *The Streets of Winter* (2004), the short story collection *A Grave in the Air* (2007), the critical collection *A Report on the Afterlife of Culture* (2008), and the essay *A Green Reef: The Impact of Climate Change* (2013). In the area of Romanian studies, he is the English translator of Mihail Sebastian's *The Accident* (2011), and the author of *Lost Province: Adventures in a Moldovan Family* (2002), which was translated into Romanian in 2005, as well as research articles on Romanian-Canadian literature.

Susan Ingram is Associate Professor in the Department of Humanities at York University. Publications such as *Berliner Chic: A Locational History of Berlin Fashion* (co-authored with Katrina Sark), *Zarathustra's Sisters: Women's Autobiography and the Shaping of Cultural History*, German translations with Markus Reisenleitner of James Donald's *Imagining the Modern City*, and Ackbar Abbas's *Hong Kong: Culture and the Politics of Disappearance*, as well as a series of co-edited volumes on the mutually constitutive cross-cultural constructions of Central Europe and North America, reflect her interest in the institutions of urban cultural modernity.

David B. MacDonald is Professor of Political Science at the University of Guelph. He has written three books related to issues of collective identity, colonialism, genocide, and the politics of memory, as well as numerous book chapters and articles on similar themes. He has also co-edited three books, and recently co-authored a political science textbook. His books include *Thinking History, Fighting Evil* (2009) and *Identity Politics in the Age of Genocide* (2008). Funded by a Social Sciences and Humanities Research Council of Canada Insight Grant, Professor MacDonald is currently comparing models of indigenous–settler relations and debates about multiculturalism and biculturalism in Canada and New Zealand. Before moving to Guelph, he was a Senior Lecturer in the Politics Department at the University of Otago, New Zealand, and before that was at the ESCP Graduate School of Management in Paris. He has a Ph.D. in international relations from the London School of Economics.

Andrei S. Markovits is the Arthur F. Thurnau Professor and the Karl W. Deutsch Collegiate Professor of Comparative Politics and German Studies in the Department of Political Science and the Department of Germanic Languages and Literatures at the University of Michigan in Ann Arbor. He is also Professor of Sociology in that university's Department of Sociology. Professor Markovits has a Ph.D. in Political Science from Columbia University. From 1976 to 1999, he worked at the Center for European Studies at Harvard University. A specialist on the politics of Western and Central Europe (Germany and Austria in particular) Markovits has published twenty books and edited volumes, well over 100 scholarly articles, more than fifty review essays, and many articles and interviews in the American and European press. Most recently, he commenced a research project on the massively changed relationship between humans and pets, dogs in particular, that has emerged in the wake of the "greening" discourse of public life in all advanced industrial societies. He focuses on the featured role of women as agents of this changed discourse. Markovits loves all sports, with a clear preference for the team sports of basketball, baseball, football, and soccer.

Spencer Morrison is a Ph.D. candidate in English at the University of Toronto, where his dissertation investigates the relationship between Cold War American fiction and the Marshall Plan. His article on Cold War Faulkner can be found in the journal American Literature.

Alla Myzelev is a Senior Lecturer in Art History at Bloomsburg University of Pennsylvania where she teaches courses on art and material culture. She is the author of *Creating Modern Living in Toronto: From Vernacular to Deco* (forthcoming). Myzelev is a co-editor (with Dr. John Potvin) of *Material Cultures, 1740–1920 The Meanings and Pleasures of Collecting* (2009) and *Furniture, Interior Design, and Contours of Modern Identity* (2010). She has published articles and essays on Russian and Ukrainian avant-garde, British and Canadian design and architecture, contemporary fiber art. She is currently editing a collection of essays that deals with display and exhibition practices of craft and design objects.

Dirk Nabers holds the chair in International Political Sociology at the University of Kiel, Germany. Previously, he was Head of the IR Reseach Programme and Academic Director of the German Institute of Global and Area Studies (GIGA) graduate school in Hamburg. He has worked as a visiting professor at the University of Otago in Dunedin, New Zealand, and the International Christian University in Tokyo, Japan. He has published widely on international relations theory and meta-theory, security, and regionalism in journals such as *International Studies Perspectives, International Studies Review, Foreign Policy Analysis, Review of International Studies,* and *Cooperation and Conflict.* He is currently completing a monograph, *Crisis and Change in World Politics.*

Jeannine M. Pitas is a Ph.D. candidate at University of Toronto's Centre for Comparative Literature, where she is finishing a dissertation on twentieth-century Latin American poets Delmira Agustini, Alejandra Pizarnik, and Marosa di Giorgio. However, Polish literature—particularly twentieth-century narrative and poetry—is one of her long-standing interests. She has studied in Poland and Uruguay on grants from the Kosciuszko and Fulbright foundations, and she is the English language translator of acclaimed Uruguayan poet Marosa di Giorgio's *The History of Violets* (2010).

Gordana Yovanovich is a Professor of Hispanic Studies at the University of Guelph. She completed high school in the former Yugoslavia and keeps her interest in the region. She is the author of *Julio Cortazar's Character Mosaic* and *Play and the Picaresque,* and the editor of *The New World Order: Corporate Agenda and Parallel Reality* and *Latin American Identity after 1980.* She has published articles on Hispanic and Yugoslavian literature and culture.

Index